Inventing the English Massacre

Inventing the English Massacre

Amboyna in History and Memory

ALISON GAMES

OXFORD
UNIVERSITY PRESS

OXFORD
UNIVERSITY PRESS

Oxford University Press is a department of the University of Oxford. It furthers
the University's objective of excellence in research, scholarship, and education
by publishing worldwide. Oxford is a registered trade mark of Oxford University
Press in the UK and certain other countries.

Published in the United States of America by Oxford University Press
198 Madison Avenue, New York, NY 10016, United States of America.

© Alison Games 2020

CIP data is on file at the Library of Congress
ISBN 978–0–19–750773–5

Contents

Acknowledgments

Just as gratifying as finishing a book is the opportunity to thank all of those who made it possible. My ability to research and complete this project benefited from the support of Georgetown University and from fellowships at four institutions. In 2013, I spent a semester as part of the "Dutch Atlantic Connections" theme group at the Netherlands Institute for Advanced Study. Although I was working on a different project, I did some preliminary archival research for this book and made my first forays into early modern Dutch sources. I thank Aviva Ben-Ur, Wim Klooster, Gert Oostindie, and Ben Schmidt for their company and their expert advice. Steve Hindle invited me to spend 2013–14 as the Robert C. Ritchie Distinguished Fellow at the Huntington Library, and it was there that I started working on this book in earnest. I thank Steve and my fellow fellows, especially Rob Harper, Julie Orlemanski, Marjorie Rubright, Stefanie Sobelle, and Valerie Traub, who contributed so much to the collegial environment there, as did Heidi Brayman, Steve Hackel, Peter Mancall, Lindsay O'Neill, and Roy and Louise Ritchie. Andrew O'Shaughnessy offered me a month's stay at the Robert H. Smith International Center for Jefferson Studies, where I dug into eighteenth-century sources in a historically appropriate setting. My thanks to Andrew and to Whitney Pippin and Christa Dierksheide for their hospitality. I finished a draft of this book while I was the Hans Kohn Member in the School of Historical Studies at the Institute for Advanced Study (IAS) in Princeton in 2017–18. I am grateful to the other members of the early modern gang, especially Tim Brook, Guillaume Calafat, Yaacov Deutsch, Marta Hanson, Erin Rowe, Jonathan Sachs, Silvia Sebastiani, and Ying Zhang, for such stimulating conversation all year. I also thank other friends and colleagues at the IAS, especially Celia Applegate, Elisheva Baumgarten, David Blackbourn, Johanna Bockman, Kathleen Coleman, Cecily Hilsdale, and Andrew Zimmerman, for making the year so fun and productive. The many creatures of the IAS woods also offered essential diversion on regular walks in the splendid company of Catherine Clark.

My debt to libraries and librarians is enormous. Thank you to the people who simultaneously safeguard precious materials and make them available to researchers. Librarians and archivists answered email queries about rare books in their holdings; they sent me illustrations of frontispieces; they helped me understand the provenance of their collections; they explained printing and book binding practices to me; they tracked down materials; they shared my enthusiasm; and they helped to make each day in the archives one of new discoveries and camaraderie. My ability to visit so many college libraries at Oxford was facilitated by an arrangement Georgetown has with Campion Hall, which provided me with an apartment one delightful summer. I thank the Campion Hall staff for welcoming me so graciously and for having my Oxford University ID waiting when I arrived, facilitating my immediate immersion in the university's treasures. Thanks also to my Georgetown colleague Emily Francomano, who occupied the flat across the hall, showed me the ropes, and helped me think about decorated woodcuts.

Early versions of chapters in this book received valuable feedback at seminars or lectures at New York University, the Newberry Library, Yale, Dartmouth, Catholic University, the University of Delaware, Penn, Middle Tennessee State University, Saginaw Valley State University, the University of Michigan, and Princeton; at seminars and workshops at the Huntington Library, the Smith Center for Jefferson Studies, and the Institute for Advanced Study; and at conferences in Ireland and Germany. I also benefited from the scholarship of the participants in the "Bloody Days" conference on massacres in comparative perspective, especially my co-organizer Sally Gordon. Many generous people at these and other gatherings asked questions that I have tried to answer or address. Paul Hammer helped me figure out how to begin. Greg Dowd asked a question that made me realize how I had to end. Jason Sharples offered invaluable feedback on conspiracies. Wendy Warren welcomed me as a regular member of the Princeton colonial Americas workshop during my year in town.

Many colleagues found Amboyna-related items in the course of their own research, and took the time to share them with me, including Deborah Hamer, Eleanor Hubbard, Matthew Mitchell, Jenny Paxton, Susanah Shaw Romney, and Suze Zijlstra. April Shelford, Erika Munkwitz, and Mitch Fraas shared their databases of books. Danny Noorlander translated some tricky manuscripts. Peter Yeandle, whom I still have not met, generously answered a query from me out of the blue when I started working on educational materials for children and pulled books off his shelves to look for answers. Jim Caudle shared his expertise in eighteenth-century print culture and book history. I also thank Rupa Mishra, Phil Stern, and Andrew Ruoss, who are fellow travelers in the worlds of the East India Companies. Adam Clulow has joined me in my fascination with and preoccupation by the Amboyna episode. It has been a strange experience to be writing a book alongside another scholar, both of us turning to an incident poorly served by historians for almost four centuries. I received a copy of Adam's book just days before I sent this one off to production, so I have not assimilated his findings here, but I urge those interested in this episode and its different regional, global, and temporal contexts to read both works together. I thank Adam for his generosity and collegiality. Several friends and colleagues participated in a manuscript workshop at Georgetown and vastly improved the final product: I thank Greg Afinogenov, Katie Benton-Cohen, Ananya Chakravarti, Amy Leonard, John McNeill, Jo Ann Moran Cruz, Simon Newman, Aviel Roshwald, and Isaac Stephens.

For their help as this book moved toward production, I thank Dan Green, Susan Ferber, and two anonymous readers. I am also grateful to three experts: Becky Wrenn, who made the maps; Christen Runge, who created composite images; and Kathleen Lynch, who designed the cover. Funds attached to the Dorothy M. Brown Distinguished Professorship were essential in furthering the research and production of this book, and I thank the generous donors who support these scholarly activities.

My travels have been facilitated by many kind house and cat sitters, including Elena Abbot, Jeanne Dushel, Oliver Horn, Erika Huckestein, Katie Johnston, Chandra Manning, Robynne Mellor, Jordan Smith, and Elizabeth Williams. They gave me peace of mind to pursue my work while they wrestled with challenges that included an elderly cat, a derecho, and the sudden failure of the locks on the front door. Friends in Europe offered abundant entertainment and hospitality: in England, Katherine and Jonathan Clark, Julie Edwards and Stefano Quadrio Curzio, and Gad Heuman; in Leiden, Rosemarijn Hoefte and Jessica Roitman. Closer to home, in addition to many people named above, I thank Tommaso Astarita, Katie Gibson, David Hancock, Robin Lumsdaine, Roderick and Michelle McDonald, Meredith McKittrick, Cindy Nickerson, Josiah Osgood, Adam Rothman, Jim Williams, and Karin Wulf. And closer still, I thank my mother, Betsy, and my brother, Tim, for their companionship and good humor. My pleasure in finishing this book and having the happy occasion to thank the community of friends and scholars who made it possible is overshadowed by the absence of one cherished member of that circle, my father, who died suddenly in 2015. I dedicate this book to his memory.

A Note on Dates and Spelling

In the seventeenth century, the English (Julian) calendar lagged ten days behind the Gregorian calendar in use on the European continent, and the English also began the new year on March 25, not January 1. While English correspondents who interacted with continental Europeans often double dated their letters (for example, July 16/26), and sometimes signaled the year during the transition period between January 1 and March 25 with slashes (for example, March 12/22, 1621/2), they did not always do so, and did not always indicate whether they were using "new style" or "old style." I have kept all dates (months and days) as authors wrote them, and I have put the years in consistent new style, with the exception of the chapter on the conspiracy, where I have followed the new style months and dates in the text in order to minimize confusion about the order of events. I have kept English spelling as in the original sources, with the exception of swapping u and v, and i and j, for greater clarity (thus unjust, not vniust).

Cast of Characters

Beomont/Beamont/Beaumont, John. 48 years old in 1623. b. Berkshire. Longtime EIC employee and merchant at the Luhu factory. Reprieved, returned to London. A well-liked man, a character in John Dryden's play, and the alleged author of two newly discovered manuscripts.

Carleton, Sir Dudley (1574–1632). English ambassador to the United Provinces in the 1620s. He became Viscount Dorchester in July 1628.

Carleton, Dudley (Junior) (1599–1654). Nephew of the above. English agent in The Hague in the 1620s.

Coen, Jan Pieterszoon (1587–1629). VOC Governor-General, 1617–1622, 1627–1629. Testy and not to be crossed.

Collins, Edward. 25 years old in 1623. b. London. EIC merchant at the Larica factory. Survived by lot. Involved in dispute in November 1624 about whether or not he was tortured. Ran the EIC's powder mills after 1624.

Coulson, Samuel. 39 years old in 1623. b. Newcastle. EIC merchant at the Hitu factory. Wrote a testimony of innocence and prayed at the execution ground. Executed.

De Bruyn, Isaack. The VOC's legal official (the "Fiscal") during the conspiracy trial.

Duncan, William. A Scot who worked for the VOC and allegedly went mad at the gravesite of the English who were executed in Amboyna. Subject of some dispute in the 1620s.

Fardo, John. 42 years old in 1623. EIC steward at the Amboyna factory. Left an oral will. Executed.

Forbes, George. b. Aberdeen, circa 1580. Steward for the VOC in Amboyna in 1623. Wrote a "True Relation" and transformed himself into an "English witness."

Hytieso. 24 years old in 1623. b. Hirado. The curious or malevolent Japanese soldier whose questions triggered the conspiracy trial. Executed.

Joosten, Jan. On the VOC council at Amboyna. Hosted the English with his family when the EIC returned to Amboyna in 1621.

Marschalck, Laurens de. Merchant at Amboyna and on the VOC council. His deposition in November 1624 started a dispute about torture.

Muschamp(e), George. Head of the English merchants when the EIC returned to Amboyna in 1621. Compelled van Speult to execute a VOC employee in June 1622, creating a crucial precondition for a conspiracy.

Peres, Augustine. 36 years old in 1623. b. Bengal. Overseer of the VOC's slaves. Executed.

Powel, John. 31 years old in 1623. b. Bristol. An assistant for the EIC at the Cambello factory. A teller of tales and a finder of men. Hired as purser of the *Swan* in September 1632.

Price, Abel. 24 years old in 1623. b. Neles, Wales. EIC barber-surgeon at the Amboyna factory. An alleged alcoholic, gambler, and arsonist with good language skills. Executed.

Ramsey, Ephraim. 21 years old in 1623. b. Carelstow, Scotland. Visited the king, shopped for clothes, traveled to The Hague, and returned to the East Indies.

Sherrock, George. 31 years old in 1623, with nine years of service with the EIC. b. Westchester. Assistant at the Hitu factory. d. 1626.

Thompson/Tomson/Thomson, Emanuel. 50 years old in 1623. b. Hamburg. EIC merchant. Heckled? Executed. His family was persistent in seeking compensation.

Towerson, Gabriel. 49 years old in 1623. b. London. Head merchant of EIC traders at Amboyna. Alleged mastermind of English, Japanese, and Indo-Portuguese plot. Executed.

Van Speult, Herman. VOC Governor of the Amboyna factory. A man on edge. Died Mocha, August 1626.

Vogel, Martin Jansz. On the VOC council at Amboyna. Allegedly suffered qualms about the executions in later years.

Webber, William. 32 years old in 1623. b. Tiverton, Devon. EIC merchant at the Larica factory. On the EIC dole in the 1620s.

Welden, Richard. EIC agent in Banda. May have believed in the English plot against the Dutch. Vouched for the translation of the trial records. Sued in London by the survivor John Powel.

Inventing the English Massacre

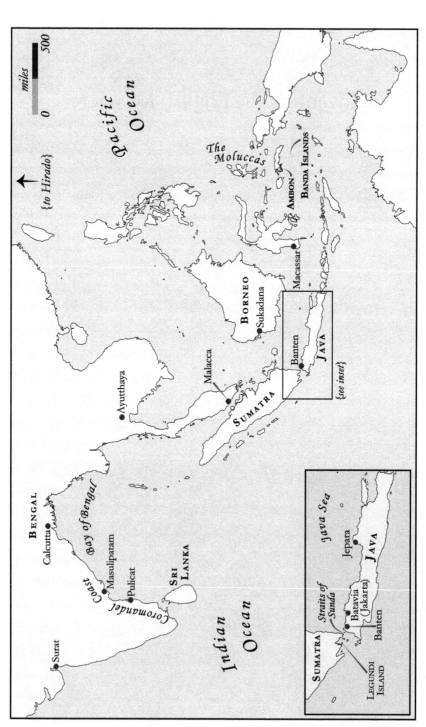

Map 1 The Indian Ocean world of the English East India Company in the seventeenth century. Map drawn by Rebecca Wrenn.

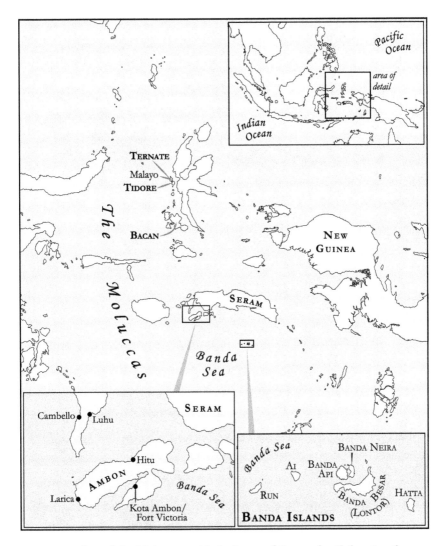

Map 2 Banda and the Moluccas, with Ambon and Seram detail showing the main trading posts. Map drawn by Rebecca Wrenn.

Introduction

Among all the things I don't know, here is what I do: after a short trial in February and March of 1623, Dutch East India Company (the *Vereenigde Oostindische Compagnie*, or VOC) officials on the island of Ambon, the heart of the international clove trade in the Indonesian archipelago, condemned twenty (or maybe twenty-one) men on charges of treason and conspiracy and beheaded them in a public execution. Ten of the condemned were employees of the English East India Company (EIC), joined since 1619 in a trading partnership with the Dutch; nine (or perhaps it was ten) were Japanese soldiers employed by the VOC; and one was a man of mixed Indian and Portuguese descent from Bengal who was the overseer of the VOC's slaves.

It had all begun with a nosy soldier. On February 22, a Japanese soldier asked, as he had before, about the size and strength of the defensive features of the main fortifications on Amboyna, the name the English and Dutch used for the island. To the Dutch, this interest was a vital "clew"; for the English who later derided the plot, it was just a sign that he was a curious fellow.[1] The VOC governor, suspicious of the soldier's recurring interest in such details and already anxious about the security of the trading post amid multiple internal and external threats, interrogated him, and then arrested all the Japanese soldiers and tortured them with fire and water, or threatened to torture them, until they confessed to plotting with English traders to kill the Dutch and take over the fort. VOC officials subsequently rounded up the EIC merchants from the houses they shared with their Dutch trading partners on Amboyna and the nearby island of Seram, and tortured or threatened them with torture until they, too, confessed that on New Year's Day they had taken an oath at the English house in the main town to get revenge on the Dutch through this plot with the Japanese. The alleged instigator of this scheme was Gabriel Towerson, the head of the English trading post and a veteran of East Indies trade who had spent two decades on and off in the service of the EIC.[2]

Execution day dawned with the thick air that promised a downpour, and a big storm blew in later that day, washing the bloodied execution ground with sheets of rain. The men marched to their deaths escorted by VOC employees and soldiers and the beating of a drum, but no one later agreed on their route nor on whether onlookers heckled them as they passed. Before the swordsman completed his grisly duties, the men sang, and they spoke, and they prayed, but no one later agreed on what they had said. And at the end of that gruesome morning, four heads stood on pikes—three Japanese, and one English—signaling restored VOC authority among a people who also cherished the heads of enemies. Somehow this unusual constellation of conspirators got to the execution ground in a land that was alien to all of them, although how and why that transpired remained clouded in controversy for centuries.

I may not understand exactly what happened at Amboyna in 1623, but almost 400 years later Walter Hicks had no doubts at all. An Australian soldier, he ended up on Ambon in 1941 as part of an Allied military force intended to secure the island, then part of the Dutch East Indies, against Japanese invasion during World War II. In an interview in 2003, Hicks explained that he had learned all about the incident he knew as the Massacre at Amboyna when he was in school. What happened, he told his interviewer, was that the Dutch had massacred a British garrison there.[3] Hicks's certainty reflected the culmination of almost four centuries of British writing about the incident, in which the Amboyna Massacre became part of the historical memory of the nation and a turning point of the British Empire.

This episode took place on a small island at the ends of the earth, from a British vantage point, and yet over the centuries it explained so much about the history of Britain itself. The Amboyna Massacre not only came to symbolize Dutch cruelty to the British, an oft-invoked tale of ruptured alliance and treachery, but also emerged by the early twentieth century as a crucial explanation for why the British Empire had a stronghold in India. Indeed, one distinguished historian declared in 1935 that it had changed the course of history.[4] Multiple innovations and inventions were vital to this surprising outcome in which the conspiracy trial at Amboyna became the linchpin of the British Empire. In the 1620s, the EIC quickly associated the trial and executions in Amboyna with European imagery of Protestant martyrs in an age of violent religious conflict and turned this conspiracy trial into a secular massacre. In repeated wars with the Dutch during the following decades, the English brandished this alleged act of perfidy as a rallying cry. The place name itself sufficed to signal all that had happened in 1623, just as today the words Sandy Hook and Dunblane conjure anguish, horror, and rage. By the eighteenth century, British writers, including the kingdom's most accomplished wordsmiths, Jonathan Swift and Daniel Defoe, invoked Amboyna as a short-hand to convey cruelty and betrayal without comment or elaboration, so certain were they that their readers would understand the significance of the word. Expanding British control in India and new acts of colonial violence in the eighteenth and nineteenth centuries prompted a reassessment of British history in the region, giving new weight to the Amboyna episode. All the while, the meaning of the word "massacre" changed, from a cruel murder to an act of mass slaughter, ultimately producing the violent incident Hicks described with such conviction. The nomenclature of massacre endures to this day, along with the certainty that an "English settlement" on the island was "wiped out" by the Dutch in 1623.[5]

The disputed incident at Amboyna mattered at the time, prompting a diplomatic crisis between staunch European allies and seeping into three wars in the seventeenth century. It mattered for another 350 years, as the British came to understand the very shape of their empire in terms of this single episode. And it matters still, because in their transformation of the judicial procedure at Amboyna into a massacre, the English East India Company invented what became the first English massacre. The intimacy, ingratitude, and treachery at the heart of how the English made sense of what had happened in 1623—all packed with emotion into a single word, Amboyna—became central and enduring features of subsequent British massacres.

A deep history of Anglo-Dutch relations fostered ties that created first the conspiracy and then the massacre: the incidents were born of alliance and intimacy, not enmity. The English and Dutch shared more than they didn't in this era. Linked by Protestantism, a related language, and for much of the era an anti-Spanish posture, the two nations often had common diplomatic interests in Europe. In the sixteenth century, Queen Elizabeth provided support for the Dutch revolt against the Spanish Habsburgs, what became the Eighty Years' War. This succor meant that in 1586, British soldiers comprised 32 percent of the army that fought under the auspices of the States General, the governing body of the United Provinces. The percentage of British troops didn't reach this level again, but still comprised 23 percent of all troops in 1621, the year the Twelve Years' Truce between the United Provinces and Habsburg Spain came to an end.[6] So many English soldiers ended up fighting on the continent during the conflict that one English contemporary described the Low Countries in 1619 as an English "university of warre."[7]

Beyond this essential military support, the two nations were enmeshed socially, religiously, and economically.[8] Merchants and artisans lived and worked and married on both sides of the North Sea. In opposition to Catholic enemies, the two nations espoused a common Protestant interest, but they adhered to different variants of this new and still-evolving set of religious practices. The United Provinces followed Calvinist doctrines while the English monarch was the head of a broad Reformed church whose policies shifted with the interests of the crown, leaving subjects in some uncertainty about which rituals and beliefs might keep one on a secure godly path to salvation or instead end at a heretic's pyre. Congregations of English dissenters lived in the United Provinces, and Dutch congregations of Protestant refugees from the war against Spain found sanctuary in England. The sixteenth century saw especially high levels of migration from the Low Countries, such a large flow of refugees from the tumult of the Eighty Years' War that people said one-third of the population in the provincial town of Norwich was Dutch.[9] In London, the Dutch, alongside the French, comprised the most sizable population of foreigners. The numbers weren't large—maybe only 1 percent of the London population was foreign born by 1635—and had dropped steadily from the late sixteenth century through the 1630s, but the Dutch presence was nonetheless pronounced in the city.[10] The Dutch and English intermarried and worked for each other. Connections forged by commerce and within dissenting religious communities enabled the English and Dutch to create bonds that transcended and occasionally circumvented official state ties between the nations. The categories of "English" and "Dutch" were themselves eroded by these deep associations, although people could be quick to identify themselves as belonging to one nation or another if necessity required them to do so.

English assistance to the Dutch in their wars against the Spanish engendered an asymmetrical relationship, one in which the English regarded themselves as the essential agents of Dutch independence and begrudged any Dutch actions that threatened English trade or stature as symptoms of a pernicious Dutch ingratitude. These sentiments intruded within Europe but proved equally pronounced around the world, as the English and Dutch nations aspired to become global powers and clashed in pursuit of this goal. The Amboyna incident emerged from this world in flux. By the middle of the seventeenth century, the on-again, off-again Protestant alliance had collapsed, and the two nations had become inveterate enemies.

Almost everywhere the English sought to establish trade beyond Europe, they had to learn not only to negotiate alliances with unfamiliar trading partners but also to cope with the constant presence of Dutch rivals. Competition over the lucrative spice trade in the Indian Ocean erupted in open warfare in 1616 and lasted until European statesmen compelled the two companies to create a trade consortium in 1619. This new arrangement made the English traders junior partners, a position that undermined their self-image as the savior of the Dutch. The forced partnership, combined with a new aggressive phase of VOC intrusion in local economies and polities, suppressed open conflict between the companies and instead spawned festering mistrust. This deepening mutual suspicion led to a decision in Amboyna in 1621 that the VOC and EIC traders should live together to further cooperation and oversight. Yet the closer the traders were physically, the greater the opportunities for strife. The result was the conspiracy of 1623, the third alleged conspiracy in the span of a year that the VOC had uncovered in the region and the second to feature possible EIC co-conspirators.

This sustained history of entanglement was a crucial precondition that both fostered conspiracy in the East Indies and ensured the incident's legacy as a massacre in Europe. A renewed English and Dutch union in Europe in June 1624, precisely at the moment news of the Amboyna executions reached each nation, hindered the ability of each company to speak openly about the violent incident in their efforts to seek redress.[11] The fragile diplomatic alliance meant that the EIC could not accuse the VOC even of ingratitude, much less use the word in print that it had already started to use privately—massacre.

It's hard to appreciate in the twenty-first century, when massacres seem ubiquitous, from mass shootings to civil wars to acts of genocide, but "massacre" was a relatively new word in the English language in the 1620s, one with capacious meanings. Massacre reached England and the English language in the wake of the French wars of religion, when a word that initially described a butcher's block came to mean the cruel murder of people. The EIC's innovation in 1624 was to attach the executions at Amboyna to the language and imagery of Protestant martyrology and in so doing to create a new kind of secular massacre in which religious differences receded in importance in favor of other features—in this instance, the treachery and ingratitude of a close ally. The EIC did not intend the word as a metaphor, nor did it apply a word whose meaning was inappropriate. For English people of the era, this episode was a literal massacre, as much a massacre as the St. Bartholomew's Day slaughter of Protestants by Catholics in France in 1572 or the murder of one-third of the English inhabitants of Virginia by Native Americans in 1622.

The implications of this word choice and the methods the EIC used to construct this judicial massacre were profound because the word itself created multiple new histories and contexts for the Amboyna episode. The nomenclature of massacre obscured two key aspects of the incident in the East Indies, its global context and the alleged conspiracy; it shaped the incident's long afterlife in British culture and imperial history; and it yoked the episode to other historical events called massacres, ultimately shaping the cultural meaning of later events. Recovering a historical context that explains what happened at Amboyna in 1623 and why the episode endured requires dismantling centuries of assumptions and certainties reflected in both English and Dutch scholarship and entangled in the legacies of the episode in British culture.

The conspiracy's first new history was evident in the 1620s, when the EIC's portrayal of the episode as a massacre detached it from its global context. The Amboyna episode was a disruptive event that revealed world history in the making. The island was long connected to distant places by regional and later global trade routes that brought waves of strangers who became trading partners or sometimes conquerors to its shores. Inhabited by a remarkable array of inhabitants by 1623—a tiny population of English traders, Japanese soldiers, VOC employees, a Portuguese remnant, Bandanese refugees, slaves and former slaves, and the Ambonese themselves—Ambon was a place uniquely formed by its role in regional and global networks and European conflicts. This context produced the conspiracy. As a massacre, however, the Amboyna incident became a story of English and Dutch relations in Europe, and it was that relationship—the alleged perfidy of Dutch allies—that cemented the incident as a massacre so far as the English public was concerned. The alleged co-conspirators—the Japanese soldiers and the Indo-Portuguese slave overseer—all but disappeared in the English accounts of the episode, an absence that only became more pronounced over the centuries as historians increasingly emphasized the European dimensions of the event. By the twentieth century, these non-European accomplices had vanished altogether in British histories of the incident.[12]

The new English terminology of massacre bequeathed a second history to the incident: it obscured the origins of the incident as a conspiracy, a terminology both disputed and shared at the time. It was a conspiracy, "premeditated," the English believed, against them by the Dutch. It was a conspiracy, a plot, the VOC was sure, by all their enemies in the region who wanted to displace them. It was treason, so named because the plot not only threatened a "horrible massacre" but would also weaken trade and thus deplete both the VOC's coffers and, more important, the strength of the United Provinces; its perpetrators deserved swift punishment.[13] It was a massacre—how could it not be?—when the English threatened to kill the Dutch and their supporters, to rip babes out of women's bellies, and to decide which infants to kill or save.[14] It was a massacre—how could it not be?—when the VOC traders appropriated legal rights and sovereignty beyond their purview, tortured their English allies, and beheaded them.

It is no wonder there was such disagreement, then and for centuries since, as the sources are a thicket of lies, half-truths, exaggerations, prevarications, epithets, contradictions, retractions, embellishments, pandering, and calumny, all deployed to serve arguments that are half-baked, half-cocked, implausible, naïve, self-serving, and vindictive. Everything was up for grabs. Contemporaries disagreed about the basic timeline of the examinations and confessions, and they quarreled above all else about whether the plot the VOC identified had even existed. Even in 1628, as he surveyed the bewildering welter of evidence around him, an English statesman lamented that the depositions were "as contrarie as night and day."[15] For all their contradictions and challenges, however, ample sources for the conspiracy exist, and they invite a systematic reappraisal of what happened at Amboyna. Indeed, the Amboyna conspiracy is unusual compared to many other conspiracies studied by historians in the survival of some alleged conspirators and in their fervent commitment to serve as living witnesses to their ordeal.

Historians of conspiracies often disagree vehemently about whether alleged plots ever took place or whether such plots were the fabrications of those who detected them.[16] The Amboyna incident has attracted similarly incompatible interpretations, although for the most part any interpretation insisting on certainty about what happened at Amboyna tends to come from someone who has not surveyed the full array of available evidence, because the only certainty that is possible is that there can be none. Historians of the Dutch East India Company tend to accept the plot as an English conspiracy.[17] Historians who specialize in the English East India Company have proven considerably more skeptical of the English plot, often dismissing it out of hand as a ridiculous fabrication. They call on the same defenses articulated in England in 1624: the plot was absurd, the fort too strong, the men too few in number, the weapons deficient, the English lived in harmony with the Dutch.[18] The most even-handed historians note that while the plot had its unlikely elements, the Dutch seem to have been certain of its reality.[19] My own assessment of the incident derives not only from an examination of over fifty manuscript depositions about the alleged conspiracy beyond the material available in the published trial record (see Appendix 1) but also from a reassessment of English and Dutch interactions in the Indonesian archipelago in the twenty years prior to the plot.

With its legacy secured in England as a massacre, the incident lost its global and conspiratorial origins, but it gained a remarkable longevity. A third new history the EIC's creation of the massacre spawned was the incident's long presence in British culture, largely a by-product of the EIC's shrewd use of print culture to disseminate its interpretation in 1624. The EIC depicted the episode as a massacre in several pamphlets, most notably *A True Relation of the Unjust, Cruell, and Barbarous Proceedings against the English* (1624), and especially through two woodcuts showing English merchants tortured with fire and water by Dutch interrogators, both made in 1624, circulated with the English and Dutch-language versions of the *True Relation*, published in a ballad, and available for purchase as individual sheets. With these works, the EIC accomplished its goal without using the word massacre, constrained at a time of alliance from launching overt criticism of an ally. Instead, it linked the ordeal of the tortured and executed traders to the suffering of Protestant martyrs, and left readers to draw the appropriate conclusions.

The two woodcuts and the EIC's pamphlets played a vital role in the long history the Amboyna Massacre enjoyed in British history and culture. The pamphlet was published twelve times as a discrete tract between 1624 and 1781 (see Appendix 2), reworked for new internal and international conflicts. The woodcuts had their own protracted afterlife, with a new version published in barely altered form as late as 1891. The texts and images were also reproduced frequently in compilations of travel accounts. The seventeenth-century woodcuts and the pamphlet stabilized one version of the story, and the print culture created what became the event's historical memory. It lived on, moreover, in a very specific way, as a tale of English martyrdom and Dutch cruelty.

But if the story endured, it slowly acquired a new shape because of the shifting meaning of the word massacre. Over the course of the seventeenth century, massacre lost its attachment to judicial execution and became a synonym for mass slaughter. Even as a slaughter, however, the story retained its core motifs of English innocence and Dutch treachery, and these two aspects acquired exaggerated importance in the context of the British empire, as did its endurance as a tale of atrocity. Almost 350 years after the first English trader called the conspiracy trial a massacre, and the Dutch who committed it cannibals, distinguished British historians and the authors of textbooks for school children continued as late as 1972 to use "atrocity" to describe what had happened.[20] The incident's afterlife spanned the entire British empire, from inception to decolonization. If it wasn't quite the Methuselah of massacres—it survived only as long as Methuselah's father, Enoch, who lived 365 years—it nonetheless showed remarkable staying power.

Why the execution of ten English traders in 1623 should have endured in British history and culture on the other side of the world for so long is a puzzle requiring some explanation. The intimacy and familiarity the English and Dutch enjoyed suggested that there could have been many other possible outcomes for this incident beyond a long and static legacy. Had the two companies not been forced into partnership in 1619, and had the companies not decided to share lodgings in the Moluccas in order to further mutual trust, the conspiracy might never have happened. Had the States General decided to pressure the VOC to pay compensation in summer 1624, there would have been no incentive for the EIC to create the texts and especially the images that so firmly lodged the incident as a massacre in British culture. Had the two nations been at war with each other in 1624, not newly joined allies against a shared enemy, the English company might have been able to say openly what it wanted about the Dutch traders and their actions. Instead, forced to mask its animosity, the EIC reached for other ways to make its point, creating a lasting image of Dutch depravity and cruelty. Had the nations not gone to war in the seventeenth century, as they did three times, the English might never have hit on the Amboyna story as the ideal way to convey Dutch perfidy, thus ensuring a renewed life for a grievance that Charles II had believed in 1664 to be consigned into oblivion. And had the Dutch not become a proxy for Whigs in British partisan politics, Amboyna might never have become such a useful way for political writers to lambaste their opponents in the seventeenth and eighteenth centuries.

Finally, the word massacre, attached to Amboyna for almost four centuries, first by English contemporaries and then by later historians, had the effect of joining the episode conceptually to other massacres, and thus created a fourth history for the incident. In the early seventeenth century, that collection of bedfellows made sense: English people in the 1620s thought of Amboyna as a massacre, like other cruel murders of the era. In the eighteenth century, historians yoked Amboyna to other acts of mass slaughter in the British Isles, notably in Ireland in 1641 and Glencoe in 1692, and by the nineteenth century, historians linked it to other alleged imperial atrocities with British victims, such as the Black Hole of Calcutta and the Uprising of 1857. At first glance, the Amboyna incident might seem to have scant resemblance to these other incidents of collective, colonial, and imperial violence. It transpired in the Indonesian archipelago, the site of many massacres, of which the Amboyna incident barely registers in terms of the number of deaths. Two years before these twenty (or twenty-one) men lost their heads in Amboyna, some 15,000 Bandanese had been displaced or murdered by invading VOC forces, one of the largest such slaughters of indigenous people by northern Europeans in this era. Ambon itself was the site of another massacre during World War II, in which 329 soldiers, mostly Australian, died, either in action or by execution at Japanese hands, in February 1942.[21] War, colonialism, and independence struggles continued to be the cause of horrific slaughters in the region, most notably the death of as many as 500,000 people in Indonesia in 1965–66.[22]

Set next to such terrible loss of life, it seems almost indulgent to explore the few judicial deaths at Amboyna in 1623, yet it turns out to be salutary—both for the history of the Amboyna incident and for the history of massacres—to think about Amboyna in light of other acts of collective violence. Historians often struggle to write about incidents called massacres because they can be obscured officially and by customary practice behind walls of silence. State officials might stonewall and misdirect in efforts to keep state-sponsored violence secret. Perpetrators might disguise the cause of death. Victims might be too weak politically and too traumatized to seek redress. The Amboyna incident is unusual in the constant reminders of the incident raised by the English survivors and their supporters. Indeed, it might seem surprising that the English chose to write for so many centuries about what looks at first glance like a crisis of national humiliation. Instead, the VOC didn't have a moment's peace, from the EIC's first protests about the executions in Batavia in 1623 to the formal negotiations in Europe in 1654. Beyond that year, the English tainted all the Dutch with the deaths at Amboyna, and not a decade passed for over 300 years without Amboyna appearing in a British pamphlet, poem, periodical, play, novel, history, schoolbook, essay, or illustration.

In its focus on the creation and legacy of the Amboyna massacre, this book explores the incident primarily in the context of British history and culture: it was the English traders who dubbed the episode a massacre, the English East India Company that creatively engaged with that word to craft a lasting story of treachery and cruelty, and English writers and historians who ensured its entrenchment in British culture for centuries. Although it took place in Southeast Asia, it has not endured as a story essential to that region's history, in contrast to other acts of seventeenth-century violence still commemorated by descendants.[23] Moreover, all of the key participants in the incident were outsiders to Ambon and to the region more generally. Although the particular Anglo-Dutch relationship created first the conspiracy and then the massacre, the Dutch had little interest in rehashing the incident after the settlement of 1654. Those interested in looking more closely at the Dutch and Japanese dimensions of the incident, at the episode's history as a conspiracy, and at the significance of the event in the context of the Dutch empire should read Adam Clulow's *Amboina, 1623: Fear and Conspiracy at the Edge of Empire*.[24]

These four histories created by the EIC's invention of the Amboyna massacre—the lost global setting, the obscured conspiracy, the puzzle of the centuries-long afterlife, and the place of the incident in a new typology of violence—together inspire the shape of the ensuing chapters that chart a new history of the incident that became known as the Amboyna Massacre. It is impossible to understand both the unusual cast of characters and the animosities that produced the episode without situating it in the Indian Ocean context where it happened. This book accordingly begins with two chapters set in the Indonesian archipelago. The first explores English and Dutch trade rivalries and how they developed as they did, manifesting themselves in such suspicion, mistrust, and violence that they could erupt in a conspiracy. The second chapter addresses the conspiracy itself, drawing on the trial records and especially on depositions mostly given by VOC employees after the conspiracy trial in Amboyna, Batavia, London, Amsterdam, and The Hague to try to understand the event as the participants themselves did. Despite this global origin, and although English and Dutch traders in Indonesia struggled with the fallout of the crisis, it was in Europe that the legacies of the episode lodged themselves most strongly. There, as the third chapter demonstrates, the English East India Company drew on its traders' characterization of the episode as a massacre to craft a powerful and tenacious interpretation of what had befallen its employees on the other side of the world. The pamphlets and images the company published transformed the incident, eliminating the non-European participants and turning a global event into a massacre, a European tale of treachery by an ungrateful ally.

For thirty years, the two East India Companies and the English and Dutch governments struggled over matters of jurisdiction and restitution before finally reaching agreement in 1654, a slow and bitter reckoning delineated in the fourth chapter. But this financial and diplomatic settlement hardly diminished the power of the story, because its afterlife was just beginning. The book's final two chapters trace the 350-year legacy of the episode in England. The fifth chapter analyzes multiple genres and eruptions of new *True Relations* in both internal and international contexts between 1624 and 1781 in order to show how Amboyna became domesticated within British culture. Widespread familiarity with the incident in the seventeenth and eighteenth centuries turned Amboyna into a shared cultural and emotional touchstone, and English convictions that the episode remained unavenged transformed it into a legend. The sixth chapter focuses on Amboyna's emergence in the nineteenth and twentieth centuries as a vital story in the history of the British Empire. By the twentieth century, historians restored the incident to the global context that had first produced it in their arguments that the massacre was the turning point in imperial history, but in important respects, the Amboyna Massacre had been transformed beyond recognition from its early history as it shifted from judicial martyrdom to a slaughter. For all the striking continuities in how writers described and invoked Amboyna, especially as a static story of Dutch cruelty and English innocence, the massacre had been reinvented.

The book's epilogue revisits the massacre's centrality in British culture. The Amboyna episode transpired at a formative moment for the English people (and, consequently, for the English language) in their emerging understanding of what massacres entailed—acts of violence with special characteristics, notably intimacy, ingratitude, and treachery. If the Amboyna massacre was not ultimately like many other massacres in terms of the manner and number of deaths, it was nonetheless foundational in producing a shared script of meaning: by the eighteenth century, it had become the first English massacre.

1

From Competition to Conspiracy

George Muschamp may not have given his all in his years of service for the English East India Company, but he had at least given his right leg, lost during the bitter fight with the Dutch over the lucrative spice trade. And for what? In 1621, after two decades of the English company's commercial competition with the VOC, and a few years of armed conflict, Muschamp found himself returning to his former home on Ambon Island in charge of English trade there but in a humiliating subordinate posture. The two companies had joined in an asymmetrical consortium and Muschamp would have to endure the ignominy of the junior partner. Every stab of phantom pain from his missing limb may have mimicked the ache of his lost status. It was almost too much to bear, and hard to make sense of, too, even for those who had lived through the rapid transition from competition to war to forced alliance. Yet there they were, yoked together in what the VOC characterized as a bad marriage. All Muschamp managed to do was safeguard what privileges he could, keep a close eye on VOC activity, and seize any opportunity to assert himself and diminish the Dutch. It wasn't much, but it would have to do. As it turned out, it would be enough, although not to achieve the outcome Muschamp had sought. Instead, his efforts deepened English and Dutch animosity and opened perilous new pathways to conflict. By 1623, Muschamp and his fellow traders, English and Dutch, had turned competition into conspiracy.

Between 1602, when the Dutch and English East India Companies began to vie for spices, and 1623, when the English traders experienced a humiliating crisis at the clove trading posts on Amboyna, EIC and VOC merchants cooperated and competed throughout the region Europeans dubbed the East Indies. It was a vast and varied terrain that included any point east of the Cape of Good Hope, reaching all the way to Japan and the Philippines. These merchants traded in India, at Surat, and on the Coromandel coast; on the Malay peninsula; on Candy, as Europeans knew Sri Lanka; on Java and Sumatra; in Japan; and at the cluster of clove-producing lands they called the Moluccas or Spice Islands. In an enormous expanse of ocean lay the smallest of motes, the chain of the Banda Islands, but these volcanic protrusions harbored the greatest wealth of all: nutmeg. Pepper was the mainstay of much of the trade in the Indonesian archipelago and vital for food preservation in Europe, but cloves, mace, and nutmeg were especially coveted commodities for food and medication alike. Europeans sought trading privileges from powerful rulers of centralized states and from local authorities in decentralized polities. When they couldn't secure concessions, those European traders with military capacity bullied their way into commercial networks. Their trading posts came and went, dismantled by rivals, evicted by local rulers, and closed by frustrated traders.

The English and Dutch companies carried the great weight of a shared history into this unfamiliar world. The ongoing conflict between the United Provinces and the Habsburgs hung over English and Dutch interactions in the East Indies, especially during the period of the Twelve Years' Truce (1609–1621), because of Dutch apprehension about a potential Anglo-Spanish alliance. Military support rendered to the Dutch since the reign of Elizabeth prompted the English to see themselves as the saviors—foster parents and nurses, as they explained in one tract—of the Dutch, and they harbored the belief that the Dutch should regularly express their gratitude.[1] This self-appointed role as savior also encouraged the English to see themselves as dominant. Financial transitions in Europe tested this asymmetrical dynamic. The rapid economic growth of the United Provinces in the 1590s led apprehensive English observers to worry that the Dutch economy might soon eclipse England's. Competition was fierce in Europe and erupted into open violence in the East Indies, where the two companies vied for the same goods in the same markets, in new and often chaotic circumstances in which each company simultaneously sought to best the other while also learning how to function in unfamiliar settings.[2]

These historical ties and decisions made in Europe, in addition to the political and commercial dynamics of the region itself, constrained English and Dutch traders in the East Indies, fettering them with European bonds that snapped on the other side of the world. The English and Dutch occasionally joined together in trading ventures, but they also fought bitterly, with especially intense eruptions of conflict over the spice trade in 1616–1620. While each accused the other of intruding on its trade, violating treaties, and acting like interlopers, at first neither company had the ability to secure its claims. The European background of alliance, set against this new sphere of competition in which the VOC came to possess the resources to acquire military dominance and the inclination to pursue that strategy, prompted sentiments of ingratitude and betrayal on all sides. This animosity was at odds with the two nations' connection in Europe. While the VOC's charter put violence at the heart of its mission, that force was supposed to target Iberian enemies of the United Provinces, not English allies. A treaty forged by diplomats and employers in Europe in 1619 and forced on the East Indies traders succeeded only in turning a hot war cold. Animosity and mistrust deepened, chronic grievances festered, and a new type of conflict erupted, one centered on conspiracies and encompassing a wide array of potential actors. The two companies began with half the world to trade in: by 1623, some of the companies' employees ended up living claustrophobically and unhappily in shared houses. Their intimacy was their undoing.

For aspiring English and Dutch traders, everything about this region was unfamiliar and each new trade opportunity another daunting interaction testing their skills and demanding social savvy. The two European companies discovered a wide array of polities, from strong centralized states to small-scale oligarchies, and had to learn different strategies for insinuating themselves in each, as they proceeded to do first in Banten, then in the Spice Islands, Ambon, and Banda. Almost everywhere they benefited from prior Portuguese presence, because local producers had already altered production practices to meet heightened European demand.

The first major port of call was Banten, which lies on the west end of Java at the Straits of Sunda. It was a vast metropolis that European visitors compared to Amsterdam and Rouen, a political capital, the most important city in the region, and the key commercial exchange point in the Indian Ocean. The city featured an enormous harbor with quiet waters sheltered from the open sea, and trade opportunities there, particularly for pepper in exchange for fabric, attracted people from all over the world. The largest foreign commercial community in residence was the Chinese, who had their own sector in the city. By 1673, Banten had a population of perhaps 150,000.[3]

VOC and EIC traders initially entered the scene like supernumeraries in a massive Wagnerian production, slipping on to a crowded stage with modest roles. One of their first challenges was making themselves known to potential trading partners who couldn't tell them apart. Part of the problem may have been that all Northern Europeans looked alike, hairy and rank when they first disembarked after their long voyages. Even other Europeans couldn't sort them out. At Amboyna in 1605, both the Dutch and the Portuguese thought the English were Dutch.[4]

This uncertainty about who was who added to the volatility of these early years of trade at Banten and sometimes posed dangers for Dutch and English newcomers. Edmund Scott, the head trader at the new English trading post there, devised a creative solution to this predicament in 1603. As Scott explained the problem, the "rude behavior" of some Dutch sailors had antagonized the Javans, who were unable to distinguish the English from the Dutch; the Javans called both Dutch and English "Englishmen," because when the Dutch first appeared there to trade, they had called themselves English.[5] Duplicity was endemic in this trading world, as revealed by this Dutch effort to deceive the Javans to enhance their own trading opportunities.

Scott worried that the Javans would end up killing some English by mistake to retaliate for bad Dutch behavior, so he devised a ritual to set the English apart. He resolved to celebrate Coronation Day on November 17 (the date of Queen Elizabeth's accession; the coronation itself took place on January 15), although at the time of the celebration in Banten in 1603 the queen had in fact died.[6] In England, November 17 had come to occupy an important place in the kingdom's national calendar, part of a cult surrounding Elizabeth and also an important feature of a new calendar of secular holidays. In parishes throughout the land, the clamor of bells announced the day, with bonfires, pageants, feasts, and processions illuminated by torches forming part of some local festivities.[7] The celebration in Banten followed a different form, marked by festive displays of flags and costumes to set the English apart from the Dutch. Fourteen Englishmen raised the cross of St. George (a flag, white, with a red cross in the middle, which usually flew over English trading establishments) above their house, donned new clothes, adorned their scarves with a gold fringe, and marched up and down in single file. When curious onlookers asked what they were doing, the English replied that they were celebrating their queen's Coronation Day. Just as they had hoped, the observers then asked why the English at the *other* house did not celebrate, too, which gave the English the opening they had sought: those people, they explained, were not English, but Dutch, and, in fact, they would not celebrate a coronation because they had no king at all, a customary slur the English hurled at the Dutch as a republican people governed (the English claimed) by merchants. When some Javans insisted that the Dutch were English, because the VOC traders had said they were when they first arrived, the English repeated that they were from a distinct country and spoke a different language. Go and talk to those people, the English urged, and you will hear their different tongue. Scott then deployed the Englishmen of the factory (as trading posts were known) to walk around the town and marketplace during the afternoon so that people could see their colorful scarves and hatbands, and from that day on, the residents of Banten understood that the English and the Dutch were different, or so Scott hoped. The English celebrated Coronation Day the following year, too (still unaware that the queen was dead), and hosted the Dutch for dinner.[8]

This holiday celebration tangibly illustrates the entanglement of people and nations like England and the United Provinces who enjoyed—or endured—close and protracted connections.[9] Scott's solution suggests what it was like for people to live inside these relationships, to be entangled, and to search for ways to distinguish themselves in alien settings where no one knew their histories, cultures, or potential value. Scott came up with language and political organization as the best way for Javans to discern the difference, first at a superficial level—by what they heard—and then at a deeper level—by what the English wanted the Javans to believe about the deficiencies of Dutch political structure. In fact, the Coronation Day celebration hardly signaled a rupture between the companies at Banten. In 1605, the EIC captain Henry Middleton urged the English traders in the city to maintain friendship with the VOC and to warn the Dutch of any talk against them by the Javans. It was to their advantage, Middleton continued, for the Javans to think the English and Dutch were "linked in one," because then they would not dare damage either nation.[10] When their interests coincided, the two companies found it strategically advantageous to cooperate, but that mutual advantage did not mean that the traders trusted each other.[11]

Middleton's invocation of the two companies as "linked in one" may have been entirely expedient and particular to the challenges the companies faced at Banten, but there were many indications in the first decade of trade in the East Indies that the two companies relied heavily on the experience and expertise acquired by the other in their efforts to navigate these challenging new commercial cultures. Competition was entangled in emulation.[12] For the most part, the English reached East Indies trading ports after the Dutch and came to rely on their experience and expertise on all manner of topics. The EIC admired clean VOC ships and deplored its own filthy ones.[13] The English learned from the VOC where particular commodities came from so they could trade more efficiently; which currencies to use in each locale; how to watch out for cheating spice traders who mixed dust with spices to boost the weight; and how to embalm cloth in lead in order to preserve it for sale. They studied model budgets so they could anticipate expenses more realistically.[14] The English seized and borrowed Dutch writings and translated them, learning important information about cartography, geography, commodities, expenses, regional trade, and alliances. One such work was the *Dialogues in the English and Malaiane Languages*, created by the VOC agent Frederick de Houtman during the eighteen months he spent in a Sumatran prison, first published in Amsterdam in 1603, then translated from Dutch into English and published in London in 1614. The dialogues commenced with an exchange signaling the commercial utility of the text, and the translator neglected to alter basic identifiers, leaving intact the sentence, "Our countrey is called Holland."[15]

But expertise went both ways, especially in terms of hiring foreign personnel. Relative prosperity and employment opportunities in the Dutch Republic kept many Dutch people at home, and so the VOC recruited heavily to find workers to ship overseas. Such men came from the European continent, especially from the Holy Roman Empire, but also from the British Isles, including the English, Welsh, and Scots.[16] The EIC hired Dutch employees, too, but normally because of their skills, not because of general staffing shortages, since England's rising population provided ample personnel for multiple overseas ventures. Because of their expertise, the EIC put two Dutch merchants in charge of its seventh voyage in 1610. Recognizing some of the unique challenges these Dutch officers might face with unfamiliar English legal practices, the company limited their authority. And because the VOC's employees were likely to "much [hate]" these two men for their English service, the EIC urged the fleet's English captain to take care to defend them.[17]

All of these close connections suggest why the Coronation Day celebration struck Scott as a desirable solution to this problem of how to distinguish the English company as an independent entity worthy of Javan trade. The occasion was amicable, yet it enabled him to make his point. The festive ritual was part of a competitive culture in which neither the English nor the Dutch companies held any particular diplomatic or commercial advantage and both struggled to find purchase. Thus the English sought not only to distinguish themselves but also to denigrate the Dutch as a people without a monarch. Dutch and English conduct suggests that they adhered to a theory about reputation that was akin to mercantilism, which imagined a world of fixed and limited resources. Theirs was also a world of limited prestige. The Dutch could enhance their status only by disparaging the English, and the English could do the same. This sensibility framed a range of dirty commercial tricks and also erupted in violent and cruel displays of dominance over

a weakened or defeated enemy. The Coronation Day celebration was anodyne, leaving no maimed bodies in its wake, but many other conflicts showed
the importance of public shame of rivals as a key strategy for securing trade
access or monopolies. Some of the most humiliating moments the English
endured in the Indies transpired around the fight over nutmeg and cloves
from 1609 to 1621.[18]

In many places in the East Indies, the English and the Dutch pursued what
was primarily a commercial rivalry, because the power of indigenous rulers
and states hindered any further aspirations. Europeans normally secured
trading privileges by winning legal rights from indigenous sovereigns. This
pattern of European diplomatic accommodation prevailed, for example, at
Banten in the first years of European trade and also in Japan. The two companies pursued the tricks of the trade available to them—underselling goods,
maligning their rivals, spreading rumors, circulating inaccurate information,
flying false flags—but they could not seize political or commercial power in
any significant way without large armed forces or potent allies.

These rivalries became violent when it came to nutmeg and cloves, for
three reasons: the value of the spices, the decentralized polities where they
were found, and the direct competition the trading companies experienced. The Moluccas were crucial for the trade in cloves, which grew in the
northern Moluccas, and starting in the sixteenth century in the southern
Moluccas (Ambon and Seram) as well. Ambon and Seram became the primary clove producing places in the seventeenth century and the VOC sought
to limit all production to Ambon to secure its monopoly.[19] Nutmeg came
from the Banda Islands, the only place in the world where the spice grew.
Both regions were far from Banten, where the two companies maintained
their administrative headquarters for trade in the Indonesian archipelago
and the Coromandel coast: it was 1,500 miles from Batavia to the Moluccas,
and about the same distance to the Banda Islands, and both places could be
reached only when the monsoons were favorable.

Europeans coveted nutmeg and cloves. They enjoyed the spices in food
preparation, and their high cost made them a prestige good, but more important still were medical applications. Europeans adhered to the Galenic
medical system that advocated keeping the body's four humors—phlegm,
blood, black bile, and yellow bile—in balance. Illness of all sorts suggested
that the humors were out of balance, and many of the purgatives and other
popular practices such as bleeding were all part of an effort to help people
restore the essential humoral equilibrium. Spices fit into this pharmacology,

and European travelers to the East Indies recorded all of the vital roles that they thought spices could play in health: cinnamon, to warm the intestines; nutmeg, to enhance memory.[20] Europeans believed that cloves improved one's vision when applied to the eye. When rubbed on the forehead, they relieved a cold. Added to food or drink, cloves stimulated the appetite, and when consumed in milk, cloves enhanced sexual experiences.[21] Elizabethan physicians had determined that nutmeg could cure flatulence, the common cold, and, crucially, plague, a menace that regularly ravaged the London population.[22] Cloves contain eugenol, which works as an anesthetic, and nutmeg has psychotropic properties.[23] Each company wanted not just access to the spices but exclusive control over the trade to safeguard against oversupplied European markets. There was plenty of cloves and nutmeg for all traders— but that was exactly the problem.

The English and the Dutch entered a rich world of enmities and alliances in the Moluccas. It was another region where they had to learn how to trade, and once again they did so simultaneously, successively, and as rivals who sought to make the case that they were the most desirable trading partners. The lessons of Banten did not always apply in these new places. The northern spice islands (Ternate, Tidore, Makian, Bacan, and Jailolo), home to cloves, were governed by two rival sultanates, based in Tidore and Ternate, whose rulers had turned to Europeans as allies in their own regional conflicts.[24] The ruler of Tidore, for example, sought English trade and alliance in addition to Portuguese alliance and seemed keenly aware of European political dynamics. He wrote James I sometime after 1604 saying that he understood that the English were allies with the King of Spain, and asked him to join with Tidore against the Dutch and Ternatans.[25] For his part, the sultan of Ternate hedged his bets, acknowledging his attachment to the Dutch but extending friendship to the English crown in his own missive in 1606.[26] Tidore and Ternate held sway over other important clove islands where Europeans traded, including Bacan and Makian.[27] Ternate was especially powerful because of its war fleets, but both Tidore and Ternate had vassal tributaries in the region, including on Ambon and Seram, two places where the English and Dutch sought to establish their own authority, thus putting Europeans and Moluccans on a collision course.[28]

In Banda (Banda Neira, Ai, Run, and Lontor [Banda Besar]) and in the southern Moluccas, where Seram and Ambon are located, the English and Dutch traders fought violently for access to and control over the trade. Leadership was decentralized in the hands of prominent traders called *orang kaya* (rich men).[29] The presence of multiple *orang kaya* looking for better allies meant that any European conquest or commercial contract proved transitory, and both companies had difficulty forming secure alliances. Bandanese and Moluccan people, moreover, faced both opportunities and terrible consequences as European newcomers took advantage of any new alliance or chance for a monopoly, sometimes resulting in murderous assaults on clove and nutmeg producers and traders and on each other. The Portuguese were the first Europeans to trade with Banda directly, but they had not been able to impose themselves there. The *orang kaya* presented a united front and refused to allow the Portuguese to erect a trading post or fortification.[30] The Dutch, in contrast, pursued the nutmeg trade aggressively and proved to be belligerent, troublesome, and often inadequate trading partners. These VOC failures and the ability of *orang kaya* to forge separate alliances with the EIC and the VOC led to conflict between the English and Dutch and imperiled the Bandanese.

As ships took nutmeg away from Banda, where monoculture had long created dependence on food imports, they brought in crucial food supplies, especially rice, and valued trading commodities, such as cloth. The Bandanese themselves constructed large ships to transport their nutmeg to markets as far as Java and Malacca in exchange for goods. They were the only Moluccan people who transported spices, and their ships were unusual in their storage capacity. At Banda, the Dutch were unable to provision the islands as other Indian Ocean merchants did and they charged excessive prices for the goods they brought. The VOC banned competitors and forced the Bandanese to rely on VOC supplies, but what they brought was both inadequate and, because of the meager supply, expensive. The Dutch, moreover, brought goods that were not appropriate to the locale, in contrast to the merchants already ensconced in the regional trade, who brought more suitable light cloths—batiks and calicoes. Regional merchants, unlike VOC traders who set fixed prices, were also willing to bargain, one of the enjoyable rituals that made commercial exchanges a pleasant and social experience.[31]

These VOC deficiencies explain in part the Bandanese eagerness to turn to the English. The Bandanese shrewdly assessed the situation of these European rivals and sought to take advantage of such opportunities as came their way. The people of Run negotiated with the English in 1617 for a rice supply, for example, at a time of famine.[32] In some cases, moreover, VOC aggression had inspired loathing for the Dutch. In 1615, one English trader reported that the Dutch would never be able to make claim to Banda, "for all the Bandeneses will lose their lives before they will be under the Hollanders."[33] A group of *orang kaya* pursued just such an English alliance in that year. In a letter to the traders at Banten, they flattered the English with praise for their reputation as a peaceful people. Alone of all rulers, the *orang kaya* wrote effusively, the king of England helps the world and harms none in matters of religion, nor aspires to overthrow other legal systems, but lives only in "peace and frindshipp" and pursues peaceful trade. This choice of compliments and the repetition of "peace" reflected some awareness of the traits the English valued in themselves, especially their emerging self-image as peaceful traders, and suggested that the *orang kaya* were perceptive observers of European intruders. The Dutch interfered with Bandanese religious practices—the islands were Muslim—and the *orang kaya* characterized the Dutch as trying to "destroy our Religion." The *orang kaya* described them as "sonnes of Whores" whose treachery produced the evocative line, "wee soe extreamely hate them." They hoped the English king would provide them with the necessary weapons to reclaim the fort at Banda Neira. And if the English helped them, the Bandanese promised all of the spices that the islands produced.[34]

Treachery became the defining attribute of trade rivalries over spices. The English were desperate to get access to nutmeg and showed a flexible view of prior VOC trade agreements. When the English asserted in 1615 that they came to Banda to trade in peace, the Dutch laughed, condemned the English as "rogues and rascals," and searched the English and their ships whenever Englishmen went ashore. And the Dutch were right to worry about the English, because during those months, whenever the English talked to local people, in Banda and on Amboyna, in some cases in secret meetings with leaders, they learned of indigenous loathing for VOC rule and listened to appeals for alliance.[35] In 1615, the VOC tried to prevent the EIC from trading at Cambello, a clove trading post on the island of Seram, where traders were eager for their business. The English managed to sneak some men into the VOC fort, and killed some Dutch but were ultimately forced out.[36] At Luhu on the island of Seram, where the VOC believed they had secured an exclusive alliance, the English traders maintained that the *orang kaya* was instead their ally. This leader "in outward show will seem to favour much the Hollanders but yet will do you all the good he can," an English merchant informed a colleague in 1615.[37] No sooner had the VOC secured treaties on Banda in 1616 and 1617 than the VOC believed that the EIC aided the Bandanese in violating them and keeping spices from the Dutch.[38] EIC members in London even raised the possibility in 1617 of the English joining with the Bandanese to expel the Dutch.[39] These continued efforts by the EIC to forge Bandanese and Moluccan alliances infuriated VOC officials, who also believed that the EIC traders armed and provisioned the Spanish, the consummate Dutch foe. In November 1617, Governor-General Laurens Real, the VOC's agent in charge of the entire region, pointed to those English alliances and contracts to endorse violence against the English.[40] Real couched this aggression as defensive, blaming the English as the provocateurs in their insistence on supporting the Bandanese.[41]

This pattern—of VOC overtures and contracts, of EIC intrusion and deception, of multiple and successive alliances with *orang kaya*—characterized European trade throughout the southern Moluccas and Banda. The Dutch were powerful enough in the East Indies by 1615 that they could make regional growers and traders too fearful to sell cloves or nutmeg to the English in Banda and the Moluccas, thwart the EIC's access to silk at Patani on the Malay peninsula, sell cloth to the Chinese below cost to hinder English trade

Figure 1.1 An illustration from 1621 showing the fortifications that European traders erected on the nutmeg and clove islands. Joris van Spilbergen, *Oost ende West-Indische spieghel* (Zutphen, 1621), plate 21. RB 9078, The Huntington Library, San Marino, California.

there, and put pressure on the ruler of Banten to rescind a plot of land he had given the English because the Dutch disliked its proximity to their own.[42] VOC strength in the region grew until in June 1617, an English trader named George Ball picked up his pen in Banten to write his friends in Japan and reported matter-of-factly that "for news, here is none but of the Hollanders."[43]

Ball's sentiments reflected the VOC's shift to an especially bellicose approach under the leadership of Jan Pieterzoon Coen, the ruthless VOC governor-general in the Indies from 1617 to 1622 and 1627 to 1629. Coen envisioned territorial occupation as central to VOC success in the region.[44] He ultimately decided, for example, to abandon the tedious negotiations with the *orang kaya* in Banda in favor of conquest.[45] Central to his aspirations to control the trade in Asia were Japanese mercenaries. European soldiers suffered high mortality rates during their long voyage to the Indies and once in the region, making local recruits desirable. The Japanese soldiers were cheaper than European soldiers, and the VOC believed them to be fiercer combatants. Altogether about 300 Japanese soldiers sailed from Hirado to serve the VOC, all on three-year contracts. Some of them may have been Christians. These employees took part in some of the VOC's major campaigns in the region, including at Tidore in 1613, Jakarta in 1619, and Banda in 1615 and 1621.[46]

In the bitter and increasingly violent disputes over trade, the former European allies found themselves at war. By May 1617, two English traders at the Siamese city of Ayutthaya dismissed the Dutch as their "mortall enemis," and in July, an EIC trader characterized the Dutch in Jakarta as his "professed enemies" who "bewitched" the English with words and drink.[47] Rumors even reached the English in Japan in June that the Dutch had poisoned an EIC officer in Banda and blamed his death on the Spanish.[48] The English instigated some of these conflicts, as one EIC captain acknowledged frankly after the VOC captured his vessel. He wasn't sorry his ship had been taken, because it was for that very reason that the president (as the EIC titled its head agent in the region) had sent him out, not only to establish a trading post but also to test the VOC. If the Dutch violated the peace by taking his ship, he argued, then the EIC could justly seek compensation.[49]

The humiliation and degradation of European rivals emerged as vital strategies in these conflicts. Flags became important symbolic targets in conflicts and another aspect of assaults on a rival's reputation. The attacks were graphic and scatological, deeply insulting and infuriating to contemporaries. In 1615 the English secured a small piece of ground at Luhu on Seram where they raised the St. George's cross, enraging the VOC.[50] The Dutch mooned the English colors, "turning up their tails."[51] Rumors reached Japan of an even more insulting treatment of an English flag seized from the trading post at Ai in 1617. According to an Englishman employed by the VOC, "the drunken, envious Holland[e]rs" ripped the flag into pieces and used the scraps as toilet paper. "(Brave men)," added the English diarist sarcastically when he recorded the news.[52] The English complained in Banten in 1618 that the Dutch stomped on their flags, shot them, and dragged them behind their ships.[53] Flags had the advantage, moreover, of making visible the humiliation and defeat of a rival and thus risked demoralizing or even enraging an ally.[54] The Dutch raised the French and English flags on one of their frigates in 1618, with the Prince of Orange's flag flying over the others, "in manner of a tryumph."[55]

The VOC likewise deployed captured EIC employees to maximize shame and discomfort. They held some English prisoners on a ship above the hatches, baked by the sun and confined in a space "where their [Dutch captors'] ordures and pisse fell upon them in the night," condemning the captives, complained an English trader, to lie like lepers in their filth. The mobility of these floating prisons offered another opportunity for the VOC to humiliate the EIC employees. The men from one captured vessel were put in specially designed cages and transported from port to port, bound in irons, so that people on land could see them, leading them, the English complained, to "beleeve, that Englishmen were their Vassals and Slaves." At a time when the two companies fought for trade, the ability to persuade local rulers and merchants that one could prove a useful ally, not just a lucrative trading partner, was essential. So to be displayed for public ridicule in numerous ports damaged English status at a time when reputations helped secure trading privileges. That the Dutch then whipped English prisoners publicly, in front of local inhabitants summoned specifically to see the punishment, drove the point home more emphatically.[56]

Richard Taylor's death was especially ignominious. The carpenter had served on the *Speedwell*, an English pinnace that the VOC seized in 1617. At the time of his capture, Taylor suffered from the gastrointestinal menace known as the bloody flux (likely dysentery). The miserable man died in the VOC's custody. Then, the English related, the Dutch took Taylor's corpse, "and put him into a bush, with his head downeward, and his heeles upward, and sayd in most barbarous manner, that there was a *stert man*, that is a man with a taile with his heeles upward, and there his carkasse rotted in the bush."

The Dutch word was "staartman," or "tailman," which was an insulting Dutch nickname for the English that the VOC employees had carried with them from Europe. It drew on the notion that the English were descended from the Devil and thus had tails.[57] The English traders felt the accumulation of insults deeply: they were not only outmatched, but unmanned, one trader lamented in a protest to the VOC's governor-general, "effeminate," like "men without hands or hearts," the constant assaults on their status simultaneous betrayals of their manhood.[58]

Some VOC and EIC traders pursued strategies to mitigate and even end these ubiquitous clashes, so expensive in lives and trade and so corrosive of whatever sentiments of amity might have remained. The traders connected the land war in Europe that had cemented their alliance in the late sixteenth century with the commercial battles in the East Indies that threatened to rupture it. The summer of 1616 gave a hint at the consequences of these trading conflicts for Anglo-Dutch relations beyond the region. An English trader reported from Banten in July that the tension in the Moluccas "hath bred such strangeness betwixt us as if we never had been acquainted." So "ridiculous" was the estrangement that the English could not count on the Dutch against their once shared enemy, the Portuguese.[59]

A major barrier to reconciliation lay in the two companies' incompatible rationales for their right to monopoly or occupation or even trade. While European legal and economic theorists such as Hugo Grotius, Thomas Mun, and John Selden sought to develop legal rationales for European conduct and claims beyond Europe during these years, company agents had to implement policies and construct logical arguments for their positions on the spot in Asia. Even orders from the two companies' headquarters at Banten were difficult to enforce, given the vast distances involved and the impediments to communication during much of the year. The traders' efforts to resolve competing claims reveal the constraints of their European relationship and the opposing philosophies that underpinned their assertions to primacy.

As they tried to figure out who had the strongest claim to coveted land, the two companies worked with different systems of debt and obligation, one financial and the other political. In their disputes with the EIC, the VOC focused on their relative financial investment. At Banda, the Dutch expected to enjoy a monopoly to compensate them for the funds they had spent subduing the islands and establishing fortifications. It was a comparative claim: if the VOC spent more than other Europeans, then their claim was more legitimate.[60] This argument was one the poorly funded EIC was ill equipped to win, and indeed the English traders offered a different type of argument, one anchored in their historical connection with the Dutch Republic.[61] The EIC's position was that the VOC owed the English for all the English lives sacrificed during the wars connected to the Dutch revolt: the accumulation of English bodies lost to defend the Dutch created an enduring debt to be called in whether in Europe or on the other side of the world. A conversation between Dutch and English traders in Japan exposed the gulf between these two points of view during a meeting about joining forces in 1616. The Dutch complained about their large investment in money and especially in lives in their trade in the Moluccas. Richard Cocks, the head of the English factory at Hirado, replied that the English could compensate the Dutch for their financial investment. When the Dutch trader queried, "what recompence shall be made for the lives of our dead men," Cocks retorted that the Dutch would do well to remember that they were greatly indebted to the English, and that for every one Dutchman who had lost his life in the conquest of the Moluccas, twenty Englishmen had died "in driveing the Spaniardes out of the Loe Cuntries & making the Hollanders a free state." In Cocks's version of this encounter, the Dutch trader had no reply to make, knowing "not well to answer, but laughed it out."[62] In November 1617 one English trader demanded how the VOC's violent attacks on the English at Banda reflected the "bandes of Amity" that linked James I and the States General and charged the VOC, on the basis of these ties, to desist in its aggression.[63] The next day another EIC trader reminded the VOC's governor-general that thousands of English had died under Elizabeth's reign, yet now he believed the Dutch wanted to cut English throats.[64]

But flinging accusations of failed amity was a game that required two players, and the Dutch were happy to join in. In 1617, the governor-general criticized the EIC for its alliance with the people of Run at Banda, when the English should have placed a greater emphasis on the old English alliance with the United Provinces.[65] After the EIC seized a VOC ship, the Black Lion, in 1618, the VOC council at Jakarta marveled at this humiliating and surprising blow, for how could such a thing happen to them when the Dutch had only ever shown friendship to the English?[66]

The positions were irreconcilable—the Dutch claiming that they had spent more in the Indies and had to be compensated with secure and sole possession; the English countering that on the other side of the world, and in the past, English people gave their lives for Dutch independence, and were owed for this sacrifice. The problem with this English argument from a VOC point of view was that gratitude seemed to be a debt that could never be repaid. The incompatibility of these lines of argument made it impossible for the traders to agree peacefully on who should withdraw and who had a legal right to possession and monopoly. Relations had reached a state of war: in November 1617 the VOC even posted a declaration of war on the door of the EIC's house at Banten.[67] VOC employees blamed the conflict on the English, who deceived and abused the Dutch in order to find ways to conquer them, or to imprison the Dutch governor-general, or even to murder him. In response, the Dutch built palisades around their trading houses and forts.[68] The Dutch had more to worry about than just the English, since they were embarking on an aggressive phase of conquest and colonization. As part of this campaign, the VOC destroyed the Javan city of Jakarta and built a new city, Batavia, on its ashes, to be the company's administrative capital. Only a peace imposed from outside brought conflict between the European companies to an end.

A treaty signed between the English and Dutch companies in Europe in 1619 was supposed to end these hostilities, costly both in lives and in trade. The companies had tried to make an agreement before, but the effort had failed.[69] It was the European context that ultimately shaped the 1619 treaty, although accounts of the violent and expensive conflicts at Banda had also spurred companies and diplomats to act. The concerns were diplomatic and financial. On the diplomatic front, the years of the Truce had provoked concerns among both the English and Dutch governments about perilous realignments in Europe. After 1618, the Prince of Orange sought the English as an ally, a concern reflecting Dutch fears of Anglo-Spanish alliance during the Twelve Years' Truce, and perhaps intensified by James I's intermittent interests in arranging a marriage between his son Charles and the Spanish Infanta.[70] Cooperation in the East Indies was one price the Dutch had to pay. Dutch diplomats were so eager to avoid war with the English that they would have sacrificed the Spice Islands.[71] The English had their own concerns, especially about the possibility of a Dutch alliance with France.[72] Moreover, the English chargé d'affaires in Spain reported that rumors in Madrid of Dutch victories over the English in both Greenland and the East Indies damaged English status among a people who valued reputation above all else.[73] James I was especially keen to secure the treaty and pushed the EIC to its negotiation and final settlement.[74] On the financial side, the VOC directors in Amsterdam worried that the companies would ruin each other and end up opening the trade to rivals.[75] The EIC, for its part, was inundated in London with complaints from the traders and in September 1618 had lodged protests

against the VOC with the Privy Council and the crown.[76] The treaty ultimately addressed these immediate European concerns about peace better
than it did the needs of EIC and VOC traders in the East Indies.

The 1619 treaty relegated the EIC to a secondary position: the VOC was
the dominant partner, paying two-thirds of expenses and earning two-
thirds of the profits in the lucrative spice trade in Banda, the Moluccas, and
Amboyna, with one-third reserved for the English company. The profits and
expenses of the pepper trade were shared equally. The two companies were
likewise supposed to contribute equally to defense, but the provisions for
breaking a tie pointed to Dutch authority, because the president of the VOC
council in Batavia got an extra vote in such an event.[77] Although the treaty
remained in place for twenty years, the need to renegotiate aspects of it and
the conflicts that followed the treaty's dissemination in the East Indies demonstrated the challenges of peace negotiations forged in Europe and then
forced on unwilling parties on the other side of the world. It was symbolically
apt that the traders in the Indian Ocean learned about the treaty in spring
1620 as an English fleet sailed from Surat to Banten for a renewed attack on
the Dutch. Neither company embraced the treaty when news arrived of this
fait accompli, and the forced peace enraged Coen.[78]

In fact, the treaty simply opened new avenues of hostility, because two
parties that had been killing each other openly were compelled not only to
make peace—hard enough to achieve—but also to join in a partnership. The
many painful humiliations of the previous conflicts made the rapprochement required by the treaty difficult to accomplish. Especially grating to the
English was that this partnership didn't look much like a partnership at all,
but instead placed the English in a subordinate position, a clear reversal of
the English interpretation of their historical relationship with the United
Provinces, whose independence the English believed they had secured.[79]
The traders found themselves in closer proximity, even sharing habitations,
and this forced intimacy fueled suspicion and mistrust. The two companies
argued repeatedly about every aspect of the treaty's provisions, including dispute resolution, cost sharing, trade strategies, and housing requirements.

The treaty may have exacerbated violence in the region in two respects.
First, the awkward end of conflict between the VOC and EIC enhanced
danger for indigenous traders in Banda and the Moluccas who had suddenly
lost allies. Second, the forced proximity the European traders endured because of the treaty's requirements likely increased mistrust and suspicion,
not only between the English and Dutch, but with other parties as well, as the

VOC worried about the newly subordinated English finding allies among the many others who chafed at VOC claims to dominion and the violence that often accompanied such claims. The eruption of conspiracies in 1622 may have been one result of how the two companies chose to implement a treaty intended to bring peace.

A wide variety of petty and serious conflicts broke out between the English and the Dutch traders even when they were acting in concert. The problems with the partnership, for both the traders and especially for indigenous people, were evident in 1621, when the VOC launched an invasion of Banda to secure a permanent monopoly of the nutmeg trade. This conquest signaled the start of a violent new phase of VOC activity in the region. Ostensibly a joint operation, as the treaty demanded, the EIC could not afford to participate; the attack in fact dislodged the English company from its remaining trading houses in Banda and wrought an unprecedented devastation. The VOC traders so mistrusted their English partners that they believed the English had leaked news of the impending attack to their old Bandanese allies.[80] The invasion destroyed the EIC's trading houses at Lontor and Run and terrified some English traders and their servants.[81] Far more calamitous was the effect of the invasion on the Bandanese population, most of whom died during the invasion.[82] The deaths numbered as many as 15,000 people, one of the largest slaughters by northern European aggressors overseas during this era. In the aftermath of this massive destruction, the Dutch uprooted nutmeg trees and brought in enslaved laborers from all around the region to replace the murdered and dispersed Bandanese, creating a new plantation system of nutmeg cultivation.[83] The ruthless display of Dutch aggression led one English merchant to worry that the VOC governor-general's main ambition was to damage the English. Only English forces equal to those of the Dutch, he thought, would protect the EIC.[84] While it is obvious that the population most terrorized in this episode was the Bandanese, the English preoccupation with their own safety, status, and trade reflected the absence of trust that defined the 1619 partnership.

Among the most frequent disputes were those about expenses. The smallest household charge might spark an objection from the English residents, leaving the VOC councilors complaining in 1621 that they were unable to tend to company business because they were so busy responding to English protests.[85] The treaty obligated the English to pay one-third of all expenditures, not just for fortifications and purchases of commodities but also for daily living. Detailed lists from Amboyna showed the range of costs the

Figure 1.2 This inflammatory illustration, published thirty years later during the First Anglo-Dutch War, depicted the violence of the VOC's assault on Banda in 1621, including the beheading of one of the Chinese servants who worked for the EIC. Abraham Woofe, *The Tyranny of the Dutch against the English* (London, 1653), frontispiece. RB 71811, The Huntington Library, San Marino, California.

companies needed to pay in March and April 1621: wages and food (rice, beef, pork, bread, oil, salt, and wine) for over 300 soldiers at the fort at Amboyna; charges for the hospital, assessments for gifts, and expenses for a school for local boys.[86] The English traders complained to their Dutch counterparts in Batavia in 1623 about what they thought were excessive charges for hospitals, schools, presents to local rulers, artisans' wages, unnecessarily extravagant food at the governor's table, and the paper decorations in the governor's house and the merchants' rooms.[87] English traders fretted that they were not getting an honest accounting of the trade, unable to see expenses until presented with a bill, nor permitted to observe the weighing of spices.[88] Another trader was convinced that the Dutch ran up expenses at Cambello.[89]

All of the EIC's protests about being overcharged and cheated would sound like any number of petty and unfounded complaints lodged by one company against the other over the years were it not for the fact that the English seem to have been correct: they *were* being cheated as part of a deliberate policy. The VOC decided to support its factories in the Moluccas on the monthly fees paid by the English, and English payments also gave the VOC vital access to specie.[90] The VOC requirement that the EIC pay in specie, not goods, infuriated the EIC, especially because the VOC paid its employees in goods. VOC employees were then able to undersell English wares in the marketplace. The VOC governor-general in Batavia explained the system to the VOC's governor in the Moluccas: even at such times as he saved some money through household economies, there was no reason to pass those savings along to the English. After all, the VOC had had to carry all the costs on its own many times: as always, if the VOC spent more, it maintained that it deserved more. In such cases, the governor-general clarified, there was no dishonor in the VOC keeping for its own benefit whatever savings it achieved through good stewardship.[91]

Physical proximity opened new opportunities for insults and for frequent reminders to the English of their secondary status, a "kinde of slaverie," the EIC council at Batavia concluded in 1622, using a metaphor that had real meaning to them as slaveholders and traders.[92] Their long acquaintance helped each company's traders goad the others, and this animosity undermined whatever strategic advantage the companies had secured through their partnership. Complaints came from all around the region in the years after the treaty. The VOC hindered EIC access to basic supplies. At Jakarta, the VOC fined the EIC president for taking wood without permission in September 1620.[93] At Banda in 1622, the VOC denied Richard Welden, the EIC's head agent there, some boards to repair a ship, nor would the governor permit him to send a letter on a VOC boat bound for Amboyna, something required by the treaty. When John Cartwright picked an orange off a tree long harvested by the English, the furious Dutch told him that if he plucked another, they would "[pluck] him out of his skinn." The Englishmen, argued the Dutch, "had noe right to the least stick uppon the land."[94]

For the EIC, the accumulation of petty insults seemed intolerable. At Amboyna, a sergeant refused to saddle horses for English traders without the VOC governor's permission.[95] Two English traders at Bacan objected in October and November of 1621 to the indignities they endured in the northern Moluccas. The trader Giles Cole griped that he had seen more friendship in the profane and raucous fishmarket of Billingsgate than he found among the Dutch.[96] A Dutch gunner invited Thomas Johnson at Bacan to drink with him, then downed most of the drink himself and flung the rest in Johnson's face, christening him, the gunner explained, in the Dutch fashion. "Either release us," Johnson implored his superior at Malayo (on Ternate), "or send ropes to end us."[97] A trader wrote plaintively from Banda that he did not know whom he could trust and thought there was no point in continuing the trade.[98]

Much of this animosity likely stemmed from two sources: English expectations and Dutch resentment. The long-standing English vision of themselves as the creator of the Dutch Republic intersected with a recurring motif in EIC correspondence about the Dutch as self-important. In 1615 and 1616, English efforts to make inroads in the trade at Banda necessitated regular meetings with the Dutch who sought to bar their way. At one meeting, the men gathered at a long table, covered with so many papers that the EIC participant joked that it looked "as if all the matters in Holland had been there to be decided."[99] After a subsequent contretemps with the Dutch in Sukadana on Borneo, he dubbed them "proud blockheads."[100] Accusations of Dutch pride were a regular refrain in the Indies and subsequently reported to the EIC in England. Traders complained in 1621 that the Dutch carried on in the Indies as if they were home in Holland, treated the English contemptuously, and ordered the people at Bacan not to do anything for the English without Dutch permission.[101] Accusations of pride say less about the accused's demeanor than about the accuser's expectations—of deference, of respect. For EIC traders living cheek to jowl with VOC partners who enjoyed a dominant position, the gap between their expectations and their new circumstances may have been jarring.

For its part, the VOC likely resented being required by the terms of the treaty to welcome the English to trading posts from which the Dutch had just dislodged them, including the clove trading posts of Cambello (Kembelu) and Luhu on Seram, and Hitu, Larica (Larike), and the main town (Kota Ambon, where the VOC had a large fortification, Fort Victoria) on Ambon. The VOC allowed the EIC to have such space as it could spare in the Moluccas, sometimes sharing houses, elsewhere letting them build houses inside or near their forts, at least at first allowing the English traders to decide which they preferred.[102] The English returned to Amboyna in 1621, two years after the Dutch there had described them as their greatest enemies.[103] Mutual suspicion continued unabated. The English, for example, did not trust the

VOC to keep them fully informed about fortifications. George Muschamp, the EIC's head merchant at Ambon, provided this essential intelligence to his employers. He sent them a "platt" in June 1621, which named and described all of the places controlled by the Dutch. He also detailed "the true plattforme of the castle, w[i]th the length, breadth, and no. of munition; according to the order given mee."[104] Had Muschamp's letter and map fallen into VOC hands, it would have provided ample justification for their chronic mistrust of EIC ambitions.

A large meeting the VOC hosted at Amboyna on February 19/March 1, 1621, manifested both this suspicion of the English and the VOC's desire to affirm its superiority. The VOC governor Herman van Speult invited all of the leaders from the places under Amboyna's jurisdiction, including Hitu, Luhu, and Cambello. Muschamp attended this event, too. It lasted for six days, during which each individual *orang kaya* affirmed his previous trade contracts and acknowledged that Prince Maurice (the Prince of Orange and the *stadthouder*, or head of state, of the United Provinces) was his ruler. He also pledged not to enter into any trade agreement with a rival nation without Dutch permission. For English witnesses, this ritual likely reminded them not just of their subservient status but indeed of their complete marginalization: the trade relationships performed before them were ties between the *orang kaya* and the VOC. Van Speult may have contrived this occasion largely, in fact, because of the important lessons of subordination for English witnesses. Only three men refused to submit to VOC authority—the representative of the sultan of Ternate, and the *orang kaya* of Luhu and Cambello, who sent deputies but failed to appear themselves because they had rebelled against the Dutch the previous year and wanted to ally themselves with the ruler of Ternate, or so Muschamp understood.[105] Ternate had its own tributary relationships with local communities and rulers and was a persistent and powerful rival to the VOC's ambitions in the southern Moluccas.

The existence of these men opposed to the Dutch—seeking allies in Ternate and likely open to other alliances—resulted in an innovative strategy for EIC and VOC cooperation: cohabitation. It was surely no coincidence that two days after this regional gathering, the EIC and VOC leaders for Amboyna devised a scheme to address the chronic mistrust between the traders in Cambello, Hitu, and Luhu. They blamed the Ambonese and Seramese people for deliberately fomenting discord between the two companies. The solution the joint council reached was to require the traders to live together in a single house at each of the three places; the men were expected to cohabit as well as help each other in times of need.[106]

Although the traders planned this scheme to prevent mistrust, in most respects, it backfired. Aggrieved English traders complained regularly about the indignities they endured when sharing their meals with the Dutch in the Amboyna trading houses. It was not just the daily assaults on their pride and the insultingly high rates the English were charged, but also the inability to find any refuge. Each meal was another occasion to take offense, each month's reckoning a reminder of the VOC's power to extract high fees. Undergirding the complaints were concerns about status. At Cambello, John Wetherall lamented that the "high commanding dutch" treated the English "more like ther slaves and servants then ther fellows and frinds."[107] The merchants were drawn into petty quarrels and controversies about matters of status such as where they were seated at meals. In their shared quarters, the Dutch asserted a right to order the English servants about. There were so many incidents to report from Amboyna, the EIC's new Amboyna governor Gabriel Towerson wrote in September 1622, that he could not possibly relate them all without using up all of the paper he possessed—and he had only three sheets left.[108]

From all of the cohabiting factories, the English traders were in agreement: the English and Dutch had to separate. An EIC trader named Humphrey Fitzherbert wrote frankly to his superiors in Batavia from Amboyna in April 1621, soon after the English had returned there, that the English had no place left, unless they were always willing to live under the Dutch. For his part, he averred, he was willing to risk his life dislodging them, and if he could get all of the traders to join him, he would attempt "the surprizall thereof."[109] What Fiztherbert threatened sounded a lot like a conspiracy. By summer 1622 the chorus had reached a crescendo. If only, John Wetherall argued from Cambello, the English could take the money from their monthly rent payment, they could establish their own comfortable houses and be spared the "contempt and greefe" in which they lived.[110] It "would be much better," Towerson explained, if the Cambello traders could live apart, producing "more love betwixt them and more for our masters profitt," and he reminded his superiors of the Treaty's seventeenth article, which provided for separate housing of both goods and people. The English in Cambello had even gone so far as to purchase some land for their separate accommodation, but van Speult was offended to learn the English had bought property without his permission, and he told Towerson to sell it.[111] Samuel Coulson weighed in from Hitu with the same complaint. As long as the English had to share a house with the Dutch, he explained, there would be no success in the region.[112]

When the English traders lamented the humiliation they endured living with the Dutch, they pointed to the spectators who witnessed their dishonor: can one, after all, be humiliated in isolation? Their degradation required an audience. That aspect of shame explains why the English complained about the presence of servants, as the Dutch subverted social hierarchies in their households, denying the English the right to command their own staff.[113] These spectators also included slaves, who were a vital part of English factory life. They worked on ships and in trading houses, but they also prepared food and attended to domestic duties, and in such positions were well placed to witness English and Dutch interactions in the shared houses.[114] The Dutch seem to have been acutely aware of the value of slaves as spectators to and participants in English debasement—and possibly also as spies—because one of the grievances the English lodged against the VOC in Batavia in 1624 was that the Dutch compelled the English merchants to accommodate their slaves in their very own rooms.[115]

In their complaints, the English traders focused solely on the perceived insults committed in front of other men, as if the traders lived in an all-male enclave. That was highly unlikely to have been the case, although it is possible that the shared houses were primarily male spaces. The servants and slaves who tended to the English, for example, seem to have been boys.[116] But the whole point of the trading posts was for European traders to establish relationships with local clove growers and sellers, and these relationships introduced the EIC traders to a host of people. The English trader John Beaumont had established just such an extensive network of friends at Amboyna, including a married couple and a woman.[117] Women were part of the web of friendships and connections the traders forged, although the EIC banned wives from its outposts. In contrast, the VOC permitted traders to bring wives with them and also allowed them to marry in the region. The VOC trader Jan Joosten lived at Amboyna with his wife and children, and his family hosted the English for over four months when the EIC first returned to Amboyna.[118] There were also many married soldiers employed by the VOC at the fort, forty-nine in 1621, according to the bill presented to the EIC.[119] None of the EIC traders at the Amboyna posts had wives with them, although Towerson was married. He had left his Armenian wife in Agra. The EIC traders in the Moluccas may well have established short- and long-term companionate unions as did counterparts elsewhere.[120] When the EIC traders explained the challenges they confronted in their shared spaces to their employers and colleagues, however, that larger social context vanished. They focused their ire on the perceived slights and insults inflicted by male housemates, before male witnesses.

The unrelenting and intimate nature of this strained cohabitation in the Amboyna factories and beyond contributed to English and Dutch proclivities to believe their trading partners plotted against them. There was nothing unusual in this era about Europeans' tendency to see conspiracies afoot in the world.[121] The sixteenth-century Protestant reformation and the ensuing religious wars boosted conspiratorial thinking as Protestants and Catholics ascribed conspiratorial actions to their enemies and believed themselves to be living in a world in which enemies plotted against their faith.[122] In the early seventeenth century, the English had to look only as far back in their history to the Gunpowder Plot of 1605, an alleged plot by Catholics to blow up Parliament, which itself inspired counter-theories that the plot was invented by Protestant officials, to confirm their conspiratorial worldviews. So embedded was this way of thinking that a character in *Gulliver's Travels* (1726) characterized English history as "'only a heap of conspiracies.'"[123] There were likewise conspiracies in the United Provinces, most recently a 1619 incident involving the Dutch statesman Johan van Oldenbarnevelt, which ended with his execution. A second incident involving the Oldenbarnevelt family, this time his two sons, transpired in 1623, when they allegedly plotted the death of Prince Maurice in an act dubbed both a treason and a conspiracy.[124]

The English and Dutch traders in the East Indies carried these sensibilities with them, but with one important difference: while conspiratorial thinking helped the English and Dutch make sense of some episodes after the fact, it turned out to be especially significant in the East Indies in the anticipation of bad acts. It became a policing strategy by the VOC, which moved to quell conspiracies (real or imagined) around the East Indies in order to secure its rule. The English traders often believed that the VOC plotted against them, devising new ways to drive them out of the spice trade altogether, while the VOC inhabited a far more perilous imagined universe composed of large-scale conspiracies by trade rivals, indigenous people, slaves, employees, insecurely conquered people, and even trading partners. The asymmetrical partnership required by the 1619 treaty fostered this situation: conspiracies thrive on proximity, which enabled alleged plotters to have familiarity with their intended victims and their habits for their plot to succeed; mistrust, which was rampant in all aspects of VOC governance, whether over violently subdued people or with poorly incorporated European trading partners; and a legal or cultural dynamic that hindered other options for redress. VOC rule in the Indies was uneasy and precarious, dependent on quelling subordinates in the most brutal ways possible. English observers provided a constant reckoning of the accumulation of bodies: 40 here, 100 there, people tortured, some beheaded, others drawn and quartered, survivors enslaved, heads on pikes. By 1622 the VOC had this system fully in place.[125]

That year witnessed periods of acute tension between the companies and within the region. Conspiracies accelerated with frightening implications especially for indigenous inhabitants but also for the English. Regular quarrels between the two companies could no longer be contained through the usual mechanisms of negotiation and co-governance as outlined by the 1619 treaty and practiced by custom. Some of these episodes involved only indigenous people; others included the English as alleged co-conspirators. One big conspiracy allegedly transpired on Banda in August 1622, led by Bandanese survivors of the 1621 invasion. Welden explained the contours of the plot: the Bandanese—despite, Welden insisted, generous treatment by the VOC governor—intended to go secretly to Seram, and before their departure planned to carry out actions against the Dutch. The scheme revealed, the VOC governor examined and tortured the ringleaders, "most intollerable tortures," Welden remarked.[126] The Dutch executed 123 men (3 quartered, and 120 decapitated) on Banda and 30 more on Ai. Others were enslaved and their possessions confiscated. The English traders agreed that this plot was a real threat and were relieved it had been revealed; still more alarming, Welden suggested that there might be "many other plotts" at work.[127] In Batavia, the EIC council condemned the plotters as "treacherous villaines" who deserved their fate.[128] Towerson learned of the Banda conspiracy in Amboyna, and he characterized the incident as a rebellion. While he might have heard the news from English traders, it is more likely, given his frequent socializing with the VOC governor, that he heard it from van Speult. If he did, van Speult may well have been trying to undermine the historical alliance between the English and Bandanese and to enhance English dependence on the Dutch as useful allies and even protectors, for Towerson believed that the English were targets as well as the Dutch, a plot twist Welden, who was in Banda, did not report.[129]

Although the English agreed with the Dutch about the existence of this Banda conspiracy and approved Dutch actions there, the VOC for its part believed that the English were sometimes complicit in anti-Dutch machinations. There were two instances involving potential English conspirators in 1622, both in Batavia, when the VOC sought to extract evidence of English connivance. Sometime in early 1622 Coen uncovered what he believed to be a plot on the part of some Bandanese to hand Batavia to the Javanese. On learning of the alleged plot, Coen tortured many Bandanese, and the English traders reported that the VOC interrogators tried to get the Bandanese to implicate the English, but to no avail. The English concluded from this incident that the Dutch were eager to entrap the English and would find any excuse to bring the English under their jurisdiction.[130]

In August 1622, at the same time as the alleged plot on Banda, a second incident happened in Batavia. It seemed like a minor episode, but its escalation signaled the tenterhooks on which the traders lived. One night two EIC employees went down to the stables, armed with swords and Japanese halberds. The corporal of the VOC guards asked them who they were, and the EIC employees replied that they were doing their rounds on the EIC president's orders, serving as an EIC night watch. The VOC guards arrested the men. The VOC's bailiff was incensed by these "improper usurpations" and resolved to torture the men to confess: the English men believed that they were expected to implicate the EIC's head agent. The VOC's sheriffs in Batavia surveyed the available evidence and decided that however much they doubted the veracity of the prisoners, they would not allow them to be tortured, only menaced with a cord. The bailiff then demanded corporal punishment for the men, but the sheriffs still refused. Instead, they pardoned and released the men and instructed the EIC's president to clarify matters for his guards. The VOC's decree, while ostensibly intended to help the Dutch keep order in Batavia, also imposed restrictions on the English that would have insulted their sense of themselves and their honor. The English president was no longer allowed to be accompanied by guards with any martial display— no beating a drum, for example, nor any of those vital performances that signaled his status. His subordinates' movements were restricted as well: his men could not visit the stable at night, but would have to spend the night there, or else keep the cattle in the English factory.[131]

These unsettling episodes revealed that VOC traders believed their EIC partners to be plotting against them in 1622. Suspicion was rampant. In the wake of reports that the English stole a ship in 1622, the VOC wrote that anyone who dared to steal would lie on oath, and the English were such skilled liars that they would deny the sun shone at high noon.[132] The EIC reciprocated the mistrust. The EIC agent at Bacan regarded the gracious behavior of the VOC head merchant there as merely part of a plot to entrap the English and characterized English and Dutch interactions as superficial, "love from the teeth outward onlye."[133] Had the English and Dutch traders paused to reflect for a moment, the most honest and perceptive men might have come to appreciate that they were looking in a mirror, each ascribing to the other identical traits.

Everything seemed to be breaking down between the two companies in 1622, even familiar protocols for administering justice. The companies had long established procedures to handle violence by their employees, especially when that violence affected the other company. Sometimes these mutual obligations placed each side in an uncomfortable position, carrying out deeds they would rather have evaded. Such was the case in Banten in 1604, when a slave in the English house was accused of killing a Dutchman. The English were distressed that they had to execute this man. Had he killed only a Javan, whose life held less value in the brutal calculus of the place and time, they would have had to pay a fine, not sacrifice the slave's life. But with a dead European (and possibly two—the story was unclear), the slave had to die. The EIC honored its obligations to the VOC, but to ensure a swift death, Edmund Scott hired the executioner and loaned him his sharp sword.[134]

When these rituals functioned properly, they enabled the companies to agree to the appropriate penalty and to remedy damaged relations through the use of public and sometimes reciprocal punishment. At Hirado in 1622 the EIC hanged one employee for murdering a Dutchman, and the VOC likewise executed a sailor for the same crime.[135] But sometimes the system broke down, and that is what happened at the shared post in Cambello in June 1622, when a VOC corporal, David Jost, and an EIC employee, George Spence, fought a duel after an "idle Argument." Jost, Muschamp explained sympathetically, suffered some bad luck when Spence died of his injuries. At Muschamp's insistence, the VOC employee was executed, shot to death by the VOC governor. Muschamp had demanded justice, but he didn't do so, he clarified, because he thought the quarrel itself had been unfair, but rather so "that ye Cuntry should take notice of it."[136] Muschamp, that is, sacrificed the life of the VOC soldier so that Seramese witnesses at Cambello could see that the EIC was capable of forcing the VOC to kill its own men. Indeed, van Speult shot Jost to death himself. Perhaps Muschamp took advantage of the few opportunities presented to him to assert EIC status. His demand for Jost's death certainly looks like an act of aggression in the face of VOC dominion. With this maneuver, Muschamp had created a crucial precondition for a conspiracy.

One person who took especially close notice of this execution was a furious van Speult, who believed that the English should have intervened on behalf of the corporal rather than demanding his execution.[137] Evidence from a later incident suggests that this custom was regularly practiced. In 1628, for example, a Dutchman at Surat found guilty of killing an English sailor was condemned to death, but at the last minute, before the man was thrown overboard and drowned, an English agent interceded and the Dutch pardoned him.[138] The Cambello incident seemed to upset van Speult beyond just the loss of Jost. It deepened his mistrust of the English: perhaps he worried that Muschamp's display was intended to show the people there that the English could be useful and powerful allies. He suspected that the English might be engaging in a conspiracy, and he wrote Coen asking for authority to carry out justice immediately, regardless of who the culprit was, if it turned out that the English were plotting against the VOC. Coen advised van Speult in turn to teach the English to stay in their place and, if necessary, to punish any violent Englishman as Corporal Jost had been punished.[139]

By the winter of 1622–23, the companies began to come to some resolution about how to navigate the daily challenges wrought by efforts to conform to the 1619 treaty. For the English, the clear solution, dictated especially by their chronic financial troubles of which the VOC was well aware, was to abandon the posts altogether and to focus on the pepper trade on Java.[140] Trade in new markets was hard, as all European newcomers had learned from their first forays in Banten and Banda. Fragile and ephemeral trading posts tended to have short life spans. The EIC closed its trading post in Japan, too, in the same year, and had other promising areas to focus on along the Coromandel Coast. But for the EIC, dealing with the VOC was also infuriating and there seemed to be no relief. "The chief plotter," the English councilors wrote their employers when they explained their decision, was Coen, and his successor was no better. The EIC believed its traders endured especially injurious conditions at Amboyna, where "wee have been as much exacted uppon as in any other, and in divers p[ar]ticulars grosslie abused." Muschamp—who had inadvertently set in motion van Speult's heightened quest for evidence of an English plot—was on his way home and wouldn't be in Amboyna to deal with the catastrophic fall-out of his actions in June. Unable to tolerate the Dutch any longer, and in poor health, he was eager to quit the region and would tell his employers all about the strife there, the endless indignities, the petty betrayals.[141] In December 1622 and January 1623, the EIC council wrote the company's head traders in Banda, Ternate, and Amboyna to inform them of its decision.[142] The EIC suspended the trade and the VOC agreed to transport the company's goods from the various factories back to Batavia.[143]

The VOC was coming up with its own strategy, the opposite of the EIC's solution of disentanglement. The VOC's position was already evident in the many conspiracies it had quelled so violently in 1622: eternal vigilance against multiple scheming enemies. The company's trading posts rapidly transformed into centers for policing. While the English traders ruminated on their mistrust of the Dutch in particular, the VOC saw enemies everywhere. In a testy letter, Coen ordered the governor of Banda not to trust even Bandanese women and children, nor indeed any of the Bandanese and Seramese men and, as for the English, trust them no more than one would an enemy.[144] The Amboyna governor stayed on his guard as well, in response to Coen's instructions for vigilance against English duplicity. In June 1622, van Speult faithfully reported that he would respond quickly if he learned of any conspiracies.[145]

Their suspicious and rigid demeanor put them at odds with the wishes of their employers in Europe. Regretting VOC traders' complaints that the English were wicked and crafty, enjoining their employees to keep the peace, and drawing on the analogies common in Dutch, the directors in Amsterdam explained in 1622 that the two companies were in a single boat and therefore were required to cooperate with each other. They similarly likened the 1619 treaty forced on them to a marriage to a quarrelsome wife: a man can't end a marriage for that reason alone, the directors argued, but rather had to make the best of the situation with all of the patience he could muster.[146] In the marital metaphor, the Dutch were the husband, the dominant partner in the conventions of the era. The directors even rebuked the VOC councilors in Batavia in 1622 for their severity against the Bandanese during the invasion the previous year: that example was sufficient, they thought, and they regretted that the council had not found a more temperate way to handle matters. Those who terrorized people had much to fear themselves, as they put it, in an analysis that went to the heart of why the VOC's governing strategies put the traders in the position of constant vigilance against plotters, and the directors told their employees to treat the English well.[147]

The traders in the Indies, living in circumstances far removed from those of their employers in Europe, were unable to find the necessary patience. The VOC regarded the English as insolent, violent, and disrespectful. In October 1622, as he prepared to return to Europe, Coen wrote the heads of the VOC factories, warning them to be on their guard against English plots and to trample any sign of insolence. All of the English were alike. It was the job of the VOC to teach them manners and keep them in check.[148] Everything the English did prompted Dutch concern in these months, including owning too many slaves at Banda, which might lead to plots against the Dutch.[149]

At his post in Amboyna, van Speult exemplified all of the stress, tension, suspicion, and touchiness of a VOC officer. The partnership and intimacy with the English had become intolerable. In this suspicious frame of mind, van Speult was ready to move on the first hint that his fears had been realized, although there were so many threats surrounding him, he had almost too many perils to choose from. Maybe he could save the day in Amboyna as the VOC's governor of Banda had done when he discovered a conspiracy there in 1622. Maybe he could finally get the evidence of English complicity that his counterparts had failed to extract in Batavia. Maybe he, too, could safeguard VOC interests and demonstrate his value to the company by protecting it from another conspiracy. He had to be vigilant. When the time came, he was ready to sift through the multiple dangers the VOC confronted on Amboyna and to piece together the conspiracy he both feared and anticipated.

2

The Amboyna Business

A distinguishing feature marked Amboyna's long, thin harbor: a sturdy fort, perched on the coast so that ships could load and unload conveniently. The building served as the center of the VOC's political and administrative activities, and in it, the Dutch governor, in consort with his council, administered justice. On its ramparts, a Japanese soldier asked revealing questions, hinting at a plot in February 1623, and in its cells the VOC interrogated and sometimes tortured his alleged co-conspirators. In its walls these men signed their confessions, heard the horrifying words condemning them to death, ate their final meal, bid farewell to the pardoned, and girded their courage to march through its gates to their deaths.

Adjacent to the structure was the town of Kota Ambon, which had grown up outside the fort when the Portuguese occupied the area and continued to expand under VOC occupation.[1] Houses clustered nearby when the VOC took over in 1605, so officials prudently moved the dwellings to create open space between the fort and the town, and it was in that space that the condemned lost their heads.[2] The town contained the English residence, not far from the fort, and a heterogeneous population. The inhabitants included Portuguese soldiers who had stayed on after the VOC conquest; some Ambonese Christians; people from other parts of Asia, including Chinese, who first appeared in the town in 1619, and the Japanese soldiers; and a population of free slaves, including people called mardijkers, who were Asians, some of whom were Christians. By 1610, the town numbered some 1,500 people.[3] Inland, above the town, the volcanic hills rise so steeply that farmers struggle to create level space for planting in the fertile soil. Rains lash the islands during the season of the eastern monsoons, and Ambon, like its neighbors, is vulnerable to powerful typhoons and occasional earthquakes. The island is mostly dry from November to April, when the western monsoons blow, and it is then that ships could find their way there from the EIC and VOC administrative center at Batavia, some 1,500 miles away. In March 1623, four recently arrived VOC ships lay at their anchors. But travel back to Java for guidance from the regional officers and the joint council

Figure 2.1 Initially built in brick by the Portuguese in 1576, the fort, along with the rest of the Portuguese-claimed territory on Ambon, was seized by the VOC in 1605. The VOC strengthened the structure and renamed it Fort Victoria in 1614. It is pictured here as viewed from the water in 1607. *Begin ende Voortgangh van de Vereenighde Nederlantsche Geoctroyeerde Oost-Indische Compagnie* ([Amsterdam], 1646), vol. 2, plate 6. RB106404, The Huntington Library, San Marino, California.

established by the 1619 treaty had to wait until the eastern monsoons, which typically begin in May.[4]

From his lodgings in the fort, Governor Herman van Speult had a lot on his mind. His post at Amboyna came with many burdens: the English regarded the man who held that office as the second most powerful officer in the Indies, after the VOC's governor-general.[5] He was responsible for the success of the clove trade, which meant regulating supply and ensuring steady cultivation. Because Ambon alone was capable of fulfilling all of Europe's clove needs, the VOC managed oversupply by ripping up and destroying clove trees elsewhere.[6] He also had to ensure that all partners and tributaries complied with their treaty obligations.[7] As part of his duties, van Speult traveled the region on annual progresses to maintain the obedience of those who lived under the

VOC's protection. By 1634, the province contained some 76,000–80,000 indigenous people on Ambon and other islands.[8]

There were, as always, concerns about regional rivals, and an unsettling incident at the trading post at Luhu showed how legitimate these fears were. Although the VOC suspected that the EIC might be in league with the Ternatans, who maintained over seventy tributary relationships, including with people on Ambon and Seram, the English had been the victims of Ternatan violence at the Luhu factory sometime between January 1 and mid-February. In an effort to recover a runaway slave who had fled to the Ternatans, John Beaumont, the head of the EIC traders there, was accosted by some Ternatans and shot in the hand. A VOC servant was killed.[9] This episode prompted the traders to close the shared factory. The EIC's goods had only recently arrived in Amboyna in the care of the VOC employee Martin Jansz Vogel, whom Gabriel Towerson, the EIC's new head trader, thanked with a present.[10]

The town held a larger percentage of Europeans than a satellite factory like Luhu, but even there, van Speult had many troubles to contend with. As always, he struggled to manage his relationship with the English traders. One glimmer of success seemed to be Towerson, who had replaced George Muschamp in September 1622. Although the trader Samuel Coulson had described van Speult's relationship with Muschamp as good, it is hard to believe it wasn't in need of some improvement after Muschamp put van Speult in the position of having to execute David Jost at Cambello in June 1622, and Muschamp himself heaved a sigh of relief when he sailed away from Amboyna.[11] That incident suggested that Muschamp might have been looking for opportunities to lord it over the VOC, but Towerson seemed to be a more malleable sort, despite his twenty years in the Indies and long familiarity with VOC traders.

Towerson's arrival held the promise of new beginnings. Like the English throughout the region, Towerson was preoccupied by his living situation. At Amboyna, he hoped to follow up on plans launched by his predecessor to buy or rent Vogel's house with its contents. Van Speult seemed eager to make the plan a reality. By letting the English have their own housing in the town, a place of respite and privacy, van Speult created a crucial precondition to the plot he already anticipated. But he wanted more than Towerson's gratitude for his assistance. He wanted presents: a chain of gold for his wife, or a hogshead of beer, and free transport in English ships, too, and he lobbied Towerson to arrange these perks. Towerson seemed swayed by van Speult's assertion that the English were in his debt, which apparently gave the EIC council at Batavia pause. His superiors warned him not to be deceived by van Speult's "dessembling frendshipp." The message was clear: do not trust the governor.[12]

So many relationships to negotiate, so many potential sources of upheaval, and it looked as if van Speult also needed to worry about the possibility of a slave conspiracy, because sitting in prison in Fort Victoria was the overseer of the VOC's slaves in Ambon, a man named Augustine Peres. Born in Bengal, he was likely Indo-Portuguese, his name suggesting a Portuguese father at least. The English account of the conspiracy turned him into a "Portingall."[13] Peres lived in Amboyna with a woman given to him as a companion by the VOC in hopes of making him more tractable, although he already had a wife elsewhere.[14] The VOC council members explained after the trial that he had been arrested "some weeks before" the discovery of the Anglo-Japanese conspiracy for using abusive language against his employers, having said, among other things, "the devil should fetch those, who had given him his stick, specially the Governor."[15] If the Dutch were troubled by thoughts of conspiracy, as their conduct throughout the region made plain, then an insulting and rebellious slave overseer who resisted the correction his employers or owners thought was their right was a frightening reminder of the personnel available to rise against them, especially because the slaves, according to one VOC trader, were used to obeying their guardian.[16] But then something happened that helped van Speult understand the threat he was really facing, more terrifying even than a rebellion raised by all the company's slaves. What exactly was the peril van Speult confronted, and how did he uncover it?

An answer to those questions requires some understanding of the evidence available and a frank acknowledgment of its myriad deficiencies. It is impossible to know for sure if any of the surviving sources were generated during the conspiracy trial itself, starting with the legal records produced by the VOC, compiled in Amboyna in late March 1623. It was a barebones document, making it difficult to recover the day-to-day activities of the council hearing the case. The record collapsed time, suggesting that all confessions were signed on the day of the torture. It dated all of the English confessions on February 26, despite the fact that the men from the outer factories were not even in the town yet on that date, and the English timeline suggests that the examinations of the English spanned five days, from February 25 through March 1.[17] The official trial record omitted some examinations and the interrogatories, too.[18] The documentation was such a mess that after the executions van Speult immediately started a clean-up operation and worked to bolster his case.[19] Other documents purportedly produced during the trial were English attestations of innocence, but all of these could well have been forgeries.[20] Many vital pieces of evidence—letters, for example, and a prayer delivered by one English trader at the execution ground—went missing during and immediately after the trial. One surviving piece of evidence— a letter by Towerson—exists only in a Dutch translation, so it is impossible to ascertain whether the English original ever existed or if the letter was invented entirely by the VOC as part of this effort to cover its tracks.

What follows is an attempt to navigate the contradictions of sources produced primarily in the aftermath of the episode, all in the context of heated diplomatic and political circumstances in Europe as the EIC, VOC, States General, Parliament, consuls, ambassadors, the Prince of Orange, and the English monarch all wrestled with the fallout of the Amboyna business, as they dubbed it. This reconstruction pieces together a sequence of events from the perspective of multiple participants, while pointing to some of the most glaring inconsistencies. It relies especially heavily on fifty depositions given after the fact by participants (six English survivors; a handful of other English deponents; assorted British employees of the VOC; and all the rest current or former VOC employees) over several years, in the East Indies, in London, in Amsterdam, and in The Hague, starting two days after the execution of the conspirators and culminating in 1631.[21] Depositions were highly controlled activities, in which deponents normally responded to a set series of questions, determined by the concerns of examiners, and, for most of these deponents, specifically by the States General. The questions, moreover, were leading and produced highly predictable and formulaic responses, but they convey a clear sense of the concerns that animated the VOC, first when van Speult assessed the dangers that surrounded him at Amboyna in 1623, and a few years later in Europe.

The imprisoned and rebellious slave overseer was among the threats that so haunted van Speult that he had nightmares, and he later told three English traders that it was a dream that led him to interrogate a Japanese soldier named Hytieso.[22] He was one of eleven or twelve mercenaries who worked for the VOC at the fort, part of a stream of about 300 soldiers hired by the VOC in Hirado, where Hytieso himself had been born, in the period between 1613 and 1623. One Wednesday night in February, during the time reserved for prayers, Hytieso asked questions about different aspects of the fort's defenses. It was not the first time the twenty-four-year old soldier had asked these questions, but this occasion prompted suspicion, whether because the soldiers he interrogated were so "younge and rawe" and foolish enough to respond or because one of those soldiers decided there was something amiss in Hytieso's interest and told the lieutenant of the fort.[23] The next day, van Speult resolved to get to the bottom of Hytieso's persistent curiosity. It was a meaningful date to van Speult and the other Dutch, for it was the anniversary of the VOC's own conquest of Amboyna from the Portuguese in 1605. How incredible, then, that God's providence enabled the Dutch to discover on that very day, eighteen years after their first conquest, that there was a plot against their rule.[24]

At his examination on February 23, Hytieso told van Speult that he had asked his questions "out of a merry disposition and for pleasure," but the governor informed him "that of necessity it must be otherwise," so he was strung up for torture, which was an essential and regulated aspect of the legal procedures the Dutch followed and used to compel confessions—not just of guilt, but especially of the true details of the intended crime. Hytieso was bound to a door frame, a cloth placed over his face, and water poured in his mouth so that he felt as if he were drowning. He might also have been tortured with fire, candles held against his armpits, elbows, and the soles of his feet. In order for a prisoner's torture to cease, the accused had to produce a plausible narrative of events. Denial, for example, only produced more torture, as most of the accused men discovered. After the torture had gone on "a while," Hytieso understandably wished it to cease, announced he would confess everything, and produced the details of a plot.[25] At first Hytieso confessed only to a Japanese conspiracy. Then, however, van Speult said (or so he later reported) that it was impossible that the Japanese could have accomplished such a task on their own, and someone asked Hytieso who his accomplices were.[26] Hytieso's answers, at least as reported after the fact by VOC employees, revealed a terrifying constellation of enemies, with the English, their servants and slaves, the Japanese, the imprisoned slave overseer, and the VOC's slaves, numbering as many as 100 people.[27] The VOC feared that such a force, planning to attack when the governor was away and the fort's ranks were depleted, or perhaps when an EIC ship arrived, promised likely success, given the English traders' ability to move freely in and out of the fort.

The outline of the plot extracted from Hytieso by torture echoed an episode in 1615, when the VOC had tried to prevent the EIC from trading at Cambello. In that instance, the English company managed to sneak some men into the fort and killed some Dutch.[28] The EIC trader Humphrey Fitzherbert seemed to have suggested another such action in Amboyna in 1621 when he proposed to join with the English traders and attempt to dislodge the VOC. [29] Aided by the feared Japanese soldiers, they could have caused more damage than in the 1615 episode. The VOC was not wrong to suspect an EIC interest in the fort, because in 1621, Muschamp had sent just such information to his employers.[30] The VOC's assumption of some kind of English plot was not entirely far-fetched.

Once Hytieso revealed this plot, and other examined Japanese soldiers confirmed it, van Speult and the men he rounded up to serve on his special council may have started to reflect anew on another prisoner then languishing in prison: the Welsh barber-surgeon, Abel Price, implicated by Hyietso. The plotters allegedly intended to set fires in different parts of the town to distract citizens. Fire was one of the most terrifying specters of life in the Indies. The English trader Edmund Scott described his fear of fire succinctly in his first years at Banten: Scott and Towerson so dreaded fire when they lived there that although they would not wake to a drum banging outside their bedroom doors, the merest whisper of fire propelled them out of their beds in terror.[31] But fire was more than a menace to safety. For those who had studied the classics, it was a sure indicator of a conspiracy under way. Livy described a slave conspiracy in 420 BCE that was to be initiated by fires, as was another major conspiracy, the Catiline conspiracy.[32]

And who better to set these fires than an arsonist already in prison? The twenty-four-year-old Price had been arrested a few days before the VOC exposed the alleged conspiracy, possibly at Towerson's request, because of his drunkenness and threatening to set a house on fire, or perhaps actually doing so. The VOC's published account of the conspiracy dubbed Price an "*Incendiary*."[33] Hytieso implicated Price, along with Peres; possibly the three men had shared a single chamber in the fort the night before the soldier's interrogation and their names were fresh in Hytieso's mind when van Speult asked under torture about his accomplices. The governor then presented Price with all the details from the Japanese soldiers' confessions—dates, times, and people with whom he had plotted. VOC interrogators tortured Price and also carried in the tortured Japanese soldiers so that their mangled bodies might prod him to confess. Thus persuaded, Price confirmed Hytieso's information and his confession filled in some crucial details for the Dutch, including the participation of the rest of the EIC's merchants and Price's meetings with the mardijkers, too. The VOC trader Jan Joosten recalled later that Price told the Dutch about the New Year's Day meeting, although that detail is not in the trial records.[34]

Nothing in the last surviving letter from the English traders in September 1622 pointed to this calamitous turn of events. It suggested instead that, while relations between EIC and VOC traders were often volatile, especially at the outer posts, on Amboyna itself VOC and EIC leaders seemed interested in cementing an amicable connection, one secured through sociability and mutual obligation. What happened between Towerson's request for presents for van Speult and his wife in September and the arrest and interrogation of all the English by van Speult in February? Why, that is, did van Speult believe that Hytieso's accomplices were employees of the English company? Whatever one's opinion of the conspiracy, it is clear that matters deteriorated in these months—whether to the point that the Dutch planned to murder the English and drive them out of the Moluccas; that the Dutch believed the English and others plotted against them in Amboyna; or that the English and the Japanese were so discontented with conditions on Amboyna that by New Year's Day they had joined in a plot with the slave overseer to take over the trading post and kill the Dutch. If Towerson or any other EIC traders had anything important to say about the corrosion of relations, their letters have not survived. Perhaps these were among the paperwork confiscated by VOC officials on February 25, 1623, when they searched the English house for incriminating evidence.

Something may have happened in December to sharpen hostilities. So, at least, a few later accounts intimate. Van Speult recalled in June 1623 that in December 1622 or January 1623, he had cautioned Towerson not to be too familiar with soldiers, slaves, and others (exactly the people involved in the alleged plot) in order to avoid arousing suspicion.[35] Two VOC employees remembered menacing remarks made by an English trader, Robert Brown, in December, when he was unable to get his horse saddled as he wished. Resentful at his difficulties, Brown threatened that soon the English would be stronger than the Dutch, and within a year would rule the fort.[36] This conversation, of course, might never have taken place, but it was precisely the type of petty conflict and boastful exchange that was omnipresent in the Indies. Its timing in December hints that tensions might have flared in that month.

It was the new beginning of Towerson's tenure as the EIC's head merchant that sparked fears of conspiracy. On New Year's Day,[37] Towerson summoned almost all of the EIC merchants to the separate English trading house at Amboyna with their accounts so that he could acquaint himself with the trade.[38] Of the eighteen EIC employees in the region, two were Scots, one was Welsh, one was from Hamburg, and fourteen came from all over England, with several from London but others from places ranging from Bristol and Devon to Newcastle. Towerson lived in the main town, along with Emanuel Thompson, a fifty-year-old Hamburg native whose language skills were invaluable to the English in their dealings with the Dutch, and five other traders, Timothy Johnson, Edward Collins, Price, Brown, and John Fardo. The traders at the remote factories traveled to the town for the meeting on pinnaces or corocoros, the outriggers common there: William Griggs from Larica, Coulson and John Clarke from Hitu, John Wetherall from Cambello, and John Beaumont from Luhu. Because the English and Dutch shared houses at Larica, Hitu, Cambello, and Luhu, their housemates would have known of their journey, and on New Year's night Towerson dined with the Dutch governor, an invitation he received during dinner with the other English, a spontaneous summons that perhaps hints at the kind of relationship the governor and Towerson enjoyed.[39] Van Speult may have been interested in companionship or surveillance or some combination of the two. Several English employees stayed in the remote factories—William Webber, John Sadler, John Powel, George Sherrock, Thomas Ladbrooke, and Ephraim Ramsey—and kept company with their VOC housemates. But despite the mistrust that had allegedly prompted van Speult to warn Towerson in December, he still took no action in response to the English meeting, which apparently did not arouse his suspicions at the time.

As Hytieso, the other Japanese soldiers, and Price divulged their alleged conspiracy on February 23–25, van Speult and his council consulted anxiously about how to proceed. The governor issued secret orders forbidding the English from leaving the island. Nor were they allowed to come into the fort's hall. The English seem to have known that the Japanese were in trouble for some kind of plot, because Thompson asked a sentinel at the fort what the Japanese had done when he dropped by to collect provisions from the store there.[40] In the cool evenings, the English in town often went to the governor's garden to exercise and play games. Towerson ran into van Speult while walking after the heat of the day, and Towerson told the governor that he knew the Japanese who worked for the VOC were imprisoned. Van Speult replied that they were up to no good, and Towerson agreed that they should be punished as they deserved.[41]

The English found out soon enough what was going on. On February 25, van Speult summoned the English who lived in the town to the fort. He

Figure 2.2 A bird's eye view of Amboyna from 1617 showing Fort Victoria, along with the variety of vessels that transported people and goods around the region. Anonymous, View of Amboyna, circa 1617. Oil on canvas, h 148.8cm × w 268.2cm, color. SK-A-4482, Rijksmuseum, Amsterdam.

reported that he was "much astonished, sorry and perplexed" to learn of the English conspiracy and professed to be loath to imprison the English but his council persuaded him to do so. The word quickly spread through town, and two VOC employees confronted Fardo that day at the smithy as he was being put in irons and asked him why he had joined this conspiracy. Fardo heaved a sigh and answered that Towerson had compelled him to support the plot or else risk losing his wages. And then Fardo allegedly lamented, "Now I am a dead man, I shall have to die." These two VOC employees testified over two years after this encounter and it would be easy to discredit their allegation, except for that distinctive phrase Fardo uttered, because it turns out to sound like something Fardo might say. English survivors who attested to his wishes in his oral will in 1624 used almost the same phrase. Fardo, one said, despaired that "he was but a dead man in England."[42]

The two VOC employees at the smithy weren't the only men with questions for their English neighbors and colleagues. Van Speult asked Towerson what kind of thanks this plot was for the friendship he had shown. In response, Towerson professed his innocence, but "so softly," Joosten recalled in 1626, "that his guilt was apparent."[43] Towerson's expression was "much abashed & altered," remembered Laurens de Marschalck in 1628.[44] Towerson requested to be imprisoned in his own house, and he remained there until the VOC council moved him with his papers to a merchant's chamber in the fort.[45] Most of the other traders were kept first at the fort and later on two VOC ships, the *Rotterdam* and the *Unicorn*. That very afternoon, the interrogations began: first Johnson, then Thompson, then Beaumont.[46]

The men from the distant posts learned about the alleged conspiracy and the English role in it on their journeys to the town. On February 25, soldiers apprehended the men from the Hitu factory, Coulson, Clarke, and Sherrock, put them in irons, and placed them on a boat to Larica, where Griggs and Sadler joined them and they all sailed to Amboyna. On his journey, Coulson talked about the conspiracy with Reynier Corcerius, a merchant at Larica. Corcerius was not sure at the time if Coulson had been accused of anything but recalled later that Coulson dismissed Towerson as a lying scoundrel.[47] Coulson continued to fume about Towerson, according to VOC witnesses. Coulson announced subsequently that if Towerson accused him, he would deny it and, furthermore, would call Towerson a rogue and tell him all of this to his face. But in this account, the story spun into one of Coulson's guilt. Jan van Nieuwpoort recalled that he had asked Coulson during his interrogation why he did not follow through on his words to accuse Towerson (precisely the kind of questioning absent from the VOC's formal trial records), and Coulson replied that his conscience told him he must speak the truth.[48]

On February 26, Coulson, Clarke, Sherrock, Sadler, and Griggs reached Amboyna. There, in the hall of the fort, they met Ramsey and Webber and asked them what had caused the VOC to suspect the English. Ramsey and Webber explained that the VOC feared a conspiracy to seize the fort. At that moment, Collins appeared from an inner chamber, soaked with water, his doublet removed, his eyes protruding from his head.[49] The last English traders to arrive in Amboyna were Powel, Wetherall, and Ladbrooke from Cambello. VOC soldiers told them that the English and Japanese had plotted to take over the fort and kill the governor and all the rest of the Dutch. On February 28, they were taken to the fort, charged with crimes, and then ushered to the smith's to have irons secured around their legs. In that condition, they couldn't walk, so they had to be carried by servants into the fort's hall, where they stayed under guard while they listened to the screams and protests of tortured men and anxiously awaited their own turn.[50]

Without torture, the VOC could never have discovered this specific plot. Even if there were a conspiracy afoot, the only confessions the examiners accepted were those they believed. The confessions, then, tell us about the plot the VOC feared and envisioned. The council believed, for example, the Japanese version that the plot would start once an English ship came into the harbor, and it rejected Timothy Johnson's version, that the plot would start when the VOC governor left Amboyna.[51] The motives that the examiners extracted from the plotters likewise give insight into what VOC officials thought would compel the alleged plotters to act. The Japanese confessed that they pledged to help the English traders in return for money. The English who confessed about Towerson's state of mind described a man moved to take revenge on the Dutch for their disparagement of the English. In this respect, in the context of confessions succeeding only if they provided what examiners wanted to hear, van Speult's anger over his execution of the Dutch corporal at Cambello in summer 1622 and his own desire for revenge raise the question of whose motivations the examiners uncovered. Van Speult's rage at Jost's death struck the survivor John Powel as his motivation for the "bloody massacre," and Powel had lived at Cambello with Spence and Jost, so he might have been a reliable source for the explosive animosities this incident engendered.[52] Whose honor? Whose revenge? As he crafted the narrative that would make the plot persuasive to his superiors, van Speult argued in June 1623 that it was "poverty" and the "inborn arrogance" of the English that led them to this plot, and the VOC's published account cited Towerson's confession that he was motivated by both *"Honour,* and *Profit."*[53]

Torture also revealed an extensive array of co-conspirators and exposed the apprehension the Dutch had about enemies within and without. Foremost were the Japanese soldiers. Although EIC employees eager to distance themselves from the conspiracy later derided the Japanese as "poore" soldiers of "meane quality," "fellowes of meane condition and such as the English regarded not nor had any acquaintance with," the English and Japanese socialized together in Amboyna, possibly communicating in Malay or Portuguese, two important regional languages.[54] So Price did at Amboyna in 1623, "alone of all the English": he gambled and drank with the Japanese soldiers and did the same with the Dutch and "other Blacks."[55] The Dutch at Amboyna regarded him as the best Malay speaker and thus believed him to be the most likely conduit between the English and Japanese plotters.[56] Two of the accused Japanese soldiers, Sidney Miguel and Pedro Congi, had possibly worked for the English before they went into Dutch service.[57] Sidney Miguel may even have served the English in Japan as an interpreter.[58]

The Japanese had skills that would enable them to take the fort, even with only ten soldiers, as outlined in their confessions. VOC employees consistently described them as "stoute and valiant" men.[59] The ferocity and prowess that made the Japanese such valuable employees to the VOC also made them dangerous enemies: the VOC directors recalled prior examples of a small number of Japanese soldiers wreaking havoc, pillaging the town of Patani on the Malay peninsula, or surprising the castle in Ayutthaya in the kingdom of Siam, taking the castle by force, and imprisoning the king, all tasks far more daunting than seizing the fort at Amboyna.[60] The Japanese also had ample motivation to support the English, since the VOC used the Japanese ruthlessly in its own military engagements and punished them harshly for any transgressions.[61] Almost every confession offered the same narrative of the plot: the Japanese soldiers, with their superior skills, would seize the fort and hand it to the English. One soldier, however, inverted the scheme, confessing that it was the Japanese who would make themselves "Masters of the Castle."[62] The fact that the first evidence of the alleged plot came from questions by a Japanese mercenary suggests the mistrust the VOC had of its own employees, despite later professions that the VOC had trusted the men. The plot contributed to the end of the trade in Japanese mercenaries in 1623.[63]

The confessions revealed co-conspirators beyond the English and Japanese, including "the Blacks," which could have referred to Ambonese, mardijkers, or people from any part of the Indian Ocean.[64] It also, of course, could refer to the VOC's slaves. Perhaps if the Japanese soldier had not divulged an Anglo-Japanese plot to conform to the intense fears of the Dutch, this dread would have manifested itself in distress about a possible slave uprising, just as Peres's incarceration suggests. The participation of the slave overseer made the plot terrifying. Slaves were a crucial labor force if the VOC was to realize its aspirations in the Indian Ocean and beyond, and Coen had considered their acquisition an urgent matter.[65] Aside from the 5,000–7,700 new slaves required annually to maintain the laboring population on Banda, for the most part the VOC employed slaves as domestic support in their factories.[66] On Amboyna, slaves were put to work during the trial; some escorted the tortured and disabled men to their prisons, or carried them on litters made of sheets, even to the place of execution, where two men carried Emanuel Thompson on a stool.[67] Slaves could find a path to freedom under the VOC. Indeed, in Kota Ambon the largest growth in the "indigenous" population came from free slaves, and by 1694, slaves themselves comprised 52.3 percent of the city's population.[68] While VOC officials initially worried in 1623 that these free slaves might join the EIC-Japanese plot, they admitted in later testimony that they had found no firm evidence linking them to the conspiracy. Resistance, however, was endemic—by the late seventeenth century, runaways formed maroon communities in the forested regions of Ambon—and the defiant slave overseer seemed to be the harbinger of a serious rebellion.[69]

The alleged plot even reached beyond Amboyna. Indeed, testimony coerced from defendants with torture suggested the ambitions of the plotters, or at least such ambitions as VOC interrogators expected them to have: Clarke confessed that he was going to go to Macassar to enlist the Spanish in a scheme to rob the smaller trading posts.[70] Although VOC employees had previously suspected Anglo-Spanish alliances in the East Indies, VOC fears of such a potential union may have been heightened by two major pieces of European news circulating in the region: the end of the Twelve Years' Truce in 1621, which opened a new phase of open conflict between the United Provinces and Spain, and rumors circulating in Amboyna "very rife and hott" in early 1623 about the effort of James I of England to secure the marriage of his son Charles with the Spanish Infanta.[71] Both developments pointed to the possibility of an Anglo-Spanish alliance, which would have been disastrous for the United Provinces. Perhaps the plot also included all of the English in the East Indies, for the VOC interrogated English traders about the culpability of Richard Welden, the EIC agent in Banda, along with the English in Batavia.[72] During the interrogations, van Speult had some forty prisoners in his custody and did not know what other enemies might exist, "either within or without."[73]

In the interrogation chamber, lowly assistants confronted the head trader and old friends and co-workers met each other with dread when the VOC summoned English traders to accuse each other; VOC and EIC rivals faced off; and housemates stood on either side of the barrier erected by torture and suspicion. On one side were the Japanese, the English, and the lone overseer of the slaves, all far from home, ensnared in an alien legal system; on the other, an assortment of traders and mariners rounded up by van Speult to serve on his special council, also far from home, but at least working within a familiar judicial system, with a legal expert (an advocate-fiscal, called the fiscal by the English), Isaack de Bruyn, to help them follow the correct procedures.[74] Some VOC council members were longtime residents with connections to the English. Joosten had spent fourteen years serving the VOC on Amboyna and lived there with his wife and children. He had befriended the English, he claimed, and when the English first came to Amboyna and had no place to live, he hosted them in his house for over four months. Pieter van Santen, Jan van Leeuwen, and Vogel all had spent enough time trading in the region to form connections with the English. Indeed, these men were crucial in helping to exonerate some of the accused English: Joosten spoke up for Powel and Ramsey.[75] Beaumont's old housemate at Luhu, van Santen, spoke up for him and for Ramsey, too. Renier [Corcerius] defended Webber.[76]

Although they objected strenuously to being tortured, the accused EIC employees themselves were no strangers to the practice. English common law prohibited it, but torture had nonetheless experienced something of a resurgence during the reign of Elizabeth, especially on Catholics. Some celebrated stories, the ones people were most likely to be familiar with, involved torture, notably the examinations connected to the Gunpowder Plot (1605) and witchcraft trials.[77] Thompson was from the Holy Roman Empire, where torture was also part of criminal investigations. Moreover, these EIC agents in the Indies had personal experience with the practice as a way of compelling confessions; for them, it was not an abstract legal policy. Towerson had participated in a sadistic dismemberment of an accused arsonist in Banten in June 1604. The English traders burned this man over every inch of his body, under his toenails and fingernails, his arms, shoulders, neck, and hands; they tore out his flesh; they broke his shin bones; they inserted iron screws in his bones, and then suddenly pulled them out; they broke all of the bones of his fingers and his toes with pincers. When the tortured man refused to emit a sound, the head trader had him put in irons and then he was tormented by insects who got in his wounds. Thinking that a single shot was too good a death for him, the English and Dutch traders tied him to a stake and shot him to pieces with their guns.[78] The English traders also knew that the Dutch used torture in their judicial proceedings in the region. They reported "most intollerable tortures" during the 1622 conspiracies on Banda and in Batavia.[79] So their predicament, however horrifying they found it, was not necessarily an unexpected development. Indeed, the EIC may have embraced the practice. Ten years after the Amboyna incident, an EIC employee familiar with the circumstances of the trial faced accusations that he and another trader had killed a man at Masulipatam with the "Amboyna torture of water." One of the English traders acknowledged that they had tortured the man but only to compel him to reveal who had stolen some pepper that belonged to the EIC: in other words, he used torture exactly as the VOC did in its own judicial proceedings, to compel people to give evidence.[80]

It was this regional context VOC employees may have had in mind when they later described the torture as "moderate and gentle," really only "a touch."[81] While VOC defenders commonly applied these descriptions to the water torture, one deponent even characterized burning someone's flesh with a candle's flame as gentle.[82] Those who made such a defense might well have believed their assessment, but those who confronted torture found it harrowing. Collins recalled that the water torture was more than anyone could endure, so awful that he could not think of any worse physical punishment. Desperate to escape it, he confessed.[83] The water torture, some survivors declared, was "more terrible & insupportable" even than the fire, although the consequences of fire lasted longer.[84]

Language barriers likely exacerbated the stress of torture and the panic men felt not just to tell the right story but to understand the questions and be understood in return. The Dutch examiners used Malay and Portuguese to examine the Japanese, and some Japanese from the town were also brought in to assist in the interrogations. Judges examined the English in both English and Dutch. The VOC council members believed that most of the English understood Dutch, but van Nieuwpoort served as an interpreter for "some words," as did George Forbes, the Scottish VOC steward, and Rowland Sollers, a Welshman who worked for the VOC.[85]

The accused men faced torture with different frames of mind and outcomes. Many tried at first to withstand it, but all eventually succumbed, shrieking and moaning in pain and distress. Beaumont heard Johnson "cry out very pitifully . . . and then loud again." He heard Thompson, both burned and virtually drowned, "roare most lamentably, and many times."[86] Beaumont himself was examined after hearing his colleagues scream and seeing them emerge drenched and shaken from the torture chamber. He saw Price, fastened in irons, carried into the torture room during Johnson's torture, probably to testify against him. Price was carried away, and Johnson's screams resumed. Johnson finally appeared, "being pittyfully wett and lamentably burned under his arme pitte and the elbowes."[87] Called in a few days later for his own interrogation, something he had likely been dreading since he first sat in the hall, Beaumont found he could endure only a brief period of torture before he confessed, although he recalled the torture as being so extensive "that his inwards did nearly crack," a characterization VOC witnesses dismissed.[88]

Of all the EIC employees, Clarke and Thompson withstood torture the longest. The English survivors reported that Clarke spent two hours in the torture chamber. He was so reluctant to confess that his examiners became enraged, testifying later that Clarke's obstinacy required them to torture him with both water and fire.[89] The English alleged that Clarke's feet were so heavily burned that fat dripped from them and caused the candles to go out.[90] A witness scoffed when asked about these details three years later, but he did concede that the candle had been poorly lit.[91] Van Speult's steward recalled in 1629 that the Dutch thought both Thompson and Clarke were witches, or housed "some enchanted characters about them," because they could withstand their torture so well, and so the examiners searched their bodies closely and shaved all of their hair in search of these creatures.[92] Allegations that the VOC interrogators thought Clarke was a witch crept into the *True Relation*, the EIC's published account of the trial, and troubled officials in the United Provinces, who asked several questions about it in subsequent depositions. The VOC deponents insisted that they cut Clarke's hair in the torture chamber not to weaken his diabolical powers, as the EIC had alleged, but rather because his long hair got in the way of the water torture. As for English allegations that the fiscal called Clarke the devil, Joosten admitted that someone said in the wake of Clarke's refusal to confess that "the Devill playes in this," but he did not remember who.[93] Joosten and his colleagues may have been thinking of the legal term, *taciturnitas*, which refers to the ability of a witch to remain silent during torture, thanks to the aid of the devil. It was for this reason that interrogators regarded severe torture as essential for witches, and that same logic may have affected the VOC's treatment of Clarke.[94]

Often fear of torture proved sufficient to compel a confession, although the accused men had difficulty finding the right story to tell. Coulson preferred to confess than to be tortured, even though he later asserted that he acknowledged behavior "that which as I shall be saved before God almightie is not true." Johnson, Coulson remembered the night before his execution, was tortured in front of Coulson to make accusations against him, and Johnson implored the interrogators to tell him what they wanted him to say, and he would speak it.[95] Johnson's effort to find out what he should confess without torture was a common strategy, according to the English survivors. Collins told his accusers that it would be a great favor if they would tell him what he needed to say, since they planned to extract it by torture, and he would prefer to spare himself that ordeal.[96]

Even advance planning did not facilitate an easy interrogation, as Wetherall discovered when he had trouble figuring out what to admit in his interrogation. On March 1, Powel, held in irons at the fort, needed "to ease him selfe," and he ran into Sherrock on his way to the privies. What's the news, he asked Sherrock, who told him the news was "heavie," with the English charged with treason and tortured. Sherrock told Powel that he himself had confessed because he was afraid of the torture. Powel reported these tidings to Wetherall, who implored Powel to confer with Sherrock about what to say to avoid torture. That very day, Wetherall was called in and tortured four times before he could manage to say what the VOC officials wanted to hear.[97] The challenge for the English was that it was not sufficient to admit guilt: the purpose of torture was to extract details of the crime, information that only the accused could know, thus showing guilt with certainty.[98] Wetherall was in a predicament, because he was prepared to plead guilty but had to produce the story his interrogators expected to hear in order for the torture to cease. He had been at Amboyna on New Year's Day, but only remembered talking with the other merchants about rotten cloth, not a plot to take over the fort. Tied up for torture, he didn't know what to say, so VOC officials obligingly read the confessions of other men to him (or so the English later claimed), and he affirmed everything they had said.[99] Powel fared better: he denied the charges made against him, and Joosten spoke up for him, saying he knew that Powel wouldn't have any part in such a plot—the only instance in any of these records of a character witness.[100]

VOC officials vigorously denied these allegations of coached confessions. Collins confessed freely, Joosten reported, ordering the fiscal to "write as I will tell you." Both Collins and Joosten enhanced the authority of their accounts by providing direct speech. In Collins's version, the fiscal rejected some of his confession, telling him "You ly." If anyone had recorded the interrogation and answers, it would have been the VOC's clerk, but the VOC provided no such record of the examinations, thus making the company vulnerable to the charges the English leveled against it about the process and enabling the EIC men to invent entire dialogues with nothing and no one to gainsay their accounts.[101]

Some of the accused produced confessions that even their examiners knew to be false, especially confessions made by those men who had not been present when the alleged plot was hatched. Threatened repeatedly with torture and hoisted onto the rack, Sherrock, the assistant at the Hitu factory, repeatedly found new stories to tell to spare himself this anguish, casting blame on Clarke, and spinning a story of intrigue for the "attentive" fiscal. Unfortunately for Sherrock, he got some of the dates of the alleged conspiracy confused and enraged his examiners, who allegedly told him that he would "be tormented with fire and water to death, and then should be drawne by the heeles to the gallows, and there hanged up."[102] These threats undermined the VOC's claims to sound judicial process. The officials who presided over the trial could not agree later on whether Sherrock was even tortured, and Sherrock himself acknowleged that several Dutch men spoke up on his behalf and said that he hadn't been at the New Year's meeting.[103] Webber, like Sherrock, had not been in Amboyna on New Year's Day, but when he was examined, he, too, confessed, and he also implicated Clarke by testifying that Clarke had sent him a letter about the plot. The alleged letter cryptically referred to a "great businesse at hand," but no one could locate the epistle. Webber's confession went awry when a VOC merchant spoke up for him, saying that he had been at Larica on New Year's Day with Webber, being "merry" with him.[104] And why did Webber and Sherrock accuse Clarke, of all the EIC traders? It's possible that Webber and Sherrock fingered him—despite their claims that the name was suggested first to them by the Dutch, and by Clarke's earlier accusations of them—because of his connection to Towerson. Clarke had been hired directly by Towerson as his servant, not by the EIC.[105] If Towerson was the culprit the VOC officials at Amboyna most wanted to implicate, then Clarke was a logical second.

The difficulties the accused men had coming up with a plausible confession suggests that if there was a plot, it might have been different from the one that the VOC expected to hear about. It may have been that the English had plotted with the slave overseer, and that that was the conspiracy the VOC should have worried about. Or perhaps the Japanese soldiers plotted with the slaves. Maybe there had been some vague English talk against the Dutch but no agreed-on plan of action. Sherrock's accusation of Clarke suggested just such animosity: he claimed that Clarke had announced that the Dutch had done the English grave wrong, and that Clarke had made a plan with Towerson to get revenge.[106] Towerson's opaque accusation of Coulson as the "principal author" and Coulson's rage against Towerson when he was being transported to Amboyna for trial suggest at least that there was a willingness by the leaders of the English traders to believe the worst of each other.[107] Or perhaps there was no conspiracy at all. All that the evidence reveals is the plot that van Speult anticipated and believed and that he could extract from the accused with threats or the application of torture.

The final confession, according to the trial record, came on March 3 from Peres, the thirty-six-year-old slave overseer, who briefly stated that two months earlier Hytieso had approached him about joining the Japanese and English in their plot.[108] With this confession, the trial procedures ended where they had begun, with the imprisoned overseer and his threatening words. Only now, after a few short days, van Speult had finally pieced together what that menace had signaled.

After all of the accused had confessed under torture, their confessions had to be written down and signed. Jan Jacobson Wyncoop remembered that the condemned had their confessions read to them, the Japanese in Malay and the English in Dutch and English. Van Santen explained that the English confessions were written in English, so that the English could sign them, and then translated into Dutch, for later use by members of the VOC council in Amboyna and authorities in the United Provinces. Thompson, the EIC merchant from Hamburg, may have assisted with the translations, according to van Santen, although it seems unlikely that Thompson was in any condition to do much translating, given the physical toll his interrogation took on him. According to Courthals, Thompson's confession, given in Dutch, was translated into English by Sollers, the Welsh employee of the VOC.[109] But the trial record and witness accounts alike suggest there were some problems with the confessions. One unnamed Englishman initially refused to sign his confession because it contained words he had not said, a report that offers credibility to the later hearsay testimony of Forbes, who claimed that Sollers told him that the council made him add words.[110] Towerson refused to sign a confession, saying he would write his own confession himself.[111] But instead, he wrote a statement of his innocence, which Forbes translated. Then Towerson wrote the same thing again, but said, according to Forbes, that if the Dutch were determined to execute him, to treat him as a gentleman.[112]

If the accused signed voluntarily and freely it may have been in part because retracting a confession was a dangerous strategy. On seeing his confession two days after his examination, Beaumont declared that nothing in it was true. After being tied up again, however, he resolved that it was better to die a quick death than to suffer more torture, so he signed the confession.[113] Fardo and Griggs, required to testify against Towerson in his presence, as it seems all of the English were, retracted their confessions when confronted with him, and then they, too, were tortured again, or so Ramsey said.[114] The VOC directors hinted at this process in a remonstrance to the States General in November 1624, in which they mentioned that after their confessions, the English were examined three or four more times.[115]

This matter of retracting confessions and professing innocence struck hard at the VOC. Confessions had to be freely given, and Dutch jurisprudence required an interval between a confession made under torture and a signed confession. In 1626, Joosten argued that people signed "voluntarily" as soon as they confessed, and that is exactly how the trial record suggests the process unfolded.[116] One VOC councilor argued in 1626 that it was impossible to consider that any judge would entice any witness to confess: such an action would be "scandalous."[117] So important were voluntary confessions that one VOC judge, Vogel, dragged himself out of his sickbed to join the council when the confessions were signed. Illness had kept him from the torture chamber, so this ritual of signing the confessions was his only opportunity to see the accused confront and accept their culpability in the plot. Their willing signatures, with no affirmations of innocence, so impressed Vogel that he signed the death sentences of men he had come to know well without any qualms at all.[118]

Five days passed between the last examination and the sentences. In their final days, the EIC men prepared for their executions through prayer, conversation, psalm-singing, and writing. Some also needed to recover physically from their torment. None seemed more grievously injured than Thompson and Clarke. The *True Relation* described Clarke's ordeal with gruesome care. After he was "martyred" with his torture, he was carried off to a dungeon, where he languished five or six days without anyone to tend to his wounds. In this condition, his injuries putrefied, "and great Maggots dropt and crept from him in a most loathsome & noysom maner."[119] Asked to respond to this accusation in later years, each VOC witness averred that the surgeon visited each prisoner daily and dressed his wounds. The VOC deponents also insisted that the prisoners were detained in pleasant conditions, not the "dirty hole" or dungeons the *True Relation* suggested. And it is true that one prisoner, Thompson, was initially housed in the VOC steward's chamber. But the steward recalled that after Thompson spent a week there without any medical attention, the steward could no longer "endure the stench or smell of his body." He complained about his foul roommate to the governor, with the result that Thompson, rather than finally getting his wounds tended, was shifted to "a secrett garrett."[120] Joosten agreed that Thompson moved from a chamber to a garret, but disputed the steward's interpretation, arguing that Thompson got everything he "craved" and recalling that Thompson was visited regularly by a doctor and in fact complained to Joosten about being "full of pain" if the doctor was late on his rounds.[121] By execution day, at any rate, his wounds had finally been bound, but Beaumont claimed that "the matter and gore blood" oozed through the bandages.[122]

The exonerated were able to visit the condemned before the execution. Powel saw Fardo, and to him Fardo proclaimed his innocence. Fardo told Powel that all that concerned him was his unjust accusation of Towerson, but Fardo had other things on his mind, too, because at some point during his imprisonment he made an oral will in the presence of Sherrock, Ramsey, and Webber.[123] Like his colleagues, he had perhaps been preoccupied by the fate of his goods, which the VOC had confiscated when the traders were arrested. Some of these items represented the culmination of their years in the Indies—credit instruments, the stocks they had been trading on their own, specie, clothing, and books. The VOC took Thomas Ladbrooke's small bit of silver and even his parrot.[124]

Fardo was unable to get paper to record his will, but others set to work writing, especially after the sentence of death had been pronounced. Three of these documents survived the trial, although all could have been forgeries made after the fact. The condemned men used whatever scraps were available to them in their incarceration, including the books traders used every day—their notebooks, their Bibles, their prayer books, and bills of exchange. They hoped these testimonies would reach England. Some efforts failed. Towerson professed his innocence on blank leaves in his Bible, covered up those leaves with other sheets, and gave the book to van Speult to pass on to Towerson's friends. Van Speult discovered the covered leaves two or three months after the execution and called Forbes to his chamber to translate. Forbes did so and never saw the Bible again.[125] Towerson wrote a letter to Coulson that has survived only in a Dutch translation: it, too, could have been a forgery created by the VOC to bolster their own case, although the content of the letter makes that seem unlikely. Towerson's accusation of Coulson is opaque (presumably a forgery would have made Towerson's intentions more clear), and the letter is full of references to Bible verses for Coulson to study and concerns about Towerson's possessions. Towerson also wrote a statement on a bill of debt to a Dutch inhabitant of Amboyna that he was condemned but was "guiltlesse of any thing that can bee justly laid to my charge." The bill was given to the creditor, who in turn gave it to Richard Welden after he paid off the debt. From their imprisonment aboard the *Rotterdam* on March 5, the day they were condemned to death, Griggs, Beaumont, Brown, and Price wrote in Griggs's tablebook (or notebook) a message specifically directed to Welden, the EIC agent singled out in some of the interrogations. They told him that they and the other English were forced to say things through torture that were not true, and that they hoped their employers would understand the wrong done them. The four men urged Welden to look out for himself, because they believed that the Dutch planned to take him into custody, too. "And so farewell; written in the dark."[126] The warning must have given Welden pause when he collected Griggs's papers, and it might explain what was otherwise strange behavior (as far as the English were concerned) in which he seemed to side with the VOC in his response to the executions.[127]

These writings not only enabled men facing their execution to assert their innocence; they also permitted the accused to make sense of what had happened to them. Coulson did just that in his *Psalmes of David*. Wetherall had given this psalm book to Towerson for the English to use at Amboyna.[128] Although Coulson himself was based at Hitu, he somehow got his hands on this book—perhaps some sympathetic friend gave it to him after VOC officials removed the goods and papers from the English house, or possibly Towerson managed to pass it along to Coulson, because he mentioned his *Book of Common Prayer* as a work Coulson seemed to have in his possession.[129] With ink and pen, Coulson set to work on March 5 as he lay in irons on board the *Rotterdam* to scratch out his defense. Coulson found blank pages in the psalm book, and on them he wrote an account of what had befallen him. Coulson proclaimed that he was "cleare of all such conspiracy" and absolved all of the other accused men as well. The explanation continued on another blank page. There, Coulson described the outlines of the trial—the examination of the Japanese, "most tiranouslie tortered" until they answered leading questions by accusing the English; the burning of the English, under their armpits and on the soles of their feet; the water torture; the forced confessions. He ended by pleading his innocence, saying of the conspiracy that "I knowe not more then the childe unborne of this bussines." Sewn up in some bedding, the book was smuggled out of Amboyna and finally made its way to the EIC in London.[130] For the most part, Coulson's writing is neat, in straight lines, handwriting that appears suspicious in light of Webber's claim that Collins could not use his hands for seven weeks after he had been tied up for torture. At the same time, the repetitions in the text— Coulson signed his name repeatedly and wrote on multiple pages—convey the strain he was likely under.[131]

By their final night, all of the condemned English traders except Thompson and Towerson gathered together in the fort. A Dutch minister came to visit them and help them prepare for the next day's ordeal, but they elected to

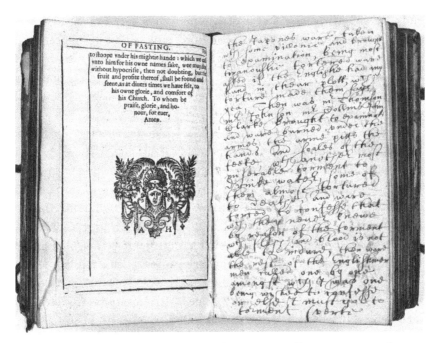

Figure 2.3 A page from Samuel Coulson's testimony of his innocence in the EIC's *The Psalmes of David in Meeter* (Edinburgh, 1611). National Archives, The Hague, States General, 1.01.02, inv. no. 12581.15.

follow their own rituals. The English allegedly declined Dutch offers of wine and preferred instead to sing psalms, pray, and comfort each other, with apologies for implicating the other men under torture.[132] But they did drink, and they also ate: Fardo had a bit of roasted chicken, and some wine, and as he savored this repast, Ramsey reported, Fardo remarked that this was his last meal.[133]

The morning of the dreadful day of execution may have dawned with the damp and heavy air that signals torrential downpours, because the skies opened during the execution in a storm so heavy that one Dutch witness described the rain as "muddy."[134] But early in the day the showers had not yet begun, and there was much business afoot. The condemned men were released from the fetters that had bound their legs for over two weeks by the same smith who had put them on.[135] That morning, a drummer walked through town to summon the soldiers, burghers, and mariners who composed the five companies that escorted the condemned to their execution.[136] The Amboyna council had been busy in the past few days, tying up loose ends. The council ensured that all of the confessions were signed and Forbes later claimed to have read Towerson's third protestation of innocence to the council on the morning of the execution.[137] The council also decided the fate of Peres's wife. They returned her to her former masters until van Speult made any further decision about her—collateral damage of the alleged conspiracy.[138]

The council also engaged in acts of mercy, tempering "justice" in the normative fashion of early modern jurisprudence. Four men had already been found not guilty in the proceedings—Ramsey, Sadler, Powel, and Ladbrooke. Next up was a pardon for Sherrock and Webber.[139] The council then offered a temporary pardon to two other men. One was John Beaumont. He was saved by his friendships, along with his age and "his silly brains," although Joosten reported that all of the men on the council wanted Beaumont, who was "old and weak," to receive a temporary pardon. Such a reprieve would enable Beaumont to care for the English goods, with the VOC's president at Batavia to make a final decision on his fate.[140] It's no surprise that so many men were willing to make a case for Beaumont, whether because of his silly brains or because those silly brains signaled the jovial disposition of a warm and charming man. Beaumont was deeply rooted in the trading community of Amboyna. As he waited aboard the *Royal Exchange* in Batavia's harbor in December 1623, prepared for the journey that would take him to England and far from a region of such sorrow and misfortune, his thoughts still turned to the friends he left behind in Amboyna. He outlined an extensive web of connections, including a likely godson, a married couple, a woman, several men, all of varied ethnicities, and still more, indeed "all the rest of our frends that inquire for us."[141] Beaumont's exoneration was consistent with that of men from the satellite factories. The traders who lived at Amboyna may have enjoyed their accommodation apart from the Dutch, but it turned out that the separate house at Amboyna doomed the English by making this private meeting possible, while the traders who lived in shared houses were more likely to have witnesses speak up for them: all seven of the traders resident at Amboyna were condemned to death, and six were executed.

The other man who won a temporary pardon acquired it by chance. The council required three of the condemned merchants, Collins, Coulson, and Thompson, to draw lots on March 8.[142] Thompson earned this "mercy" because, several officials said, he was old and had asked for pardon—admitting his crime, conceding that he deserved to die, and begging to be saved.[143] He even offered to perform "the fowlest worke of one of the meanest slaves" if his life were spared, a suggestion of assimilation to regional norms in which slavery was an alternative to a death sentence.[144] While the council left no explanation for their choice of Collins and Coulson, there are several possibilities. Coulson seems to have been well known and well liked. Both Collins and Coulson, moreover, implicated Towerson to his face, episodes singled out as significant in the various depositions and accounts.[145] Collins even told Towerson in detail what he had confessed, thus perhaps helpfully signaling to Towerson what he needed to say in order to spare himself torture.[146] Collins won the draw. For all the rest of the condemned EIC employees, Japanese soldiers, and Peres, the judges involved in the examinations pronounced the sentence of death.[147]

Both Thompson and Towerson, still housed separately from the rest of the condemned men, received VOC visitors in their final hours. Joosten, who had known Towerson well, visited him an hour before the execution and wished him "eternall happinesse." The two men drank some Spanish wine and toasted each other, and Towerson bequeathed two geese to Joosten's daughter. Then Joosten walked down the hall to pay a final call on Thompson and the rest of the English. Thompson implored Joosten to intercede for him, but Joosten said that that time had passed.[148] Thompson made the same plea to Vogel, another old acquaintance.[149] Vogel, Joosten, and van Leeuwen, all judges in the Amboyna affair, denied they heard any professions of innocence, but Jacob Bigwell, a VOC employee who had been an occasional visitor to the English house, saw Towerson and Thompson thirty minutes before their deaths and recalled that they asked him to attest to their innocence before the EIC if he ever came to England, as he later did.[150]

These assertions of innocence explain why the last moments of the English, Japanese, and Peres were clouded in controversy. While it is possible to discern basic movements—the men gathered together in the fort's hall, marched to the execution ground, spoke some words, and were beheaded— the divergent opinions of witnesses were at their most pronounced about what happened on execution day. The dispute over what transpired at the execution ground stands in contrast to observations of the executions of religious "martyrs" in Europe during the sixteenth and seventeenth centuries, when accounts by even the most religiously or politically opposed observers often produced a common narrative, of people embracing their deaths, exhorting the crowd, and singing psalms of joy as the flames lapped at the hems of their gowns.[151]

The disputed accounts focused on the condemned men's professions of innocence, while still at the fort, as they walked to their deaths, and as they awaited the Japanese swordsman's fatal blow. All of the men involved in signing the execution warrant for the condemned denied at every turn, in every context, that the English or Japanese or Peres ever expressed their innocence. As Joosten insisted, had any of the condemned claimed he was innocent, then the execution would have been delayed.[152] The VOC councilors consistently depicted the condemned as penitent and resigned.

The English accounts of the execution rested entirely on hearsay (their sources were several British employees of the VOC), because none of the pardoned men saw the execution. But the English accounts were also supported by numerous depositions from VOC employees in 1628 and 1629 that confirmed some of what the English believed happened on that day.[153] The men who gave these depositions had originally been solicited to do so by the EIC's agents in the United Provinces. The first depositions offered an interpretation favorable to the EIC's depiction of the event. Then VOC supporters solicited second, and sometimes third, depositions from these same men in order to bring their testimony back into agreement with the VOC's interpretation of the episode. In the first depositions, the witnesses relied on some hearsay. In the second round, they retracted the hearsay, but continued to attest to what they had seen—and they had seen at least one of the condemned assert his innocence.[154]

Before they left the fort, all of the men crowded into its hall. The English and Japanese saw each other for the first time since the interrogations. It was a bustling and somewhat chaotic scene, in which VOC witnesses were not entirely sure who was able to talk to whom, despite soldiers standing between different groups to keep them apart. The acquitted English and the condemned also had the opportunity to talk and to say farewell. When Towerson joined the other condemned men, they apologized to him, and again to the rest of the traders, for implicating each other in the conspiracy. The condemned had the chance to pass some final messages on to their acquitted and pardoned comrades. Finally able to talk to his EIC colleagues, Thompson asked Beaumont to take the news of his innocence with him back to England.[155]

At last the dolorous march to the execution ground commenced. Not everyone was able to walk after the ravages of torture. The council members who signed the death warrant argued that Thompson, like the other men, had been well treated, and in Jacob Coper's words, all of the men went "lustely and well" to their executions.[156] But four VOC employees attested that they saw Thompson carried to the execution, his feet "so shrunck with the fire" that two Japanese (or two "Blacks" or "slaves") carried him on a stool.[157] Several VOC employees at Amboyna knew who Thompson was even if they didn't know his name: they referred to him as the Hamburger (he had been born in Hamburg), domini (which could have meant minister or master), and the "ould man" in their depositions. The procession had not gone far before the heckling began. *Schellem* (rogue), the onlookers called out, reproaching the condemned for their perfidy.[158] "Schelm" was a word of Dutch or Belgian origin that was also in English usage, although it was rare.[159] These hecklers were likely Dutch onlookers, not only because of the linguistic evidence (anyone else would likely have called out in Malay or Portuguese), but also because three Dutch deponents testified in 1628 that the "common people of Amboyna" believed the alleged plot was impossible.[160] As he was carried on his stool through the fort's gate, Thompson responded to the attacks, probably in Dutch, which would explain how widely understood his comments were by Dutch-speaking witnesses. He denied he was a thief or a traitor and proclaimed that he died an honest man.[161] The VOC councilors denounced this story, claiming no one called Thompson a rogue, and that he never asked for anything but mercy.[162] Thompson seems to have been pursuing two strategies to save his life— admitting guilt, and pleading with his friends for mercy; and when that failed, denying his guilt, perhaps with the knowledge that Roman-Dutch law required the guilt of the condemned to be assured.

When the VOC marched the condemned to the execution ground, they adhered to conventions that prevailed in Europe. This was an age of public burning, of processions by the condemned to their grisly deaths, of cheering and recoiling crowds at execution grounds. The guards may not have taken the circuitous and humiliating route through town that the English survivors described, "in manner of a triumph & soe back to ye place of execucon."[163] Every VOC deponent rejected this claim, except for one deponent who testified that he was so moved with compassion for the condemned men that he followed them to church (a detour evident in no other account) as they walked about 150 paces to their execution.[164] Everyone else agreed that the condemned marched straight to the execution ground, itself a mere stone's throw from the fort, via the ordinary route.[165] The Japanese prisoners would also have found such a procession familiar. In Tokugawa Japan, the condemned paraded through the streets to the execution ground, accompanied by banners describing their crimes and punishment. From the

1620s on, with a few exceptions, neither torture nor executions were public occasions.[166]

On the matter of the disputed itinerary, it is hard to believe that van Speult could possibly have resisted the impulse to march the men through town. After all, he had accomplished what VOC leaders at Batavia had failed to do: he had managed to implicate the English traders in a plot. He was a hero. Moreover, he had uncovered a threat so insidious, so broad ranging, that the plotters represented key elements in VOC trading society—not just English trading partners, but also Japanese soldiers and the company's slaves. This story was his creation, his great triumph, because it was the story he was prepared to accept when the accused tried to confess to the right plot. Part of his goal in the public executions at Amboyna, as opposed to moving the whole process to Batavia (which would have been consistent with the 1619 treaty and as the EIC later insisted was proper), may have been to deter future plotters and to display VOC authority.[167] Perhaps there were multiple intended audiences, including the powerful Ternatans and all the regional people who were their tributaries. Why would van Speult hesitate to maximize the opportunity to broadcast his success and his authority—his imperial triumph, just as the English complained? Moreover, he finally had his rejoinder to the enraging incident in June 1622 when he had to execute a VOC soldier at the EIC head trader's request. With this procession, he made clear who held the upper hand in Amboyna.

Once the men reached the execution ground, they prayed, and they sang. Many also had final words, although what they had to say was the subject of considerable dispute. The EIC's published account asserted that all of the men, the English, the Japanese, and Peres, proclaimed their innocence. The VOC councilors uniformly rejected such claims. Wyncoop deposed that only two English spoke—Thompson and Price—and both prayed for mercy.[168] Peres prayed over his rosary and kissed the cross, swearing his innocence of this crime, but adding that he thought God was just in punishing him, because he was a bigamist, with a wife in his native country and a second that van Speult had given him (forced on him, so Peres said) in Amboyna.[169] The condemned Japanese, Joosten recalled, "went singing to theire death," and according to van Nieuwpoort competed to be the first to die.[170] Towerson was the first of the English to be executed. He had some unexpected things to say: according to a VOC witness, he wished van Speult "a long life & happy government."[171] He also took the opportunity to blame Price and other EIC employees for engaging in such bad conduct that God had chosen to punish them in this manner, even if they were not guilty of the crime of which they had been accused.[172] After the other condemned English witnessed his violent end, and perhaps wrestled with some anger at Towerson's rebuke, Coulson collected himself. He read a prayer from a book, in the English custom, VOC witnesses explained, and after his prayer, the English sang a psalm.[173] He also delivered a prayer he had composed himself, in English.[174] According to the *True Relation* and the hearsay of witnesses, this prayer proclaimed his innocence. It was because of these professions of English innocence that the States General worried about the scrap of paper on which Coulson had allegedly written his prayer, so in 1626 and 1628, they asked the VOC councilors about this piece of paper and its contents. The deponents consistently denied that Coulson made any profession of innocence, and all those who knew what had happened to the paper agreed that it ended up in van Speult's hands where, like almost every other document produced by the English that van Speult got hold of during this period, it disappeared.[175] The depositions make it clear that listeners did not know what Coulson said: some witnesses were not close enough to hear him, some could not understand what he said, and most did not understand English.

The English may or may not have prayed to God to give signs of his displeasure, and it may or may not have been Towerson or Thompson who gave such a prayer, two points on which there was no agreement. One deponent suggested that it was in fact van Speult who sought a sign from above. But whoever called on the deity for action, it did rain—heavy, muddy rain, the kind of torrential downpour that comes with wind so fierce that a witness compared it to a tempest or typhoon and that caused two ships in the harbor to drag their anchors some distance.[176] At the end of this day, at the gallows soaked with the blood of twenty men and a drenching rain, the Dutch set four heads on pikes—those of Hytieso, Sidney Miguel, Pedro Congi, and Towerson—the man who revealed the conspiracy through his questions, the two men who may have earlier worked for the English and perhaps functioned as important conduits, and the alleged instigator of the plot.[177]

In both Europe and Japan, the head was a trophy of the state, brandished to terrorize people, whether subjects or enemies. The English employed heads to just such effect in Ireland in the sixteenth century. They adorned the facade of Dublin castle with the heads of Irish leaders and soldiers, and, in one notorious instance, the English commander Humphrey Gilbert forced conquered Irish to walk a gauntlet of heads.[178] The Japanese, too, exhibited the heads of condemned people. An EIC trader remarked on just such a display on a journey to Edo in the summer of 1616. On one side of the river before they reached Kyoto, the English traders saw a man who had been crucified for committing murder. Further down the river, they spied eight to ten heads displayed on the side of the highway.[179] So all of the condemned men would have understood the message VOC authorities sought to convey when they placed four heads on pikes for public show.

But the heads of enemies had a special symbolic significance in the Moluccas, too. Ambon was populated by headhunting people, as was the neighboring island of Seram.[180] People marked major life transitions with freshly decapitated heads. War, as the Dutch trader and later Ambon governor Artus Gijsels explained in a 1621 account, was not about conquest but rather seizing prisoners or heads, with the heads displayed in a village's ceremonial hall.[181] The Dutch understood the local cultural significance of heads. When a Ternatan fleet killed forty Spaniards in February 1622, the commander decorated the stern of his vessel with Spanish heads and traveled to the VOC fort at Malayo on Ternate, where the VOC showed its approval by responding with a nine-shot salute.[182]

When the Dutch raised these four head on pikes for public spectacle, they both adhered to traditional rituals of victors in Europe and conformed to the norms of the headhunting people whose territory they occupied. The heads remained on display, like the head trophies of the island's inhabitants. Some men who arrived on Dutch ships eight days after the event noticed the heads on the gallows and even claimed to see blood there despite the heavy rains on execution day.[183] Towerson's head, complained some English merchants in February 1626, was still on display on the gallows at Amboyna three years after his execution.[184]

Although the executions were over, the legal process was not yet complete. Van Speult may have been concerned that he had not assembled a suitable legal trail. He quickly organized three further depositions that spoke to English guilt, although they were weak statements that could have persuaded only someone prepared to believe the deponents. Two men attested, for example, that they had heard talk four months earlier that sounded like a threat against the Dutch, although they weren't entirely sure because of language difficulties.[185] Finally, on March 29 the trial records were collated in Amboyna. Just two months later, six bilingual men, three from each company, certified the linguistic accuracy of the translation.[186]

Van Speult also seems to have been working to create a coherent narrative of the conspiracy to supplement the confessions. He told his superiors in multiple letters between June and September about a plot in which the English joined with all the people of the area, at Luhu and elsewhere on Seram, including with Ternatans and with some Bandanese, too. He conveyed a picture of an island under siege, fled by deserters, surrounded by enemies plotting rebellion.[187] This broad plot contributed to confusion and suspicion later, in Batavia and in Europe, because none of these people were interrogated or punished. At least one of the accused English also believed that the VOC feared an EIC plot with natives of the region.[188] Whatever van Speult had hoped to accomplish with the public executions, he doesn't seem to have quelled unrest in the region, unless he invented the unrest for his superiors in order to justify his behavior.

The eight EIC employees who were pardoned or reprieved had to stay on Amboyna in the company of those who had suspected and tortured them until the eastern monsoon arrived in May and vessels could make their way to Batavia. Some of them were clearly on edge. Sherrock, exonerated by multiple witnesses, begged for pardon on his knees before Frederick Houtman, at the time the VOC governor of Ternate, who had traveled to Amboyna in April 1623, and declared his debt to the VOC for the kindness shown him.[189] Beaumont and Collins (the two men who had secured only temporary pardons) perceived themselves as still in Dutch custody and still in hostile company, not only in Amboyna, where they endured some awkward meals, but also on their journey from Amboyna, because while on the ship to Batavia they affirmed their guilt. Collins prudently escaped from this vessel to an English boat that passed by in the large Batavia harbor, and he went straight to the English house in Batavia to tell his amazing news. It turned out, however, that the EIC council had already heard it thanks to a letter Powel had managed to send en route from Macassar.[190] Beaumont reached Batavia sick and lame, and once he came before the VOC council he had to confess again, or, as he put it, "to alledge the untruth," for fear he would have been tortured had he refused.[191] In December the survivors finally boarded two different ships and started the long journey to Europe. And then, in the early summer of 1624, when the tale of the Amboyna business reached England, the riveting and unexpected story of the executions found a new life. The massacre the Dutch thought they had detected and escaped through God's wonderful providence turned into the Amboyna massacre of English innocents that would haunt Anglo-Dutch relations for centuries to come.

3

Inventing the Amboyna Massacre

During the throes of the wet season in 1623, the men on the EIC council in Batavia prepared for the annual departure of the homeward-bound fleet. They were responsible for trade from Japan to Masulipatam and everywhere in between, so before the ships sailed they had extensive reports to complete, in multiple copies in case one went astray. In addition to personal letters to family, friends, and individual company members, the council members wrote a long missive to their employers about their activities since their last communication—commercial successes and disappointments, informative details about commodities, conflicts with rivals, mishaps and opportunities, and always a dolorous litany of death and disease. The December 1623 letter was characteristically long at thirty-one tightly written folio pages, but the council had some unexpected developments to report. The second page hinted vaguely at executions, and the letter touched occasionally on the violent fate of some of the traders, but it wasn't until twenty-six pages in that the authors turned their attention to the shocking news from the Amboyna trading post. Readers in London must have been on tenterhooks before they finally got to the main event: the execution of ten EIC employees, the exoneration of six, and the temporary pardon of two more, all as part of an alleged treasonous plot with Japanese and Indo-Portuguese co-conspirators, ten of whom also died. As the council members gathered their thoughts and their sentiments that day and the next and searched for the best way to describe what had happened, they landed on some powerful words. It was a "bloody massacre" and a "butcherlie execution," and the Dutch who committed the offense were "Canniballs."[1]

The company's predilection to frame the event as a massacre, first in Batavia and then in London, turned out to be a brilliant, if politically risky, strategy in its quest for restitution and maybe a touch of revenge. This rhetorical innovation showed the EIC making use of a relatively new word and concept in the early seventeenth century, wedding it to this international incident, and creating a powerful and enduring framework that launched a new trajectory for the conspiracy trial from the other side of the world. By casting the conspiracy as a massacre, the EIC transformed the episode into a European story, a crisis produced by European conflict that required resolution in Europe. A massacre entailed a cruel death, but also vital to the emerging definition of a massacre was the idea of the innocent victim, a role the executed English assumed and an image that had a counterpart in Dutch perfidy. These men were martyrs, accompanied by relics and signs of God's providence. To these three attributes, so vital to a massacre, the EIC added treachery. These crucial elements were firmly in place by summer 1624 and appeared in print by November. By February 1625, even as the English government moved to quell anti-Dutch sentiment in London, the rhetorical work had been accomplished, and the "Amboyna massacre" had become a fixture.

The context in which the EIC trader John Goninge employed the word "massacre" in December 1623 suggests what made this terminology seem appropriate to the men in Batavia. He identified three key features. First, there was the violence, "the bloody massacre." Second, there were blameless, defenseless victims, the "poore innocent servants at Amboyna." Third, there was the fear and uncertainty of Dutch authority, which Goninge compared to a yoke, an important metaphor of bondage with biblical roots.[2] The executions at Amboyna embodied the asymmetrical relations between the two companies as they had been codified in the 1619 treaty, which had created a new dynamic that overturned everything the English had come to believe about their historical connection to the Dutch.

The English in Europe picked up on Goninge's characterization, uncertainly at first, largely because of how they learned about the incident. News traveled slowly across the world.[3] The first report reached the Netherlands at the end of May 1624. Dudley Carleton, the English ambassador to The Hague, wrote the English secretary of state on May 28 to report news of "a treason of the inhabitants w[i]th some English joyned to them against the fort of Amboyna," the word "*treason*" revealing the VOC's perspective on the affair. Carleton questioned the truth of the treason, reported the execution of the merchants, and noted the receipt of a relation of events there, a brief account that he included with his letter.[4] The story itself was confusing, with such an extensive array of potential conspirators that rumors circulated that even some Dutch might have been involved, or so Carleton later heard in the Netherlands, in addition to rumors of Moluccan participation.[5]

But once the news reached Europe, it started to move quickly via the mouths and pens of EIC employees. By May 29, the EIC received letters from their employees at Batavia, and two days later, the Company referred to the Amboyna actions as "these most injurious crueltyes" and a "slaughter."[6] By June 5 the London-based newswriter John Chamberlain, who made a living writing personal newsletters in an era of formal news censorship, noted recent reports in the capital of how "barbarously" the Dutch had treated the English merchants.[7] By June 16, the EIC's ship *Elizabeth* finally anchored at Plymouth after almost six months' travel, and one EIC employee fresh back from the Indies wrote the company from there to report the "murderinge" at Amboyna.[8] Finally, the survivors themselves, seven of whom returned to England that summer, made their way to London. They were the most important source of news, and they played a vital role in shaping the interpretation of the episode as a massacre. By July 7, when the Admiralty court started to depose them about their ordeal, the "massacre" had become a certainty. Among the questions posed to each man was the eleventh: "whether hee beleiveth in his conscience, that the blody and murderous massacre predeposed, was premeditated by the Dutch."[9]

This was, to be sure, a world replete with massacres, or, at least, episodes that modern readers might dub massacres. But words change their meaning, and that was the case with "massacre," which was relatively new in this era. It is of French origin and originally described the chopping blocks commonly used by butchers, but in 1556 "massacre" appeared in a French pamphlet to describe a purge of heretics in Provence in 1545. French Protestants then began to use the term regularly to characterize the violent sectarian strife in France; the word, with its new meaning, reached the English through translations of French Protestant pamphlets, especially those written in the wake of the murder of Protestants on St. Bartholomew's Day in 1572.[10] The word appeared in print in English as early as 1510, a virtually inexplicable manifestation, because otherwise the word didn't appear in print again until 1567, suggesting it was not in wide circulation.[11] Early dictionaries show multiple related meanings of the word—not just murder or slaughter of many people, but certain kinds of murders: cruel (1599) or horrible (1605).[12] By the time of the playwright Christopher Marlowe's 1593 play about the St. Bartholomew's Day incident, *The Massacre in Paris*, the word had become familiar in England with a meaning understood to apply to certain types of murders. It was still used infrequently by 1624, when news of the events at Amboyna reached England, and it probably still had traces of its French pronunciation, with the accent placed on the second syllable.

Between 1473 and 1624, only ten unique works were published in England with the word "massacre" in the title, and one with massacre featured prominently in a subtitle.[13] For the most part, these books deployed "massacre" in the context of either a mass murder of unsuspecting people (as was the case with the St. Bartholomew's Day episode), the threat of terrible death and destruction (in the Gunpowder Plot), or some violent and depraved murder (of a three-year-old boy, whose sister's tongue was cut out by the predators). Between 1624 and 1641, when the first publications appeared about widespread violence in Ireland, most books with massacre in the title were reprints of the first text about the Gunpowder Plot.[14] These varied usages suggest that there were multiple types of massacres: all might be cruel murders, but those murders transpired in different ways. The EIC made its distinctive contribution to the English meaning of "massacre" in how it linked the judicial execution of its employees in the Indonesian archipelago to the mass murder of religious dissenters in Europe and in deepening the association of massacre with treachery and betrayal.

In the twenty-first century, "massacre" is a synonym for "slaughter," but the words were not so close in this earlier era. Slaughter was a considerably older word that showed up in English dictionaries as early as 1475, while massacre's first definition was in 1593.[15] Three of the best known compilations in the English language in this era, the Geneva Bible, the King James Bible, and the works of Shakespeare, attest to both the relative frequency and different meanings of the words. The Geneva Bible was an English translation of the Bible, first printed in Geneva in 1560 and then in England in 1575. Massacre is not in the 1561 edition at all, in contrast to 68 uses of slaughter.[16] The King James Bible (1611) contains slaughter 77 times. "Massacre" appears twice, in 2 Kings 11 and in the Apocrypha, 1 Maccabees 1:24.[17] Likewise, slaughter shows up 78 times in Shakespeare's complete works; massacre, only 8. For the most part, Shakespeare used massacre as a synonym for slaughter or mass murder (with the exception of Hamlet's well-known invocation against "self-slaughter"); in Henry VI, Part I, he even paired the words "massacres and ruthless slaughters."[18] One exception, however, intimates the special meaning massacre might convey. In Richard III, Sir James Tyrrel announces the deaths of the two princes in the tower as a "piteous massacre." A few words later, he elaborates by calling the killing a "ruthless piece of butchery."[19] The English traders had also called the Amboyna deaths an act of butchery, "an inhumaine and butcher execution."[20]

The pairing of "butcher" and "massacre" does not seem to have been accidental. In fact, the association of the two words says something important not just about the linguistic origins of "massacre" in a butcher's block but also about the sentiments users may have attached to such violence. Butchery cemented an association of massacre with intimate violence—in this era, one butchered something in proximity, by hand—and that subtle understanding of a massacre as the butchery of humans might similarly explain why the English deplored the Dutch for acting like cannibals at Amboyna. Contemporary depictions of the people of the Americas whom Europeans regarded as cannibals may have assisted in this series of logical steps from butcher to massacre to cannibal, because popular images depicted Americans butchering humans for easy consumption and grilling. Cannibalism had emerged as the era's ultimate symbol of barbarism by the mid-sixteenth century.[21] English assessments in 1623 and 1624 of the Dutch at Amboyna as cannibals both linked the word massacre to its origin in butchery and associated the Dutch with savagery.[22] "Cannibal" also had associations in Europe with the killing of martyrs. The 1563 edition of John Foxe's *Actes and Monuments*, a Protestant martyrology, contains a poem that describes Edmund Bonner, the Bishop of London, as a cannibal for having killed 300 martyrs in three years.[23]

Yet not all mass murders or cruel murders, or even murders by the Dutch, were massacres. The English, for example, had disapproved of the VOC's murder of the Bandanese on Run in 1621, yet the traders stopped short of characterizing the event as a massacre, the very word that one of the same men used in a letter the next day to describe what had happened to the English at Amboyna.[24] Likewise, the English deplored the violence inflicted on EIC employees during the period of open strife with the VOC in the 1610s. More English were wounded and killed, and far more suffered long-term imprisonment, between 1617 and 1621 than was the case with the whirlwind if brutal Amboyna trial. The number of English killed on the *Sampson*, attacked by the Dutch in July 1619, numbered eleven, for example, and thirty-five were wounded. And there were some terrifying ordeals, too, including the assault on Lontor in 1621, where the Dutch seized the English along with their Chinese servants, and beheaded three of the Chinese.[25] The EIC condemned the Dutch as ungrateful. They were barbarous, cruel, inhumane. They were bad Christians, even "Pagan-like"; they oppressed the English.[26] Yet the EIC did not describe these incidents as massacres.

Figure 3.1 American "cannibals" butchering and grilling people. Theodor de Bry, *Dritte Buch Americae, darinn Brasilia durch Johann Staden auss eigener Erfahrung in teutsch beschrieben* ([Frankfurt], 1593), p. 48. G159 .B8 pt. 3a E141, Library of Congress.

The association of *massacre* with the 1623 conspiracy trial had two likely causes, one in the entangled history of the English and the Dutch, and the second in the recent global history of the English. Both factors make it clear that the relationship between killer and killed at a specific moment in time played a vital role in making a murder a massacre. In 1619 the English and Dutch were in open conflict in the Indies, but in 1623, they were allies and partners. By putting the English on trial, the Dutch asserted a superior authority over them, a prerogative that flouted both the 1619 treaty and, more important, English notions of their historical connection. That bitterness infused the title of the EIC's published account of the trial, which proclaimed the "unjust, cruell, and barbarous proceedings" of the Dutch.[27]

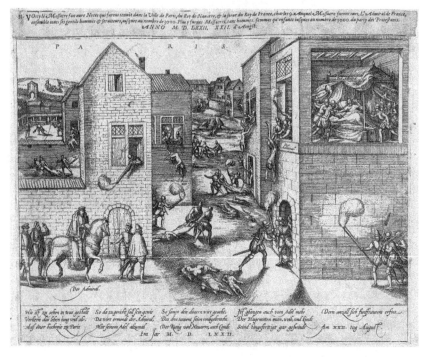

Figure 3.2 An artist's rendering of the event Protestants called the St. Bartholomew's Day Massacre (1572). Franz Hogenberg, "Hie ist zu sehen in was gestalt" (Cologne, 1573). Call # ART 266905. Used by permission of the Folger Shakespeare Library.

A second cause for the EIC's interpretation might pertain to the remote location where the incident took place. One of the few books that came off English presses about massacres before 1624 concerned an episode that occurred in 1622 in the colony of Virginia, and this pamphlet—and this event—help explain how and why in the summer of 1624 the EIC decided to embrace its employees' description of the Amboyna conspiracy and advance an argument that the trial was a massacre. In this attack, one-third of the English colonists were killed by a Pamunkey leader, Opechancanough, and his soldiers during a period when the English thought they were at peace. Instead, their allies showed what the English characterized as treachery—bearing gifts, but armed and ready to strike—and attacked the English invaders in the midst of their morning chores.[28] The Virginia episode's large-scale violence conformed closely to European accounts of unexpected attacks on civilians by their neighbors, especially the massacres connected

Figure 3.3 An artist's rendering of the 1622 Virginia "massacre." Matthaus Merian, "The massacre of the settlers in 1622," from Theodor De Bry, *America*, Part 13 (Frankfurt, 1628), p. 42. RB122220, The Huntington Library, San Marino, California.

to the French wars of religion. A near contemporary depiction of the event in 1628 made that connection emphatically. In 1622, this Virginia attack was the most recent experience the English had as victims of a massacre along the continental model—a mass attack by allies on people the English regarded as unprepared and innocent civilians—and it was the first event as the word evolved in English to feature multiple English victims.[29] Several works about the Virginia massacre in 1622, including a pamphlet, a ballad, a poem, and a play, made it clear that massacres were something that could happen to the English when they were far from home, vulnerable, and dwelling uncomfortably among untrustworthy allies. Those at the center of government perceived the paired struggles. So, at least, Sir Francis Nethersole, an English politician and diplomat with extensive experience in continental diplomacy, reported to Carleton (in The Hague) from London in June of 1624, as the news of Amboyna festered in the capital. The Virginia Company, he wrote, was ready to be dissolved in the wake of the 1622 attack, and as for the East India Company, it was so dismayed by the "outrage" at Amboyna that it contemplated giving up trade there as well.[30]

By summer 1624, then, the EIC may have drawn on this new familiarity with massacres as something experienced by English people overseas in its assessment of the Amboyna episode. The word was central to the July depositions at the High Court of Admiralty, and that same month Carleton lamented the "bloudy massacre" in his correspondence.[31] The Venetian ambassador picked up the term by October 1624, when he informed the Doge that the English still complained about the event they called the massacre.[32] But if the word was so commonly embraced that foreign ambassadors knew to use it, sanctioned printed works about the episode did not use it at all to describe what had happened, because the rapid emergence in English hands of the event as a massacre posed political and diplomatic hardship at a precarious moment. At the very instant news arrived about the execution of the English traders, James I was in the process of signing a treaty of defense with the United Provinces. He signed this treaty on June 5, 1624, after delaying a week to assimilate the tidings from Amboyna.[33] The EIC thus crafted its massacre carefully, cautiously, and without using the word.

When the word "massacre" appeared in printed works about Amboyna, it didn't apply to the English as victims: instead, it applied to the Dutch. The author of *An Answer Unto the Dutch Pamphlet*, one of the pamphlets the EIC wrote and published in 1624, described Dutch fears of a "massacre" by the people of Run, one of the Banda islands.[34] The only time the word massacre appeared to describe the feared plot at Amboyna was in the VOC's official record of the trial, in which the English trader Timothy Johnson confessed that he met with Japanese and other English several times to discuss their plot of taking the fort and "massacring those of the Low-Countries."[35] The VOC called the episode a massacre, too, in its condemnation of the culprits at Amboyna, sentencing the English and Japanese for "having conceived and complotted together a horrible massacre & treason" against the Dutch.[36]

The new alliance made it risky for each company to put forward its interpretation of events, hindering attempts for revenge or compensation for injuries suffered in the East Indies.[37] The EIC pressured the crown to pursue restitution through diplomatic channels, and indeed while the Dutch government courted English support, the States General promised to investigate matters and punish the guilty. This diplomatic tension meant that the path to publication for both companies was perilous and protracted. The VOC had been quick to circulate an account of the conspiracy. By May 28, the English ambassador at The Hague had in his hands a brief manuscript sent to him by the States. This work was shorter than the manuscript for *Waerachtich verhael vande tijdinghen gecomen uut de Oost-Indien*, which appeared in England in a French version sometime in May or June. It was printed in the United Provinces soon thereafter.[38] The EIC translated and published this text in 1624 as *A True Declaration of the Newes that came out of the East-Indies*. The EIC's account, published as *A True Relation of the Unjust, Cruell, and Barbarous Proceedings against the English at Amboyna In the East-Indies, by the Neatherlandish Governour and Councel there* (London, 1624), started circulating in manuscript in July. As the title indicates, this account provided a narrative of the events of the trial, with some discussion of the aftermath in the region. The company's agent at Delft soon set to work having a Dutch translation made in "the sharpest style the translation would beare."[39] The EIC wanted to publish its *True Relation* right away, and company members presented the Dutch "libel" at court in August to make their case.[40] The EIC's agent in Amsterdam was relieved to learn in August that the EIC had not yet published its version, since at the time he was trying to get the published Dutch account suppressed, which the States General agreed to do.[41] On August 18 (in the Dutch calendar) the States General ordered the destruction of this work, condemned it as libelous, and offered a reward for the identity of the printer or author.[42]

The EIC took care to ensure that its own account was published simultaneously in English and Dutch, and it funded a large print run, determining in October 1624 to have 2,000 English copies and 1,000 Dutch copies published.[43] The EIC sought to get the *True Relation* into the hands of men with power, those able to make decisions and carry out diplomacy. The English text was printed in October, and on December 10, EIC members learned that their book about "the crueltyes of the dutch" had been published in both English and Dutch and was in circulation in England and in the Netherlands.[44] This printed version was a three-part text. It included the *True Relation*, an English translation of the VOC's account, the *True Declaration*, and an English response (*An Answer unto the Dutch Pamphlet*). The EIC could thus address the monarch's concerns about antagonizing an ally by publishing the VOC's own account. While each company resorted to print, manuscript texts also continued to circulate, including a copy of the trial records, a remonstrance the VOC sent the States General in November

1624 in response to the States' rebuke of the VOC's conduct, and the EIC's reply to the VOC remonstrance.[45]

In all of these works from 1624, printed and manuscript, the VOC and EIC argued about a few core points. They focused on the plausibility of the plot and especially on matters of legal process. The English objected to the torture used, both mock drowning with water and flames placed on tender flesh, since they professed to be unaccustomed to such violence in their own criminal law procedures, and they leveled charges of cruelty against the Dutch.[46] The two companies believed that the incident had different historical and geographic origins, too. For the VOC, the conspiracy was embedded in a pattern of animosity in the region and thus the *True Declaration* commenced with an account of treachery by the people of the powerful and clove-rich Sultanate of Ternate, in the chain of islands north of Amboyna, who had been intermittent allies and rivals of the Dutch.[47] Certain of the innocence of its employees at Amboyna, the EIC cast the men as victims of a Dutch plot, rendering the conflict as national and ethnic, another chapter in English and Dutch relations.[48] The English thus transformed the Amboyna episode from the regional conspiracy the VOC had dreaded in the Spice Islands, one involving Spanish, English, Japanese, enslaved, and Moluccan forces, into a massacre, something that concerned only the English and the Dutch. The *True Relation* depicted the event as a betrayal of the harmony between the two nations enshrined in the treaty signed by the two companies in 1619.[49]

The important and potentially dangerous role that Amboyna played in European politics as an incident that could rupture the new Anglo-Dutch alliance is evident in the publication history of the *True Relation* in 1624.[50] Three unique versions came off the presses in that year. One was the authorized East India Company account in English. This was the work that the printer Nathaniel Newbury entered in the Stationers' Company register on October 14, 1624.[51] The Stationers' Company controlled printing in the capital, and all books required licenses and official approval. It was the Stationers' Company's responsibility to ensure that publications were not offensive.[52] The EIC's pamphlet was one of several hundred books to come off English presses in that year, maybe as many as 500 in London alone.[53] The English version had two separate printings in 1624, with the second printing labeled "the second impression" on its title page, and it contained corrections from the first impression listed on its errata page. The work continued to circulate in manuscript, as a student at Cambridge University saw both printed and manuscript versions by November 1.[54]

The company published the work as a quarto, a customary format for a pamphlet in this era and a comfortable shape to hold, easy to read, and not so long that the book feels overwhelming.[55] The font is big enough for the far-sighted and the language is plain, even in discussions of legal matters. Thanks to the survivors, the account is full of direct speech and personalized details that bring the traders and their ordeal to life. The title page was unadorned by an image, but instead was filled with words: it listed the titles of the three pamphlets, all printed together as one work, along with the publication information and the assertion that the text was "Published by Authoritie."[56] Together these words advance a clear political and moral position, all while giving the appearance of balance—a gesture to the tender sensibilities of an ally—since the EIC included the VOC's pamphlet in its own text.

The second version was the authorized account translated into Dutch and printed sometime after November. It reproduced the complete text of the authorized English version, and it, too, showed its official imprint with the EIC's seal. The Dutch-language version concluded with its own distinct letter to the reader, which explained that since the *True Relation* had been first printed in English, a new Declaration to the States General by the VOC appeared, a reference to the remonstrance the VOC presented to the States in November 1624.[57]

The third version was printed at the college of St. Omer, the largest of three English Jesuit institutions located in the Spanish Netherlands, and this edition was part of a Habsburg campaign to sever the new Anglo-Dutch alliance. The College boasted a large press and published works for an English audience. Many such works were shipped to England in the early 1620s, when English laws were relaxed during the period of the Anglo-Spanish match. The St. Omer's pamphlet was one of the press's overtly political works.[58]

It is possible—indeed, probable—that the St. Omer version of the *True Relation* was actually printed just before the EIC's version. The English government's agent in Brussels reported in early October 1624 on a concerted campaign by interests there, especially Catholic ones, to "animate" England against the Dutch. As part of that effort, the provocateurs sought to publish an account of the Amboyna incident and, to that end, hoped to find an English printer to accomplish their goal.[59] Had the EIC's *True Relation* been in print and in circulation already, there wouldn't have been much need for the St. Omer version. Whoever hoped to publish the book had a copy of

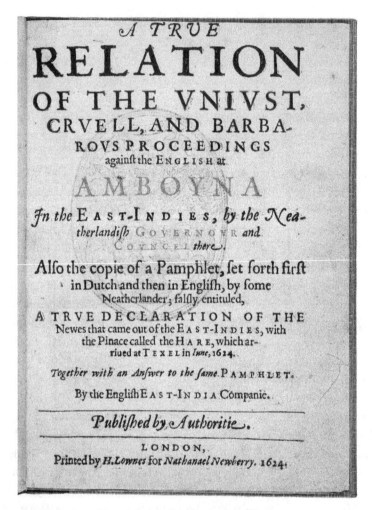

Figure 3.4 Title page, *True Relation* (London, 1624, first impression). Call # STC 7451 copy 1. Used by permission of the Folger Shakespeare Library.

one of the many manuscript "True Relations" in circulation and in this particular case had obtained it from Jean Baptiste van Male, who represented the Infanta Isabel in London. Part of the title proclaimed the text's history: it *hath byn lately delivered to the Kings most Excellent Majesty.* The EIC had presented its manuscript "True Relation" to the king in July. Often authors worried about losing control of a manuscript when they handed it to a printer, and the EIC was so anxious about an unauthorized version that it ordered the press to be broken after its pamphlet was printed. But in the case

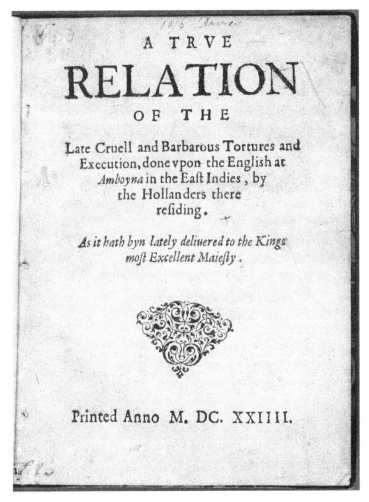

A TRVE

RELATION

OF THE

Late Cruell and Barbarous Tortures and
Execution, done vpon the English at
Amboyna in the Eaſt Indies , by
the Hollanders there
reſiding.

*As it hath byn lately deliuered to the Kings
moſt Excellent Maieſty .*

Printed Anno M. DC. XXIIII.

Figure 3.5 Title page, *True Relation* ([St. Omer], 1624). Although not identified
on its cover with a place of publication, the pamphlet carried the press's
distinctive "tailpiece," the ornament that adorns book covers. RB433817, The
Huntington Library, San Marino, California.

of this manuscript, multiple copies circulated for several months before (and
after) the work was printed in England, and for that reason it was vulnerable
to being scooped, as seems to have been likely in this case.[60]

The appearance of the St. Omer *True Relation* in 1624, one year after the
marriage negotiations broke down and Catholic hopes of a new Anglo-
Spanish union collapsed, suggests that English Catholics had not yet given

up on driving a wedge between England and the United Provinces and that the new Anglo-Dutch alliance in June 1624 may have inspired more vigorous efforts on the part of Habsburg sympathizers. The publication of the Amboyna text by the Jesuit press explains why the English and Dutch governments were so agitated about the conspiracy trial on the other side of the world: they feared the Spanish might use the affair to sever their alliance. The St. Omer version for the most part followed the text of the authorized *True Relation*, with four exceptions. Two were relatively minor. First, the St. Omer edition included only the *True Relation*, not the other items printed with it (the VOC's *True Declaration* and the EIC's response to this text) in the EIC's authorized version. Second, there are many small variations in wording and punctuation between the two texts, almost inevitably the result of errors in manuscript copying. In the St. Omer work, for example, John Beaumont's "Bowells were ready to breake," whereas in the London edition, his "inwards were ready to crack."[61]

The third difference between the two texts was a two-paragraph omission in the St. Omer version that signaled its political agenda. These paragraphs concern the Indo-Portuguese and Japanese victims of the Dutch proceedings at Amboyna. In its *True Relation*, the English East India Company carefully named these men, identifying who was condemned and who was spared, although the author seemed skeptical that anyone would care, and added the names "(if any be curious to know them)." In the St. Omer edition, there is no mention of these individuals by name and fate. Instead, it skips from the list of the names of the English who were condemned and spared to a description of a black velvet cloth deployed to cradle Gabriel Towerson's decapitated head.[62] The absence of these other victims, who equaled the English in numbers and whose presence was so important in VOC accounts of the conspiracy and its aftermath, tightened the focus of the conflict on the two European nations, which was precisely why the printing house at St. Omer wanted to publish the text.

The final divergence between the two texts makes explicit the purpose of the St. Omer volume. The EIC's *True Relation* contains an Epistle to the Reader. So, too, does the St. Omer edition, but the compiler wrote his own text, which emphatically asserted that Dutch perfidy, so evident in the "Tragicall Cruelty" at Amboyna, was not limited to the trade centers of the East Indies. Instead, the English should shun all "barbarous shores" where the Dutch "beare sway," for the Dutch rejected the ties of religion, humanity, alliance, and gratitude in their betrayal of their English friends. The author embraced his English nationality and implored his readers to do the same, and to show their solidarity with the Amboyna dead ("our English Merchants") by resisting continued affiliation with the Dutch.[63] Nationality, not religious affiliation, should determine alliances. The St. Omer version made its plea unfettered by the constraints that made it difficult for the EIC to speak or write freely in England.

The same international interests eager to sever the Anglo-Dutch alliance produced another work that was published in 1624, a newssheet with text and four images entitled *The moste savage and horrible cruelties lately practised by the Hollanders; upon the English, in the East-Indies*.[64] The publication, a news print or illustrated broadside, was an ephemeral genre and few survive.[65] This work is almost certainly that described in a letter some members of the EIC wrote Carleton in February 1625, after a visit to the Privy Council, which questioned them about four items connected to Amboyna. One of those items was a work published in Europe, "expressinge in effigie the severall tortures inflicted uppon the English at Amboyna and Lantore."[66] It was published in "Presborow," or Pressburg (present-day Bratislava), then the capital of Hungary and within the Habsburg Empire. The printer, I. M. Armstrong, seems to have been English. He obviously worked with a highly skilled engraver, because the news print contains four illustrations so meticulously crafted that emotions come through clearly. The engraver added a fourth image to the three Amboyna scenes: the violence against the English and their Chinese servants during the VOC's invasion of Lontor in 1621.

The broadside was printed in English, in Roman (not Gothic) font, and clearly targeted at an English audience. It never could have been licensed for publication in England because of the author's agenda to deter Britons from signing up for military service. The author described the Dutch as "vilanous wretches," and "monsters": they showed "divelish malice & vilanie," more than ever known before. By failing to get revenge, the English were humiliated before the world. Moreover, the broadside continued, English people traveling abroad have been asked if the kingdom was populated by lunatics, residents of "Bedlems or mad-howses," because how else could one explain why 6,000 soldiers (as per the treaty signed in June 1624) were available to serve in Holland given how the Dutch had treated the English in the East Indies? The reference to the soldiers indicates the likely audience for these two continental works: the thousands of British soldiers serving in Dutch regiments.[67] Were the Habsburgs able to discourage Britons from volunteering for this service, it would severely hinder Dutch military capacity, or else require the

Figure 3.6 *The Most Savage and Horrible Cruelties Lately Practised by the Hollanders; upon the English, in the East-Indies* (Presborow [Pressburg], 1624). National Archives, The Hague, States General, 1.01.02, inv. no. 12551.62-3.

United Provinces to spend precious funds hiring soldiers. It would also put James I in the position of failing to meet his treaty obligations.

These Habsburg-sponsored works illustrate the utility of Amboyna for those hoping to sever the Anglo-Dutch alliance at a precarious moment, and they also explain why the two companies had to censor themselves as they produced their own pamphlets. Printers in St. Omer and Pressburg were free to say what they wanted about the Dutch, but neither the EIC nor the VOC had such latitude. Some things could not be printed or displayed in England during these years of alliance—notably direct accusations of Dutch

ingratitude or admonitions to shun Dutch connections. The English company produced pamphlets; it commissioned a painting; it may have played
a role in a play and in a ballad. Yet none of the works it sanctioned—at least
those that have survived—employed the word massacre to describe Dutch
actions. The most common way to describe the incident (generally called the
"business" or the "fact" in extant records) was with the adjective "bloody."[68]
It was the "bloody execucon";[69] "bloudy accident";[70] "bloodie proceedings";[71] "bloody inhumanitie";[72] "bloudy tortures";[73] "bloudy and treacherous villany";[74] "bloudy fact";[75] "bloudie murther";[76] "bloudy butchery";[77]
"bluody passages";[78] and "bloudy accon."[79] A 1624 broadside ballad about
the incident excelled in its use of the term, with "bloody gore," "cruell and
bloody usage," "bloody body," "bloody deeds," and "bloody Tragedy" in its
short space.[80] The word was everywhere, on the lips of the family members
of the executed, statesmen, EIC company members, and the king himself. By
1676, an author could wrap the whole thing up as "the old story of bloody
Amboyna."[81]

But if the EIC did not use the word massacre to describe the deaths at
Amboyna, their publications in fall 1624—the three-part pamphlet and
two woodcuts—nonetheless made that assessment clear. The EIC's *True
Relation* was a powerful book—one reader described himself as reading it
in tears—but the text alone was not sufficient to make the EIC's case.[82] The
most persuasive work was done through two woodcuts, one that adorned the
English-language English pamphlet and another for the Dutch-language edition, both of which showed traders enduring torture. These woodcuts closely
resembled the 1624 Pressburg work, but it is difficult to determine with certainty which came first.[83] The EIC's woodcuts came as separately printed
sheets that a purchaser asked a binder to sew or stitch into the pamphlet.[84]
The pictures, purchased or viewed on their own or with the pamphlet, also
enabled the *True Relation* to straddle the divide between the literate and
nonliterate.

The illustrations conveyed directly what the EIC was hesitant to utter. The
Amboyna massacre wasn't, of course, a mass slaughter akin to those of the
religious wars nor like the incident in Virginia, but the English believed it to
be a cruel or horrible murder. The EIC fused these different components of
"massacre" in how it told and depicted the story of the traders' fate: the company yoked the Amboyna deaths, characterized by torture and a judicial process, to the martyrology central to the murders and executions of Protestants,
a history so recent in England that the last person burned as a heretic had

Figure 3.7 *True Relation* (London, 1624), frontispiece. RB437335, The Huntington Library, San Marino, California.

been executed just twelve years earlier.[85] In so doing, the EIC created a new kind of massacre, one connected to judicial execution, and contributed to the evolving meaning of the word. It also created a secular version of the religious massacre, and in the company's executed employees it created secular martyrs, men who died for commercial conflict at the hands of a treacherous ally, not for a religious cause.

The woodcut for the English-language edition provides a narrative of events to display the ordeal the English endured, from forced confessions to

Figure 3.8 *Een waer verhael* ([London], 1624), frontispiece. (c) The British Library Board, 9055.b.11.

execution. Placed prominently in the center of the image was an English merchant, clad only in loose breeches below a stomach distended from the water
torture, splayed spread-eagled on a frame, hands and legs fastened closely.
One Dutchman pours water in his mouth, while a second man deploys a
long torch to burn the trader under his right armpit, an image that might
have been intended to invoke the lance thrust by a Roman soldier into the
right side of Christ. Candles scorch his soles. A second scene at the bottom
left depicts a harried looking man, staring directly at the viewer, clad only

in a drape of fabric around his genitals, his unkempt hair shaggy around his forlorn face. Water drops seem to fall from his head: he is a victim of the water torture. He languishes, barefoot and bareheaded, a state of undress that conveyed the vulnerability of the imprisoned men awaiting their fate, in contrast to the well-clad Dutch. Finally, at the bottom right, is the final episode of the depicted drama. A composed merchant, still half-naked but his beard trimmed to a perfect point, kneels on the ground, his hands bound and clasped in prayer, before a Dutch executioner poised to sever his head from his body with a sword.

The image collapses multiple scenes and events. It renders the actual execution as a private event, an intimate encounter between executioner and condemned. In this claustrophobic setting, a torturer hovering over the accused, an executioner looming over the condemned, the intimacy at the heart of a massacre as a particular type of violent death is vivid. In fact, the condemned men were all marched to the public place of execution and beheaded by a Japanese executioner. The creator removed any distinctive features of the locale, placing all the action in a room with European architectural features. The woodcut, moreover, eliminates non-Europeans entirely—whether Japanese soldiers as executioners or alleged conspirators, the slave overseer, or Moluccans, crafting a tale of English and Dutch conflict when there was a much more complex cast of characters involved. The images are thus at best a partial truth and were a vital aspect of the transformation of the event into an Anglo-Dutch story and into a massacre. For the English, the episode was a massacre specifically because of the conduct of the Dutch; the presence of the Japanese co-conspirators was largely irrelevant. The absence of the Japanese soldiers or other non-Europeans intimates whether an author or creator was part of the transformation of this episode into a massacre.

In the Dutch-language version of the EIC's *True Relation*, this woodcut is joined by a companion image with an emphasis on fire.[86] Four candles held aloft and placed under feet and armpits torment the central figure. One Dutch man seems to be making an incision in the Englishman's side, probably a reference to survivors' reports of gunpowder placed in their cut flesh. A dungeon beneath a tiled floor reveals figures, not even discernible as men, who peer out, clinging to the grate.

The creators borrowed heavily from familiar images of martyrology. Christianity was based on the ordeal of the afflicted and tortured body and the transcendence promised by faith: the central figure of the faith was the scourged, humiliated, tortured, and executed son of God. European artists had long made the ordeal of Christ and of others who suffered for their faith—martyrs—central to their work, whether in massive canvases, devotional works, or stained glass. But those images also circulated in accessible print forms, especially with the rise of printing and the spread of literacy, and ensured that viewers of the EIC's woodcuts had a context in which to make sense of the images they saw. The trader splayed across the doorway in the shape of an X, for example, echoed the martyrdom of Saint Andrew in the first century CE. Legend had him bound to an X-shaped cross (called a saltire, now known as the Saint Andrew's cross). Like the EIC traders, Saint Andrew was bound, not nailed, to the cross. He survived the culling of saints that accompanied England's reformation: the Book of Common Prayer listed his feast day on November 30.[87] A British Protestant, literate or not, would have recognized the image easily and understood the association between the fate of the Amboyna traders and a saint's martyrdom.

The best-known English text concerned with martyrology may have inspired the execution scene: John Foxe's authoritative and ubiquitous *Actes and Monuments*, which appeared in six editions between 1563 and 1596.[88] In the 1583 edition, a woodcut shows a scene of multiple tortures inflicted on the bishops of the early church. In the midst of a scene of flagellation, immolation, mauling by lions, and a range of other torments, an executioner raises aloft a sword above his right shoulder over a kneeling man, whose hands are opened as if in supplication. In the Amboyna woodcut, the picture is reversed, with the executioner holding the sword over his left shoulder.

Overall, the images in Foxe's compendium contrast with the Amboyna illustrations. Foxe tended to depict single-action scenes, not woodcuts that told a story. The vast majority of Foxe's pictures are of people in fires, with cartouches over their heads in which inspiring final words appear. There are few scenes of torture. The martyrs are almost universally composed and dignified.[89] Foxe's martyrs deliberately insert their bodies in fires, welcoming their deaths: the famous example of Thomas Cranmer putting his hand in the flames of his execution pyre to atone for having earlier signed a recantation of his faith memorialized the cleansing ritual of fire. Where, then, did the inspiration for the depiction of this harried, tormented Englishman at Amboyna come from, and what purpose might it have served? This was, after all, the East India Company's first use of woodcuts in its works, and surely every element of the picture warranted considerable discussion—none of which appears in the surviving court minutes.

Figure 3.9 This image from John Foxe, *Actes and Monuments*, was a possible inspiration for the creator of the EIC's woodcut shown in Figure 3.7: note the executed man at the center of this illustration. The flagellated martyr on the right also shows a slight resemblance to the figure of the Englishman recovering from the water torture. John Foxe, *Actes and Monuments* (London, 1583), 780. Call # STC 11225. Used by permission of the Folger Shakespeare Library.

The EIC's woodcuts ensured that English and Dutch readers, literate and il-literate alike, understood the message of the pamphlets. Moreover, the Dutch had their own emerging tradition of Protestant martyrology, a product of their ordeal under Habsburg rule. As part of their critique of Spanish violence ("tyr-anny," as the Dutch styled it), Dutch printers discovered and resuscitated the writings of Bartolomé de las Casas, a Dominican friar who criticized Spanish cruelty toward the indigenous people of the Caribbean and Central America in the early- to mid-sixteenth century. An initial Dutch translation in 1578 was followed by twenty-five more, many accompanied by graphic illustrations of violence, before war came to an end in 1648. These works created what has come to be known as the Black Legend, an interpretation of Spanish conquest in the Americas that emphasizes cruelty and violence. Once it was safe for the Dutch to criticize the Spanish openly, as opposed to condemning them for their conduct on the other side of the world, depictions of Spaniards torturing and murdering the Dutch also appeared in multiple printed books in the United Provinces.[90] Both the English and Dutch, then, had print cultures that prominently featured the tortured and mutilated bodies of Protestant martyrs, making these woodcuts familiar and comprehensible to viewers.

In the context of the era's shared visual imagery of Protestant suffering, the two woodcuts made it clear to English and Dutch viewers that the English traders at Amboyna died as martyrs. Merchants might not seem a likely contender for such status, but by the beginning of the seventeenth century, merchants had acquired a reputation as people who served the nation, and Foxe had expanded the categories of people who could achieve martyrdom.[91] His compendium showcased learned divines and steadfast Protestants of all ranks and occupations, male and female. What made the EIC traders martyrs was especially their ordeal with torture: each time the word "martyred" appeared in the text of the *True Relation*, the author linked it to the physical suffering of the accused men, and it served as a synonym for "tortured." Clarke and Thompson, for example, were "mangled and martyred." The word even encompassed the Japanese soldiers, their tortured bodies "martyred with fire and water" persuading a frightened Abel Price to confess.[92] Towerson moved beyond martyr, his behavior described as "godly" in an EIC manuscript written in 1624–25 and printed in 1632.[93] The association of martyrdom with physical suffering left opaque the issue of whether the traders sacrificed themselves for a noble or transcendent cause (certainly they showed no such conviction in their confessions), in contrast to the assurance of executed Protestants, who died steadfast in their faith.

Assisting the *True Relation* in advancing the EIC's case that the episode was a massacre and its victims were martyrs was a broadside ballad, *Newes out of East India*, which was published after the *True Relation*, probably some time between November 1624 and February 1625.[94] A woodcut accompanied the ballad, as was typical of the genre. Frequently ballad illustrations came from formulaic woodblocks and the same stock image appeared in multiple ballads on vaguely related topics. In this case, the printer did not choose an old recycled woodblock but instead adorned the ballad with a slightly modified version of the EIC's first woodcut. Seventeenth-century ballads often dealt briefly with issues explored at greater length in pamphlets, as was the case with the Amboyna ballad. It rendered the English ordeal in verse as a song to be sung and it was a good way to spread news of the incident to those who could neither afford nor read a printed book. It was to be sung to the tune "Bragendery," long believed to be lost, but possibly the melody survived as the tune "Oh Women Monstrous Women," or "Oh Folly Desperate Folly." Text at the end of the ballad referred readers to the *True Relation* and instructed them where to buy it. This note suggested that the ballad's creator imagined multiple constituencies: London-based readers curious about the episode and with financial resources to purchase the *True Relation*; singers, both those with physical access to the ballad's text, and those who joined in only at the refrain, once they got the hang of the tune and the lyrics; and listeners, either too shy to sing along, or unable to carry a tune, or passing by and hearing the song in snatches.[95]

The ballad continued the distortion of the story evident in the woodcut that accompanied it with a lurid and almost entirely fictitious account of the different tortures experienced by ten English men. They were racked, strangled, confined so tightly in iron chains that blood gushed from their bodies, whipped and then covered in salt and vinegar, tortured with water, bound with cords, tormented with burning pincers, and burned with candles until the dripping fat from the body extinguished the candles' flames, a detail lifted from the tortures of John Clarke and Emanuel Thompson as described in the *True Relation*. Each man confessed to relieve his misery and then was hanged, not beheaded. The ballad did not neglect to point out that the Dutch confiscated English goods. The ballad included not only the woodcut, which became an indispensable feature of all accounts of the incident, but also a list of the dead. It recorded the names and occupations of the ten executed English men and the eight pardoned English men, plus a ninth, "A Portingall," and noted that "nyne native Indians" also died with the ten English. It is odd that the ballad listed the "Portingall" and the "nyne native Indians," since they were otherwise missing in the lyrics. There were obviously no Japanese soldiers, since they had been turned into "Indians," but more crucially there was no Japanese soldier asking questions to launch the legal process. Instead, in the ballad's account, the Dutch simply called the English in for questioning, without provocation, an interpretation of the incident that remained entrenched in English histories as late as the 1970s.

The emotional and rhetorical power of the ballad lay not in the poetic quality of its verse, which staggered gamely on from one stanza to the next, but in the special qualities that accompany a collectively sung, repetitive composition. If the tune has been correctly identified, it was a simple one, since, aside from the refrain, it used only three different notes. For all the lugubrious quality of the text, the tune itself is brisk and jaunty, something that might sound appropriate coming from a bright brass instrument, until it reaches the refrain. Then it slides into an awkward descending line in a minor key. It would have been an easy matter for even the most unskilled singer to pick up the tune and to join in. Twenty-one stanzas ended with the same two-line refrain: "Oh heaven looke downe, upon poore innocent soules," a turn of phrase that echoed John Goninge's 1623 assessment of the "poore innocent servants at Amboyna." Thus, twenty-one times a singer or a listener approached the English experience as one of injustice. It is easy enough to conjecture that for many people, the only time they sang this song was during the refrain, participating in the communal music-making only to invoke English innocence, a quality that was the hallmark of the martyr, central to religious massacres of the era, and applied to a new secular variant.

A second vital aspect of turning the incident into a massacre were signs of divine Providence. The miracles connected to Amboyna were not performed by the martyrs themselves—such actions would have refuted core tenets of Protestantism—but, rather, were "miracles of retribution," which also featured prominently in Foxe's *Actes and Monuments* in the form of punishments inflicted on those who tormented Protestants.[96] Abundant evidence pointed to providential punishment at Amboyna. The VOC governor who condemned the English later fell sick and died; a terrible storm hit the island on execution day, tearing ships from their anchors; great sickness befell the island at a season that was normally salubrious; a Scot who worked for the VOC and had implicated the English in the plot went crazy.[97] The *True Relation* delineated these punishments (except for van Speult's death, which was a later story of retribution) and so did the ballad, which savored the tale of the man who "fell starke mad" at the graveyard.[98] Over time, the tales of sickness became embellished. First reports had 1,000 dead, a number that swelled in subsequent accounts to 4,000–5,000 dead out of a population of 20,000, and the highest mortality, one man attested in 1628, fell in the areas around the fort, where the English were imprisoned and tortured.[99] The subsequent death of van Speult in the Red Sea particularly fascinated the English, who researched his condition and maintained a list with biographical information about each of the VOC judges. They concluded that van Speult suffered from the pox (they likely meant syphilis) when he came to Amboyna, clear evidence of his depravity and God's judgment of him.[100] All these misfortunes the English credited to Thompson's prediction on the scaffold that God would give signs of English innocence, and the *True Relation* professed that the Ambonese believed these hardships to be indications of God's displeasure for Dutch tyranny.[101]

These English tales of God's punishment agitated Dutch officials in Europe. The Dutch, after all, were heirs to the same tradition of Protestant martyrology, and they knew what these accounts of miracles were intended to signal to readers: the innocence of the English, the injustice of the Dutch, and God's wrath. They wanted answers about these miracles, so carefully detailed in the *True Relation*, and in order to get them, they included questions about the storm, the sickness, and especially the fate of Duncan, the Scot who allegedly went to the English gravesite a few days after the execution, fell down, and rose up mad, both in the 139 questions they set their employees to answer in Batavia in 1626 and in the 186 questions they posed to the same men in The Hague in 1628. Duncan's fate was particularly troubling, as this kind of madness was a sure sign of God's justice.

The VOC men answered each question in their depositions. Duncan, in the English account, was likely remorseful because he had made an allegation during the proceedings that suggested there had been a longtime English plot to take over the fort. Left unsaid in the English version was Duncan's perhaps greater culpability as a Scot, one who shared a king with the English and who might have owed them greater loyalty. Guilt-ridden, Duncan allegedly died the death of a crazed penitent. The VOC trader Jan Joosten had no reply to make to this tale but observed in 1626 that he thought this story that Duncan arose "stark mad" was "rather ridiculous." Jan Jacobsen Wyncoop agreed that he had never heard such a "fabulous" story. Jan van Leeuwan reported that Duncan left Amboyna for Batavia with a cargo of iron, and people (including the captain of Amboyna's garrison, Martin Jansz Vogel) saw him in Batavia, so he could not have died as the English described. Roeland Tieller finished the narrative arc with reports that Duncan returned to Amboyna from Batavia, and Tieller himself talked to him there.[102] They also spoke about the weather. What of the terrible darkness that obscured the sky at the time of execution, or the great storm? Joosten remarked that it was just the usual rain of the monsoon. What of the Dutch ships driven off their anchors? Only one ship was driven off its anchor, but it was soon corrected. As for the allegations of a terrible sickness, Joosten insisted the mortality rate among the Dutch was the same as usual for that time of year, but that before the execution, the native Ambonese, as well as the VOC's enemies on Seram, had endured a pestilence called "louki louki," and many subjects and enemies died of this disease after the execution. Wyncoop referred his interrogators to a list naming the dead contained in a book that he had sent to Batavia himself.[103] The care with which Dutch officials in Europe sought answers to these questions about the alleged miracles suggests the powerful narrative the EIC had created in a providential framework the company shared with fellow Protestants. Miracles were a sure sign of a massacre.

A third component of the transformation of this episode into a massacre was the existence of relics. The Amboyna episode produced several relics, although these objects were not the bloody detritus of executed martyrs characteristic of the Catholic tradition. Nor was the velvet cloth that cradled Towerson's decapitated head a suitable relic, although to the English it was an important indicator of Dutch parsimony. In the *True Relation*, the English accused the Dutch of charging them for the velvet cloth, a matter that vexed the States General enough that they subsequently interrogated VOC officials about the fabric.[104] Instead, in keeping with the legal and diplomatic battle over process and justice that ensued in Europe, the Amboyna relics were the attestations of innocence written by the condemned men as they awaited execution: a statement Towerson added to a bill of debt owed a Dutch inhabitant of Amboyna; the attestation by four men in William Griggs's account book; and the lengthy memorial crafted by Samuel Coulson in the EIC's *Psalmes of David*. These documents became evidence in the protracted struggle by the English company to receive restitution. The objects reached England in June and July 1624: they were mentioned and quoted extensively in the depositions in July 1624, and later quoted in full in the *True Relation*.[105]

But the texts were more than an accumulation of words that spoke to English innocence. They were tangible objects—a sacred book, a scrap of paper, a merchant's accounting, "yet extant under the hands of the severall parties," the *True Relation* explained.[106] They represented the detritus of a factory's records and the final words of six condemned men. The States General requested these items as evidence in their proceedings. The EIC opposed sending the originals in case such action might make it look as if the company was submitting itself to the authority of the United Province, so instead had copies made. Charles I ultimately instructed the company to send the original documents, not the copies.[107]

To comply with the king's orders, some English men gathered to attest to the legitimacy of these texts. These witnesses explained the chain of custody. John Cappur, an EIC employee not involved in the Amboyna episode, knew the *Psalmes of David* as company property from his time working in Cambello. The survivor John Powel studied this book and said he believed it was Coulson's, and he had seen it with Coulson before he died. An English survivor placed the book in Richard Welden's hands in Amboyna; Welden took the book to Batavia and brought it with him to England. After Welden's arrival, the book landed in the custody of Andrew Ellam, a merchant of London. The witnesses were also deposed about the authenticity of the handwriting, addressing head-on the possibility that the documents were forged.[108] Finally, the EIC shipped the relics to the United Provinces, with copies kept in England in the Privy Council's chest.[109]

These martyrs, their relics, and God's punishment made clear what could not be said openly in England in 1624: the Amboyna episode was a massacre, and the Dutch were its perpetrators, cannibals bent on destroying the English whose only offense had ever been their selfless generosity to the Dutch. These charges were incendiary.

Even at the time it was published, with its cruel and barbarous proceedings, its martyred traders, and its outraged call for justice, the *True Relation* closely hewed the line that distinguished appropriate criticism of an ally and a breach of that amity. The EIC's efforts, moreover, risked encouraging an anti-Dutch faction at court. One reader of the work in November 1624 thought the text would not be published quickly for these reasons. "I suppose," he told his brother, "it will breed a generall distast if not enmity betweene us and them."[110] After all, the EIC had received permission to print its *True Relation* provided, the king adjured, that the book harbor "no bitternes against the States."[111] Indeed, the work seems to have slid quietly into public notice in November, but by February 1625 a transformed political situation hindered the EIC's ongoing and broad-ranging campaign for restitution. The EIC had extended its activities beyond the *True Relation* and sought to publicize its employees' ordeal in multiple genres. But in February, at the behest of Dutch ministers and the ambassadors of the States General, authorities suppressed a play, destroyed a painting, revoked the license given just days earlier for a reprinted sermon, and posted guards against anti-Dutch riots around Shrove Tuesday, a holiday when apprentices traditionally rioted. It fell on March 1 in that year.[112] The story behind the suppressions reveals both the complex international ties of the era and the awkward diplomatic moment.

The shifting climate derived from a variety of circumstances. First and foremost, the EIC's anti-Dutch posture could not make headway against entrenched and powerful pro-Dutch sentiments. It seems that when news of

Amboyna first reached London in summer 1624, the nation was still consumed by anti-Spanish feelings in the wake of the embarrassing failure of the Spanish match and was not prepared to rally against the Dutch.[113] Moreover, the long-standing ties between the two nations provided multiple mechanisms that enabled concerned people to minimize the impact of the executions. Amid English outrage at the brutal treatment of the English merchants, for example, a brave voice was even raised in defense of the Dutch, calling on the English to cherish their shared Protestantism above the terrible strains caused by this rupture. A Puritan named Thomas Scott wrote a pamphlet designed to bring the English and Dutch back into harmony.[114] Scott's inclination to defend the Dutch in the wake of an event almost universally deplored in England revealed the deep and historic ties between the two nations and, for some Protestants, a shared Calvinism.

Scott's strenuous effort to assert amicable relations received ample reinforcement from similar labors by the crown, the Prince of Orange, the States General, and the Privy Council, all of whom remained eager to stand behind the newly signed treaty of mutual defense. It was for precisely this reason that the EIC and VOC had to tread so carefully in their own publication efforts. The EIC faced especially powerful resistance from Prince Charles and the Duke of Buckingham, both of whom were determined to start a war with Spain. They had returned from the failed Spanish match in October 1623 to acclaim, and they jockeyed for more power at court in James's final months. Their concern was the fate of the Palatinate, a territory in the Holy Roman Empire, and the problem a dynastic one that drew England into a maelstrom of continental conflicts. Charles's sister (and James's daughter) Elizabeth had married Frederick V, the Elector Palatine, who had accepted the crown of Bohemia at the behest of Protestants and thus threw himself into direct conflict with Ferdinand II, the Holy Roman Emperor and cousin of the king of Spain. Charles and Buckingham wanted England to enter the war on behalf of the Elector. Buckingham emerged as the leader of a Protestant interest keen on war, and both Charles and Buckingham worked to marginalize James I—and, needless to say, to quell any anti-Dutch feelings or actions.[115]

But by the winter of 1624–25, new anti-Dutch sentiments had emerged in England, especially London. This hostility might have been part of a general growing xenophobia, because in January the Court of Alderman, the body that regulated the city of London, determined that no alien, or son or grandson of an alien, could become a citizen of London.[116] By February this hostility specifically targeted the Dutch. Bad news from Holland combined with lingering anger over Amboyna. Reports of starving soldiers serving under the command of Ernst von Mansfeld during his trouble-plagued winter effort to relieve the Dutch stronghold at Breda discouraged Englishmen from enlisting for service in the United Provinces, but so too, a newswriter argued, did these men chafe at how the Dutch, "the basest of people in matter of courage" treated the English, compelling them to endure the "barbarous cruelty" of Amboyna without giving any hint that they condemned the action. Adding insult to injury, the main legal official at Amboyna had returned to Amsterdam, where he was able to walk around with impunity. The result of all these sentiments, the newswriter concluded, was that the Dutch had "almost lost the hearts of their best friends here." The capital city was full of Dutch, so the potential for an enraged Londoner to find a target for his aggression was high. In an attempt to temper this rising Hollandophobia, a Dutch minister in London delivered a sermon critical of VOC actions at Amboyna in February. It was this concern, and especially anxiety about possible riots on May Day, that led these leaders of the Dutch community to protest the many cultural artifacts currently in gestation or already in circulation, all connected to Amboyna.[117]

The Amboyna crisis revealed a strong and deep strand of Hollandophobia in London, if not more broadly in England. The 1620s may have been the moment when an intense anti-Spanish sentiment in England started to shift toward anti-Dutch sentiment. In that respect, the *True Relation* and accompanying works may not have shaped a changing English sensibility, defining, that is, English identity in terms of an anti-Dutch stance, so much as clarified and reflected a process already under way. To be sure, these sentiments were just the seeds of what would flourish thirty years later, and authors of printed works usually censored themselves from expressing these anti-Dutch feelings openly. Manuscripts, however, sometimes revealed more frank sentiments. One such item was a manuscript titled "A Discourse of the Busines of Amboyna in A.d. 1624."[118] With no certain author, it is hard to place this text fully in its context, but it was written in response to another work by the Dutch sympathizer and Puritan Thomas Scott, *The Belgick Pismire* (1623). The author of the "Discourse" explained he had recently read this work and was agitated by its pro-Dutch contents. The author assumed that his reader was familiar with the *True Relation*, because he did not want to bore him by repeating details there.[119]

The manuscript "Discourse of the Busines of Amboyna" was unprint-
able in 1624. It contained standard caricatures of the Dutch, deploring their
drunkenness, greed, atheism, betrayal, cruelty, and deceit, but the author
embellished these traits by drawing on evidence from Amboyna. While the
Dutch professed to be Christians, he mocked that they observed the Sabbath
in Amboyna by torturing John Clarke. Far from being England's ally, they
were instead her sword. He singled out two VOC officials at Amboyna, van
Speult and the fiscal, Isaack de Bruyn, for particular opprobrium, claiming
personal knowledge of each, and pondering what a coat of arms for the fiscal
might look like when he returned to the Netherlands and was knighted for his
service, before declaring that it would have two devils on it. The devil, in fact,
had a great affinity for the Dutch. The only people he preferred more were
cannibals. The anonymous author's final image contained a world of loathing
in a single, memorable metaphor. For anyone with just a little chamber, who
might like to put something small in that room that represents all of the evil
in the world, the thing to do, he advised, is to find a picture of a Dutch person
and have it made into a statue, thus capturing in a single object all the world's
abhorrent traits—atheism, treachery, murder, deceit, envy, malice, drunkenness, and greed.[120]

The anger described by Chamberlain and the cruel and mocking tone of
this unpublished work suggest the tensions during the winter months. The
destruction, suppression, and demise of multiple cultural works—a painting,
a sermon, and a play— that interpreted the Amboyna episode punctuated
this atmosphere. The EIC had commissioned a massive painting, which
the company envisioned as part of its efforts to prompt Parliament to assist
them in their suit, though it also claimed that it sought to keep the painting
in its own building, "a perpetual memory of that most bloudy and treacherous villany."[121] The artist was Richard Greenbury, who was probably in his
early to mid-twenties when he got this commission and was already suffi-
ciently well established to have been hired by the crown two years earlier.
Given his facility with portraiture, it is tempting to imagine his work on the
large Amboyna canvas, in which the EIC charged him to display "the whole
manner of torturing the English at Amboyna."[122] He had at his service seven
Amboyna survivors, eager to render their assistance to the company in its
push for restitution. Did they offer themselves to Greenbury as models? Did
they stand by his side, describing the sights they saw, the sounds they heard?
It's impossible to know, because Greenbury made a tactical mistake, perhaps
swept away by his own Hollandophobia. He embedded a history of English

and Dutch relations in his canvas by deciding to paint a petition from the Dutch to Queen Elizabeth seeking help during their resistance against the Habsburgs. Such a document signaled the succor provided by the English and therefore highlighted the ingratitude and betrayal of the Dutch in the present moment. But this theme of ingratitude was a dangerous one for the EIC to emphasize, and the company required him to paint over this item in February 1625.[123]

That solution, however, was not sufficient to safeguard the canvas. The Dutch ambassadors in London lodged complaints about the EIC's activities, and the Privy Council summoned company officers on February 18 to question them about the painting. The Dutch, the Privy Council reported, were concerned that the company planned to display the painting before Parliament, which would further rile an already agitated membership. Company members conceded that they had planned to do just that, but complied with the council's request to keep the work locked in a room. The painting was apparently effective at evoking distress in those who saw it, because company members reported that people left their viewing shaken and distraught, with one woman, allegedly a widow of one of the men executed at Amboyna, fainting at the sight. The company was ordered not to display Greenbury's canvas publicly until Shrove Tuesday had passed. It so troubled state officials that none other than the Duke of Buckingham, that ardent Dutch advocate, sent for it at the end of February, and it was never seen again.[124]

In that same month, authorities recalled a sermon whose epistle invoked the "savage hearts" of the Dutch at Amboyna soon after they had licensed it. *The Stripping of Joseph*, first delivered in 1618, was licensed on February 3, 1625, and published by February 16.[125] The pamphlet included an introduction, characterized as a "consolatory Epistle," written by Thomas Myriell, the pastor of Saint Stephen's church in London, and dedicated to the EIC in light of the wrongs it had endured at the hands of the Dutch in Amboyna. Myriell presented twenty-four vellum-bound copies to the company at its meeting on February 18.[126] In his epistle, Myriell analyzed the source of conflicts between men and anchored them in the deadly sins. He turned first to examples of Spanish cruelty in Peru, calling on the newly emerging Black Legend, something familiar in England, too, especially after the first English-language edition of Las Casas was published in 1583.[127] Still more troubling were instances when people of the same religion, and those with whom one was at peace, turned on each other, and "practised most exquisite torments upon the innocent bodies of their Friends and Confederates." Such the Dutch did to the English, in their "inhumane and wolvish butchering up" of the EIC's employees at Amboyna.[128] Myriell, in other words, turned the Dutch into Spaniards, a sentiment antithetical to the pro-Dutch diplomatic and political posture in England in February 1625.[129]

But Myriell did something more, too. Along with his transformation of England's Dutch allies into tyrants as cruel as the Spanish in the Americas, this action probably explains why the work ended up being recalled. The work concluded with a final note to the reader from "a Friend of the Publisher." Perhaps the note was added after the license had been granted, because it is unlikely to have slipped by the censors, or perhaps they were duped and told that the sermon would be published without a new introduction and epistle.[130] The author, identified only as H. D., emphasized how appropriate the current moment was for this reprinted sermon. The blood of the English, *"miserably macerated and massacred,"* cried out for vengeance against the Dutch.[131]

"Miserably macerated and massacred." There it was in print, that word, massacre, that the EIC, more attuned to the precarious moment, had avoided in its own publications. It was too strong, too much, and another author fell foul of the political environment. It was in this context that Samuel Purchas tried to bring his four-volume compilation of voyages, *Purchas His Pilgrimes*, to press.[132] He, too, found that state concerns about excessive anti-Dutch fervor hindered the book's smooth publication. This work, which Purchas had presented to the EIC in January, contained numerous accounts of English and Dutch activities in the East Indies, all from the English point of view, and some highly critical of Dutch traders and their conduct. Showing how quickly authors and printers could work, Purchas even managed to include a short version of the EIC's *True Relation* in the *Pilgrimes*. In his discussion of the incident, Purchas referred readers to the *True Relation*, but highlighted a few vital particulars, notably the condemned men's professions of innocence, their written testimonials of the same, and their piety before death.[133] But the political context had changed as Purchas worked, and he had qualms that some of the anti-Dutch elements of his book were too stark. Page headings captured the tone perhaps too powerfully: "Heathens more kind then Hollanders, to the English," and "English love and aide to the Dutch, ill requited." Purchas suffered pangs of writer's remorse, but it was too late and too expensive to reprint so many pages. He reached a compromise with his printer, who had already balked at including an epistle Purchas wanted

to insert that explained the aggression of the Dutch against the English in the Indies. He made special inserts for thirty "presentation" copies, special volumes given to the four men to whom the work was dedicated as well as other patrons. These inserts included little flaps of paper, generic cancel slips that read "English voyages to the East Indies," to be pasted on top of problematic page headings. The printer also redid two pages for these special copies.[134] Purchas and his printer were right to worry about Dutch reactions to these headings. In 1628, the States General's ambassadors complained to the king about the work, and in 1630, the Dutch ambassador listed the offensive page headings, including a few ("uncharitable purposes of the Dutch," "Hollanders more cruel than Spaniards") that Purchas had not flagged for concealment with a cancel slip.[135]

The end of February, after the suppressed painting, the recalled sermon, and the hindered publication of Purchas, saw a final clamping down on anti-Dutch sentiment inspired by the Amboyna episode. More dangerous still to public order was a play about the cruelty of the Dutch toward the English in a variety of places, including Greenland and Amboyna. The English government, worried that a dramatic performance of the Amboyna tortures might spark anti-Dutch riots in London, especially with Shrove Tuesday

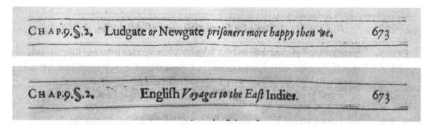

Figure 3.10 The image on the top shows a page heading as originally printed in Samuel Purchas's travel compendium, with the text suggesting that the English in the East Indies were less happy living under the Dutch than were those miserable people incarcerated in England's infamous prisons; the image below shows the corrected version with its anodyne message printed on the cancel slip as found in the Archbishop of Canterbury's presentation copy.
Top: detail from Samuel Purchas, *Hakluytus Posthumus or Purchas his Pilgrimes* (London, 1625), vol. 1, p. 673. Call # STC 20509 copy 2. Used by permission of the Folger Shakespeare Library; Bottom: detail from Samuel Purchas, *Hakluytus Posthumus or Purchas his Pilgrimes* (London, 1625), vol. 1, p. 673. Shelfmark ZZ 1625.1, Lambeth Palace Library.

approaching, banned its performance. The play, presumably, was therefore intended for a public performance.[136] No script has yet been found, but a contemporary described it as showing "the matter w[i]th all circumstances."[137] The public anger reached such a pitch that the government hired 800 guards to keep watch in the city.[138] These anti-Dutch sentiments did nothing to alter English foreign policy. Later that year, Charles and Buckingham finally got their war with Spain. The English signed a military alliance with the Dutch in September, and in October thousands of English soldiers readied for what turned out to be a disastrous attack on Cadiz.

The EIC may have been disappointed in 1625 that its efforts and expense came to naught, but it turned out that to ensure the longevity of the Amboyna Massacre, the EIC had little need of the painting, the sermon, the play, or Samuel Purchas and his wandering pilgrims. The company's tasks of persuading people that the executions were a massacre, and of entrenching that interpretation in English public culture, had been accomplished by November 1624 with the distribution of the *True Relation* and, especially, the woodcuts depicting tortured traders. The EIC had wedded judicial execution—murder—to religious slaughter to create a new and distinctive type of English massacre, a commercial conflict suffused with religious motifs. The company's strategy had long-term consequences, shaping a British history of massacres and making this one incident something that endured at the heart of English politics and, much later, imperial history. What the company failed to accomplish, however, was what it most earnestly sought: compensation for its losses in the East Indies trade.[139] That goal would take thirty years to achieve, and it was thanks to the EIC's efforts in 1624 and 1625 and the public life the EIC created for its employees' execution that the incident remained alive for those three decades.

4

The Reckoning

The EIC's quest for compensation began in Batavia with angry and bitter sentiments, just as it would end thirty-one years later in England. On June 20/30, 1623, as the VOC council in Batavia caught up on its correspondence, the arrival of an EIC delegation interrupted its work. The agitated English traders had made their way through town clutching a letter they had just received via Macassar from John Powel, one of the English traders at Amboyna. In it, Powel shared the stunning news that ten of the company's employees and ten Japanese soldiers who worked for the VOC had been executed at Amboyna on charges of plotting with some natives of the country against the Dutch, and that the senior trader's severed head stood atop the gallows.

The English traders must have been distraught when they reached the VOC headquarters, because they had already passed the day grappling with Powel's "most lamentable and unexpected newse" of an event they characterized as an "inhumaine and butcher execution." In a 390-word summary of their meeting, the English used the words "blood" or "bloodie" four times. It seemed perfectly plausible that the Dutch were plotting against them in Batavia, too, and they were keen to avoid "the lyk bloody attempts against us." After "serious deliberation," they resolved to show Powel's letter to the VOC's governor-general. Off they went, in a likely violation of the social norms they observed, since the VOC traders characterized the visit as unexpected. The EIC emissaries put the VOC employees on the defensive, briefly in limbo as they awaited further evidence to enable them to respond to these allegations of cruelty, although they declared their certainty that the governor of Amboyna would never have proceeded without adequate proof. It was an encounter fraught with emotion, the shocked and angry English traders and the surprised and defensive VOC council, all urgently in need of more information, the elusive "truth" of the affair.[1]

This initial exchange of news in Batavia established a thirty-one-year pattern of accusations, retorts, and negotiations as participants, companies, and public officials all sought to find some common understanding of what had happened and thereby some mutually satisfactory resolution to the affair.

As news traveled with the East Indies fleets from Batavia to Europe, queries returned across the globe, requiring the depositions of company employees in the East Indies and in Europe. Some of the EIC traders dedicated themselves to their employers' service as mobile witnesses. The fallout from Amboyna transpired in part at this individual level. It also took place whenever governing bodies assembled, trading companies met, and people picked up a pamphlet or gazed at a woodcut of a tortured body. In all these settings, a shared understanding remained out of reach.

The intimacy of the EIC and VOC traders' living conditions, their employers' forced partnership, and the renewed Anglo-Dutch alliance in Europe that led the English crown to place adjudication of the incident in Dutch hands together hindered an easy resolution and in fact furthered hostilities. Had the companies and nations been less enmeshed politically, economically, diplomatically, religiously, and culturally, there may have been less urgency to reach agreement about what had happened at Amboyna. What the two companies and especially the men who had participated in the judicial process at Amboyna sought was in essence a conversion to their point of view. No existing English or Dutch judicial process could achieve such an outcome, one akin to the type of enforced communal harmony pursued in this era by Reformed Protestants who banished those who were likely to disagree with them and enjoined covenanters to live in peace and love.[2] A secular court could declare guilt and order payment and punishment, and the English welcomed such judgments, but they wanted more than compensation and retribution: they wanted those judged guilty to accept the error of their ways. The Dutch likewise sought recognition of the terrible conspiracy they had confronted.[3] Alliance so effectively hindered resolution that a settlement came only by compulsion at the end of war in 1654. The English shared this financial connotation of a "reckoning" with the Dutch, for whom *de rekening* meant the bill. But settling that bill was only part of the solution the English desired. Reckoning held other meanings, too, including a final judgment. In this regard, the reckoning remained incomplete, with opinions on the matter unchanged from 1623. This unsettled situation enabled the lurid and incendiary tale of Amboyna to endure as a cultural touchstone and an unavenged injury.

The Amboyna conspiracy had a mild impact in the region where it had taken place, a perspective difficult to appreciate given the near simultaneous reorientation of English trade in these years away from Indonesia and spices (with the notable exception of pepper) and toward India, the EIC's later stronghold. Historians came to treat the Amboyna episode as the cause of this shift, the incident through which to understand the ultimate shape of the British Empire, but at most it only accelerated a process already under way. The Amboyna incident ultimately fit into the EIC's plans for the pepper trade, conveniently enabling them to justify the separation from the VOC that the English had long sought. The short-term consequences of the Amboyna incident in the East Indies were twofold: suspicion and separation. Both companies remained certain of conspiracies and stayed on their guard, inhabitants still of a world of great peril, but in a pattern of vacillation between animosity and union that was consistent with the period before 1623.

The EIC's immediate concerns in Batavia were safeguarding their employers' property and further information, precisely the subjects that animated company members and diplomats in Europe for the next three decades. The first issue was easily accomplished by dispatching a delegate to close down the Amboyna trading post, a mission completed by May 1624. The council also instructed this man to gather information about the "wrongfull execution" of the English, but urged him to "be very circumspect" in his inquiries in order not to give the governor any reason to move against him. The truth would eventually be revealed, the council maintained optimistically, but those closed accounts hardly signaled any resolution of what had happened at the factory.[4] More knowledge about the alleged conspiracy did not lead to rapprochement, as it seemed instead only to harden each company's initial response to news of the episode. The EIC and VOC traders didn't agree about whether there had been a plot or who might have been involved. During that summer of 1623 the companies' leaders in Batavia met frequently and heatedly about the incident, fighting even about English access to the trial records.[5]

A climate of suspicion pervaded both the English and Dutch factories, because each company believed that plotting continued. While the VOC council reported to its employers in Amsterdam in 1624 that it regretted the procedure followed by the Amboyna governor, the council did not doubt that there had been an English conspiracy. Rather, it wished clemency had been afforded to men from a country that was their neighbor, an invocation of a European relationship, not of ties forged in the Indies.[6] Everything in the VOC's experience of governing the region and dealing with the EIC predisposed the traders to accept the veracity of the Amboyna plot. As far as the council was concerned, the threat was real and ongoing.[7]

Rumors heightened anxieties. The very day after the VOC traders in Batavia received their surprising visit from the EIC, they noted that an Englishman had announced that the English would soon enter and leave the fortress at Batavia as freely as the Dutch did, which they thought might have been a veiled threat. What the Dutch learned within the next week confirmed their need for vigilance, as they reported that an English groom had warned a free citizen of Batavia that a massacre would take place there soon.[8] The VOC council also believed that there was another plot similar to that at Amboyna, this one featuring the people of Luhu, long regarded as untrustworthy by the VOC, seeking to join forces with the EIC trader Richard Welden.[9]

The EIC traders likewise saw plots arrayed against them. The council was certain of Dutch schemes to "trap [them] into false accusations." Its suspicions increased thanks to a rumor carried by an Englishman who worked for the VOC, who warned the EIC that the governor-general plotted "some great villany" against the English. Because this informant was "somewhat in drinke" when relaying this news, the English were not sure whether to believe him, although "their cruell proceedings against us elsewhere may give us just cause to doubt ye worst."[10] Little incidents hinted at the tensions that permeated the trading post. In September 1624, an English trader reported a scuffle in Banten on his way home one night. When the night watch asked who passed, he replied, "a friend." A squabble then ensued in which the watchman retorted in Dutch that the English were not friends before he finally allowed the Englishman to pass by.[11]

It wasn't only Amboyna that created such a barrier between the companies. The usual petty insults and quarrels characteristic of the years since the 1619 treaty had forced an unequal partnership on the companies continued.[12] In a 1623 protest filed by the English against the Dutch, the executions at Amboyna ranked only third, after English allegations that the Dutch overcharged them for customs and did not allow them to buy slaves at Banda.[13] But if it wasn't only Amboyna, it was mostly Amboyna that caused this rupture. Indeed, by January 1624 the VOC council characterized the EIC's sentiments as so bitter as to be impossible to describe.[14]

In this deepening culture of animosity, the companies tried to develop strategies for a productive working relationship that would enable trade to flourish. The only policy guaranteed to prevent future conflict was to separate, in contrast to the scheme devised in Amboyna in 1621 that security lay in proximity. The problem was that the companies had competing visions of what separation entailed. The EIC traders believed themselves to be free to pursue their own interests and no longer bound by the requirements of the 1619 treaty; they refused to contribute to the common defense or to joint trade, and they denied responsibility for matters covered by the 1619 treaty.[15] The English wanted physical distance between the companies and freedom to trade independently, but the VOC wanted physical proximity and oversight with minimal daily interaction. The VOC council fumed about being forced to deal with the English, comparing them to a difficult wife.[16] It believed that the English were picking quarrels, deliberately ignoring Dutch instructions about regulating their slaves in order to find another source of disagreement.[17] The VOC council attributed this behavior to English greed, because it believed that the English always wanted more than their fair share.[18] But the VOC council knew well that it was Amboyna that festered, not mere avarice, and feared in 1625 that if the English ever managed to get the upper hand in Batavia, they would utterly destroy the Dutch.[19]

The culmination of this mutual mistrust was the decision by the EIC council in 1624 to move the entire operation to another location, Lagundy (Legundi), an island in the Straits of Sunda, the body of water separating Java from Sumatra. VOC officials in Batavia averred in 1625 that the EIC dubbed this new location "an anti-batavia."[20] Although the EIC council initially envisioned a permanent relocation, at the last minute the English traders hedged their bets, deciding not to sell their house and property in Batavia.[21] VOC personnel interfered with the move in a variety of ways, by requiring the EIC to prove the status of each slave the traders hoped to transport, among other impediments.[22] They hoped the English would take a VOC employee with them to their new settlement—possibly to help, as the Dutch insisted, but perhaps also to spy, since the VOC maintained a frigate at Batavia ready to keep an eye on what the English were up to.[23]

These hindrances did not deter the English from launching their new venture in November 1624, but the escapade turned into a disaster. All went well at first, but then everyone fell sick from a pestilence so dangerous that the English reported that if a dog or cat licked the blood of the ill, the poor creatures swelled up, burst, and died. In desperation, the traders sent a ship to Batavia in May 1625 for help, and the VOC came and evacuated them. Given this unfortunate turn of events, the EIC officers concluded that they must learn to live in peace with the VOC, and they resettled in Batavia. The Dutch, also apparently eager for a new beginning, welcomed them and provided a brick building for their use. The companies reached a new rapprochement, resolving in Batavia in August 1625 to join forces "as a bullwarke" against their shared enemies.[24]

Both companies tried to be on their best behavior, motivated by continued proximity and common enemies but also by stern instructions that had just arrived from their employers in Europe who were shocked at the catastrophic breakdown in the trading partnership revealed by the Amboyna incident. VOC directors' orders in 1624 and 1625 to maintain harmonious relationships accompanied those adjuring their employees not to trust the other company, even with such conventional courtesies as mail delivery.[25] Chastened, the VOC traders in Batavia pledged in fall 1625 to work on their friendship with the English.[26] For their part, the English believed their friendship with the Dutch strengthened during this time, despite impediments, or so they told their employers in October.[27] Most expressions of harmony appeared in letters to Europe, suggesting that the two councils may have been trying to persuade their employers that they were obeying instructions to get along.

The two companies nonetheless continued to harbor diametrically opposed views of what had happened at Amboyna. EIC employees claimed in 1626 that the Dutch were burdened by Amboyna, condemned by the world, but were trying to put the episode behind them.[28] In contrast to English allegations that the Dutch were ashamed, the Dutch themselves showed continued belief in the Amboyna plot. They seemed to harbor no doubts whatsoever that the English were likely still plotting against them. After the Lagundy debacle, the VOC believed the English to be incapable of causing too much trouble at Batavia because of their weakness, but stayed on guard, noting a troubling shift from their initial friendliness when they returned to Batavia to "bitter and sharp writings" by December 1626. The VOC council reported continued threats of English conspiracy to the directors that month, likening the English to an animal frozen with cold who, warmed by a kind farmer, paid the farmer back with aggression, and the company despaired of ever having a secure friendship with the EIC.[29]

That both companies still tried to make their connection as amicable as possible despite these enduring animosities is evident in various social occasions they shared, with each putting its best foot forward, showing "heartie affection" as if there had been no prior and ongoing conflict.[30] At a dinner engagement in 1626 before the European-bound fleet set sail, all the VOC traders even apologized to the English—or so the English interpreted their actions—and expressed hopes for future harmony. This occasion might have given cause for optimism, except the English traders noted that it followed such "strangenes" that the two companies had avoided the usual public rituals that marked the fleet's departure.[31]

One cause of the "strangenes" might have been all the legal activity under way at the VOC factory. In 1625, VOC officers started scrambling to comply with the States General's orders to gather information, including depositions by the members of the Amboyna council, who had to be called back from their various posts in the region and sent to Holland.[32] Their employers also wanted more information, although their own review of the materials sent to them in 1624 inclined them to believe van Speult's assessment of the situation. They urged the traders to gather all the evidence they could, even the tiniest scrap, so that they could satisfy English representatives in Europe.[33]

The depositions began in March 1625 with a trickle, which soon became a flood. In Batavia, Jan van Nieuwpoort was deposed in March; in September, by which time the English had returned from Lagundy, seven members of the VOC council in Amboyna, including van Speult, Wyncoop, van Leeuwen, Cravanger, van Santen, van Nieuwpoort, and Corthals, collectively testified in answer to ten questions.[34] Another VOC employee was deposed in September, followed by van Santen for a second time in October. The biggest round of depositions occurred in December 1626, when five men who had sat in judgment in Amboyna (Joosten, Wyncoop, Tieller, van Leeuwen, and Vogel) answered 139 questions set by the States General, all prompted by the English company's published *True Relation* and the EIC's *Answer* to the VOC's *True Declaration*.[35] It was impossible for either company to get any distance from the incident, with the men coming to town for questioning that tapped into some of the most sensitive issues raised by the trial: Did fluids dripping from John Clarke's tortured body extinguish candles? Did the VOC charge the EIC for the velvet cloth under Gabriel Towerson's decapitated head? Did the condemned men profess their innocence? Did they march through town on a lengthy and humiliating public tour to the execution ground? Were they heckled along the way?

The EIC traders tried to stay on top of the deponents' movements, especially when they learned that the judges had been summoned to Europe, and the men were especially agitated about van Speult, who arrived in Batavia in August 1625, soon after the EIC had returned from Lagundy. The English protested when the VOC appointed van Speult as general of the VOC fleet bound for Persia—an honor for a man they regarded as a murderer. The VOC council insisted it would send him back to Holland from Surat, as ordered by the States General, but the English worried that the VOC planned instead to help van Speult avoid any accountability for his role in the trial, because the EIC observed that van Speult could get home to Holland more efficiently from Batavia.[36] For its part, the VOC council worried about van Speult's safety and warned him to keep his distance from the English, whom they suspected might try to take him into custody.[37]

The animosities surrounding the Amboyna episode accompanied van Speult as he traveled to India, where his presence in Surat undermined a tentative plan in April 1626 for a joint English and Dutch mission against the Portuguese. The VOC head at Surat believed that the English withdrew from this enterprise specifically because of van Speult's support for it.[38] In van Speult's own account of this matter, he attributed English hesitation to a theme familiar to him from his time at Amboyna—complaints about the distribution of expenses.[39] Van Speult's death in 1626 deprived the English of the reckoning they envisioned for him in Europe.

All of the complaints and machinations in Batavia after the Amboyna crisis of 1623 resembled the strained cohabitation of the period before 1623, making Amboyna an example of the kind of conflict that could break out in trading posts among these European allies forced into a cooperative trade agreement they disliked. Within the acrimonious relations of the English and Dutch, however, lay new commercial opportunities for the English. Despite the assertions of harmony in Batavia after the Lagundy failure, the English traders continued to seek another home base. In 1627, the English left Batavia for Banten, which became their headquarters until 1682, a move the VOC protested as it had the Lagundy experiment.[40] While perpetrators of violence often gained immediate advantages from their actions, victims, too, sometimes identified long-term strategic benefits in their ordeal. That had been the case in Virginia in 1622, in the wake of the attack that left one-third of the English inhabitants dead, when policy makers for the colony decided that they could pursue a new strategy of unfettered aggression in the wake of this assault.[41] Likewise, the Amboyna episode might have been useful strategically as the EIC's regional directors violated the 1619 treaty and endeavored to secure their pepper trade with a new administrative base at Banten. There was little firm footing, however, as the two companies shifted about the region, always acutely aware of the other's movements in a world crowded with non-Europeans and an array of competing interests. In this unsettled context, with each company adhering to mutually incompatible interpretations of the Amboyna episode, no resolution was possible and no reckoning could be achieved. A firm conclusion required action in Europe and took thirty-one years and one war to achieve. Central to this settlement were six of the English survivors.

The letter that John Powel had sent from Macassar to his bosses and colleagues in Batavia signaled the vital role the EIC traders who survived the Amboyna conspiracy trial played in shaping the kind of reckoning the English and especially the EIC in Europe believed they were due. These men began as the accused, emerged as survivors, and became witnesses. The transition from accused to survivor commenced during the trial itself. The interrogations at Amboyna sought to divide the English from each other. This division was essential in order to compel people to point the finger at others: self-incrimination alone was useless, as a conspiracy of one was a sign of a failed judicial process. But the interrogations also linked them as a group joined in a nefarious plot. Theirs was a shared ordeal. Before their execution, they engaged in a round of mutual apologies, with each forgiving the other for incriminating them (or so the survivors reported) because, perhaps, of a keen understanding of how each reached this plight. Most of the English went to their deaths carrying this wrenching emotional weight of confession, apology, and forgiveness, surely along with apprehension about their impending executions. But the eight survivors carried this weight, too, not to the execution ground, but, for seven of them, back to Europe, to their families, friends, and employers there.

Torture was essential to this new identity, although most of the survivors had not been tortured. Nonetheless, torture and the fear of it punctuated their confinement and shaped their memories. John Beaumont set the scene effectively: he recalled how he had waited outside the interrogation chamber while first Timothy Johnson and then Emanuel Thompson were examined. He heard their cries and saw Johnson carried out. Beaumont himself was tied up, a linen cloth fastened around his neck, and threatened with the water, but before his interrogators compelled him to speak, they released him. The next occasion, he again waited in a corridor and heard John Fardo cry out. Beaumont then endured the water torture, until he confessed that he had been present for the plotters' meeting on New Year's Day. When it came time to endorse his confession, he first renounced it, but then was afraid of more torture, so signed it.[42]

Torture victims endure a plight beyond their physical ordeal. Those who speak—revealing truths or falsehoods—can bring their physical agony to an end, but at the cost of other values they might cherish, whether honesty, physical strength, loyalty, or secrecy.[43] They might produce terrible harm for others—and still their own death. Certainly the survivors had done their share of incriminating others. George Sherrock and William Webber did so despite not even having been in Amboyna when the alleged meeting happened, and their accusation of John Clarke subjected him to extensive torture. Whether because of this shared bond, or for other reasons, Webber and Sherrock formed an especially close connection. Once back in England, Sherrock made Webber his executor, and Webber cared for Sherrock when he fell mortally ill in 1626.[44] The tortured men were frank about the pressures that forced them to incriminate others. On the eve of their execution, four condemned men wrote a memo in which they warned the English merchants who came after them to Amboyna to be vigilant, because the Dutch were determined to ensnare them, too. The Dutch had asked about them, "which if they had tortured us, we must have confessed [implicated] you also."[45] They wrote unapologetically, in a simple assertion of fact.

The survivors' common ordeal continued in Amboyna and Batavia as they were compelled to act in ways that undercut their attestations of innocence and instead confirmed the VOC's certainty of their culpability. Sherrock prostrated himself before a VOC official and proclaimed his debt to the Dutch for not punishing him for his guilt. Beaumont performed a similar ritual in Batavia in the summer of 1623. These accounts of English professions of guilt and gratitude circulated in manuscript by the winter of 1624–25, leaving some English survivors under continued clouds of suspicion and shame.[46] Beaumont and Edward Collins had additional legal complications: both had confessed and had been only temporarily reprieved. EIC officials in Batavia sent them to Europe so that they could clear their names.[47]

Through this collection of experiences—torture, self-incrimination, accusation of others, a death sentence, and especially a shared reprieve—the accused became survivors. They may have been wrestling with what is known today as survivor's guilt, the keen awareness of the fine line between life and death and of the role of fate in making such determinations. Beaumont was pulled back across that line by the friendships he had forged during his career in the Indies. Collins won his life by casting lots, no clearer indication of how chance determined who lived and died. Webber and Sherrock received last-minute pardons. All four had been prepared to join their colleagues in the march to the execution ground. Their ardent desire to speak, to be heard, to witness with their bodies, their eyes, and their voices, once back in England may have derived not only from rage at their ordeal but also from a desire to speak for the dead, whose fate they almost shared, and to help the families of the dead get their own reckoning.

They soon found opportunities to act on behalf of the dead in numerous depositions about their colleagues' confiscated estates. In September, Collins and Beaumont testified before the Admiralty court about Thompson's estate, including his hens and hogs, clothes and bedding, and his "pretty library of books." In October, Webber, Sherrock, and Ephraim Ramsey were deposed before the Consistory Court in London about the oral will Fardo had made while imprisoned with them in Amboyna. At some point, some survivors testified about Johnson's estate, because his father mentioned the depositions, and presumably there were similar legal actions taken on behalf of all of the executed men.[48] In their July depositions before the Admiralty court, some of the witnesses provided almost verbatim speech from the dead, allowing their final words and thoughts to live on in the formal text the EIC published.[49]

The survivors also needed to speak for themselves. They wanted restitution for their losses in the Indies. Powel claimed to have lost 2,000 ryals (or £500). Thomas Ladbrooke requested 30 ryals (or £8) and compensation for the loss of his parrot, whose value he did not assess—suggesting that the bird may have been a pet and companion.[50] Their pursuit of these individual reckonings intersected with the company's own financial damages. When Sherrock complained that he had lost everything at Amboyna, the company agreed to consider his request, but reminded him that the company, too, had suffered a great loss.[51]

In the summer and fall of 1624 these men regularly showed up at EIC court meetings to navigate their new status, determined to demonstrate their value to the company when they returned to London in 1624. On June 30, they attended an EIC court meeting.[52] A week later, six of them commenced their most important service: they told their story in depositions before the High Court of Admiralty. These legal statements became the basis for the *True Relation*.[53] Their utility derived in large part from what they had to say about their ordeal.

While the two companies disagreed on almost every detail, disputes about torture especially animated the English. In November 1624, the EIC learned that a newly returned VOC employee, Laurens de Marschalck, had given a deposition in which he refuted Collins's claims of torture. Collins reiterated his earlier account, insisting that he had been tortured with water. Webber, Sherrock, and Ramsey all confirmed Collins's story, although Webber saw only the aftermath—Collins drenched with water. All four men were ready to go to the United Provinces to challenge Marschalck's account, and Collins himself accompanied two EIC members to the king's palace at Newmarket to tell the monarch personally of the VOC's distortions.[54] The special sensitivity of the English to the irregularity of judicial torture is suggested by the £10 the company granted Ramsey in September for having been tortured.[55]

Torture marked these men: so, at least, their families believed. Collins's wife argued in 1652 that he never recovered from the injuries inflicted on him. Never again was he "his owne man," she recalled, but was dependent on physicians, whose charges consumed his estate.[56] Sarah Collins's desire for financial relief may have encouraged her to exaggerate both her husband's plight and his personal qualities, but her insistence that he suffered because of the torture he endured indicates an argument she found advantageous to make and hints at contemporary English ideas about torture's effect on those who suffered. It might not have been only his physical health she considered, but his state of mind, too.

These disputes over torture and other matters kept most of the men from returning to their jobs in the spice trade as they had envisioned. In November, Webber and Sherrock applied for positions with the fleet that had carried them to Europe.[57] The EIC was unsure when it might be prudent to send the men back. During the fall of 1624, as the VOC continued to challenge the EIC's account of the Amboyna incident, it became clear to the English company that it might be helpful to keep the survivors on hand, "in a readines." All of the men were expected to be at the disposal of the commissioners investigating the Amboyna incident, hinting at the process that made them witnesses.[58] This necessity placed the men in limbo: Powel, Webber, Ramsey, and Sherrock explained that they were unable to find work because they needed to be available in case they were called to testify against the Dutch. Four of the men, Beaumont, Powel, Ramsey, and Webber, lived in London, but Sherrock and Collins did not and had no reason to be there aside from waiting for the company to require their service in the Amboyna matter. As late as October 1625, the EIC still thought it might be possible to let the men return and even resolved to send Ramsey on the *Exchange* as a purser's mate, but ultimately Ramsey did not go.[59] The only one of the "Amboyna men," as they were soon dubbed in the company records, who returned to the Indies was Ladbrooke, who received 20 shillings from the poor box in light of his losses at Amboyna.[60] Instead, the men remained in London on the company dole, although the EIC sought to support them at minimal expense. In

December 1624, the company granted the witnesses 10 shillings per week for those who were not otherwise receiving wages.[61]

Some found regular positions with the company. It turned out that surviving the ordeal and proving one's use to the company were splendid ways to rehabilitate a shady reputation. In the East Indies, company officers reported of Powel, Sherrock, Webber, and Ramsey in 1623 that "neither their sufficiencie nor good carriage have deserve[d] o[u]r commendation," and dismissed Collins as untrustworthy and a cheat.[62] Collins improbably ended up working in the counting house, but ultimately he found steady work as the clerk of the EIC's powder mills. The company regarded Powel within three months of his return as worthy of board and wages in light of his "quallity," despite the disparaging reference he brought home.[63] The EIC praised Sherrock in September 1624 as "an honest dilligent young man," in contrast to the opinion of him in the East Indies, where the English council at Batavia had urged the head trader at Amboyna in December 1622 not to trust him.[64] Webber ended up hired to track down runaways—men who had committed to go to the Indies but then disappeared. Sickness made him unable to carry out his position in 1627, and the company finally decided to give the job to someone else, but to continue paying Webber a weekly allowance. The EIC's minutes note his status as an "ancient servant" of the company, but perhaps his value as an Amboyna survivor also contributed to this decision; his allowance simply continued an existing practice by the company to support the Amboyna men.[65]

One of the most important services the witnesses performed was inspecting VOC ships that had been apprehended by English authorities along the coast in search of men who had participated in the Amboyna trial. Stopping VOC ships was a long-standing practice by the English, employed as a way to compel restitution for various infractions, and in 1624, to the surprise of the VOC's directors, James I decreed that VOC ships should be detained.[66] Powel and Ramsey began inspecting ships in April 1625 and performed this service through 1628. Powel turned out to be accident prone, tumbling into the hold of one ship and damaging his arm, and falling off a horse while riding to Harwich on company business and suffering a "rupture" in another instance.[67] They were supposed to inspect passengers and crew, looking particularly for any of the VOC employees who had passed sentence on the English at Amboyna. Van Speult was a special target, although he never made it back to Europe, and in fall 1627 the English learned of his death.[68]

Eventually, the witnesses acquired various perks for their service. The EIC created incentives for them to show their utility: to come up with helpful information about the injuries they had endured, to provide more ammunition to use against the VOC, to be ready to testify with their words and their bodies to their injuries, to serve as living reminders of the treatment inflicted on them. Four days after his deposition in July 1624, the company gave Sherrock £10 in response to his petition for assistance and questioned him again about the tortures inflicted at Amboyna. He agreeably produced some new details, explaining that the Dutch placed gunpowder in incisions in Englishmen's bodies, and then set the powder on fire, a detail possibly invented for the company.[69] Perhaps he was eager to show his worth; perhaps he was trying to overcome the burden of his incrimination of Clarke with his helpfulness; perhaps he realized how to keep these stipends coming his way. By 1626, the company rewarded Powel with the status of the company's freedom, something normally purchased but that could also be conferred by company members.[70]

The witnesses found numerous ways to demonstrate their value to the EIC, but they were also motivated by their own investment in the story they had told. Powel's need to be believed led him in to a protracted lawsuit against Richard Welden, the EIC's agent at Banda. Both men had returned to England in summer 1624 on the same ship, and it seems likely that a mutual dislike festered on the long voyage.[71] Powel sued Welden that summer to recover 446 ryals (approximately £110 in 1623) worth of goods and slaves he accused Welden of having taken from him, but the suit revealed that his grievances went far beyond this financial loss. Powel regarded Welden as too sympathetic to the VOC. Welden had imprisoned Powel and Sherrock in the Indies "only for reporting truely the cruelty of the dutch towardes them and other English men in Amboyna." Moreover, Powel accused Welden of endorsing Dutch actions, giving them presents, and drinking to van Speult's health. None of these matters had anything to do with the financial damages Powel claimed, but Powel's indignation that Welden belittled and denied his suffering and sided with those who had incarcerated him and killed his companions incensed him. All of Welden's actions undermined Powel's story of what had happened—that he was the innocent victim of a VOC plot. Welden defended himself vigorously, arguing that he, too, was vulnerable to the VOC at those moments. He might even have believed the possibility of an EIC plot when he first reached Amboyna, because he knew well the acrimonious circumstances in which the traders lived, although he didn't offer this explanation for his behavior to the EIC in London. None of Welden's defense appeased Powel. He seethed. He characterized his own attitude toward Welden, and that of the other English survivors, as "detestacon." And Powel's grievances and Welden's conduct left the EIC members who heard them "much moved." Under pressure from his employers, Welden apologized and insisted he had never doubted the innocence of his comrades.[72] The EIC had no such leverage over the VOC.

Powel's rage reflected the plight of the survivors, men who had lost so much—all but their lives—in Amboyna and whose accounts the VOC spurned in so many particulars. He was not the only one who wanted to look his doubters in the eye and make them hear his tale. Welden was a convenient scapegoat for English anger, but several of the witnesses wanted to go to The Hague and participate in the judicial process under way in the States General, an idea they had first proposed in November 1624 when the VOC denied torturing Collins. Their journey was entangled in a diplomatic impasse surrounding the adjudication of the EIC's claims, because James I had decided to let the States General administer justice in the matter, a gesture of trust for a reaffirmed alliance.

After initial indications that the States General took the EIC's complaints seriously and sought to appease first James and then Charles with tangible action during a time of renewed alliance, English representatives in the United Provinces grew skeptical. The English ambassador, Dudley Carleton, wrestled with the Amboyna matter, among many other pressing concerns. Carleton was often accompanied by his nephew, also Dudley Carleton, who may have been especially well prepared for the linguistic, cultural, and political challenges of this post thanks to his first marriage to a Dutch woman whose father was the secretary of the States General. The two Carletons found able assistance in two EIC agents, Robert Barlow in Amsterdam and Edward Misselden in Delft. Barlow and Misselden reported regularly on their sense of the mood of people, including the VOC directors, about Amboyna.[73]

All of these people weighed in on the matter of sending over the EIC witnesses, a dilemma that intensified in 1627. By that year, Carleton (Junior) worried that the States had come to dismiss the importance of Amboyna, condemning only the hasty punishment inflicted by the VOC council at Amboyna but accepting the council's interpretation of events there.[74] The VOC matched EIC outrage and lobbying activity and petitioned the States General in 1626 for redress of the "intollerable wronges" the company had endured at the hands of English subjects.[75] The VOC directors maintained in 1627 that a great injustice had been done to them, first by the original plot, and then by how the English misinterpreted their judicial process, and finally by the English response—detaining VOC ships and demanding that the judges (as the English described the VOC's council at Amboyna) return to Europe.[76] It was a low period for the EIC, but the king insisted that the company wait for the States General's legal process to be completed. That summer, however, Ramsey put himself forward to go to Holland. If the Dutch were ready to carry out justice on the men responsible for the "bloody massacre," he wanted to be there and see for himself that the right people were punished. The EIC embraced his suggestion and allocated funds to defray his expenses, because Ramsey was looking for justice, but first he needed to get some new clothes. Powel was ready to go, too, but Ramsey was so enthusiastic that he went shopping, buying clothing and other sundries for his trip to Holland, and presenting the bill to the surprised company in June.[77]

Like so many English hopes for justice, Ramsey's preparations for a reckoning in The Hague were premature. Everyone agreed, EIC and VOC alike, that what had happened at Amboyna had been a "trayterous plott," but no one agreed about whether the witnesses should go.[78] In 1627, the EIC couldn't agree on whether it would help or hurt its cause and the company's status to let the men appear before the States General.[79] Throughout 1628, the subject animated the EIC, its agents, the Privy Council, the monarch, the VOC, the States General, and the English representative to the States, who took it upon himself to read through all of the EIC and VOC depositions and declared in despair that the facts of the matter were "as contrarie as night and day."[80] The English witnesses' absence infused the VOC deponents with such confidence that they returned from their interrogations in spring 1628 in The Hague "in great Jollity," certain that nothing would be done to them. The VOC employees denied everything in the English depositions, according to Misselden, rejoiced in beheading the "English traitors," and, after being dismissed by the States General's judges, "are gon laughing home."[81] Moreover, the failure of the English witnesses to travel struck people in the United Provinces as a serious and troubling issue.[82] The VOC directors marveled that the English required the men on the Amboyna council to travel around the world to give testimony in Holland, but the English witnesses refused to sail across the North Sea.[83] The debate over the witnesses raged while the crown arranged for the relics of the episode—Coulson's prayer book, Towerson's bill of sale, and Griggs's account book—to be transported with certificates of authenticity to the EIC agent at Delft, and there they sat.

Carleton (Junior) puzzled why the States had not asked to see the items, and finally he collected the materials and personally delivered them to the head judge.[84] Carleton thought it might be helpful to get the witnesses to The Hague, if the king would permit it, and the monarch came around to that point of view by November 1628.[85] The EIC's agents had a clear sense of how matters stood in the United Provinces and urged their employers to send the witnesses, with Barlow pleading the case "ernestly" in April 1629.[86]

The witnesses finally journeyed to the United Provinces in November 1629, accompanying Sir Henry Vane when he traveled with his family not as an ambassador sent to deal with the States General, but rather as Charles's personal envoy to the Prince of Orange.[87] The group consisted of five men: Collins, Ramsey, Powel, Beaumont, and a most improbable fifth, a Scot named George Forbes who had worked for the VOC in multiple capacities. While all of the men who made careers for themselves as Amboyna witnesses had enjoyed some acts of reinvention, no one's refashioning was more impressive than Forbes's. By 1621, Forbes was the steward of the VOC house in Amboyna.[88] He served occasionally as an interpreter during the conspiracy trial. He returned to Holland on the *Golden Lion*, but his ship was detained at Portsmouth in September 1627. It was a red-letter day for Powel in his years of inspecting ships, or perhaps it was for Ramsey, because he was also in Portsmouth that fall: someone noticed Forbes and two other VOC employees with Amboyna connections.[89] Despite Forbes's insistence that they would find fair treatment in England, the other men retorted that they feared being torn to pieces in the streets of London, showing how ill will continued to fester in the capital, and they escaped Portsmouth before the EIC obtained a warrant to hold them.[90]

Forbes transformed himself into an EIC ally, a case he made in a series of speeches and depositions, including before the Privy Council in 1627, and in a five-page narrative, his own "True Relation . . . by an honest, true, and impartial ear and eye witness." He professed agreement with the English view that the alleged plot was "utterly impossible." Forbes added some new details that addressed especially sensitive subjects for the English, including the torture of Thompson and Clarke, and Towerson's interrogation, all of which he claimed to have witnessed. Forbes had also translated letters that Towerson had received at Amboyna, none of which offered any hint at a plot. The EIC's insistence that the condemned men denied their guilt had been repeatedly refuted by the VOC, but Forbes claimed he had been present when the sentence was read against the English and he heard them profess their innocence steadfastly until their deaths. Forbes even provided new information about a lost and otherwise unknown relic: Towerson's Bible, in which Forbes said Towerson had written a statement of his innocence. Finally, Forbes confirmed something the EIC had long suspected: that the VOC council found out sometime after the first arrests but before the executions that the EIC intended to close the Amboyna factory, yet continued with the trial. Everything about Forbes's testimony served to confirm the EIC's suspicions that the nefarious VOC had plotted against its traders in Amboyna and to fuel the company's desire for compensation.[91]

If Forbes invented the whole tale, it was a shrewd performance guaranteed to win him supporters because it conformed perfectly to the image the English had crafted both of themselves and of the VOC. His perceptiveness may have been a result of being present in Batavia when the VOC council members were deposed in response to questions from the States General in 1626: that is, he may have already known what subjects most irritated the EIC. By attaching himself to the English survivors, Forbes transformed himself from a Scots VOC employee to one of the Amboyna men, someone who might assist the EIC in its quest for justice, and off he went to The Hague. There the English survivors became "the witnesses," and sometimes "the English wittnesses," although two of them, Forbes and Ramsey, were Scots.[92] The VOC directors had their own word to describe them: they were "accomplices" to an insidious plot.[93]

Vane raised the business of Amboyna soon after his arrival with the five men, but within a few weeks, he had grown so discouraged about the possibility of any real progress that he told the Prince of Orange he wasn't going to pursue the subject further. Over the winter months, Vane carried out his own research into the matter. Dismayed by the contradictions he saw in all the depositions, he saw little hope of resolution and came to believe that the king had made a big error letting the States control the judicial process.[94] To comply with the king's orders governing the English witnesses, Vane enforced strict conditions for their appearance before the States. The witnesses could not be examined about subjects beyond their original 1624 depositions, nor without the ambassador present.[95] These restrictions placed the witnesses in an awkward position, ordered by Vane never to act without consulting him, then commanded by the judges to appear. In fact, Vane never approved their examination, and the men lingered, running up expenses.[96] After three months, Vane couldn't understand why the witnesses were still with him, and after four months, he finally had orders to send them back.[97] They stayed away so long that Forbes's wife became dependent on the EIC for support.[98] Yet still they remained in The Hague: perhaps they wanted to, because it was not until August that Vane, whose patience had long since been exhausted, described them as impatient.[99] Finally, Vane sent them home at the end of August 1630.[100]

The stay was likely frustrating for these men, some of whom had been eager for several years to testify about their experiences in Amboyna in front of a Dutch audience. Several of them likely spoke Dutch, or so their examiners in Amboyna had claimed. Forbes was fluent, and Beaumont probably knew some Dutch from his friendships with VOC merchants and his long East Indies career. It is easy to imagine that they all traveled about, possibly looking up old friends or acquaintances, and chatting with them in Dutch or English or even Malay and other Indian Ocean languages in which Beaumont at least was proficient.[101] Perhaps they even confronted the VOC judges in informal settings, in taverns or private homes.

Powel seems to have continued his career as a searcher, because his name appeared along with that of Forbes as witnesses to a deposition in Amsterdam on July 8, 1630. The English searcher and the Scot with something to prove must have joined the EIC agent Robert Barlow in an activity that had occupied him on and off for two years: procuring depositions by former VOC employees in hopes of obtaining further evidence about some of the sticking points of the process. Did the English continue to assert their innocence, and did the local people and the VOC employees themselves find the plot plausible? The depositions also revealed English interest in whether the VOC council members at Amboyna came to regret their actions ("any sorrow, grief, repentance, or gnawing of conscience," as the interrogatories put it in 1628), and that was the main point of this 1630 deposition, arranged by Barlow, but perhaps facilitated by Forbes and Powel, who may have been looking for likely candidates to help advance their cause. This deposition is the only one solicited by Barlow that has turned up for this period when the witnesses were in town. In it, a man named Hendrick (or Henry, since he was from Yarmouth in England) Alban, previously a soldier for the VOC first at Amboyna and later at Batavia in 1628, testified about the state of mind of Martin Jansz Vogel, one of the Amboyna judges and Alban's employer. Although in his 1626 deposition in Batavia, Vogel asserted he had no doubts about English culpability, he may have been haunted by uncertainty. So, at least, Alban claimed. He stated that he heard Vogel say that he thought he had served justice in Amboyna, or else perhaps he had been deceived by his fellow council members. Vogel also professed reluctance to go to the Netherlands, despite repeated orders to do so.[102] Vogel's alleged pangs of conscience conformed to the EIC's interpretation of events, but this deposition did little in the end to advance the witnesses' or the company's cause.

The witnesses' failed trip signaled not just a thwarted reckoning but also coincided with deteriorating relations between the companies, which the VOC directors believed to be worse than ever in 1631.[103] The Amsterdam chamber's decision to christen one of its new ships the *Amboina* in 1629 might simply have been a continuation of an existing pattern to name ships after places, or the name could have been intended to antagonize the English.[104] Exacerbating this conflict were the incompatible visions each company held of itself in relationship to the other. The VOC directors in 1631 regarded the English as ungrateful to them for all of their assistance.[105]

The witnesses, meanwhile, were back in London complaining about how their time in The Hague depleted their estates. The company later rebuked them for their "lavish & exorbitant expences," but that might just have been the complaining of a tightfisted employer, not an indication that the men were living the high life.[106] The company was reluctant to cut them off completely, hoping still in the fall of 1630 that there might soon be a settlement, so it granted the men their old allowance of 10 shillings per week for another six months, as long as they were always ready to assist the company. The EIC extended the same deal to Forbes.[107] Collins returned to his job in the powder mill, but the EIC terminated the payments for the other men at the end of September 1631 and Powel, Beaumont, and Ramsey were forced to find new positions after devoting seven years to the company's service as witnesses.[108] It wasn't just employment they had secured during those years: it was also status, recognition of their losses and suffering, and perhaps even a new identity. They had even acquired some celebrity, with Ramsey and Collins meeting the king so that they could tell him about "the busines."[109] But their value derived from their willingness to yoke themselves to a single story and a single episode in their lives.

When that chapter came to an end, they had to find a way to move on. Some resumed plans interrupted in 1624, when they had first sought positions back in the Indies. After discovering Forbes and two other VOC men on the *Golden Lion* at Plymouth in 1627 and later tracking down a helpful VOC deponent in Holland in 1630, Powel probably could have parlayed his special skills into a new career as a witch finder. Instead, by summer 1632 he planned to return to the Indies as a purser on the *Swan*. Ramsey likely returned to the

Indies at the same time. In anticipation of this trip—knowing all too well the peril such employment posed— Ramsey made his will, and, hoping still for restitution, he left whatever might be due him for his losses in the East Indies to his sister.[110] All the witnesses had spent almost a decade in limbo with little to show, no financial compensation, and no conviction that they had won justice in their suit. Their time in Holland had been expensive, costing £100 each, or so they alleged in petitions to the king, Privy Council, and the EIC that conveyed their frustration. Assured that their presence in Holland could help the Dutch see reason in the case, they were restricted from ever testifying, spent nine months waiting, remained uncompensated for their losses in the Indies, and incurred further debts in Holland.[111] All they achieved was the painful discovery, soon before Powel sailed, that the States General had reached an unsatisfying decision. In March 1632, the Dutch ambassador personally notified Charles I that the States General had found the VOC judges at Amboyna to be guilty "of a serious offence," but there was insufficient evidence to prove murder or treason or lèse majesté, as the English had hoped. The English witnesses might have provided that evidence, but never testified. The States General judges sentenced the VOC judges to prison.[112]

The decision marked a waystation in a bitter legal battle, one that signaled the virtual impossibility that any resolution might bring with it a shared interpretation of events. With this disappointment over the judicial decision, and no reckoning for their alleged financial losses in the Indies, the EIC turned, as it had in 1624, to the press. The company published two works in 1632. First, it reprinted the *True Relation*, accompanied as before by the VOC's *True Declaration* and the EIC's *Answer to the True Declaration*, exactly as in the two authorized 1624 impressions. The texts themselves were unchanged, merely a "third impression," as the title page professed. With the reproduction of the original epistle to the reader, the pamphlet thus presented the incident exactly as it had in 1624, as if it had just happened and was an immediate and recent grievance. Second, the EIC published three texts on "the Massacre of Amboyna" that had been circulating in manuscript since 1624 and that the company had tried to bring to print in 1627: the VOC's record of the Amboyna trial, the VOC's Remonstrance to the States General in November 1624 (a refutation of the *True Relation*), and the EIC's response to the Remonstrance.[113] These three texts, like the *True Relation* and its two accompanying texts, were published as a single work.

The EIC had republished the *True Relation* even before it learned of the States General's decision in the matter. In September 1631, the Privy Council

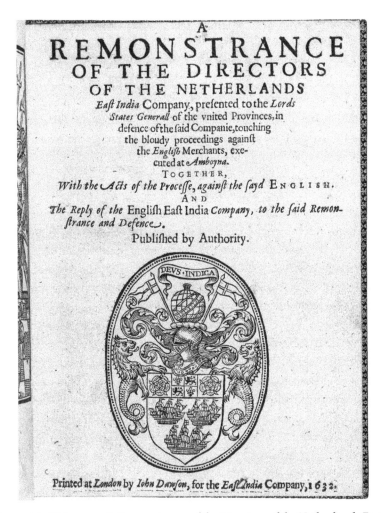

Figure 4.1 Title page, *A Remonstrance of the Directors of the Netherlands East India Company* (London, 1632). Call # STC 7450a. Used by permission of the Folger Shakespeare Library.

issued a warrant suppressing the work, but then lifted it in October.[114] By early April 1632, the Dutch ambassadors in London lodged complaints. The Lord Treasurer told them, they reported to the States, that because the EIC remained uncompensated for the incident, the company had permission to publish these texts. The ambassadors added that the permission came from the secretary of state himself, who was deeply agitated by the affair. Indeed, he was "so violent" about it that, when asked to reply to the ambassadors' queries about various wrongs the Dutch had allegedly endured, he simply answered, "AMBOINA."[115]

The two publications were linked not only thematically, advancing familiar subjects of Dutch ingratitude and perfidy, but also physically. A book buyer in this era purchased unbound texts, and then took them to his or her preferred binder, making choices about binding material, embossing, and other aesthetic and financial considerations. This practice enabled buyers to gather texts with a common theme into a single volume. Wear patterns and evidence of original binding on surviving copies of these two works show that they were often bound together.[116]

These texts recapitulated familiar themes but offered an important innovation: their accompanying image. This time, the printer used the woodcut that the EIC had employed in its 1624 Dutch language translation, *Een waer verhael*. This version focused on the fires placed under the feet and armpits of the English. The 1632 woodcuts likely came from the same block that produced the 1624 illustration: they show degradation along the lower left edge, suggesting some deterioration in the original block over the intervening years. Possibly the EIC came to believe that this new image was more powerful; perhaps it wanted to give readers something different in a text that was otherwise an exact reproduction of the 1624 version; perhaps the other woodblock was lost or too heavily degraded.[117] The illustration appears twice, as a frontispiece and as an endpage. The prose work is thus wrapped in identical illustrations.

The revival of the woodcut, with its heightened focus on torture, and its double appearance seems to attest to its significance. So, too, do the markings that survive on two-thirds of the extant frontispieces, where printers added red ink at carefully chosen places. It appears at the tips of candles; on the tortured man's hands; on his feet; at the incision in his chest. The red drips down below the hands, to suggest blood, although there is no evidence that the Dutch nailed the English to the doorframe. The uniformity of the ink pattern indicates that the ink was added in the printing process with a stencil. This process added costs to production: extra labor, red ink, which in mid-seventeenth-century London cost considerably more than black ink, and additional materials.[118]

The markings enhanced the qualities of martyrdom. The ink marks on the hand highlight what look like stigmata. The woodcut's presence sewn into surviving copies of the *Remonstrance*, a work that was not printed with the image, conveys its importance to readers and book buyers.[119] It is possible,

Figure 4.2 In black and white, the red ink on the original woodcut appears as dark splotches. Compare with Figure 3.8 to see the differences between the two woodcuts. *True Relation* (London, 1632), frontispiece. X 991.3 EA7T1632, The Rare Book & Manuscript Library, University of Illinois at Urbana-Champaign.

given the fact that one-third of surviving woodcuts do not have the red marks, that the printer added the red ink to copies printed after the official decision of the States General became public. With its dripping blood, the woodcut was a fitting punctuation to EIC sentiments in 1632, with anger at the mild punishment meted out to men they regarded as murderers and no financial restitution for their claims of lost trade in the Indies. In contrast to their 1624 publication practices, the EIC did not translate the 1632 texts into Dutch, so the envisioned audience was English.

For all the EIC's efforts, between 1632 and 1651 there was little headway on the many outstanding claims between the two companies, and efforts to mediate the companies' disagreements were entangled in the other issues that stood between the English crown and the States General. Indeed, it was a perilous moment for the EIC as it faced growing state intrusion in its affairs, specifically in light of the sympathy Charles I showed for merchants who sought to challenge the company's monopoly.[120] In 1637, both the VOC and EIC complained about their frustration at advancing their causes.[121] Successive English ambassadors wrestled with the issue in the 1640s, as did commissioners appointed by the companies. The betrothal and marriage of Charles's eldest daughter, Mary, and William of Orange in 1641 inspired optimism that relations between the two nations would improve, but that did not lead to a resolution on the Amboyna incident.[122] In 1643, it looked as if William Boswell, the English ambassador at The Hague, might be able to resolve the matter, but the case of the Banda island of Run emerged as a more important issue at the time.[123] All that resulted in this era was something unlikely to facilitate resolution: for the first time since the quickly suppressed sermon of February 1625, "massacred" appeared in print in 1646 to describe the Englishmen who died at Amboyna, followed in a few short years by "Massacre at *Amboyna*."[124] And then the distractions of the English Civil War and the volatile relationships between crown, Parliament, and the United Provinces made progress difficult in the 1640s.

The push for a final reckoning of the Amboyna losses began in 1650, and did so, ironically, with the promise of an Anglo-Dutch alliance. The English Civil War and two deaths, first the execution of Charles I in November 1649, an act opposed by the shocked Dutch, and then the death of William II, the head of state of the United Provinces, in November 1650, established the crucial context. William II was Charles I's son-in-law and Charles II's brother-in-law, and he had pushed the provinces toward active support for the Stuarts. In the wake of William's death, the English anticipated a new and more amicable relationship with the United Provinces, and some of the individual provinces recognized the English Commonwealth for the first time. In November 1650 the EIC seized the momentum of a potential union and petitioned Parliament with a catalogue of its accumulated losses, including the deaths of its employees, hoping that Parliament would keep the company's losses in mind as commissioners sought to repair the two nations' divisions.[125] But the promise of union soon collapsed. English agents who sailed to The Hague in spring 1651 were unsucessful in their negotiations. Their diplomatic failure sparked Parliament to pass its first Navigation Acts in October 1651, a set of regulations that placed Dutch commercial interests at a disadvantage. In this turbulent era, the representatives of the Dutch government arrived in December 1651 hoping to make peace, but they were confronted instead by hostility from both the Rump Parliament and the English polity.[126]

By the time the Dutch commissioners arrived, no EIC employee from the 1623 episode seems to have been alive or in London. The only man left standing by then was the Scot, George Forbes, who lived in two rooms in the EIC's almshouse, supported by a generous allowance, in return for which he was to say morning and evening prayers and keep things in good order.[127] The families or executors of four of the survivors and two of the executed men petitioned the Council of State for compensation in 1652. Some of these families had been assiduously pressing their claims since June 1624, when the kin of six executed men first began to approach the EIC and the English government for compensation and assistance.[128] This later round of petitions to the Council of State commenced in January 1652, with claims from Sarah Collins, the widow of Edward, and her two children; and Thomas Billingsley, a nephew of Emanuel Thompson, and a member of the most persistent family in terms of seeking reparations.[129] They were joined by three other petitioners in April, from the families and executors of the survivors Webber, Sherrock, and Powel, and of the executed trader Samuel Coulson, whose brother declared in a succinct summation of the long-standing English position that Samuel had been "murthered on purpose and upon designe" to expel the English.[130] These three petitions were part of a deluge in April by family members of EIC employees and by the EIC itself, all making claims against the VOC for injuries dating back thirty-five years.[131]

These petitions signaled a fleeting optimism that the two nations might achieve a rapprochement. The VOC directors were similarly encouraged in April 1652 that relations with England might improve but urged their employees in Asia to remain vigilant. They were right to have been cautious.[132] Instead of the anticipated alliance, the two nations lapsed into war, what became the first of three Anglo-Dutch wars in the seventeenth century. With war came pamphlets outlining the English justification for the conflict, and Amboyna featured prominently in these texts. Amboyna may have been especially important in a conflict in which the religious differences so central to recent European wars were not present as motivating factors, nor was this a dynastic conflict, in which warring nations staked claims based on gene-alogy. Without such justifications to legitimize their aggression, the English looked for other rationales. One approach that emerged by mid-century cen-tered on accusations of cruelty, leveled at the Spanish as the English justified their conquest of Jamaica in 1655 and at the Dutch when the English justi-fied the attack on New Netherland in 1664.[133] But the unrevenged injury at Amboyna seems to have played such a role a few years earlier as an animating factor in this first Anglo-Dutch conflict. By 1652, Amboyna had become such an essential way for the English to think about their relationship with the Dutch that Parliament mentioned the "cruel and bloody Business" in its rationale for the war.[134]

Some anti-Dutch works may have been published even before the Dutch commissioners arrived, including another version of the *True Relation,* printed in London in 1651, possibly in the wake of the Navigation Acts. This version, unlike the 1624 and 1632 imprints, was not an exact copy. It was tiny, one-third the size of the original quarto volumes, and it was not printed by the EIC but rather arranged by the Council of State. It also contained some new material, notably a prefatory letter and concluding remarks.[135] Just as the Dutch delegation landed, an English periodical, the *French Intelligencer,* published a short account that professed to be a "further testimony" asserting the innocence of the men who had endured "*Martyrdome*" in Amboyna. The text was that found in William Griggs's notebook and first published in the 1624 *True Relation.* It was hardly new, nor was it unfamiliar, but it was an efficient way to generate hostility toward the Dutch.[136] This recycling of old Amboyna texts, moreover, was a harbinger of what was to come.

Many anti-Dutch wartime pamphleteers hewed to the EIC's estab-lished practice of recycling old information and reworking old images, but there were four innovations in the war years connected to the portrayal of Amboyna and its shifting place in print culture. First, new anti-Dutch works written in the context of the war absorbed Amboyna as an iconic episode of Dutch cruelty. Thus, the Amboyna episode started to move beyond a problem unique or particular to the EIC's interest and became part of an English critique of the Dutch. As part of that transition, Amboyna emerged as a way for the English to understand challenges they faced beyond Europe, and thus a metaphor for global conflicts with the Dutch, which was a second innovation of this era. Third, English authors used the Amboyna story to make their own political critique of the English government. Finally, images cemented their importance to the English interpretation of Amboyna. These four developments of 1651–54 ultimately facilitated the endurance of the story of Amboyna beyond the formal resolution reached in the wake of the Treaty of Westminster of 1654.

Between 1652 and 1654, at least twenty-four English works were published that discussed the Amboyna incident as part of a larger enterprise to critique the Dutch. These pamphlets were part of an explosion of political texts written during this war.[137] They advanced two key themes: the familiar argument that the VOC's treatment of the EIC traders at Amboyna revealed the enormous ingratitude of the Dutch Republic for English assistance over the past century; and a lament that the EIC had still received no satisfaction for the claims it pressed for restitution.[138] In these works, Amboyna stood out as the consummate example of Dutch perfidy. The EIC appreciated these works and arranged to purchase fifty copies of one such book, Abraham Woofe's *The Tyranny of the Dutch against the English* (London, 1653).[139]

As these new texts joined the 1651 *True Relation*, the EIC no longer had any proprietary claim to the story of Amboyna, nor indeed to the company's own account of it, the original 1624 *True Relation*, that had brought the affair to public attention. This process of detachment of the *True Relation* from specific EIC grievances ensured that the work lived on; writers reworked it multiple times over the next 130 years, with a final appearance in 1781 during the Fourth Anglo-Dutch War. The printer James Moxon produced the first such reworking in 1652. He provided a new title: *A Memento for Holland: or A True and Exact History of the most Villainous and Barbarous Cruelties used on the English Merchants residing at Amboyna in the East-Indies, by the Netherland Governor and conucel* [sic] *there.* The subtitle makes obvious the connection to the EIC's *True Relation*, but Moxon was not yet done. The subtitle continued with the most lurid highlights of the episode: *Wherein is shewed What Tortures were used to make them confess a Conspiracy they were never guilty of; by putting them on the Rack, and by a Water torture to suffocate them; and by burning them under their Arm-pits, and Soals of their Feet, till their fat by dropping extinguished the Candles.* The new title had a double meaning: a memento was a memory or a reminder, but it could also mean a warning, and the dual meanings served the author's purpose in this case, signaling to the ambassadors from the United Provinces that the matter was ever-present in English sentiments.[140] The *Memento* did not include the two texts normally printed with the *True Relation* (the *True Declaration* and the EIC's answer to it); it was a stand-alone, something that became the norm in all subsequent reworkings of the iconic text.

As the political and diplomatic exigencies of the first Anglo-Dutch War detached Amboyna from parochial EIC concerns, it became a proxy for Dutch conduct beyond the East Indies. Moxon's letter to the reader modeled this transition. In it, he reminded the reader of the ingratitude of the Dutch to the English, not only in this example of Amboyna but at the present day. During England's "unhappy Troubles," he explained, the Dutch made no effort to help the English "recover [their] Rights and Liberties," but rather assisted those—that is, the king—who sought to enslave them.[141] He thus built on the legacy of Amboyna to make a timeless indictment of the Dutch character. An invocation in a 1652 work of "Amboyna-like cruelties" perpetrated by the Dutch likewise signaled this transition in Amboyna's function as part of a more general way to criticize the Dutch.[142]

Consistent with this approach, a brief pamphlet about an incident in New England in 1653 drew on the Amboyna example to emphasize the alleged treachery of the Dutch. Dubbed *The Second Part of the Tragedy of Amboyna*, the pamphlet echoed the *True Relation* explicitly in its subtitle: *or, a True Relation of a Most Bloody, Treacherous, and Cruel Design of the Dutch in the New-Netherlands in America. For the total Ruining and Murthering of the English Colonies in New-England.*[143] According to the text, English colonists on Long Island believed that Peter Stuyvesant, the governor of New Netherland, and Dutch colonists were plotting with the Narragansetts to destroy the English during the First Anglo-Dutch War. In just the same way that the original Amboyna pamphlets played up the theme of Dutch ingratitude for English assistance, this pamphlet remarked on English generosity to Dutch settlers in New Netherland when they most needed help and deplored the Dutch for their perfidy, clear evidence, the author noted, that "Amboyna's treacherous Cruelty" stretched from east to west. But the English in essence inverted the conspiracy narrative of 1623, putting themselves in the vulnerable spot the VOC had occupied in Amboyna, surrounded by treacherous people. The English pamphlet closely resembled the VOC's *True Declaration* in multiple respects: in terms of the nefarious conspiracy it imagined between the Dutch and the "barbarous Indians"; in the remarkable divine providence that sent a "revealing Deliverer" to tell the English about the plot against them (the role inadvertently played in 1623 by the Japanese soldier who asked his questions and thus revealed the plot on an anniversary day special to the Dutch); and the miraculous rescue of the English from their peril.[144] The directors of the Dutch West India Company dismissed this pamphlet as a "shameless and lying libel" and proclaimed the text so despicable that even the devil himself could not have produced it.[145]

The flurry of publication activity in the early 1650s revealed how meanings of Amboyna had become both crystallized and transformed. For the English, it had become a "byword" for deception, ingratitude, and cruelty.[146] But it was becoming much more than that thirty years after the fact. The incident was embedded not only in an intertwined history of English and Dutch relations but also in England's own history. Amboyna invited an internal reckoning and provided a new vantage point on monarchy for a nation in turmoil. If the incident revealed Dutch cruelty and injustice, it also exposed English weakness.[147] The new material in the 1651 *True Relation* argued that if Amboyna had indeed become a sign of English weakness, the fault lay in James I and in monarchy more generally, not in the character of the English people, an analysis of the early Stuart dynasty that became entrenched in eighteenth-century English histories. While it is hardly surprising that someone might deploy a historical event to make a contemporary point, this pamphlet was the first time Amboyna played such a role in a reassessment of England's own past. Invoking a parliamentarian critique of the Stuarts, the compiler argued that James was weak, distracted by his desire for luxury and his eagerness to please his "*Catemit*" (a reference to the Duke of Buckingham), and easily bought by the Dutch.[148]

A final feature of Amboyna pamphlets in these war years was the continued importance of the image of the tortured trader, but with a renewed emphasis on execution, perhaps a reflection of the execution of Charles I a few years earlier. The 1651 *True Relation* rejected the illustration that had circulated in 1632 of the blood-spattered trader and returned instead to a new engraving of the scene depicted in the 1624 English-language editions, with its narrative of torture, recovery, and a dignified execution. In the 1652 *Memento*, that same version appeared again, virtually identical to the 1651 engraving, although rendered in a crude woodcut. Execution scenes littered works in the 1650s. One printing of the 1651 *True Relation* contained new illustrative features, notably decorations around the letters I and S. One shows a scene of execution; the other shows a slaughter. Even a 1652 English broadside collage showed the same execution scene in the middle of a cryptic array of Dutch horrors connected to the murder of Isaac Dorislaw, the English ambassador to The Hague, by English royalists in 1649. In the Dutch-language version of this same work, an engraver removed the figure of the frazzled English trader and instead added two decapitated figures, drawing out the execution narrative to its brutal culmination.[149] The popularity of the Amboyna execution scenes, and their essential link to the text they accompanied, is suggested by a

 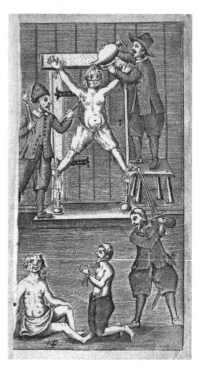

Figure 4.3 Frontispieces from two *True Relations* printed a year apart. The woodcut on the left is from *A Memento for Holland* (London, 1652), frontispiece. Shelfmark LH.1.6 (3). By permission of the President and Fellows of Corpus Christi College, Oxford. The engraving on the right comes from the *True Relation* (London, 1651), frontispiece. Call # 150-313q. Used by permission of the Folger Shakespeare Library. The 1665 *True Relation* featured the same engraving depicted here on the right, but the quarto-sized 1665 edition had enough space on the page to add a poem beneath the image.

surviving manuscript version of the *True Relation*, with its own hand-drawn version of the woodcut. A cataloguer's note says that the manuscript copied the 1632 *True Relation* verbatim, but it is more likely that the creator copied the 1651 version, given the virtually identical illustrations.[150]

These accumulated words and images suggest that English sentiments in the 1650s were just where they had been when the agitated English traders marched to the VOC house in Batavia in June 1623 looking for answers and explanations. It was not only suspicion and mistrust that continued to characterize so many Anglo-Dutch interactions but also an entrenched

Figure 4.4 There were two printings of the 1651 *True Relation*. One printing showed these execution scenes around the letters S and I at the beginning of each separate section of the pamphlet. *True Relation* (London, 1651), prefatory material, pp. 2, 3. Shelfmark LH.1.45. By permission of the President and Fellows of Corpus Christi College, Oxford.

commitment to the least generous interpretation of events. Moreover, ideas about the original Amboyna incident had not altered at all. These hardened—and shared—sentiments manifested themselves in the war years in several ways. As had been true in the 1620s, English and Dutch publications continued to be in apparent conversation with each other. Four Amboyna publications appeared in the United Provinces in 1652, three in defense of the VOC and one in support of the EIC. The VOC's account from 1624, *Waerachtigh Verhael*, was reprinted in the Netherlands twice in 1652. One edition noted specifically that its purpose was to respond to a pro-English pamphlet, the *Anatomia*.[151] This work was a Dutch-language version of the EIC's *Answer to the True Declaration*, which had originally been published in English and Dutch in 1624 as part of the three-part *True Relation*. Another 1652 pamphlet, *Engelsche-Duymdrayery*, contained a dialogue between two characters, the Hollander and the Traveler, who had just come from London and who wanted to know the true story of Amboyna. This dialogue was a popular genre in the Netherlands, the *praatje*. The Hollander convinced the skeptical Traveler of the existence of the Anglo-Japanese plot, and the Traveler pledged to defend the VOC with his last drop of blood.[152] Finally, a brief, six-page pamphlet summarized the conspiracy from the VOC point of view.[153] These works trod familiar ground, with an innovation only in

Figure 4.5 Both the English and Dutch language versions of this 1652 broadside placed Amboyna at the center of the action. These scenes are highlighted here, with the rest of the engravings in slightly darker relief. Top image: *Dr. Dorislow's ghost, presented by time to unmask the vizards of the Hollanders* (London, 1652). Photo courtesy of the Morgan Library and Museum, New York. Used by permission of The Morgan Library and Museum. PML 145850.25. Bequest of Gordan N. Ray, 1987. Bottom image: *De geest van Dr. Dooreslaer wordt door de tijdt vertoont, en ontmomt 't aensicht der Hollanderen* (1652). RP-P-OB-75.328, Rijksmuseum, Amsterdam. Combined photo created by Christen Runge.

Figure 4.6 This illustration in a manuscript "True Relation" showed a close resemblance to the woodcut and engraving featured in Figure 4.3. (c) The British Library Board, Sloane 3645, f. 177recto.

the genre used in *Engelsche-Duymdrayery*. One of the nation's most distinguished legal theorists, Dirck Graswinckel, also set to work compiling a massive book that summarized the Amboyna episode. He gathered the relevant papers with the aim of justifying the procedures followed there, but as the war's end loomed, he could not get permission to publish it. Only a treaty finally silenced the war of words.[154]

But if these works communicated with each other, they did so by reiterating the same account that had been rejected for thirty years by their counterparts. They manifested the enduring intransigence of the two companies and spoke, moreover, to a second feature of these years: a deep gulf of understanding. This chasm manifested itself during preliminary negotiations in 1652, when the VOC reminded the EIC agents of how helpful the Dutch had been during the Lagundy crisis twenty-seven years earlier. The EIC acknowledged this vital succor, but it was not enough: the VOC wanted its assistance "registered in the public records of England." The VOC had long complained that the EIC was ungrateful for the Dutch rescue at Lagundy, a reproof dating to 1626.[155] To this request in 1652, the EIC retorted that while it appreciated the help at Lagundy, the English were in that predicament only because the Dutch had shown such cruelty at Amboyna and Banda.[156] This exchange revealed that the long-standing and mutual sentiments of ingratitude that had helped produce the Amboyna conspiracy in 1623 remained entrenched, part of an emotional reckoning that could find no resolution.

English and Dutch diplomats who gathered to forge a treaty had to wrangle these incompatible sentiments, which intruded in a third and final conflict: how to characterize the episode at Amboyna. Most of the treaty had nothing to do with Amboyna, of course, but the incident required some resolution. Foremost for the Dutch was what to call the Amboyna episode. The States of Overijssel, a province in the central part of the Netherlands, ratified the articles of the treaty in February 1654 but did not approve of the suggested terminology. Rather than the characterization of the incident as "*the murder of the English at Amboina*," the States preferred "*The disorders that happened; or, were committed; or, the perpetrated facts at Amboina*, or any the like and least offensive expressions."[157] A few days later the States General echoed the States of Overijssel's choice and similarly suggested more anodyne and passive phrasing. Omit, they proposed, that "odious word of *murther*."[158] These protests were in vain: the treaty employed the preferred English perspective, "*Homicidii Anglorum in Amboyna*," in what was ultimately the 27th article.[159]

The Treaty of Westminster made provisions for the English and Dutch to appoint commissioners to adjudicate the two companies' many long-standing claims against each other. The commissioners met in England in the summer of 1654, and by August 30 (English style), they reached a decision: the VOC was required to pay £85,000 to the EIC, and £3,615 to the estates of those who had suffered at Amboyna.[160] An informant who read the Dutch ambassadors' letters reported their great relief at being rid of the Amboyna episode at such a modest cost.[161] Of the eighteen EIC traders ensnared in the legal proceedings at Amboyna, twelve had estates whose claims were settled in this resolution. Seven of these twelve were survivors of the episode, which meant that all of the survivors except Sadler received payouts, and only half of the executed men.[162]

The two companies had finally secured the financial settlement they wanted, and so too had twelve executors. But as the conflicts in the Indies over shared expenses in 1620–22 revealed, accounting was rarely only a financial enterprise, and a bill paid in full seldom quelled disputes.[163] Traders brought anger and suspicion to each month's reckoning, worrying about being cheated, stewing about shirkers, fretting about loss of honor and advantage, and fuming over displays of ingratitude. Accounting for the two companies was always emotional as well as financial. Treaties offered another type of reckoning, one that bound nations and sought to distill a range of disputes into formal and mutually agreeable prose. In 1654, the EIC received a financial reckoning. It emerged by compulsion at the negotiating table despite persistent and intractable disagreements about what had happened at Amboyna, but it turned out that the emotional reckoning lingered for decades. Amboyna's aftermath had come to an end, but its afterlife, forged in the pamphlets and the violent images that both created and publicized the event, was just beginning.

5

Domesticating Amboyna

In 1664, as tensions between the English and Dutch portended another war, Charles II and the Dutch ambassador struggled to prevent the conflict. The monarch recalled the Treaty of Westminster of 1654, in which so many old Dutch injuries to the English had been resolved. The love the English harbored for the United Provinces, the king assured the ambassador, enabled them to cast these offenses, prime among them the incident at Amboyna, into "oblivion."[1] It was too late. The Amboyna business had already become ubiquitous by the 1650s, well known to populations as diverse as raucous audiences at London plays or English soldiers bent on revenge, and the peace of 1654 had done little if anything to hinder the story's spread.

There were many reasons for the incident's remarkable longevity. Two more conflicts—the Second (1665–67) and Third (1672–74) Anglo-Dutch Wars—provided new occasions to reprise the tale, but the story transcended the war years and its tenacity owed still more to its rapid entrenchment in English domestic and political culture. The Amboyna story moved on two parallel and sometimes intertwined tracks. The political lesson of Amboyna, articulated during times of conflict with the Dutch and in six new *True Relations* that appeared between 1665 and 1781, continued to be one of ingratitude, although writers occasionally emphasized other aspects of the episode to highlight themes resonant with their contemporary moment—treachery, for example, or the lack of fidelity the Dutch showed to treaties with the English. In most forms of popular culture, however, the key lesson of Amboyna was cruelty, a result of the emotional impact of the illustration of the tortured trader and what readers took to be most significant about the episode— torture. Between 1624, when news first reached England, and 1781, when the last bespoke *True Relation* was published, the episode made appearances in multiple contexts: in virtually identical pamphlets that targeted Dutch opponents and, after 1688, internal political enemies; in plays and poems; in comedy and drama; in fiction and essays. Authors sometimes engaged creatively with the original pamphlets yet still left the core aspects of the story unchanged. The reappearance of the *True Relation*, always accompanied by an image of the tortured trader, familiarized new generations of readers with the tale and its graphic violence. All collectively made "Amboyna" such a familiar cultural touchstone that by the eighteenth century authors assumed readers knew exactly what the word signaled. Amboyna's persistent appearance through 1781, accompanied by occasional eruptions of Amboyna pamphlets, in 1665–67, 1672–74, 1688, 1711–13, 1767, and 1781, culminated in the domestication of the story as a familiar and consistent tale of cruelty and, at the end of the period, as a legend of unavenged injury.

Relying on printed works to discern Amboyna's presence in popular culture is admittedly an imperfect method and offers only a partial glimpse at how English people may have responded to and understood the incident. For the most part, in terms of identifying a popular response beyond texts, all that comes through is anger—the wrath in London so strong that authorities feared riots in 1625, for example, or that led two VOC employees detained in Portsmouth to flee lest they be murdered in the streets in 1627. But sometimes one gets a glimpse of specific knowledge about the incident. In 1631, for example, two English soldiers in Germany overheard eighteen Dutch soldiers boasting about participating in the interrogations and perhaps even the torture of the English at Amboyna. The English soldiers then gathered their comrades and lay in wait for the Dutchmen. They executed sixteen on the spot, "in revenge of the blood" of those English who had died in 1623. Showing a close familiarity with the procedure used at Amboyna, the English soldiers compelled the two survivors to draw lots as three English merchants had been forced to do in 1623 in order to determine who should live to carry the news of this English revenge to the States General.[2]

This combination of features—detailed knowledge and emotional responses—emerges clearly in a range of surviving printed works. Between the first reports of the incident in Europe and the conclusion of the Third Anglo-Dutch War in 1674, the Amboyna story became securely lodged in many aspects of popular culture, in both humorous and dramatic forms that showed authors responding to the image of the tortured trader, the key texts that established the massacre, and the theme of cruelty. These varied forms, however, had a common feature. It didn't matter what the genre, the celebrity of the author, the high or low audience, comedy or tragedy— it was torture that stood out, and it was the *True Relation* and its various illustrations that directly affected how readers and viewers made sense of the violence of the episode.

Multiple works that had nothing at all to do with Anglo-Dutch relations or with the story of Amboyna sometimes revealed that authors had seen one of the many circulating illustrations of torture and were inspired by it to draw conclusions about subjects as diverse as medical remedies, the relative merits of art or poetry, and etiquette. Take the physician Stephen Bradwell, whose compendium of medical treatments was published in 1633. He had the notion that the best way to cure someone of the hydrophobia that resulted from the bite of a rabid dog was to force the patient to deal with water, either by making him swim, or making him drink. The problem was that patients fearful of water were unlikely to cooperate. Here Bradwell drew inspiration from Amboyna. After seeing a picture of the water torture, he devised a scheme to compel reluctant patients to consume some water—always taking care, he reminded his reader, that the patient was able to breathe. Bradwell could only have seen two different illustrations at the time he wrote, and it is likely he was describing the 1624 English-language edition woodcut. "Thus," Bradwell concluded, "have I out of a wicked weed sucked Honey for Health; and from an inhumane torture extracted ease in a grievous sicknesse."[3] The historian William Sanderson had also seen an Amboyna image, although in his case he saw Greenbury's painting before it was destroyed in 1625. It was a work so "monstrous" that he thought it should be burned, and it led him to conclude, in answer to that age-old debate, that art was more powerful than poetry.[4] The illustration and description of the water torture even inspired some etiquette advice. Do not, wrote an author in 1673, compel your guests to drink more than they want, because to do so smacks of the "*Barbarity*" shown by the Dutch at Amboyna. His details about how the water torture worked in Amboyna, with distended stomachs and bulging eyes, closely echoed the published accounts.[5]

The torture was such a central part of the Amboyna story that it could endure even in humorous renderings and even during times of war, although the lighthearted invocations didn't appear until after the legal settlement in 1654. In a 1668 comedy, *Sullen Lovers, or, The Impertinents*, the dreadful singing of Sir Positive At-all prompted another character to complain that it was more painful than the torture at Amboyna.[6] There was an effusion of such comic sentiments during the Third Anglo-Dutch War. A prologue in a 1672 collection of verse, *Covent Garden Drolery*, compared theater critics to the Dutch at Amboyna, who in their assiduous dissection of each scene and word of dialogue behaved like the Dutch when they racked English bodies.[7] In 1673, an author likened a beggar's cry of pain to the roar of a man tortured at Amboyna; the use of the metaphor was humorous in this context, as the author sought to mock the beggar's claim to injury and thus saw the cry as feigned.[8] There was even a comic play, part of a daily series of "Farces Drolls and Comical Entertainments," titled "The Dutch Cruelties at Amboyna," which was performed with "the Humours of the Valiant Welch-Man" in November 1672.[9] A short sketch that emphasized physical comedy and humor, this genre of the droll took its inspiration from plays early in the seventeenth century: it is possible that "the Humours of the Valiant Welch-Man" was based on a 1615 play, The Valiant Welshman, and perhaps even possible that the Amboyna sketch was based on the never-performed Amboyna play of 1624–25, or even another unknown show.[10] Only the chance survival of a single playbill reveals the existence of this comic entertainment, and it is impossible to guess all the many ways in which the Amboyna incident might have been depicted on stage.

This focus on torture reached its apogee in a play written during the Third Anglo-Dutch War, Amboyna: A Tragedy (1673), by John Dryden, a poet and playwright who was a major literary figure and poet laureate.[11] Dryden's play has become popular among literary critics because its setting, themes, and characters speak so effectively to English interactions with non-English people and English anxieties about their status in a globalizing world. This play, however, was not the first dramatic work to touch on Amboyna, and situating Dryden's Amboyna in its historical context demonstrates the intimate familiarity authors had with the incident (and assumed their audiences shared) and the changing political environment that enabled Dryden to showcase torture.

The very first effort to depict the story on the London stage had been suppressed in 1625, and subsequent works in that decade only touched on the incident. Two plays from 1626 contained casual references that suggest the authors' conviction that audiences would understand the allusions. One play noted how men were "pepper'd" (tortured) at Amboyna, while a second had a character who called out, "Yes, for Amboyna, and the Justice there!"[12] The justice may have referred to the acts of divine retribution that befell Amboyna after the executions—the sickness, the storm, the mad Scot—and, if so, then the playwright assumed the Amboyna incident was not only still on the minds of his London audience but also that theatergoers would understand justice as the retribution visited by God on that place in 1623, not the absence of justice that the English traders believed they had found there.[13]

In the difficult years of the 1630s, when the EIC learned of the disappointing actions of the States General, another playwright, an EIC employee named Walter Mountfort, wrote about the incident in a 1633 play, *The Launching of the Mary*.[14] Mountfort was not a professional playwright but a company man, a clerk who had been in the service of the EIC on and off since 1615. After a short period working in the East Indies, Mountfort sailed for Europe in April 1632, and it was during this long voyage across the globe that he wrote his play. Set in the busy area of the Blackwall shipyard, the play's main storyline concerned the launching of an EIC ship, the *Mary*.[15] The play has two subplots, one about three women who were left on their own in London when their husbands went to the Indies, and a second about five men who work in the shipyard. These workers serve as mouthpieces for anti-Dutch language, something that had become increasingly common on stage in the wake of the Amboyna incident.[16] The Hollandophobia appears early in the play, when a character named the Admiral obliquely invoked the Amboyna story as "the unmatcht vile, miserable, torture, / Those dutch inflicted on some English men."[17]

Mountfort's amateurism may have made him especially likely to compose a play that audience members wanted to see.[18] Amboyna may still have been on the minds of the EIC's employees, not just in London, where the decision of the States General smarted in 1632, but also overseas, where details remained fresh in the minds of employees. Perhaps Mountfort had spoken to men about the affair when he was in Persia, and perhaps on the journey home the subject came up again. Perhaps his fellow passengers asked him to read his work-in-progress aloud, as a way to enliven the tedious months of the voyage, and if so, perhaps they corrected his memory. The executed men may have been their friends and colleagues, and Mountfort may have been settling scores on their behalf.

Nonetheless, Mountfort struggled to get his play licensed. He knew enough not to refer explicitly to Amboyna, it seems, but he wanted to convey his anger at the event. Securing a license for a play was a back-and-forth process, in which the Master of the Revels, at the time Sir Henry Herbert, read the text, marked scenes for deletion or emendation, and sent the work back to the author. When the company of players (probably the second Prince Charles Company) submitted Mountfort's play to Herbert, he excised passages that pertained to the Dutch, particularly offensive remarks about the Amboyna judges. Herbert licensed the text in June 1633, with the caveat that these changes had to be made if the play was to be performed.[19]

Although Mountfort struggled to see his play on stage, authors continued to believe that the story belonged in the theater. Evidence from the 1650s suggests an intensifying interest in bringing the story to the public. James Shirley wrote a play in 1630, published in 1633 as *A Contention for Honour and Riches*, which he reworked and then published as *Honoria and Mammon* in 1659. The original play had no reference to Amboyna, but the 1659 version mentioned the punishments the Dutch concocted there.[20] His inclusion of Amboyna may have been a response to an effort in 1653–54 by William Davenant, another English poet laureate and playwright, to persuade the Puritan Parliament to reopen England's theaters by pointing out how much it would inspire spectators if they could see, among other things, the cruelties of England's enemies enacted on stage. The only example Davenant provided to bolster his argument was the case of Amboyna.[21]

Davenant's belief in the power of Amboyna on stage to shape public sentiment achieved delayed fruition in Dryden's play.[22] Charles II may have asked Dryden to write the play as a way to stir up anti-Dutch feelings, just as Davenant had hoped the Amboyna episode might do during an earlier war with the Dutch.[23] Amboyna—the real incident—was packed with people. Dryden stripped the story down to a few protagonists. He reduced the English survivors only to John Beaumont, killed off Edward Collins, enhanced Dutch perfidy by having the Dutch torture a woman, and removed some of the more eloquent figures from the original trial, notably Samuel Coulson. He also added a love story and created two female characters: Ysabinda, an Ambonese woman whose name may have been a misreading of Tsabinda, one of the Japanese co-conspirators; and Julia, the wife of the slave overseer Augustine Peres.[24] Turning the episode into a romance may not seem like an obvious choice, but Dryden's decision made the play consistent with other dramatic and literary works of the era and especially with his own tragedies, all of which contained love stories. Moreover, Dryden might simply have wanted to ensure that the play would appeal to audiences.[25] Whatever his reasons, Dryden's decision enabled him to find new ways to illustrate Dutch depravity.

Mountford and Dryden, the amateur and the professional, separated by forty years, literary credentials, and political contexts, nonetheless covered much of the same ground and spoke to similar themes. Moreover, their works had common features that suggested a widely shared understanding of the story. Both men, for example, dwelled on Dutch excess. Mountfort's play condemned the Dutch as drunkards and renamed Herman van Speult

"Harman van Spew[e]d."[26] The Dutch in Dryden's play were fat, venal, grotesque people.[27] The son of the Dutch general raped Towerson's companion, Ysabinda, in the first rape depicted in a Restoration play.[28] Dryden even turned the Dutch into cannibals. The character Harmon (the VOC governor, an obvious variant on the historical figure, Herman van Speult) requested the candle used for torturing the English so that he could light his pipe at the very point where the candle's wick had fed on English fat. He then passed the candle along to a merchant, who exclaimed, "oh the Tobacco tasts Divinely after it."[29] In Dryden's repugnant image, the Dutch fed their smoking habit with English fat and ingested English drippings with their tobacco. Dryden's depiction evoked the language deployed by the English merchants at Batavia who had scorned the Dutch as "Canniballs."[30]

The two authors likewise demonstrated detailed knowledge of the trial. In Mountfort's play, one character named five of the judges, described the torture, and then recited the English defense against the conspiracy accusations from 1624. His list of weapons precisely matched the information in the EIC's pamphlets.[31] Dryden relied on printed accounts, too, including the *True Relation* and John Darell's *True and Compendious Narration* (1665).[32] His play thus consisted of a recycled story likely also performed with recycled scenery, including a torture rack borrowed from another play, Davanant's *Cruelty of the Spaniards in Peru* (1658).[33] A final detail conveys deep familiarity with the episode—the use of a single word, *schellam*, which appears in both plays. Rarely used in English, schellam had direct associations with Amboyna; it was the insult—rogue, scoundrel—allegedly called out when the condemned men processed to their executions.[34] Mountfort put the word in the mouth of an English character: "o. that Harman van Speult *is een schellam in Zijn Hart*" (Harman van Speult is a scoundrel in his heart).[35] It was not uncommon for English audiences to hear bits of Dutch in plays, which occasionally featured Dutch characters who spoke in broken English, to comic effect. They sometimes also spoke in Dutch.[36] What's unusual about Mountfort's play is that the Dutch was spoken by an actor portraying an English character, without comic intent. It is highly unlikely, then, that Mountfort's choice was accidental or coincidental. Rather, it likely reflected the word's familiarity at the time because of its association with Amboyna, not just in the wake of the 1632 printing of the *Reply to the Remonstrance*, but also earlier, when it circulated in manuscript. Dryden had the Fiscal say the word. He announced that he had devised a plot against the "*Skellum English*."[37]

But for all they shared, Dryden could do what Mountfort could not amid his travails with the Master of the Revels. In 1673, in the throes of war, Dryden had no need to disguise the setting, the alleged villains, or their conduct. Dryden brought the lurid story to life and enabled an audience to see enacted what they may have previously only read or imagined. He turned the Dutch into cannibals and depicted torture on stage. Near the end of the play, a scene opens to show "the English Tortur'd, and the Dutch tormenting them." Soon after this shocking revelation, the Dutch led Beaumont on stage with matches tied to his hands. The intrepid fellow told the Dutch to bring on more torture.[38]

When Beaumont emerged on stage in Dryden's drama, he enacted what had become most memorable about Amboyna by 1674: the torture.[39] Cruelty, symbolized by torture, ultimately trumped ingratitude as the main lesson of Amboyna, but these two lines of interpretation converged during the war years, because war pamphlets continued to emphasize ingratitude. It was a theme central to the reckoning achieved in 1654, and it re-emerged during the two successive conflicts with the Dutch. Only eleven years lapsed after the Treaty of Westminster in 1654 before the Second Anglo-Dutch War broke out; when that war ended, it was only another five years before the start of a third conflict. In each episode, English writers eager to attack the Dutch picked up just where they had left off in 1654, both in reprinting or revising the *True Relation*, under old and new titles, in assimilating Amboyna as the preeminent example even in an expanding collection of Dutch atrocities, and in their heavy reliance on the image of the tortured trader. Authors and compilers showed little creative engagement with the story during the war years; rather, they reproduced the early texts and adapted or copied the original image, thus revealing the important role print culture played in enabling the story to endure. Moreover, these works solidified a single interpretation of the story, all harking back to the 1624 *True Relation*.

Each crisis saw the publication of another version of the *True Relation*, although the work had its last printing under its original title in 1665.[40] None of the wartime pamphlets contained the two supplementary texts (the *True Declaration* and the EIC's *Answer* to it) found in the 1624, 1632, and 1651 editions, and the complete *True Relation*, with the three linked texts, did not return to print until 1745 in a collection of travel narratives, a volume that also contained the 1632 *Remonstrance* and its two accompanying texts.[41] By the Third Anglo-Dutch War, the *True Relation* had a new title, *The Emblem of Ingratitude: or The Hollanders insolencies and cruelties detected* (1672), which had a second printing in the same year as *The Emblem of ingratitude. A true relation of the unjust, cruel, and barbarous proceedings against the English at Amboyna*.[42] The distinguished Yale librarian and bibliographer Donald Goddard Wing attributed this work to "John Beamont, of Amboyna," possibly because a manuscript note on the cover of the Yale library copy credits the work to him.[43] Beaumont was one of the survivors of the 1623 conspiracy trial but sadly not the author of a newly discovered manuscript, since this book was simply a repackaged *True Relation*, with some added material about other examples of bad Dutch behavior.[44]

These gently reworked *True Relations*, along with other pamphlets, continued to emphasize Dutch ingratitude. In 1666, for example, Charles Molloy titled his anti-Dutch work, *Hollands Ingratitude*.[45] One author of a 1665 translation of Grotius's *De Rebus Belgicis* likened the Dutch to "an ungrateful Snake," showing only violence to the English who had nurtured them.[46] In the same year, an author derided the Dutch as a people whose ingratitude was as "abominable" as their profits from fishing illicitly in English waters were large.[47] And of course "Beamont's" work, *The Emblem of Ingratitude*, placed the sentiment right in the title, showing the continued importance of that historical and political dimension of Anglo-Dutch relations during the third war. Ingratitude rested on an asymmetrical relationship, an unpaid debt owed to a patron; it was a moral sentiment, in that it spoke to the offense of not honoring one's obligations, but it was also a political sentiment that pointed to the betrayed loyalty of an underling.[48]

Although the wars produced new grievances to lament, the dominance of Amboyna in anti-Dutch war pamphlets showed that it remained the most enduring injury. Authors like "Beamont" identified new Dutch offenses, especially Dutch aggression in the African trade, but *The Emblem of Ingratitude* still devoted two-thirds of its pages to Amboyna.[49] Pamphleteers likewise revealed their debt to the Amboyna story in frequent invocations of the affair. Some, like Robert Codrington in *His Majesties Propriety* (1665), reproduced almost the complete *True Relation*.[50]

The new images accompanying pamphlets in the second and third wars both reflected the array of offenses ascribed to the Dutch and asserted the primacy of Amboyna. John Darell, a former EIC employee, mentioned the Amboyna incident only briefly in his 1665 work, *A True and Compendious Narration; or (Second Part of Amboyney)*. He focused instead on other acts of VOC violence, especially the sinking of two English ships, the *Katherine* and the *Dragon*. The work's frontispiece, a four-part image, displayed multiple Dutch affronts. Darell added new personnel to the otherwise familiar Amboyna image, showing three praying figures awaiting their execution.[51] But the classic Amboyna image continued to feature prominently. Each new *True Relation* contained an image. The 1665 *True Relation* reproduced the same engraving as the 1651 *True Relation*. *The Emblem of Ingratitude* featured an illustration nearly identical to the 1624 English-language woodcut. Henry Stubbe combined the two main Amboyna images in a diptych spanning two quarto pages in the second of two pamphlets he wrote during the Third Anglo-Dutch War.[52] Stubbe's diptych suggested that it was not possible to integrate all of the themes of Amboyna into one single work: only a two-part illustration could do justice to the lessons English artists and writers hoped to convey.

The conclusion of the third war brought peace between England and the United Provinces that would last for over a century, but that era of amity did not bring an end to the story, because of Amboyna's status as the consummate illustration of cruelty. Both ingratitude and cruelty co-existed, of course; a 1673 book about gypsies, for example, mentioned Amboyna as a story of both Dutch cruelty and ingratitude.[53] And like ingratitude, cruelty had a political dimension. It was an important element of English justifications of their wars of the mid-seventeenth century and was deployed against both the Spanish and the Dutch.[54] The period of the Third Anglo-Dutch War seems to have been an important moment in this transition from ingratitude to cruelty, and Dryden's play may have played a role in the transition, or perhaps simply have reflected a process already under way. The work's full title was *Amboyna, or the Cruelties of the Dutch to the English Merchants*. The emphasis on Amboyna as the epitome of cruelty emerged in some improbable places, including an introduction to a verse adaptation of one of Aesop's fables (The Dog and the Sheep) in 1681.[55]

A book on extreme passions published in 1683 conveyed this crystallized assessment of Amboyna as an illustrative tale of cruelty. A London bookseller and author named Nathaniel Crouch, writing under his pseudonym Robert Burton, or R. B., composed a work titled *Unparalleld Varieties: or, The Matchless Actions and Passions of Mankind* which investigated a range of admirable and malign behaviors. Crouch made a career as something of a "hack writer," in the words of one biographer, who specialized in placing ideas from high culture in the hands of a broad and new audience. *Unparalleld Varieties* demonstrated this process, as it integrated a prodigious array of examples from the classical world with recent injuries such as Amboyna. The incident

Figure 5.1 An array of cruelties by the Dutch, including the Amboyna incident, from a pamphlet during the Second Anglo-Dutch War. J. D., *A True and Compendious Narration; or (Second Part of Amboyney) of Sundry Notorious or Remarkable Injuries, Insolencies, and Acts of Hostility* ... (London, 1665), frontispiece. RB123579, The Huntington Library, San Marino, California.

Figure 5.2 This frontispiece from the 1672 version of the *True Relation* closely followed the model of the 1624 and 1651 illustrations. Note the manuscript caption. [John Beamont], *The Emblem of Ingratitude* (London, 1672), frontispiece. Call # B1580. Used by permission of the Folger Shakespeare Library.

featured in the work's fifth section, where Crouch explored "The Tremendous Consequences of Cowardice, Barbarity, and Treachery," and it was his twenty-first example. It kept company with a variety of tales of deliberate cruelty, following, for example, a discussion of Demetrius of Syria having 800 prisoners in Jerusalem killed in front of their mothers, after which he put

Figure 5.3 The left side of Stubbe's diptych shows a trader enduring the water torture, while the right image combines the two common depictions of the Amboyna episode, one showing the torture and execution sequence, and the other featuring the tortured trader above imprisoned men. Henry Stubbe, *A Further Justification of the Present War against the United Netherlands* (London, 1673), opposite p. 134. RB138352, The Huntington Library, San Marino, California.

the mothers to death. The author recapitulated the version of the Amboyna story as related in a work by the historian William Sanderson in 1656 and he dutifully cited his source. Consistent with his emphasis on cruelty, Crouch lavished attention on the repugnant details of the Amboyna torture.[56]

Crouch's book also contained a new illustration, the first creative reworking of the Amboyna story since 1624. The creator rejected previous images' tight focus on the tortured trader in a chamber that could have been anywhere. Instead, the artist devised a scene that suggests an actual (if imagined) location, with land, sky, sea, and ships. The top third of the image showed the miracles described in the 1624 texts and repeated in Crouch's own brief account: the storm that arose at the time of the execution and allegedly dashed VOC ships and caused some to lose their anchors, and the alleged madness of a Scot who became unhinged at the gravesite of the English. No other

The Cruelties of the Hollanders upon the Englich at Amboyna. Page .207.

K

Figure 5.4 This elaborate illustration showing the alleged acts of divine retribution at Amboyna appeared in R. B., *Unparalleld Varieties: or, The Matchless Actions and Passions of Mankind* (London, 1683), opposite p. 212. AG241.C7 1683 midi Copy 1, Library of Congress. This work was published four times between 1683 and 1724. The 1683 and 1685 editions used this illustration; the 1699 and 1728 editions used a cruder version that occupied only half of the page, but still showed the miracles. A later version of the *True Relation*, Richard Hall, *The History of the Barbarous Cruelties* ([London], 1712), recycled this image.

extant image from before 1683 showed these features. The illustration's caption, moreover, hints at the new assessment of Amboyna: "The Cruelties of the Hollanders upon the English at Amboyna."[57]

It was no accident that a study of cruelty produced this innovative image, because this defining attribute was becoming Amboyna's new legacy. Further evidence for this new interpretation appears in an unlikely set of sources: library catalogues. Printers produced such catalogues for a variety of purposes: sometimes owners wanted published catalogues of their private libraries, but more often they were sales catalogues, in which a bookseller might list the contents of private libraries just acquired for auction, or simply those works available for purchase at his establishment. Some circulating libraries also had published catalogues.[58] Out of 71 of the 1624, 1632, 1651, and 1665 *True Relations* identified in 119 different sales and library catalogues between 1664 and 1800, cataloguers retitled 47 with cruelty, and 9 with a variant of barbarous. Almost 60 times, that is, in a pattern evident from the 1680s, people charged with creating a catalogue for a private library, an auction, or a circulating library looked at a volume titled *A True Relation of the unjust, cruell, and barbarous proceedings against the English at Amboyna by the Netherlandish Govornour and Councel there* (1624, 1632, 1651, 1665) and renamed it.[59] The pattern persisted with *True Relations* published under different titles, such as *The Emblem of Ingratitude*.[60]

These catalogues suggest that the association of Amboyna with cruelty expanded over the course of the eighteenth century. Searchable seventeenth-century library catalogues are few in number, but they indicate that Amboyna works were still catalogued by their actual titles. Between 1664 and 1700, less than half (42 percent) of likely copies of the *True Relation* were retitled to emphasize cruelty or barbarity. The Massachusetts cleric Increase Mather, for example, owned a quarto described as "Relation of Proceedings of Dutch at Amboyna," according to his 1664 catalogue. This work was presumably a *True Relation* from 1624 or 1632.[61] Late-seventeenth-century catalogues suggest the transition to cruelty.[62] The diarist and naval officer Samuel Pepys acquired a 1651 *True Relation* sometime after 1700 and called it "Barbaritys of the Dutch towards the English at Amboyna."[63] By the middle of the eighteenth century, cataloguers described 80 percent to 90 percent of Amboyna pamphlets in this way, as books about barbarity or cruelty.

This short-circuit—in which what the hands held, the eyes saw, and the brain processed consistently produced a title used by none of the books— conveyed a universal understanding of what the point of these Amboyna texts was. Even works that were not solely about Amboyna shared a similar fate. Cataloguers consistently described Henry Stubbe's two pamphlets from the Third Anglo-Dutch War, *A Justification of the Present War against the United Netherlands* (1672) and *A Further Justification of the Present War* (1673), as a variation along the lines of "Stubbes' Justification and cruelties of the Dutch at Amboyna," despite the fact that neither book had the word cruel nor cruelty in its title, nor even Amboyna; in fact, the 1672 volume's subtitle lamented continued Dutch ingratitude, and the 1673 volume had no subtitle at all.[64] In many cases, this generic title makes it difficult to figure out which book a given catalogue cites, surely undermining the basic point of creating such a record.[65]

With the defining attribute of cruelty, the Amboyna story acquired resonance beyond specific EIC or English grievances, beyond warfare, beyond an international incident, and potentially beyond the Dutch. Several examples attest to Amboyna's utility as a general metaphor for cruelty between the mid-seventeenth and late eighteenth centuries. A massive compendium published in 1668 about those who suffered for the Protestant faith contained a description of an Englishman whose servants endured "*Amboyna* Cruelties in *Chancery-lane*," when English officials coerced them to reveal information about their employer and his goods.[66] In 1673, an author used Amboyna as Crouch did ten years later, as an illustration of "the Barbarous and Savage cruelty of some men."[67] Accusations of Amboyna-like cruelties targeted the British themselves for their actions in Bengal in 1772.[68] In 1782, Americans compared the vicious behavior of the king's army in the United States during the Revolutionary War to the cruelty seen at Amboyna or Calcutta, presumably invoking the Black Hole (an incident in which some British prisoners suffocated in close quarters in 1756) and turning the British into perpetrators, not victims, of violence in colonial settings.[69] Another American, Jedidiah Morse, invoked the Amboyna massacre and other examples of European cruelty to make a statement in 1791 about universal human attributes: he argued that *all* people have the capacity for cruelty.[70]

These many uses of Amboyna as a metaphor for universal cruelty committed by a wide array of people, including the British, suggested that the tale of the Amboyna massacre had transcended its origins during this era of peace with the Dutch, but that was not in fact the case. As all of the library catalogue descriptions made clear, Amboyna's defining feature was the cruelty of the Dutch, and it was that dimension of the story that gave Amboyna continued political resonance in British politics. Between 1688 and 1713, British political writers deployed the story to critique internal opponents, and they did so in two moments of crisis, the so-called Glorious Revolution of 1688, when the English deposed James II and invited William of Orange and his wife, Mary, James's oldest daughter, to rule in his place; and the struggle to bring an end to British participation in the War of the Spanish Succession (1701–14), a European conflict sparked by disputes about who should acquire the Spanish throne. Authors resurrected and reapplied the original Amboyna texts in new settings. The story maintained its core features, but new applications revealed a paradigm shift, because it turned out that the cruelty of the Dutch was a convenient way to indict the conduct of some English, too. In each moment, Tories—first as supporters of the Stuart monarchy, and then as opponents of continued involvement in the war—returned to the printed accounts of Amboyna to critique their political opponents. They deployed the violence and cruelty at Amboyna to define the values they ascribed not just to the Dutch, but also to fellow Britons, Whigs.

The upheaval of 1688 marked both the sudden end of James II's reign and the return of the *True Relation* as a discrete text for the first time since 1672. James had been on the throne for only three years, but he had failed to secure enough support and his religious faith concerned those troubled by a Catholic head of the Church of England.[71] As early as the 1670s a Whig interest had developed among those opposed to his future ascension to the throne. Their opponents, Tories, were willing to accept James as their monarch. The Amboyna story turned out to be a helpful way for Tories to indict Whigs, becoming a proxy for domestic conflict, and especially so when William and Mary invaded England in 1688. Elkanah Settle composed a new *True Relation* to make the Tory case. An English playwright and poet who had initially been a man of strong Whig convictions, he experienced a change of heart after 1682 and became an advocate of the Tory position and James II's right to the throne.[72] William and Mary's invasion inspired Settle to publish *Insignia Bataviae: or, the Dutch Trophies Display'd; Being Exact Relations of the Unjust, Horrid, and most Barbarous Proceedings of the Dutch Against the English in the East-Indies* in 1688.[73] Based on the text in *The Emblem of Ingratitude*, the *Insignia* invited the reader to ponder the violence the Dutch had used to seize control at Amboyna and to imagine the greater horror they would visit on England.[74] It was obvious whom Settle regarded as despotic: not the Catholics dreaded by the Whigs, but the Protestant Dutch opposed by the Tories. Settle included the essential engraving of a tortured trader, but his version offered one key embellishment that showed

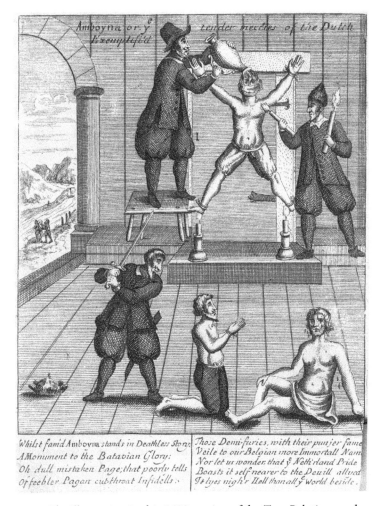

Figure 5.5 The illustration in this 1688 version of the *True Relation* was larger than the book it accompanied and had to be sewn in, with a bottom flap folded up. The crown on the floor next to the kneeling man facing execution was an important addition to the iconic depiction of the tortured trader. Elkanah Settle, *Insignia Bataviae* (London, 1688), frontispiece. RB 16176, The Huntington Library, San Marino, California.

the Amboyna incident's application to these new political circumstances. He placed a crown on the ground by the kneeling trader. This cast-aside crown, next to a man kneeling beneath his executioner, could only refer to the deposed monarch, James II.

Settle's decision to put the Amboyna story to work to discredit his Whig opponents and their support for what he regarded as a Dutch invasion established a pattern that Tories emulated vigorously during the War of the Spanish Succession, when Amboyna served a Tory campaign to end British involvement with the conflict. The war did not conclude until a series of treaties in 1713 and 1714, though discussions about the peace commenced in 1706. In 1709, preliminary peace negotiations had failed, and that disappointment increased British hostility to the Dutch. The English and Dutch were allies in the war, so the appearance of the Amboyna pamphlets seems unexpected if one does not appreciate the British political context in which the Dutch were a proxy for the Whigs. Tory animosity for the Dutch had increased during the final years of William's reign (he died in 1702), amid concerns that William placed Dutch interests above those of the English after the death of Mary in 1694. Anti-Dutch sentiments were also furthered by the 1709 Barrier Treaty, which committed the English to guaranteeing a barrier of Dutch garrisons that would protect the Dutch from French aggression. The Dutch in turn committed to a Protestant succession in England via the Hanovers, the first of whom came to the throne after the death of Queen Anne in 1714. The treaty obligated both parties to continue the war just when much of the English public had turned against it.[75] The Whigs pressed to keep fighting, but in 1710, the Whigs lost control of the House of Commons, and the new government wanted to push for peace. Tories pursued a public campaign, launched with a pamphlet, *The Conduct of the Allies* (1711), published anonymously by Jonathan Swift.[76] A flurry of pamphlets between 1711 and 1713 disputed the nature and value of the alliance and the character of the Dutch, and thus emphasized a new aspect of the old Amboyna tale, the VOC's betrayal of the 1619 treaty in its usurpation of authority over the English traders.

Amboyna was an important element of several of these works. Eleven Tory pamphlets mentioned Amboyna. Some authors did so only in passing, invoking Amboyna as a shorthand reminder of Dutch treachery.[77] These authors suggested, for example, that the English might have to fear a "second *Amboyna* reward," or confront "Merchants *A la Mode Amboina*."[78] One pamphleteer believed that Amboyna was the most important example of Dutch ingratitude, an incident that "ought to be Printed in deep Characters in the Hearts of all True *English* Men."[79] *The Examiner*, which Jonathan Swift edited, investigated the subject of Dutch ingratitude weekly.[80] But Amboyna also took pride of place in several pamphlets, a reflection of the continued familiarity and accessibility of the 1620s texts. Amboyna adorned titles and title pages. The full title of *The Dutch won't let us have Dunkirk* (one of the barrier towns) continued *And the reasons why those that Massacred the English at Amboyna, so Malitiously and Barbarously; Thwart the General Peace of Europe, and the Advantage and Welfair of Great Britain at this Time.* Beyond its prominent place on the title page, Amboyna appeared many times in the pamphlet and served as the main evidence that the Dutch were treacherous, preferring to massacre the English again rather than let them have Dunkirk.[81]

Three reprints of earlier works and three modestly reworked images attested to the applicability of Amboyna during this political crisis almost ninety years after the original episode. Writers reprised the strategies of the pamphlets of the first three Anglo-Dutch wars, but with different targets (British Whigs, not the Dutch) and aims (peace, not war). Like Settle, they had little new to say about Amboyna and simply wanted to use the familiar story to illustrate the unreliability of the Dutch as allies and the treachery of the Whigs who supported them. The use of Amboyna in this conflict—to sever an Anglo-Dutch alliance—echoed the Habsburg scheme to deploy Amboyna to the same effect almost a century earlier by sponsoring the publication of the *True Relation* at St. Omer in 1624 and a newssheet and likewise emphasizing the theme of Dutch treachery.

The 1624 *True Relation* made a comeback in two pamphlets. One work, *Dutch Alliances: or, a Plain Proof of their Observance of Treaties* (1712), professed to be a recently discovered manuscript by John Beaumont, the same survivor credited with the authorship of *The Emblem of Ingratitude* in 1672. Although the title page asserted that this manuscript was "never before printed," in fact the text recapitulated the 1624 *True Relation.* In a statement revealing how removed the incident was from its origins as a conspiracy, the author deliberately omitted the list of the Japanese who were executed, because, he explained, "To mention the Names of the *Japanese,* will be needless."[82] *Dutch Alliances* also had two illustrations, both adaptations of earlier Amboyna images. The second reworking of the *True Relation* was Richard Hall's *The History of the Barbarous Cruelties and Massacres, Committed by the Dutch in the East-Indies* (1712), which primarily consisted of a complete *True Relation* intercut with the VOC trial record, something originally published in the 1632 *Authentick Copy,* but which had not been reprinted since that year. Hall clearly had a copy of this book, and he used it to create what he may have thought was a more sensible narrative, explaining this decision as an effort to show his fairness to the Dutch—although, he added, anyone could see that these were false confessions extracted through torture. Hall's pamphlet also reproduced Crouch's image with a new caption.[83]

But these Tory Amboyna pamphlets emphasized a different aspect of the Amboyna episode, the alleged violations of the 1619 treaty, to warn people about the perils of any agreement with the Dutch. *Dutch Alliances* even put the issue right in the title. Just as the Dutch had violated the 1619 treaty, so too would they sabotage the English in this later accord. A 1712 publication, *The History of the Dutch Usurpations*, was essentially a reprint of a 1672 work, *The Dutch Usurpation*, but it enhanced the Amboyna elements by placing Amboyna in the title, in contrast to the 1672 original, and also flagged the issue of Dutch behavior in treaties. The full title in 1712 featured cruelty, ingratitude, and treachery all together. It continued, *Their Maxims and*

Figure 5.6 Frontispiece and illustration from John Beaumont, *Dutch Alliances, or, A Plain Proof of their Observance of Treaties* (London, 1712). College Pamphlets 910.1, General Collection, Beinecke Rare Book and Manuscript Library, Yale University.

Politicks in Point of Government, and their remarkable ingratitude to England. Particularly their unheard of Cruelties at Amboyna, and the Debates theron in the English Council, in the Reign of King James I. With their usual Method of managing Treaties.[84]

Whig pamphleteers who responded to this collection of Tory books made scant reference to Amboyna, since it served them so poorly in their attack on the Tory position, but two authors addressed it explicitly. One reprised the *True Declaration*, the VOC account of what had transpired at Amboyna, which had not been printed in English in England since 1651.[85] Thus the two works, the *True Relation* and the *True Declaration*, were back in conversation in 1712 as they had been in 1624 and again during the First Anglo-Dutch War in the 1650s. In *The Dutch Better Friends than the French*, the author confronted the incident head-on as he worked his way systematically and relatively even-handedly through different objections made to the Dutch. He dismissed the incident, both in his word choice—it happened to "some *Englishmen*" (whose number he reduced by half) on a "little Island" far distant from Britain—and in his questioning the certainty of their innocence. Even if the English had been wrongly executed, he argued that the incident had transpired almost a century ago, and vengeance could not be exacted on subsequent generations.[86]

This surge of publications connected to Amboyna at such a remove from the original incident shows some key themes that are central to understanding its longevity: the continued assumption by authors that readers were familiar with the episode not only in general but also in its particular details; the enduring utility of the original texts; the continued complexity and urgency of Anglo-Dutch relations; and the power of the image. As Swift's pamphlet showed, Tories and Whigs didn't have to talk about Amboyna in their pamphlets: that so many authors found it useful shows the episode's entrenchment as a cultural touchstone.

In the ensuing decades, Amboyna was everywhere. Not a decade passed without a casual reference in a novel, a poem, a joke, rhymes of dubious merit (such as Amboyna/joina), essays, and histories.[87] A quirky essay about reincarnation epitomized the broad utility and ubiquity of the story. An author of a 1756 article found he could not enjoy lobster without being haunted by the possibility that people were reincarnated as animals. Then, however, he imagined that perhaps the lobsters had once been Dutch people at Amboyna, and he was able to set aside his distress at seeing the poor creatures boiled alive and ate up enthusiastically.[88]

Passing invocations of Amboyna in popular literary works of the eighteenth century indicated authors' assumptions that their readers knew exactly what the place name signaled. Between 1719 and 1726, Amboyna appeared in novels by Jonathan Swift and Daniel Defoe.[89] Defoe and Swift were highly invested in the Whig and Tory pamphlet disputes of the early eighteenth century, and Amboyna, of course, was familiar to them. But they assumed that their readers knew what the word meant, too, because they did not coddle them with much explanation. In each instance, the word served a clear purpose, as an emotional shorthand to evoke a sympathetic response in the reader and to inspire a deeper understanding of the predicament and sensibility of the novel's hero. In Defoe's *The Life, Adventures, and Pyracies, of the Famous Captain Singleton* (1720), the pirate protagonist sailed to the Spice Islands. He captured a Dutch ship heading for Amboyna, but then found he could barely prevent his crew from murdering the captured crew, "as soon as they heard them say, they belonged to *Amboyna*, the Reason I suppose any one will guess."[90] Defoe evoked Amboyna more vividly in *The Farther Adventures of Robinson Crusoe* (1719). At one point on his travels, Crusoe acquired a ship that turned out to have been stolen and had been used by pirates. He was terrified he might be mistaken for a pirate himself, and fear, "that blind useless Passion," gripped him, wreaking havoc on his imagination. On restless nights when dreams arrived they proved to be nightmares of gibbets and death. This disabling anxiety prompted thoughts of Amboyna, amid his terror that the Dutch would seize the vessel. He dreaded the tortures that would make him confess, and then an execution, "with a formal Appearance of Justice; and that they might be tempted to do this, for the Gain of our Ship and Cargo." Crusoe's horror conjured all that the English had come to believe about Amboyna, distilled in three elements: the torture compelling men to make false confessions; the execution after an illicit trial; and, finally, the Dutch plot to steal English goods—a motive revealed.[91] Swift offered the least explanation of all. In *Gulliver's Travels* (1726), Lemuel Gulliver, disguised as a shipwrecked Dutch merchant, sought his way home from Luggnagg and did so via Japan. The discreet Gulliver secured a ship at Nagasaki called the *Amboyna*. Swift—and Gulliver—said nothing further about the significance of the name, but it was hardly accidental and it sufficed to convey to a reader that Gulliver found himself in a vulnerable and dangerous position.[92]

Defoe and Swift published their famous works a century after the Amboyna incident, in the wake of the familiarity possibly enhanced during the War of the Spanish Succession. But the story continued to have salience beyond this era. It appeared in the novel *Chrysal: or, the Adventures of a Guinea*, by Charles Johnstone, an Irish author, once again in a context that assumed a reader's knowledge. Published in 1760, *Chrysal* was one of the bestsellers of that era, going through twenty-four editions in the eighteenth century alone, and five editions just in the period from 1760 to 1763.[93] The book is told from the point of view of a guinea coin as it passed from owner to owner, and its style of digressions and detail and its nods to contemporary fashions and people were popular in its time. It was one of fifty-nine such works (it-narratives, or novels of circulation) published before 1800, told from the point of view of objects as different as a rupee and a hackney coach.[94] *Chrysal* encompassed everything about its particular historical moment, and in this historical moment, people knew of Amboyna. The reference appears in a conversation in The Hague between the guinea's current owner, a Jew named Aminadab, and a Dutchman named Van Hogen, a play on the title for members of the States General, *hooge en mogende herren* (high and mighty lords) and also on a derisive name the English used for the Dutch at the time, Hogen Mogen. Van Hogen complained about the current predations of English pirates blockading Dutch ports and proposed it was time for "*another AMBOYNA affair*" to give the Dutch both satisfaction and revenge, repeating the interpretation also advanced in *Robinson Crusoe* that Amboyna was a deliberate plot by the Dutch. Neither character bothered to explain what or where Amboyna was, indicating that Johnstone assumed his reader already had all the necessary knowledge of the incident and what it communicated about the character of the Dutch (although he did help his reader by locating the incident in the 1620s).[95]

Defoe, Swift, and Johnstone could safely assume their readers knew what they intended to convey with each Amboyna reference because a well-read person of the eighteenth century had many opportunities to learn about the incident. A spate of publications in the mid-1740s enabled English readers to draw on newly accessible Amboyna texts. The original pamphlets of 1624 (the complete *True Relation*) and 1632 (the complete *Remonstrance*) were reproduced in their entirety in 1745 in *A Collection of Voyages and Travels . . . From the curious and valuable library of the late Earl of Oxford*.[96] A travel account, *A Voyage to the South-Seas* (1745), included a brief version of the *True Relation* in its appendix; and a new edition of John Harris's *Navigantium* (or *Voyages*) (1744–48), a collection of travel accounts, reproduced the *True Relation* and its companion pamphlets from 1624 along with a new engraving.[97] Harris's work had originally been published in 1705, but the 1740s edition was the first to contain an Amboyna illustration.

Part of the process of Amboyna's domestication was its diffusion in printed works around the Anglophone world. The personal libraries of readers as distant from Britain as Virginia, Jamaica, and India reveal just how easily far-flung British subjects could get access to works that mentioned Amboyna, whether in passing or at length. Thomas Jefferson had an extensive and well-documented library at his home in Virginia, and he possessed a variety of books that touched on the incident.[98] He owned histories by David Hume and Catharine Macaulay. Both historians used Amboyna to illustrate the deficiencies of the early Stuarts, with Hume rebuking James I for failing to get satisfaction at the time for the Amboyna affair, and Macaulay arguing that the failure continued after the 1654 treaty.[99] In 1771, Jefferson compiled a list of books appropriate for a private library: four of the items had Amboyna content—Hume's history, Dryden's collected works (including the play, *Amboyna*), Swift's works (including *Gulliver*), and the novel *Chrysal*, which he misattributed to Smollet.[100] His contemporary, Thomas Thistlewood, an overseer and planter in Jamaica between 1750 and 1786, was also an avid reader. He, too, owned *Chrysal*, and Harris's *Voyages*; the *Harleian Miscellany*, which contained a reprint of De Britaine's *Dutch Usurpation* (1672); two Chronologies (a genre of history, structured by date) that listed Amboyna; and a collection of Swift's works, including *Gulliver's Travels*. Moreover, Thistlewood had at least two Amboyna engravings to ponder from his Jamaican perch, assuming no one had cut them out of his books.[101] Readers in Calcutta in the same period had access to at least two copies of Harris's *Voyages* and eight of Hume's *History* and could have learned about the incident from those works, if it weren't already part of the folklore connected to the EIC and the Calcutta community.[102] The contents of these dispersed libraries suggest that it is hard to envision an educated person in the eighteenth-century Anglophone world who did not know the story, given its sometimes lengthy appearance in the major histories of the era, Dryden's play (a staple in lending libraries), and the brief references in *Gulliver's Travels*, *Chrysal*, *The Life of Captain Singleton*, and *Farther Adventures of Robinson Crusoe*.

This widespread familiarity established a crucial context for the final eruptions of Amboyna-related pamphlets in the final decades of the eighteenth century. In each instance, the story shifted back to the Dutch, away from internal British political rivals. The Amboyna story proved to be supple,

The Torments inflicted by the Dutch on the English in Amboyna.

The condition of the English in the Dungeon & their Execution.

Figure 5.7 This engraving followed the trend established by Stubbe in 1673 (see Figure 5.3) and replicated in *Dutch Alliances* in 1712 (Figure 5.6) in showing two separate aspects of the Amboyna scene. It was frequently reproduced in the eighteenth century. John Harris, *Navigantium atque bibliotheca; or, A complete collection of voyages and travels* (London, 1744–48), vol. 1, opposite p. 879. Call # G160.H3 Cage. Used by permission of the Folger Shakespeare Library.

something writers deployed to make critiques of both English opponents and Dutch allies.

Two eruptions (one a minor flare-up featuring only a reprint, and the second an extended, months-long episode featuring two reworked 1624 pamphlets) took place in the context of the Seven Years' War, during which the Dutch were neutral, a continuation of the peace secured in 1674. In the first episode in 1759, the precipitating spark came from Bengal. After the alleged horror of the Black Hole in 1756 and the Battle of Plassey in 1757 (a key victory by the EIC over the French and the nawab of Bengal), the English had replaced the nawab, Siraj-ud-Daulah, with a man more to their liking, Mir Jafar. But Jafar chafed at British authority and realized that he had a potential ally in the Dutch, who had a VOC factory at Chinsura and resented British regulation of shipping on the Ganges. Encouraged by Jafar, the Dutch planned to gather enough troops from the East Indies to enable them to frustrate British actions. Robert Clive, an EIC administrator and soldier who became a national hero, learned of this plan and ordered the Dutch forces attacked and destroyed in 1759. At the end of his lengthy account of this conflict, Clive compared the incident to Amboyna and argued that had the Dutch won the day, the English would soon have forgotten all about Amboyna in light of the envisioned later tragedy—just the kind of warning Settle had offered his countrymen in 1688.[103]

News of Clive's victory over the Dutch inspired an anonymous author to call this incident "a sequel to the Tragedy of Amboyna," an episode that showed that the Dutch had sought "to commit another Amboyna act upon Calcutta" through this plot.[104] Amboyna aficionados keeping track would have realized that this was at least the third sequel to Amboyna. Like the original event, all such sequels took place outside Europe: the second part of Amboyna that had transpired in New England in 1653, and the "Second Part of Amboyney" (the sinking of two ships, the Katherine and the Dragon in the East Indies) that John Darell described in his True and Compendious Narration (1665). These texts signaled what had become thoroughly internalized by the time of this third sequel in 1759—that beyond Europe, British traders and travelers had to be especially vigilant against Dutch deception and cruelty.

So obvious in Britain was the connection between the 1759 incident in Bengal and the Amboyna episode that a periodical called the Universal Magazine of Pleasure and Knowledge reprinted the 1624 True Relation along with parts of the Answer to the True Declaration (essentially an abridged version of the account in Harris's *Voyages*) in the wake of the incident. The text was retitled, as had become the norm by that period, "The History of the Cruelties exercised by the Dutch on the English at Amboyna." The periodical also reproduced the engraving in Harris's *Voyages*. The introduction to the account linked the incident in India to the ongoing global conflict of the Seven Years' War. It explained how Dutch neutrality looked more like support for an enemy. The author accused the Dutch of shirking their responsibilities and supporting Britain's enemies through trade and provisioning, despite the sacrifices the British had made on behalf of the Dutch especially during William's reign—an updated version of the accusations of ingratitude levied by the English against the Dutch in the early seventeenth century.[105]

This context of British frustration with Dutch neutrality during the Seven Years' War and the atmosphere engendered by the episode in 1759 might help explain another eruption of Amboyna publications in 1767, when the incident reappeared with the reproduction of two of the 1624 texts, reformulated in thirty letters published between February and August in the *Public Advertiser* by a correspondent who dubbed himself Gabriel Touwerson.[106] The author claimed descent from the executed EIC head trader Gabriel Towerson. This *nom de plume* was consistent with a publishing practice in which authors asserted authority by direct connection to the episode, as had been the case in the 1672 and 1712 pamphlets allegedly written by Beaumont. Authors gestured toward memory by inventing fictitious authors with personal knowledge of the episode, but the print culture of the seventeenth century in fact formed the basis of the memory.

The Touwerson letters appeared at another moment of official English and Dutch neutrality, but there were continued strains, especially over commerce and fishing. Benjamin Franklin invoked Amboyna in a piece he wrote while he was in London, published in the *London Chronicle* in 1767, that reflected on tensions with multiple constituencies in that year—the Dutch, the Portuguese, and the American colonies, although Franklin derided all the conflicts as molehills turned into mountains.[107] The author of one anti-Dutch text believed that the new administration of William Pitt the Elder in the 1760s offered the possibility that the government might even act on these anti-Dutch sentiments, thus inspiring this eruption of anti-Dutch letters in which Amboyna played its familiar and essential role.[108]

The circumstances that occasioned Touwerson's letters ostensibly had nothing to do with Amboyna or the East Indies. Instead, it all began with a book published in 1766, *The Dutch Displayed; or, a Succinct Account of the*

Barbarities, Rapines and Injustices, committed by the subjects of Holland upon those of England.[109] The work concerned a legal case launched seventy years earlier by an Englishman in the Dutch colony of Suriname named Jeronimy Clifford. The thrust of the book was that the Dutch had been unfair in their treatment of Clifford. The first eight pages of the sixty-eight-page pamphlet consisted of an abridged *True Relation*, and the first third of the pamphlet developed other aspects of the Amboyna incident. The author argued that the Amboyna episode was an early example of Dutch cruelty, the worst instance one could imagine, and that Dutch treatment of Clifford was consistent with that history of violence, which the author proceeded to trace from Amboyna in 1623 through the Bengal episode in 1759 up to the alleged violations of neutrality during the recent war. The book even featured an illustration of the Amboyna tortures, the only illustration in the entire work and powerful evidence of how Amboyna had come to signify all negative associations with the Dutch. It was based on the 1744 engraving in Harris's *Voyages*, an image that had just been reproduced in the *Universal Magazine* in 1760, then reworked in 1766 for the *Dutch Displayed* before appearing in yet another travel compilation in 1767.[110] The work inspired two other pamphlets, one replying to the *Dutch Displayed*, titled *A Short and Modest Reply*, and then a second that responded to the *Reply*.[111]

Touwerson was agitated by the *Short and Modest Reply*. In the course of coming to the "Displayer's" defense, he started with Amboyna. His thirty letters followed a formula. The author reached back to two texts published in 1624, but he did not reproduce the text almost every other Amboyna pamphlet did, the 1624 *True Relation*. Instead, he reproduced the English translation of the VOC account, the *True Declaration*, and then the EIC's reply to it, *An Answer unto the Dutch Pamphlet*. Touwerson did something innovative, repackaging the pamphlets in the same way that Hall had done in his 1712 *History of the Barbarous Cruelties*. His letters had three parts. First, each contained an excerpt from the *True Declaration*. Then he added the relevant excerpt from *An Answer*, responding to that specific issue. Finally, he summed everything up in his own voice, explaining that the situation was similar in Suriname, and so the reader could understand the terrible plight of Clifford.

As Touwerson's letters indicate, eighteenth-century British authors did not simply reproduce the early texts but engaged with the original works in new ways, reorganizing the information they contained but always making the same timeless and familiar point about Dutch cruelty and perfidy.

Occasionally, however, the times called for a *True Relation*, not a cut-and-paste pastiche. The original text made a twelfth and final appearance as a bespoke political tract during the Fourth Anglo-Dutch War (1780–84). The main provocation in this conflict as far as the British were concerned was Dutch neutrality. Just as had been the case in the Seven Years' War, the British objected to Dutch trade with Britain's enemies during the American War of Independence. Relations had deteriorated since 1778, and Britain declared war in 1780.[112] Fighting ensued in the West Indies, the East Indies, Europe, and the Cape Colony. It had become evident that any tension with the Dutch required a *True Relation*, and a final version came off the press in 1781: *The Cries of British Blood, or, An authentic narrative of the horrid massacre of the English by the Dutch at Amboyna* . . . The text followed the distillations of the eighteenth-century version as seen in Harris's 1744 *Voyages*, and the pamphlet also featured an engraved frontispiece that largely followed the Harris template.[113]

The pamphlet had two intertwined goals. First, it sought to persuade readers that the Amboyna incident remained unrevenged. The money the VOC had paid in 1654 was insufficient to match English losses, and the cruelty of the Dutch was especially egregious in light of all the Dutch owed the English. That was a familiar argument about ingratitude, offered in an over-wrought introduction that preceded the *True Relation*. The second purpose of the work was to prod the British to seize the territory the Dutch held in the Indian Ocean, starting with the Cape Colony and reaching all the way to the Dutch East Indies. To that end, the pamphlet provided brief ethnographic descriptions of places ranging from Banten to Banda, with pithy remarks about how much the people of each locale loathed the Dutch. The ambition was premature, as it wasn't until the wars of the revolutionary and Napoleonic eras that the British seized some of these places, but the author's connection between the "Amboyna Massacre" and future territorial conquests at the expense of the Dutch showed the fusion of a long-past injury with imagined future territorial ambitions. The author of the *Dutch Displayed* had made a similar pitch a few years earlier, proposing that the British take the opportunity of multiple tensions with the Dutch in the 1760s to return the ruler of Banten (in exile in Bengal at the time) to his throne and thus restore the British to their trading post there, too.[114]

Although the pamphlet echoed familiar themes, its invocation of blood and its call for revenge revealed that the Amboyna episode had become the stuff of legend. Legends feature violent death, often at a distance; inadequate

The Cruelties Inflicted on the English at Amboyna.

Published as the Act directs for T Lovewell, Stationer,

Nº 158, St John Street, Clerkenwell.

Figure 5.8 *The Cries of British Blood* (London, 1781), frontispiece. Call number 9913 c4. This image is reproduced courtesy of the National Library of Ireland.

or nonexistent compensation; and a demand for revenge.[115] All of these qualities had become core elements of how the British made sense of the incident during the 160 years since the executions, and they converged in this final *True Relation* in 1781. First, the emergence of Amboyna as a story of cruelty, not just ingratitude, cemented the importance of violent death as the key lesson of the incident. The three Amboyna sequels that took place far from Europe signaled the centrality of remote locations as part of English associations with the episode. Second, the English had long complained

about inadequate compensation, an injury that intersected with calls for revenge. Those promoting war with the United Provinces in 1665 and again in
1672 had made just that complaint about the settlement of 1654 to prod their
countrymen to war. The 1665 *True Relation* even featured a new poem, un-
derneath its engraved frontispiece, which described the torment the traders
endured and called for vengeance. Animosity may even have intensified, despite the financial settlement. George Downing wrote two discourses about
affairs with the United Provinces, in 1664 and 1672. He added material to the
later version about Amboyna, suggesting his perception that the unavenged
injury had grown in importance and offense.[116] Despite the century of peace
inaugurated by the 1674 treaty, feelings of injustice lingered, and English
writers regularly cast blame on the Dutch for the English inability to move
beyond the incident. In 1730, for example, an article in the *Boston Gazette*
maintained that the Dutch had refused to accept any responsibility for bad
conduct at Amboyna. In 1766, an author insisted that the English would
have been able to forget Amboyna were it not for the fact that the Dutch kept
acting in such hostile and greedy ways.[117] These lingering injuries fostered
enthusiasm for revenge, action demonstrated as early as 1631 in the attack by
English soldiers on the continent, and the third vital element of the legend.
Blood had been a hallmark of the Amboyna incident since 1624, when
"bloody" emerged as the indispensable adjective to describe the episode.
Drops of blood, in expensive red ink, had adorned most of the woodcuts in
the 1632 *True Relation*. But in the 1781 text, as the author explained, "the
blood of our ancestors cries aloud for vengeance to this present day."[118]
Legends insinuate themselves into national histories, and Amboyna had
done just that, a process evident by the end of the eighteenth century in the
multiple genres in which authors repeated and embellished the story of the
massacre or simply invoked the place name that all on its own had come to
stand in for everything that the English believed about the cruel violence and
treachery that happened there.

   The Cries of British Blood concluded a long era that had begun with the
EIC's publications in 1624. The book marked a final eruption, the last *True
Relation* reworked as a distinct and unique pamphlet published for political
purposes, although still with the same basic text, still focused on the Dutch,
and still with the essential illustration of the tortured trader. The original text
and the iconic image had been repurposed multiple times to target the Dutch
during wartime and English political rivals at times of Anglo-Dutch alliance.
All the while the tale of cruelty had taken on a life of its own, insinuating itself

into English culture, as comedy, as tragedy, and as a shorthand to convey a long Anglo-Dutch relationship. The recourse to Amboyna as a constant and chronic way to reflect on Dutch relations suggests an almost atavistic instinct in an era when Britons were otherwise and more obviously consumed by the nation's relationship with France.[119] In the centuries to come, the tale of the Amboyna massacre became a touchstone of a different sort, one that spoke not just to an old European past but also to Britain's increasing engagement with the world. The Amboyna Massacre then became a story of empire, the context in which the incident had first emerged but which authors had found of little salience in the first 150 years since it took place.

6

Legacies

Reinvention and the Linchpin of Empire

"Hicksey!" The call reached the Australian prisoner-of-war Walter Hicks as he served on a work patrol to clear an overgrown sports field on Ambon Island. Hicks had sailed to Ambon as a member of the 2/21st Battalion, which had been dispatched to help defend the island and other positions in the Dutch East Indies from Japanese attack. The Australians were among 4,500 troops stationed on Ambon, but it was not enough to repel the Japanese invaders, and Hicks had been imprisoned by the Japanese along with surviving members of his battalion since February 1942. The cry came from a mate who was working to remove a memorial stone to Englishmen who had been massacred in 1623, and he summoned Hicks to take a look. Hicks, who described himself as a history lover, remembered the incident well from his education in Melbourne, and when he had first learned he would be part of this Ambon occupation force, he recalled the island's history in some detail. In an interview in 2003, Hicksey explained that the story of the massacre stuck in his head. Some dates do, he remarked, like 55 BC, or 1066, or August 4, 1914, all iconic symbols of a British-oriented education, but for him, the memorable date was 1623. That, he told his interviewer, was the year that the Dutch had massacred a British garrison in Ambon.[1]

However removed that version of the story was from what had transpired in Amboyna in 1623, there was nothing wrong with Walter Hicks's memory. His account was perfectly consistent with the history of the Amboyna incident as it had developed over the course of the centuries. By the twentieth century, when Hicks learned his history, the tale of the Amboyna massacre had changed in two important ways from the EIC's creation of it in 1624. First, it had been reinvented as a slaughter, becoming a different type of violent act from the legal procedure and executions in 1623. Second, it had been restored both to a history of the British Empire and to a real geographic location, a real island, where, historians had come to argue, a massacre had transpired that explained the ultimate configuration of the British Empire. The

Japanese had long since disappeared from the British version of the story. Had Hicks learned about their original alliance with the English in the alleged 1623 conspiracy, he might well have pondered his wartime predicament with a sense of irony, that 300 years after the original incident it was now the English and Dutch who were allies, and the Japanese who had become the enemy.

Hicks's version of the Amboyna massacre, remote from the actual events of 1623, emerged from a process simultaneous with the repetition of the story during its first 170 years: reinvention. It's surprising that reinvention could happen in light of the constant replication of the original texts, but it turned out that what all of the eighteenth-century readers and writers had come to understand about Amboyna, and especially about the event as a massacre, was different from what the English East India Company had worked so hard to describe in 1624. The core lessons were the same—Dutch cruelty and treachery—but the legal trial and judicial executions had been transformed into a slaughter, despite the persistence and ubiquity of the illustrations of tortured traders. This reassessment was essential for Amboyna's new place in imperial history.

In the years since the episode, authors introduced many minor factual errors into the story. Some authors mixed up proper names; several located the event in the wrong year (ranging from 1618 to 1624), with many writers by the eighteenth century especially confused about the old style dating practices of an earlier era. One author had van Speult reaching the English coast and brought before the Admiralty, not dying in the Indian Ocean. Another killed off John Beaumont, one of the eight English survivors. A 1796 issue of the *Britannic Magazine* had the slave overseer, the "Portuguese" man in the English versions, confessing early on alongside a Japanese soldier, both of whom the author put in English service, instead of testifying last, as the trial record suggested. Fictitious tortures had been introduced as early as the ballad in 1624–25, which had men whipped, scourged, and hanged. None of these errors had any impact on the overall interpretation or meaning of the story as a tale of Dutch ingratitude or cruelty.[2] Other authors invented facts, especially when the story of Amboyna was useful in international conflicts. In 1672, the Hollandophobe George Downing had the condemned English traders wanting to take the sacrament before their executions to show their innocence, but the Dutch forbade it.[3] Another wartime pamphlet declared that the VOC enslaved any English and Japanese they met.[4]

The primary reason interpretive errors appeared was not because of English bias against the Dutch but rather because of the changing meaning of the word *massacre*. In the early seventeenth century, the word was capacious. A massacre was a cruel death, a topic on which there was universal agreement, but that cruel death could occur in a variety of ways. A massacre encompassed the averted deaths of the Gunpowder Plot (1605), the mass killing in Virginia in 1622, and the legal process at Amboyna in 1623. A major event that the English called a massacre and that looked a lot like the Virginia incident took place in Ireland in 1641, when the Irish rose in rebellion and attacked the Protestant plantations in Ulster, killing perhaps 10,000 and displacing thousands more. The Ireland episode's history resembled Amboyna's in a variety of ways. It, too, came to be defined by a key text, John Temple's 1646 work, *The Irish Rebellion*, which characterized the Irish and the English in stark opposition to each other. The work's subtitle also invoked, perhaps consciously, the language of the Amboyna pamphlet, with a reference to *"the barbarous cruelties and bloody massacres"* that had transpired in Ireland, although "barbarous cruelty" was a common phrase of the era. Like Amboyna, the Irish violence produced martyrs for an English nation baying for revenge, although at the hands of Catholics in the Irish case, and the Protestantism of the English dead mattered in ways it hadn't in the Amboyna episode. And like Amboyna, the Irish story acquired a long afterlife, although unlike Amboyna its legacies found traction in a much more volatile political environment.[5]

In the mid-seventeenth century, however, "massacre" continued to be associated with a death connected to a legal process, as was evident in the execution of Charles I in 1649. Those opposed to the death decried the process and denied the legitimacy of the adjudicating body to deliver sentence: the death was a massacre, and Charles I a martyr. In 1661, the Virginia colonial assembly declared January 30, the day of Charles's execution, to be a day of fasting in the king's honor, "soe bloodly massacred" by the previous government.[6] The 1662 *Book of Common Prayer* marked January 30 to commemorate his martyrdom.[7]

The connection of massacre with the type of judicial violence at Amboyna or the execution of Charles I slowly came to be superseded by the word's association with killing—or slaughtering—large numbers of people. The transition began in the 1650s, when John Milton described the Dutch "slaughter" of English men in the East Indies as part of the damages the EIC sustained before the First Anglo-Dutch War, although he may have been thinking not only of Amboyna. In 1662, Henry Foulis connected "the horrible slaughter of *Amboyna*" with the St. Bartholomew's Day massacre of 1572. By the end of the seventeenth century, the association of massacre with mass slaughter became more entrenched. In 1672, the statesman George Villiers, the Duke of Buckingham, accused the Dutch of having massacred and enslaved the English in the East Indies.[8] The author of the epistle in the *Stripping of Joseph* in 1625 had also described the English as "massacred," but he meant something different—tortured and cruelly killed—than later authors like Villiers who meant slaughtered.

Once massacre became a synonym for slaughter, it was easy for authors to assume the same kind of destruction at Amboyna that had been visited on victims in the large-scale massacres of Paris (1572) or Ireland (1641). They had already linked Amboyna to these episodes as another type of cruel death, but now it became a slaughter, too. Indeed, by the eighteenth century, British historians generally used massacre in this sense of slaughter.[9] David Hume classified the Amboyna incident as a massacre, like that of the Huguenots in France or the English Protestants in Ireland, and Catharine Macaulay used massacre as a verb to describe what happened to the English at Amboyna.[10] In one retelling of the original Amboyna story in 1797, an informant claimed that the Dutch had expelled the English from their factory in 1623 "with the most unexampled barbarity, torturing, and otherwise putting to death hundreds." Ten had become hundreds; so too had the era prior to 1623 become one of "profound peace," whose rupture made the Dutch violence seem more shocking and treacherous.[11]

No less an authority than the *Encyclopedia Britannica* became hopelessly entangled in the story. The first edition of the *Encyclopedia* in 1777 provided a short entry for Amboyna, locating the island in the East Indies and then adding that what distinguished the place was "the cruel usage and expulsion of the English factors by the Dutch" in James I's reign. Subsequent editions showed the transformation of the incident into a different kind of massacre. By the third edition, a lengthy entry summarized the original English version of the story, with some of the additional tortures that had started to creep into the story over time. The 1842 edition placed the event in 1622, lost sight of the violence and negotiations that produced the 1619 trade-sharing arrangement, simply saying that the English had tried to share the island since 1615, and described the conflict as a dispute between "settlers," which led to the Dutch killing the English through cruel tortures and "[expelling] all the English settlers." By 1875 the venerable work described the incident as the result of the Dutch destroying an English settlement at Cambello in an episode called "the 'Amboyna massacre,'" an interpretation that endured through the 1945 edition and continues to be a common version of the Amboyna incident in reference works as recently as 2015. Drawing on some Dutch sources, the 1953 edition elaborated with still more errors: it too told of a British settlement at Cambello, established in 1615, but in 1623 the Dutch claimed that they had discovered that the British were conspiring in a native revolt on Seram and Run. As a result, the Dutch "massacred the settlement." These embellishments cumulatively turned what had been the shared English and Dutch house at the Cambello trading post in 1623 into an "English settlement," and transformed the English traders into settlers. The legal procedure vanished, as did the Japanese and the overseer of the slaves, and a slaughter replaced them. The contemporary Britannica Online does a much better job with its "Amboina Massacre" entry, but problems continue with the entry for "Ambon," where a reader learns that the Dutch "destroyed a British settlement."[12]

If the narrative of the massacre had changed, so too had its significance, although it was not immediately apparent in the late eighteenth century how or why. The iconic Amboyna image—a tortured English trader in a small chamber, crowded by other Europeans—placed the most memorable aspects of the 1623 conspiracy trial in a room that could be anywhere or nowhere. Amboyna had insinuated itself into English culture as a familiar reference that spoke persistently to the behavior of the Dutch, and not to the specific experiences of a handful of English traders who dwelled among non-Europeans on the other side of the world, as of course they had at Amboyna in 1623. But from the 1790s through the mid-twentieth century, Amboyna's physical locale—the fact that it was an island in the Indonesian archipelago and once the site of a potentially lucrative trade for the EIC, as well as the status and occupations of the executed men—became important in the role it ultimately came to play in nineteenth- and twentieth-century histories of the British Empire.

For a brief period, the British even held the island, achieving the grand geographic ambition outlined in the 1781 version of the *True Relation, The Cries of British Blood*. They seized Ambon from the Dutch in 1796, just after the United Provinces had been invaded by the French army, with the support of Dutch Republicans, resulting in the creation of the Batavian Republic. In the same year, Britain claimed the Dutch territories of Berbice and Demerara on the South American coast, all acquisitions facilitated by the upheaval of the war with France and also prodded by the loss of America in the previous decade. During this era of conquest, the British navy named a brig the *Amboyna* in 1800, a riposte of sorts to the VOC ship, the *Amboina*, in 1629. The ship's name would no longer conjure the horror and sympathy Swift had sought to invoke when he had Gulliver travel on a ship of the same name. But the British restored Amboyna to the Dutch at the end of the Napoleonic Wars, and once again the clove island slipped beyond Britain's grasp.[13]

That moment of return and its aftermath in the 1810s and 1820s revealed competing interpretative strands about Amboyna in the early nineteenth century: detachment from the graphic violence savored in an earlier era; continued resonance with the East India Company; and derision in some quarters in domestic politics. Two versions of the *True Relation* and a speech in Parliament revealed the diverse opinions. In 1813, an abridged *True Relation* appeared in a multi-volume collection of travel accounts. Titled "Account of the Massacre of Amboina, in 1623," this version closely followed Harris's account in his 1744 *Voyages* and also drew on Purchas's *Pilgrimes* (1625). There was nothing unusual about the story of Amboyna appearing in a travel compilation, a trend dating to 1625 with Purchas and especially common in the eighteenth century. But this compiler—a Scot named Robert Kerr—both drew a familiar lesson from the story and discerned a new interpretation.[14] When Kerr created this work, the British still held Amboyna. He agreed with the argument dating back to the 1620s that the incident was part of a VOC scheme to grab all the spice trade, but he also reflected on a more recent history and concluded that the Dutch loss of Amboyna and other territories was an appropriate punishment for Dutch submission to French republicanism.[15]

Kerr also found old aspects of the story distasteful, most notably the torture. He explained that there were many sources available for his anthology, but he preferred the abridged version he used, which he thought was "quite sufficient on so disgusting a subject, especially so long after the events which it records."[16] "Disgusting" also characterized his response to the "minute description" of the torture, which he chose to omit.[17] The contrast with both seventeenth- and eighteenth-century versions and reprints of the *True Relation*, which sometimes placed the details of the torture in a work's title, and illustrated it with graphic and occasionally red ink-spattered drawings, is marked. Torture, in fact, had originally made these men martyrs and had made the incident a massacre. That Kerr could exclude the torture details reveals how much had changed about how Britons understood the incident, perhaps in part because it was hard to reconcile the story of judicial torture with the new understanding of what a massacre entailed. No doubt because of his admitted disgust with the graphic aspects of the story, Kerr also left out the illustration of the tortured trader, which otherwise was a staple of reprinted *True Relations*.

But if Kerr shied away from a full reprinting of the details of the traders' ordeal and pointed to the incident's distance in time, those who had commercial and strategic concerns in the East Indies held different sentiments. The *Asiatic Journal*, a monthly publication established in 1816 for readers interested in India, showed an ongoing commitment to anti-Dutch sentiments, especially those associated with Amboyna. In April 1821 the periodical reprinted the *True Relation*, and in September, a report from a British officer who had been to Amboyna inspired the author to observe, as had Captain Singleton in Defoe's novel just a century earlier, that "there is something in the very mention of this Government and this Island, in connection with each other, which rouses an Englishman's feelings, and recals associations that he would willingly, for the sake of human nature, have blotted out from his recollection, if not from the records of history."[18] The 1821 publications signaled a continued emotional investment with the sentiments first expressed in the 1620s, including a nationalistic repudiation of the Dutch violence there, while Kerr, in contrast, characterized the whole episode as remote in time.

As for the EIC, it too held the memory close, but the company was only a shadow of what it had once been. Intense anti-monopoly campaigns in Britain in the 1780s and 1790s had sought to dismantle the company's monopoly on trade. By 1813, the EIC awaited the outcome of its charter renewal with an uncertainty soon confirmed by the government's decision: the company lost almost all its trading privileges, keeping only the tea trade to Canton, and was left with one main purpose, as bureaucrats in India. All that was left was a "bureaucratic shell."[19] To be sure, the India bureaucracy was substantial, and the EIC also controlled the military, but the company's fortunes were on the wane.

The Amboyna incident remained part of the EIC's institutional memory and political toolkit, and EIC agents in fact sought to use the episode in 1824 to pressure Parliament to act on their behalf. The problem the House of Commons grappled with was the fallout of the treaty that had restored Dutch territory at the conclusion of the Napoleonic Wars. The EIC protested the return and wanted to make their own treaties. George Canning, the leader of the House of Commons, delivered a speech to the House in which he described his difficult dealings with members of the company. Company members complained to him about "the grasping disposition" of Dutch authorities, who were determined, they argued, to expel the English from the trade, just as the EIC had claimed in the 1620s. Canning reported that he tried assiduously to get evidence of this Dutch conduct from the EIC, but to no avail. All he heard were general claims of Dutch greed. He asked in vain for facts, but the EIC replied with "an obscure kind of reference to the 'massacre of Amboyna.'" He then laughed at the EIC's invocation of the incident.[20]

It is impossible to imagine a member of the House of Commons laughing at the incident in 1624, right after it had happened, when statesmen were moved to tears and a woman allegedly fainted at the sight of Greenbury's painting; even in 1724, it would be inconceivable. It was in 1719, after all, that Defoe gave Robinson Crusoe a terrifying nightmare about Amboyna, and in 1726 that Swift inflicted Gulliver with a journey on a ship whose name signaled horror and peril—not amusement. Canning's mockery reduced the incident to a source of entertainment at the EIC's expense, that the company could marshal such improbable evidence to support its allegations against the Dutch in 1824. If seventeenth- and eighteenth-century writers had domesticated the incident, making it a central hallmark of English cultural memory, in the nineteenth century it was domesticated in a different fashion, tamed, subdued, and turned for some into a silly relic of the past.

Canning's derision, Kerr's disgust, the EIC's embrace—all exposed a gulf in opinion on the meaning of the incident in the early nineteenth century and yet a continued engagement and familiarity with it. Although Canning's laughter in the House of Commons suggested a contemporary dismissal of the story, by the middle of the nineteenth century the Amboyna massacre had in fact begun to acquire a more consistent and stable place in British history. In domestic histories, it conveyed, as it always had, the weaknesses of the early Stuart monarchs. In imperial history, however, Amboyna played a more powerful role: it was the linchpin that explained Britain's focus on India.

Throughout the seventeenth and eighteenth centuries, British writers who drew on the story of Amboyna had done so for two main purposes: to criticize the Dutch as a cruel, ungrateful, and treacherous people, and to attack British political opponents. By the early nineteenth century, the massacre no longer served these purposes, but by mid-century, amateur and professional historians alike started to write explicitly about Amboyna in the context of the English activity overseas. The fact that the three Amboyna "sequels" took place beyond Europe—in New England (1653), in the East Indies (1665), and in Bengal (1759)—suggested that Britons intuitively associated Amboyna with English experiences in overseas locales. In this vein, Sir Dalby Thomas, the Royal African Company's agent at Cape Coast Castle, had characterized the rival Dutch there in 1706 as "the greatest Amboina Rogues in the World."[21] In the nineteenth century, writers began to make the association between Amboyna and Empire more systematically.

Important publishing developments in the nineteenth century enabled Amboyna to become familiar to new swaths of society, which in turn facilitated its integration into British history, as did the growing importance of India. The most significant publishing landmark in the nineteenth century for the history of Amboyna was the appearance in 1860 of the first volume of the *Calendar of State Papers Colonial* (East and West Indies) series, edited by W. Noel Sainsbury.[22] The books placed records that existed only in manuscript in British repositories, especially state and company papers, in the hands of people with library or personal access, and popular periodicals reviewed the volumes as they were published. The volume that covered the period of the Amboyna incident and the news first reaching London (volume 4) was published in 1878. This issue of the *Calendar* was a detailed and comprehensive work, with lengthy letters abstracted with care and the various manuscript accounts of the conspiracy reprinted almost in full. A review of the volume in the *Edinburgh Review* in 1880 suggested avid interest in these materials. The critic noted that the Amboyna incident was "one of the foulest massacres which a high-spirited nation has ever permitted to remain unavenged," and then the reviewer recapitulated the *True Relation*.[23]

This expanded and detailed familiarity with Britain's colonial and imperial past intersected with a strong commitment to local history, whose culmination was the massive Victoria County History project that launched in 1899 and aspired to produce a uniform history for every English county.[24] Regional periodicals sprang up as part of this interest in local history and offered a new way for Britons to identify with the event. The story of Amboyna as experienced by the Newcastle-born trader Samuel Coulson, for example, appeared in *The Monthly Chronicle of North-Country Lore and Legend*, a magazine published in Newcastle-on-Tyne, in 1891, thanks to the easy access the published *Calendar of State Papers Colonial* provided to Coulson's biography. A crude illustration of a tortured trader accompanied this brief tale, with the core motifs of the original woodcut. The image indicates that the author was not content with the report in the *Calendar* (which did not reproduce the woodcut) but went to the trouble of finding one of the many existing images to prepare his own version.[25]

Historians' association of Amboyna with India also tightened in this era. This connection is neither obvious nor intuitive, even if in the seventeenth century both Amboyna and India had fallen within the EIC's charter. Ambon is 3,200 miles from Calcutta, for example, and the island itself was just one of

Figure 6.1 This late nineteenth-century illustration accompanying an article about Samuel Coulson suggested the continued importance of the image of the tortured trader almost 260 years after the original incident. James Clephan, "The Massacre of Amboyna, 1623," *The Monthly Chronicle of North-Country Lore and Legend*, May, 1891, p. 196. Image courtesy of University of Michigan Library (Special Collections Research Center).

many places where the EIC traded in the seventeenth century. Robert Clive, a historical figure indelibly linked to India, had helped to forge the connection between the two places after the rout of the VOC in Bengal in 1759, and John Malcolm's popular three-volume biography of Clive, published in 1836, reproduced the complete account in which Clive likened his actions to Amboyna.[26] Biographers of Clive drew on Malcolm's work for decades and wrote of Clive achieving revenge for Amboyna in that episode, an interpretation that still endures in some quarters and that replicates the language of unrequited injury that permeated the 1781 version of the *True Relation, The Cries of British Blood*.[27]

But there was a more concrete set of connections, too, between the small island in the Moluccas and India, the place that had become the centerpiece of the British Empire and the most populous region of the world under British dominion. Some 40 million subjects lived there under the rule of the East India Company by 1815.[28] The EIC's commercial authority might have been on the wane, but India's economy was robust and growing. A large British population in India, especially soldiers and administrators trained for their respective tasks by British institutions, also thickened connections between Britain and India. This context in which the significance of India to Britain's interests was both obvious and expanding put new attention on antecedents to British occupation there. The Amboyna incident offered contemporaries a crucial explanation for how the British ended up in India: not lured by avarice, but pushed out of the Spice Islands by the Dutch, with India but a consolation prize in a set of European conflicts. Mid-nineteenth-century historians incorporated the Amboyna incident in their histories of the British Empire, using Amboyna as a way to assert that the jealous Dutch sought to drive the English out of the spice trade. Unlike many of their predecessors and successors, these historians tended to include the Japanese accomplices in their narratives.[29] One of the nineteenth-century historians drew carefully on a variety of published sources, but somehow managed to turn the Japanese soldiers into Javanese, an error that suggests a lack of familiarity with the admittedly unusual seventeenth-century context that produced the original collection of co-conspirators.[30]

For these writers, the Amboyna massacre also became a way for Britons to make sense of ongoing resistance to British occupation in India, even if in fact the original episode emerged from a very different kind of resistance to British claims. The new meaning of massacre as slaughter may have contributed to the expanding utility of the Amboyna incident. The Rebellion of

1857, a massive uprising in India against British rule, may have further entrenched the association of Amboyna and India. A late-nineteenth-century
history connected the "frightful massacre at Amboyna" of the seventeenth
century with the "tragedy of the Black Hole at Calcutta" of the eighteenth
century (which allegedly resulted in the deaths of forty-three people), and
"the crimes connected with the Sepoy mutiny" in 1857 as common sources of
horror to the British.[31] The story of the Black Hole had itself been revived in
the 1840s by the historian Thomas Macaulay in an essay on Clive, becoming
"one of the founding myths of empire," and the connection later historians
drew between the Black Hole and the Amboyna Massacre attested to the important role these paired tales of atrocity played in creating a version of imperial history marked by both violence and innocent British victims.[32]

The Amboyna story became a staple tale of empire by the end of its third
century, returning in some respects to the global context that produced it
but for purposes far removed from its origins. This new understanding of
Amboyna's place in British history derived from the emergence of history
as a profession in the 1880s; the rise of imperial history as a subject; the attention that the South African or Anglo-Boer War (1899–1902) placed on
the English relationship with the Dutch; concerns sparked during that same
conflict about the physical and patriotic preparation of British youth for
battle and citizenship, which led to a surge of educational activity to train
children in the history of empire; and the participation of professional imperial historians in producing books for the young. None of these variables in
isolation could have explained how ubiquitous Amboyna became; together,
they ensured that Amboyna continued to be a story not just about the British
Empire, but specifically about the Dutch influence on the British Empire and
the British turn to India.

The first and vital ingredient for the Amboyna Massacre's new trajectory
was the South African War, which contributed to a surge of enthusiasm for
imperial history and inspired renewed attention on the Anglo-Dutch connection. The Boers (the word means farmers in Dutch) were descendants of
Dutch migrants in the seventeenth century. Although Britain had secured its
claim over the Cape Colony in 1814, the majority of the European-descended
population remained Dutch. The South African Republic and the Orange
Free State were independent polities with Boer majorities but sizable numbers of British inhabitants, too. In the conflict, the Boer states sought to fend
off British aggression with a preemptive attack. Works written during this
period suggest that the conflict had prompted a reappraisal of Britain's long

history with the Dutch Republic, and Amboyna featured in that reassessment. George Peel, a Member of Parliament and author, published a deeply partisan work entitled *The Enemies of England* in 1902 in which he systematically explored various nations' hostilities toward England. Peel considered seven centuries of occasionally embittered relations between England and the Netherlands, from the founding of Amsterdam to the Boer War. He pointed to the seventeenth century as the period of greatest animosity, and in that period, of course, no greater depredation existed than the terrible "slaughter" of the English at Amboyna.[33] No one showed more hostility than the Canadian author Beckles Willson, whose *Ledger and Sword* (1903) was a history of the East India Company that reveled in anti-Dutch language and interpretations. His narrative of the events at Amboyna recapitulated the *True Relation*, with the addition of verbatim dialogue, all drawn loosely from the dialogue included in the 1624 *True Relation* and rendered with inflammatory verbs ("moaned," "snarled") and adjectives ("astounded," "staggering") to convey the sentiments he harbored. He characterized the incident as a "monument to the crafty and bloodthirsty policy of the Dutch." Gratuitous insults adorned the text, and Willson conceded in his introduction that readers might disagree with his assessment of Dutch actions in the seventeenth century.[34] Symptomatic of the mood of the times, one book reviewer even rebuked a Dutch scholar in 1900 for being insufficiently critical of his countrymen in his analysis of the massacre.[35] The cumulative depiction of the Dutch as stubborn, proud, cruel, and envious could have come right out of a pamphlet written during one of the three Anglo-Dutch wars of the seventeenth century, as indeed Willson's text virtually did with its verbatim copying of the *True Relation*.[36]

The war, with its renewed attention on a history of English and Dutch interactions, and especially a deepened interest in the conflicts of the seventeenth century, also had implications for educational materials and programs for the young because of wartime concerns that malnourished British youth were ill-equipped for the rigors of military duty. Moreover, they demonstrated insufficient patriotism and connection to empire. A lack of volunteers led one observer to worry in 1903 that the national curriculum might not be doing enough to educate children about the privileges and responsibilities their citizenship afforded. Two consequences of such concerns were a surge of jingoism and more attention to history education. Children's schoolbooks and recreational reading conveyed common values, in which authors pushed history (whether through specific history books or general reading books) as a way to promote an "emotional attachment" to the empire. The League of the Empire and similar organizations established during and after the war years produced teaching materials and sponsored occasions such as Empire Day, competitions connected to aspects of imperial history, and a gamut of activities all intended to promote pride in empire.[37]

Undergirding these new educational materials was the emergence of history as a profession, starting in the 1880s, and especially important was a coterie of scholars dedicated to the history of the British Empire. They included the Regius Professor of History at Cambridge J. R. Seeley (1834–1895); A. P. Newton (1873–1942), who held the Rhodes Professorship in Imperial History at King's College London; Hugh Egerton (1855–1927), who held the first chair in colonial history at Oxford; and Charles Lucas (1853–1931). These men produced works of scholarship, and some of them also contributed to didactic materials for the young. As imperial history became a more important subject by the late nineteenth century for professional historians and for the young for civic and patriotic purposes, the Amboyna Massacre, invigorated perhaps by the circumstances of the South African War, came to play a modest but enduring role in that larger narrative. Egerton's assessment in 1903 of the "massacre of Amboyna" as having "practically secured" the East Indies spice trade for the Dutch is characteristic of the conclusions these scholars drew about the incident.[38]

The version of the Amboyna story that featured in these works by professional historians almost universally omitted the Japanese and instead drew on the story to examine English connections with the Dutch.[39] The disappearance of the Japanese and the intense focus instead on Europeans indicated what British scholars in this era understood to be significant about imperial history: European experiences around the world could be explained primarily by looking at other Europeans. If the English abandoned the Spice Islands, therefore, the explanation must lie in competition with the Dutch, not in any other impediments the English might have faced in their trading enterprises around the region, including their own failures. The Amboyna Massacre ended its career in British culture as a story of the British Empire, but historians rendered it in such a way as to make the global forces that had created it utterly opaque.

But Amboyna had a still more insidious legacy. As an imperial origin myth, the Amboyna story functioned as a funhouse mirror. In British hands, the episode had remained a tale of Dutch brutality, irrational violence driven by jealousy, with English victims. The massacre hinged on these innocent traders—the martyrs of 1623. As a turning point of empire, it put English innocence at the center of a national fiction that disguised and distorted the violence that was the hallmark of Britain's own imperial aggression. This tale of murdered innocents created a foundation for an imperial history that ignored ruthless violence committed by Europeans in favor of multiple episodes recounting the unjust suffering of English victims—first at Amboyna, Britons believed, and then at Calcutta in 1756 and throughout India in 1857. An empire composed of British martyrs not only fabricated a history of sacrifice for a glorious cause but also dictated a future plan of action, a script for steadfast determination and retaliation, and created a lineage that linked the modern British Empire to the Protestant struggles delineated so powerfully in John Foxe's *Actes and Monuments*.

Professional historians of this era were not entirely consistent in their treatment of the incident, as evident in *The Cambridge History of the British Empire*, a multi-volume, multi-authored work whose publication commenced in 1929. The work highlights how key scholars made sense of the episode in this era. Even a single chapter might contain mutually incompatible interpretations. A.P. Newton, one of the work's co-editors and contributors, distanced himself from the old seventeenth-century interpretation by describing the incident as a " 'massacre' " in its own quotation marks, but he also embraced elements of the original English perspective when he characterized Dutch behavior in the incident as "evil usage." In the same volume, J. Holland Rose dubbed the episode both one of many "annoyances" and an "outrage." J. A. Williamson dismissed it as "shameful." Both Newton and Rose revealed their effort to deploy the detachment important to the profession (" 'massacre' " and "annoyance") while their invocation of "evil" and "outrage" suggested that they still remained in thrall of the lingering jingoism that had come to define imperial history since the late nineteenth century.[40] As for where it belonged geographically in imperial history, a helpful chronology appended to the work's fourth volume on British India answered the question by including the "Massacre of Amboyna" in that region's history.[41] Thus the era's definitive work on imperial history struggled to present a single interpretation of the incident and located the main purpose of its history in India.

A. P. Newton turned out to have had a lot to say about Amboyna, and his interest encapsulates the intersection between professional historians, imperial history, and educational materials. In 1935, he wrote a short piece about the episode, an event "long remembered among the most tragic episodes in history," which was accompanied by an illustration showing the original

True Relation's title page and the 1624 Dutch-language version's woodcut, for a popular periodical, the *Saturday Review*. The Amboyna story, specifically its "commercial martyrs," served the foundation of the British Empire, he argued, because after Amboyna the EIC turned its attention to India. Indeed, with this violent episode "the course of history was changed."[42] Finally, Newton answered a question that dated to the first invocations of the executed traders as martyrs in 1624: what was the cause they had been martyred to? Newton made it clear that the cause was the British Empire and the trade that both animated and sustained it. His use of "martyrs," moreover, undermined the professional distance he signaled in the 1929 *Cambridge History* with " 'massacre' "—because martyrs were an essential and defining feature of massacres. Newton also wrote *A Junior History of the British Empire Oversea* (1933), a book for "boys and girls in many parts of the globe." Newton wanted to illustrate the breadth of the empire as well as the importance of cooperation as an imperial value that held together people who were scattered around the globe and otherwise characterized by their "diversity and complexity." In this work of 279 pages, Amboyna received about 1 1/5 pages, much more than the three sentences Newton allotted to another staple tale of cruelty, the Black Hole of Calcutta. Newton's assessment of Amboyna as "the most atrocious crime in the struggle for Asiatic trade," as he dubbed it, distilled the English interpretation as it had been forged in 1624 and parroted in the twentieth century: the Dutch levied false accusations against the English and tortured them, making some men confess "what they knew was false," almost a verbatim echo of the *True Relation*. The men died before a crowd of thousands in "shame and cruelty," and the EIC gave up the spice trade. Amboyna deserved this attention, Newton made clear, just as he did in the *Cambridge History* and his *Saturday Review* piece, because the incident "was a real turning-point in our history in Asia."[43]

With his *Junior History*, Newton participated in the surge of children's book publishing between 1880 and 1940 that focused on imperial history. These history books were part of a shift in history education in this era away from the rote imparting of knowledge to the didactic use of history as a mechanism to instill imperial enthusiasm and a sense of connection and belonging, just as Newton had sought to do in his *Junior History*. Amboyna didn't appear in all history books nor in some of the most popular, so it was clearly not an indispensable aspect of British imperial history. There was nary a mention of Amboyna, for example, in one of the big sellers of the period, R. B. Mowat's *A New History of Great Britain* (1926).[44] But it did appear in the other most frequently used book for older children in the 1920s, G. T. Warner and C. H. K. Marten's *The Groundwork of British History* (1900).[45] Amboyna featured in other popular books of the era, too, including Charles Lucas's *The British Empire* (1915), a work designed for adult education, and J. F. Bright's *History of England* (1890).[46]

When authors of educational works discussed the Massacre of Amboyna, as they called it, the episode spoke to two aspects of British history: internal and imperial. First, it illustrated, as it had for writers such as Hume and Macaulay in the eighteenth century, the weaknesses of the early Stuarts and the conflicts with the Dutch of that era. Arthur Flux, who prepared teaching materials for educators in the first years of the twentieth century, urged pupil teachers in 1902 to be sure to understand that a key component of the First Anglo-Dutch War was the recovery of damages for the "massacre of Amboyna," something he characterized as a "barbarous act" in a history he published in 1906.[47]

Amboyna was also part of imperial history, a tale of violence and treachery that fit into a pattern of resistance to English occupation. In his 1899 history for students and general readers deficient in English history, William Harrison Woodward likened the impact of the "murder" and "judicial murders" at Amboyna on English people of the time with that of Cawnpore on the English of the mid-nineteenth century, a reference to the Great Rebellion of 1857 which modern historians have described as the key event for imperial histories of this era.[48] George Southgate also set the Amboyna incident in the context of other violent episodes of empire in his enduring work, *The British Empire*, first published in 1936, with reprints and new editions until 1972. Southgate identified Amboyna as the first imperial massacre, followed by Boston (1770), Patna (1763), Cawnpore (1857), and Amritsar (1919). At least Southgate provided a mixed set of violent incidents—two committed by British forces, one by the Dutch, and two alleged atrocities by Indians resisting British occupation.[49] Above all, the Dutch violence at Amboyna explained the EIC's shift to India, the pivot on which the empire rested.[50]

The interpretations of Amboyna in these educational works shared two key features: they explained Dutch actions through their jealousy of the English, and they omitted the Japanese soldiers. Many authors were vague about why the Dutch had wanted to kill the English and how the English died. H. E. Marshall, author of an enormously popular children's book called *Our Island Story* (1905), also wrote *Our Empire Story* (1908), in which she simply remarked that "suddenly one day" the Dutch jealousy of the English overflowed, and they seized, imprisoned, tortured, and executed the

English.[51] With very rare exceptions, in none of these works is there any reference to the Japanese, but only the sudden actions of the envious Dutch, eager to drive the English out of the trade.[52]

For the most part these children's books were very cryptic about what exactly had happened at the trading post. The League of the Empire produced history books for all student levels. In each of the three works they produced for the youngest children through more advanced learners, the League's authors mentioned the "'massacre'" that transpired at Amboyna, but provided few specifics.[53] With the exception of Newton and Marshall, who provided enough lurid details, drawn directly if imprecisely from the *True Relation*, to entertain the most ghoulish child, the discussions of the incident were brief. Otherwise, curious children might have been deeply frustrated by what they learned—or didn't learn—about the massacre. Robert Rayner, author of *A Concise History of Britain to 1939* (1938), provided a clue about how more information about the incident might have been transmitted to children. An experienced teacher, he explained in his preface, knew that some information was better learned through reading, while other material could be conveyed orally. His textbook drew on his own classroom experiences and he provided a separate section of notes that he envisioned as complementary to the narrative in his text. Amboyna turned up in his notes accompanying a chapter about the period 1603–88. Rayner assumed teachers already knew enough about the incident (which his notes identified as an incident sparked by Dutch jealousy) that they could tell children about it in class.[54]

Some of these schoolbooks made it clear that the incident was a trial featuring torture, while others suggested that the episode resembled a massacre. Southgate, for example, wrote that "an English outpost at Amboyna was overwhelmed and its occupants were put to death," the choice of "overwhelmed" suggesting a military attack, while Rayner's text, in 1938 and in subsequent editions, declared that the Dutch "[murdered] a number of English merchants."[55] Those murdered merchants meant that the story of Amboyna did not always align perfectly with the aims of these imperial schoolbooks, which tended to emphasize heroes, men of action, those who stood down enemies and pursued deeds of derring-do.[56] Amboyna's executed traders had served as heroes in their seventeenth-century moment and for the next half-century, signaled most vividly in Dryden's staged depiction of the martyred trader Gabriel Towerson in 1673, but these tortured men could not compete with the active military heroes adored in a later era.

Newton's "commercial martyrs" seemed to find no traction as subjects of biographies for children.

The Amboyna Massacre was only one small story in history books for children and scholars of all ages, all chock full of events and characters, and all part of a broad effort sparked by the South African War to inculcate an attachment to empire through history education. And yet, as Hicksey's recollections in 2003 suggest, Amboyna played its own special role in cementing that attachment and in fostering a sense of imperial belonging, at least for one Australian veteran whose military career drew him into that imperial history in a tangible way. He remembered the story of Amboyna so well, including the island passing back to British control during the Napoleonic wars, and even that the English and Dutch used different names for the place, that in his mind's eye he could locate the passage about two-thirds of the way down the page of his schoolbook. Maybe it was even Southgate's history he had read, because that is where Amboyna appears in the 1936 edition, the year Hicks started at Melbourne High School. Although Southgate did not talk about a garrison, he did speak of an "outpost" that was "overwhelmed."[57] When his mate summoned Hicks to look at the white stone memorial to what he remembered as twenty-three British men who had been massacred on Amboyna, he saw something his excited friend had thought said John Hicks. The stone in fact read, Hicks later explained, "HIJCKS."[58] With the "IJ" it's possible that the name was even Dutch. There was no John Hicks killed at Amboyna in 1623 and it isn't clear what memorial stone Hicks and his comrades stumbled on. But what matters is that the story was important enough to Hicks that he inserted himself in it, showing the exact emotional attachment to empire that educators had hoped to impart. It wasn't John Hicks, but it was almost John Hicks, and thus perhaps Amboyna was a story about Walter Hicks, too.

A vital aspect of these educational works, beyond their interpretive frameworks that promoted imperial identification and pride in children and adult learners, and the familiarity an imperial subject in the armed forces might discover as he arrived in a strange land, was their long shelf life. The exigencies of World War II and its aftermath meant that there was little funding or supplies available for new editions or printings, and so the old works limped along. Books written during the 1930s, for example, continued to be reprinted into the 1970s, including George Southgate's popular *The British Empire*, first published in 1936. The 1972 edition replicates the same language as the 1936 work, with both "atrocity" and "Massacre of Amboyna." The longevity of such works suggests that even after a revolution in history education in the

1960s, children continued to learn British imperial history from textbooks whose main lines of argument had been shaped in the early twentieth century.[59] The result was the tenacity of the Amboyna incident as a real massacre (or slaughter), not a "massacre," and as an atrocity. This characterization also persisted in old scholarly works that continued to be reprinted. J. R. Seeley's *Expansion of England*, first published in 1883, was in print until 1956. This book, based on two sets of undergraduate lectures Seeley had delivered at Cambridge, was regarded at the time and thereafter as the foundational work in the field of imperial history. Although Seeley had almost nothing to say about the episode, his casual reference to the "massacre of Amboyna" as responsible for launching the seventeenth-century "duel with Holland" kept the story and the old interpretation of 1623 alive. And given the key place Amboyna occupied in British history and in British education, it probably wasn't an obscure reference to his readers even in the mid-twentieth century.[60]

Amid the focus on Amboyna as a massacre in British books and histories in the almost four centuries since it transpired, it is easy to forget all that the story once entailed. Long gone in English accounts were the alleged co-conspirators, their disappearance contributing to a narrative of inexplicable Dutch aggression and envy, of cruelty without provocation. Also long forgotten were the event's origins as a conspiracy. That was the VOC's perspective in a world full of conspiracies, and it was once the EIC's, too, because they were sure that the VOC had plotted against them, maybe even with support in Holland. But the story of the Amboyna conspiracy never persisted—or, at least, it did not endure among the English-speaking people who were heirs to the Amboyna Massacre.

This ongoing English characterization of the episode as a massacre enraged two Dutch historians in the first half of the twentieth century, F. W. Stapel in 1923 and W. Ph. Coolhaas in 1942.[61] Both scholars did what none of their English counterparts did: they looked at manuscripts. Both historians conceded that there were many problems in the legal materials compiled by the VOC council in Amboyna, but they nevertheless endorsed the probability of the plot, with Stapel willing to concede only that Coulson might not have been culpable. Their serious engagement with the original sources may explain why Coolhaas was so incensed by the lazy assessments of his British contemporaries, respected historians like Newton and Rose who based their interpretation of the incident on an inherited tradition and the EIC's pamphlets. The English East India Company's archives, available to historians like Newton, contained all that a scholar needed to create a richer history of the episode, but such was not their agenda.

Coolhaas and Stapel fought a losing battle. Even after the historian D. K. Bassett published a thorough and well-researched article in 1960 that dismantled the long-standing claims that the EIC gave up on the spice trade after and because of the incident in Amboyna, historians have continued to misunderstand what happened there, forever tripped up by the word massacre.[62] Historians might no longer write of the incident as an atrocity, but the massacre endures. To this day, scholars have had trouble getting some basic facts straight about the episode, whether they examine Dutch or English sources or both. Some of those facts might be of little consequence, such as how many people were executed, but others reflect an important misunderstanding of the context of the conspiracy, including whether the Japanese worked for the English or the Dutch, and whether the Dutch physically destroyed the English residences at Amboyna and elsewhere in a slaughter.[63] It's no wonder there are so many lingering errors, because for nonspecialists there are few reputable reference works that can explain the history adequately.[64]

In the modern era, even as serious historians tend to demonstrate more caution in how they characterize the "massacre," libraries around the world rely on a shared subject classification system devised by the Library of Congress that promulgates the ancient EIC interpretation. For the Library of Congress itself, the books about the episode have "Ambon (Indonesia) History" and "Ambon Island (Indonesia) Early Works to 1800," as their subject classification, but librarians in most institutions generally add more details when they catalogue books about this episode, including a date and a description. It's a modern version of the eighteenth-century phenomenon, in which those who made library catalogues described Amboyna books as works about the cruelties of the Dutch, whatever the title of the book itself. The twenty-first-century equivalent is the cataloguing of seventeenth-century Amboyna books as works about a massacre, despite the absence of that word in the book titles. At the British Library, for example, the 1632 *True Relation* appears under the subject heading "Ambon Island (Indonesia)—Massacre, 1623."[65] The English victory in terminology and conceptualization is so complete that the incident has become a massacre even in the Netherlands, where Leiden University has the subject heading "Ambon (Indonesia) History Massacre, 1624 Early works to 1800" for the 1624 *Een Waer Verhael*.[66] How fitting that the year is wrong, too, one of the many little errors characteristic of the legacy of the alleged conspiracy. The English at Amboyna may have lost their heads, but they still got the last word.

Epilogue

The First English Massacre

The Amboyna episode didn't start out as the first English massacre, but by the eighteenth century that is what it had become.[1] When the incident took place in 1623, there were already events called massacres with English victims, including the large-scale attack in Virginia in 1622, and the cruel "murther and massacre" of a child and the torture of his sister in England in 1606.[2] The Gunpowder Plot in 1605 was "a traiterous and bloody intended Massacre."[3] But these incidents did not stand the test of time as *massacres*, especially as the word's meaning changed to denote slaughter. The Gunpowder Plot maintains a central place in British history, but it is no longer remembered as an averted massacre. The fate of the Virginia incident is more puzzling, primarily because Virginia was an iconic massacre, just the type of violence the word defined then and later. Its disappearance in contemporary works marking important events in English history suggests that that episode had quickly become immaterial to English interests. It didn't speak to an enduring historical relationship that needed constant management over the course of several more centuries, as was true for Amboyna. When mass slaughters of civilians took place in Ireland in 1641 and 1649, observers then and later connected the two episodes not to what might seem a logical point of comparison for the deaths of British subjects in colonial locales—Virginia—but to Amboyna, as a writer named Robert Dixon did in 1683 for the 1641 episode and as the Duke of Ormond did in 1649 when reflecting on violence in that year in Drogheda.[4]

Before Amboyna could become the first English massacre, however, it needed to be lodged firmly in calendars of national events as a significant episode in English history. This process began in almanacs, popular, cheap, and easily available books that perform a number of useful tasks and often include chronologies of significant events.[5] Almanacs offered handy ways for people to remember historical events and to ponder their relationship to one another as the names and dates marched up and down a page in tidy columns. Several seventeenth-century almanacs included Amboyna. George Wharton's *Gesta Britannorum and Calendarium Ecclesiasticum* listed "*Amboyna's* bloudy cruelty" or "Amboyna's *bloody* Cruelty" in the 1657, 1663, and 1666 editions, although he located the event in 1624.[6] Wharton did not include the Virginia massacre. Nor did *Englands Remembrancer* (1676), which was a list of important events and "Remarkable Passages," where "*Amboyna's* bloody cruelty" appeared for 1624.[7] A New England visitor and chronicler named John Josselyn created a rare seventeenth-century chronology that included Virginia and Amboyna in an appendix to his travel account. Many of the events in his chronology took place in the Americas. He recorded that "The Natives in *Virginia* murdered about 340 *English*" in 1621. His listing for 1622 included nine items, all American except for his notation that "The *Dutch* tortured the *English* at *Amboina*, 1623." Josselyn's inclusion of Amboyna among other American episodes suggests that he might have been unsure of where Amboyna was, or that Amboyna was so important that it belonged in any timeline, or even that he conflated events from different parts of the world.[8] Eighteenth-century chronologies continued to record "*Amboyna's* bloody cruelty" or even the "Dutch Massacre" for the year 1624 or thereabouts.[9] One 1775 chronology listed the event in both 1622 ("The Dutch massacre the English at Amboyna") and 1624 ("The cruelty of the Dutch at Amboyna").[10]

These chronologies show contemporaries working out how to fit Amboyna into English history. It had clearly found a spot in the march of time, but how important was it? Jonathan Swift had some thoughts on this matter. In 1713, he linked Amboyna to the Spanish Armada and the Gunpowder Plot, joining the small-scale episode in the Indonesian archipelago to two vital moments in English history when external and internal foes threatened to destroy the kingdom.[11] A derisive commentator mocking the radical British politician and writer John Wilkes in the wake of an incident called the massacre at St. George's Fields in 1768, in which British troops seeking to disperse a gathering of those protesting Wilkes's imprisonment shot and killed a handful of people, showed how eighteenth-century Britons might associate Amboyna with other events, and the relative importance they assigned Amboyna. He dismissed the St. George's massacre by sarcastically invoking the St. Bartholomew murders (1572), Amboyna, and Ireland as massacres that would be eclipsed by this latest horror—intending, of course, for his reader to draw the opposite conclusion.[12]

Some of these chronologies also organized events by category, not just by year, and it was in these ways of structuring past events that Amboyna's place as the first English massacre becomes evident. The 1775 *Historical and Chronological Remembrancer* included six massacres under that heading. Amboyna was the first of three massacres with English (and Scottish) victims, followed by Ireland in 1641 and Glencoe in Scotland in 1692 (the murder of members of the MacDonald clan by government forces, all entangled in relations with the Campbell clan, and an incident long considered the embodiment of treachery).[13] *Tablets of Memory* sometimes added other massacres to the list, but Amboyna continued to be the first chronological episode with English victims.[14] The historian David Hume yoked Amboyna to other massacres, signaling the significance of the event in the sweep of European and English history: his index of "Massacres" includes "of Jews in England . . . of Hugonots in France . . . at Amboyna . . . of Protestants in Ireland."[15] Even a US chronology, James Hardie's *American Remembrancer* (1795), omitted the Virginia incident in 1622 for Amboyna in its list of "Massacres, horrid." The entry contained several incidents, starting with the classical world and progressing grimly from the St. Bartholomew's Day massacre to Amboyna and Ireland and on to the contemporary era. Hardie's record included several North American episodes, including the Boston Massacre, several murders of American Indians by colonists, and two massacres of colonists by Indians, including in Virginia in 1644, but not 1622.[16]

These chronologies and indexes made apparent that the Amboyna Massacre had become the first English massacre despite prior claimants. Indeed, there were many reasons aside from these earlier episodes that the Amboyna incident should not have stood the test of time at all. With the EIC initially constrained in its observance of the event by a strong diplomatic alliance between England and the United Provinces, with no lingering connection to the massacre locale, and with such a small number of victims, Amboyna had few of the attributes that helped other incidents either endure from the moment they transpired or subsequently acquire historical salience.

It didn't, for example, achieve the memory boost other events gained with special commemorative sermons and anniversary days. The Irish Parliament passed a law in 1662 that required mandatory attendance at an anniversary sermon in all parishes each October 23 in recognition of the events of 1641. Special prayers for this day remained in the Irish version of the *Book of Common Prayer* until 1859.[17] The Boston Massacre (1770) enjoyed an annual commemorative address only until 1783, but during those years, the

Massacre served a crucial political and social purpose in Massachusetts.[18] Even the Gunpowder Plot, the forgotten averted massacre, remains in the British holiday calendar as Guy Fawkes Day, marked with fireworks and bonfires, although with less anti-Catholicism than the first three centuries of commemoration. The only sermon published in Amboyna's honor was a recycled text and it ended up recalled by authorities days after its publication in 1625 because its harsh anti-Dutch rhetoric threatened the diplomatic alliance between England and the United Provinces.

It didn't experience a revival of interest after a period of quiet, as other incidents did. These revivals often reflected an ongoing concern with reinterpreting the meaning of the episode. The Boston Massacre, for example, became a source of discomfort soon after the American Revolution because it smacked of mob activity. Bostonians distanced themselves from the story, and when Bostonians finally dedicated a statue in honor of the episode in 1888, the speaker at the dedication ceremony argued carefully that Boston was not a "mobbish" place. But starting in the 1840s, the Boston Massacre became a story of profound interest to African Americans who found their own place in United States history in the story of one of the decedents, Crispus Attucks. The episode also became a metaphor for other acts of violence, including the Kent State incident in 1970, in which US National Guard troops shot into a gathering of college students, killing four. Even the iconic image of the Boston Massacre changed over time, with Paul Revere's famous 1770 engraving of passive Bostonians under fire displaced by later depictions showing more chaos and more aggression on the part of Bostonians.[19] In contrast, the story of Amboyna was static, constant, its twelve *True Relations* over 160 years, its twenty or more images, all speaking to a single interpretation of English innocence and Dutch treachery, even when massacre had turned into slaughter.

It didn't provide an accessible physical landmark for English visitors who wished to honor the dead. Places have been important to massacres probably since the first blow felled the first victim: they provide locations to mourn the dead and can become pilgrimage or devotional sites. That such places mattered to the English is suggested in Edward Waterhouse's 1622 pamphlet about the Virginia massacre, in which he named both the victims, each "'a glorious martyr,'" and also the location where each died.[20] Victorian Britons mapped the spot where British subjects had allegedly been imprisoned in the Black Hole of Calcutta.[21] In the United States, the National Park Service has a careful process for locating sites of violence and inscribing

The Massacre perpetrated in King Street Boston on March 5ᵗʰ 1770, in which Mess.ʳˢ Sam.ˡ Gray, Sam.ˡ Maverick, James Caldwell, Crispus Attucks Patrick Carr were Killed, six others Wounded, two of them Mortally.

Figure E.1 This familiar image of the Boston Massacre showed passive Bostonians under fire, a central aspect of the interpretation of the event as a massacre with martyred innocents. *A short narrative of the horrid massacre in Boston* (London, 1770), frontispiece. LC-USZ62-45554, Library of Congress.

them with historical markers. These locales can become important senti-mental landscapes, even many years after an incident took place. The Sand Creek Massacre in Colorado in 1864, for example, became a National Park Service site in 2007, after an exhaustive process to identify the correct spot.[22] Sometimes an entire town can become a commemorative site. The French village of Oradour-sur-Glane became a national monument after the murder

Figure E.2 This depiction of the Boston Massacre, created over eighty years after the incident, conveyed a new interpretation of the event, one featuring active and aggressive Bostonians. Crispus Attucks is shown here at the center. Boston Massacre, March 5th 1770. Lithograph by J. H. Bufford's Lith., after W. Champney (Boston, 1856). Collection of the Massachusetts Historical Society.

of most of its population during World War II, and as a monument, the village has both sustained and shaped cultural traditions around the horror that happened there.[23] Locales can be so important that authorities attempting to suppress information about a massacre might go so far as to deny the place ever existed, as Portuguese officials did in the wake of the Wiriyamu massacre of 400 people in Mozambique in 1972; they even created a fictitious town.[24] A ghoulish tourist could construct a macabre tour of massacre sites (real and alleged) within the former British Empire alone, from Glencoe to Kolkata, from Drogheda to Boston. Unlike these other episodes, the Amboyna massacre didn't provide a sacred spot that became a place of pilgrimage, one that permitted visitors to reflect on the event and to ponder its lessons for their own different era. The island was too remote for the English, who stopped trading there in 1623, and the many illustrations of the execution scene, most of them tightly focused on a torture chamber, suggested that a specific locale was irrelevant to the story and meaning of the massacre. The history of the episode could be easily revived as a story indelibly linked to a location, however, as Walter Hicks's World War II memories revealed.

For all that the Amboyna Massacre took place in the context of European global expansion, it also did not become entangled in disputed memories of colonialism. At the beginning of the twentieth century, for example, the story of the Black Hole of Calcutta, first deployed by white Britons as an illustrative tale of Indian cruelty, attracted the interest of nationalist Indian historians eager to get to the bottom of the incident and to tell its history anew.[25] The Amboyna incident wasn't a story of imperial slaughter first suppressed by perpetrators and then brought to light by the advocates of the dead, as has been true of so many such incidents over the centuries. The English and the Dutch argued openly, in judicial proceedings and in voluminous writings. It was a contested story, but the Dutch lost interest in it after 1654 and left the story in the hands of the English, theirs to repeat and embellish for centuries to come. Nor, in an age of sectarian violence, did the European perpetrators and victims at Amboyna have opposing faiths that explained the violence to contemporaries, but instead a shared Protestantism.

It didn't have large numbers of dead to mourn, and eighteenth-century chronologies that recorded the multiple deaths for other episodes provided no such accounting for Amboyna. In light of the horrifying loss of life in other massacres, especially the violent deaths of children, the Amboyna incident might not appear to have especially sympathetic victims, for all that their quirky individuality endures in the surviving records. It might even be easy to feel little compassion for most of the executed men—the Japanese soldiers, who were crucial instruments of repression in a violent VOC regime; the EIC merchants, men who have come to be seen as agents of a brutal imperialism, and some of whom had behaved with sadistic violence during their careers in the East Indies. Perhaps Gabriel Towerson's torture and execution at Amboyna look like just retribution for his vicious torture and dismembering of a Chinese man at Banten in 1604.[26] The English East India Company turned Towerson into a martyr and dubbed him "godly," but readers can readily discern the flawed humanity of him and his compatriots.

If it didn't have so many features that either together or cumulatively might contribute to an episode's longevity, what *did* it have? It benefited from a static and consistent story. Repeated conflicts with the Dutch, or in which the Dutch served as a proxy in British politics, over a long period generated almost continual utility for the tale, and the English recapitulated it in the same way. Even if the story proved supple enough to apply in some new contexts, it retained core features that made it immediately recognizable. It still conveyed the old themes of Dutch cruelty and betrayal even after writers understood the episode as a slaughter. It was, moreover, despite the legal and financial settlement in 1654, unrevenged as far as many writers were concerned well into the nineteenth century, and thus the stuff of legend. The many printed works that lodged Amboyna firmly in British culture together constructed a historical memory of the incident. This coherence made the Amboyna incident, indeed the mere invocation of the word itself, a constant and shared emotional touchstone.

Virtually identical illustrations reinforced this uniform narrative of treachery and violence. The images with their common motifs speak to the timeless aspect of the tale. The existence of copies of the *True Relation* bound with the images from different editions attests both to the importance of the images and to book buyers' or collectors' perceptions that the text was incomplete without it. Middlebury College in Vermont owns a first impression of the *True Relation* (1624): bound with it is not the 1624 woodcut that normally accompanied the English-language edition, which possibly fell out of the copy over the years, or was removed, but rather the illustration from Henry Stubbe's 1673 work, *A Further Justification of the Present War Against the United Netherlands*.[27] In 1935, the *Saturday Review* published an illustration of the title page from the English-language first impression of the *True Relation*, accompanied by the 1624 Dutch-language edition woodcut.[28] The Sutro Library at San Francisco State University, meanwhile, owns a 1632 *True Relation*. The book is missing its original woodcut and instead is bound with the engraving found in Harris's *Voyages* (see Figure 5.7), which is so large it has to be folded to fit into the book.[29] All of these combinations of text and image suggest that whatever the particular edition of the text, whatever the historical moment it was first rewritten, reprinted, and rebound, it required an illustration with its timeless motifs of torture and execution in order to be considered complete.

Above all, the Amboyna Massacre transpired at a formative moment, just as the word massacre became common in the English language, which meant that the Amboyna incident came to define the key attributes of a massacre for the English people. Amboyna's legacy for other massacres lay in shaping how Britons understood the relationship between victim and perpetrator and the kind of violence that might make a massacre. The origins of the word in a butcher's block associated butchery with the act of massacring, a connection that EIC traders in Batavia made the very day they heard of the incident. The linkage of butchery and Amboyna became common over the years, with George Downing making the association as late as 1672.[30] This connection forged an enduring association of massacre with intimate violence, placing proximity and a particular kind of relationship at the heart of the murders that became massacres. It also spoke to an especially inhumane and cruel death in an era when cannibals—the consummate butchers of humans— were the epitome of barbarism. This reflection on the intimacy and cruelty of deaths as massacres might explain why James Butler, the Duke of Ormond, associated violence in Drogheda in 1649 with Amboyna. At Drogheda, Oliver Cromwell issued the order for no quarter for soldiers, and perhaps 600 to 700 civilians were killed as well during the siege. It was another sectarian killing along the lines of the sixteenth-century French conflicts that pro- duced the word massacre in the first place, but that wasn't how Butler made sense of the violence, nor did he look back to the violence in Virginia in 1622 nor even that in Ireland a few years earlier in 1641. Instead, he described the horrors of Drogheda as like the "cruelties" and "inhumanity" he had read about in Amboyna, or those described in Foxe's *Book of Martyrs*.[31]

In their assessment of what happened at Amboyna and of the fraught Anglo-Dutch entanglement that produced and deepened the crisis, the English added ingratitude to intimacy and cruelty. The English events that came to be called massacres were never just about violent deaths. They were also about ruptured connections between individuals but especially be- tween groups—of kin, of neighbors, of distinct and rival political and social communities—who already shared a relationship. Those emotional and his- torical links turned murders into massacres. With its occurrence during a time of commercial union, and with the deep history of Anglo-Dutch ties, the Amboyna Massacre contributed this connotation of rupture from its inception and deepened it throughout the seventeenth century, when the English dwelled on the ingratitude of the Dutch, not just the cruelty and in- justice of their actions. The Amboyna massacre created a script, not of ac- tion, but of meaning, one that shaped the selection of the other incidents that followed in its wake. It was a script that called both for innocent victims and cruelty, features that are pervasive in modern assessments of massacres, and for a prior historical relationship, one in which accusations of ingratitude and betrayal can take hold and explain what happened. Amboyna's legacy as the first English massacre was to place this emotional dimension of ruptured intimate relations into subsequent events that came to be called massacres in the Anglophone world. Ireland in 1641 and Glencoe in 1692, the chronological successors to Amboyna in eighteenth-century indexes, did not transpire between strangers but between intimates, whose relationship defined the violence that ensued and whose treachery made each killing a massacre and an enduring symbol of betrayal and cruelty.[32]

The eighteenth-century English assessment of Amboyna as a massacre came in part out of a misunderstanding of a changing word. Perhaps the common eighteenth-century meaning of mass slaughter is sufficient for understanding what the Amboyna massacre meant to Britons in that era. But perhaps there was something more. Perhaps massacre was not a fully satisfactory synonym for slaughter after all. Perhaps tucked inside that word were remnants of an older meaning forged in the seventeenth century, with its associations of intimacy, treachery, and ingratitude, and perhaps those remnants lingered long after the 1623 incident, encouraging those who heard of a massacre to look both beyond and within the violence for the sundered personal relationships that produced the cataclysm. And perhaps that is why the word massacre speaks to us still.

Deposition Abbreviations

Alban 1630	Deposition of Hendrik Alban, Stadsarchief Amsterdam, 5075. Archief van de Notarissen ter Standplaats Amsterdam, inv. 847 (Notaris J. Steijns). Testimony, July 8, 1630
Bailiff et al. 1625	Deposition of the bailiff and sheriffs of Batavia, October 7, 1625, IOR I/3/14, CCXXIII
Barens 1629	Deposition of Harmon Barens, March 17, 1629, IOR G/21/2, pt. 3
Beaumont 1624	Deposition of John Beaumont before the Admiralty Court, July 7, 1624, IOR G/21/2, pt. 3
Beaumont 1628	Deposition of John Beaumont about English documents (the "relics") from Amboyna [October 10, 1628], IOR G/21/2, pt. 3
Bigwell 1631A	Deposition of Monsieur Violett, March 6, 1631, London, IOR G/21/2, pt. 3
Bigwell 1631B	Deposition of Jacob Bigwell alias Violett [butcher at Amboyna], March 13, 1631, London, IOR G/21/2, pt. 3
Cappur 1628	Deposition of John Cappur about English documents (the "relics") in Amboyna, [October 10, 1628], IOR G/21/2, pt. 3
Carsten 1623	Deposition of Lubbert Carsten [or Coursten], Amboyna, March 11, 1623, IOR I/3/14, CCXXIII
Collins 1624	Deposition of Edward Collins before the Admiralty Court, July 7, 1624, IOR G/21/2, pt. 3
Coper 1628	Deposition of Jacob Coper in answer to 186 questions, The Hague, February 28, 1628, IOR G/21/2, pt. 3
Corcerius 1625	Deposition of Reynier Corcerius, Batavia, September 13, 1625, IOR I/3/14, CCXXIII
Corthals 1628	Deposition of Vincent Corthals in answer to 186 questions, The Hague, March 17, 1628, IOR G/21/2, pt. 3
Cravanger 1628	Deposition of Herman Cravanger in answer to 186 questions, The Hague, March 21, 1628, IOR G/21/2, pt. 3
Devenijns and Jocket 1623	Deposition of Gillis Devenijns and Christoffel Jocket, Amboyna, March 11, 1623, IOR I/3/14, CCXXIII
Duncan 1623	Deposition of William Donchert [Duncan], Amboyna, March 14, 1623, IOR I/3/14, CCXXIII
Ellam 1628	Deposition of Andrew Ellam about English documents (the "relics") [October 10, 1628], IOR G/21/2, pt. 3
Forbes 1627	Deposition of George Forbes at Whitehall, October 30, 1627, CO 77/4/40
Forbes 1628	Deposition of George Forbes about English documents (the "relics") from Amboyna [October 10, 1628], IOR G/21/2, pt. 3

Forbes, "True Relation"	George Forbes, "A true relation of the Netherlands Honourable East India Company's Agents proceedings against the English at Amboyna, by an honest, true, and impartial ear and eye witness, who did serve the foresaid Honourable Netherlands Company within the Castle at that instant" [November 1629], CO 77/4/75
Ideson 1629	Deposition of Ide Ideson, February 28, 1629, IOR G/21/2, pt. 3
Jauss and Sanderson 1625	Deposition of Thomiss Jauss [Jansz?] and Willem van Sanderson, Amboyna, May 24, 1625, IOR I/3/14, CCXXIII
Jochums 1629	Deposition of Frans Jochums, March 8, 1629, IOR G/21/2, pt. 3
Joosten 1626	Deposition of Jan Joosten on 139 articles, Batavia, December 2, 1626, IOR I/3/14, CCXXXIV
Joosten 1628	Deposition of Jan Joosten in answer to 186 questions, The Hague, February 9, 1628, IOR G/21/2, pt. 3
Marschalck 1624	Deposition of Laurens de Marschalck, Delft, November 4, 1624. French translation in SP 84/121, f. 27
Marschalck 1628	Deposition of Laurens de Marschalck in answer to 186 questions, The Hague, March 2, 1628, IOR G/21/2, pt. 3
Marschalck et al. 1623	Deposition of Laurens de Marschalk, Reynier Corcerius, and Herman Cravanger, Amboyna, March 24, 1623, IOR I/3/14, CCXXIII
Pieters 1629	Deposition of Erasmus Pieters, March 1, 1629, IOR G/21/2, pt. 3
Powel 1624	Deposition of John Powel before the Admiralty Court, July 9, 1624, IOR G/21/2, pt. 3
Powel 1628	Deposition of John Powel about English documents from Amboyna, October 10, 1628, IOR G/21/2, pt. 3
Ramsey 1624	Deposition of Ephraim Ramsey before the Admiralty Court, July 13, 1624, IOR G/21/2, pt. 3
Ramsey 1628	Deposition of Ephraim Ramsey about English documents (the "relics") from Amboyna, [October 10, 1628], IOR G/21/2, pt. 3
Sherrock 1624	Deposition of George Sherrock before the Admiralty Court, July 12, 1624, IOR G/21/2, pt. 3
Thomas 1629A	Deposition of Cornelius Thomas, Amsterdam, February 17, 1629, IOR G/21/2, pt. 3
Thomas 1629B	Deposition of Cornelius Thomas, February 26, 1629, IOR G/21/2, pt. 3
Tieller 1626	Deposition of Roeland Tieller on 139 articles, Batavia, nd, IOR I/3/14, CCXXXIV
Tieller 1628	Deposition of Roeland Tieller in answer to 186 questions, The Hague, February 1628, IOR G/21/2, pt. 3
Van Leeuwen 1626	Deposition of Jan van Leeuwen on 139 articles, Batavia, nd, IOR I/3/14, CCXXXIV
Van Leeuwen 1628	Deposition of Jan van Leeuwen in answer to 186 questions, The Hague, March 15, 1628, IOR G/21/2, pt. 3

Van Nieuwpoort 1625	Deposition of John [Jan] van Nieuwpoort, Batavia, October 4, 1625, IOR I/3/14, CCXXIII
Van Nieuwpoort 1628	Deposition of Jan van Nieuwpoort in answer to 186 questions, The Hague, April 3, 1628, IOR G/21/2, pt. 3
Van Santen 1625	Deposition of Pieter van Santen, Batavia, October 4, 1625, IOR I/3/14, CCXXIII
Van Santen 1628	Deposition of Pieter van Santen in answer to 186 questions, The Hague, March 9, 1628, IOR G/21/2, pt. 3
Van Speult et al. 1625	Collective deposition of Herman van Speult, Jan Janss Wyncoop, Jan van Leeuwen, Herman Cravanger, Pieter van Santen, Jan van Niewcoop [should be Nieuwpoort], and Vincent Corthals, in answer to ten questions, Batavia, September 10, 1625, IOR I/3/14, CCXXIII
Vander Knijck et al. 1628	Deposition of Lambrecht Vander Knijck, Jenrian Casperson, and Lambert Wiggerson, Amsterdam, March 31, 1628, IOR G/21/2, pt. 3
Vogel 1626	Deposition of Martin Janss Vogel on 139 articles, Batavia, nd, IOR I/3/14, CCXXXIV
Webber 1624	Deposition of William Webber before the Admiralty Court, July 10, 1624, IOR G/21/2, pt. 3
Wiggerson 1629	Deposition of Lambert Wiggerson, (nd; sometime after February 17, 1629), IOR G/21/2, pt. 3
Wyncoop 1626	Deposition of Jan Jacobsen Wyncoop on 139 articles, Batavia, 1626, IOR I/3/14, CCXXXIV
Wyncoop 1628	Deposition of Jan Jacobs Wyncoop in answer to 186 questions, The Hague, April 7, 1628, IOR G/21/2, pt. 3 [in two translations, one of which has marginal responses by the English survivors]

APPENDIX 2

True Relations

Printed *True Relations*: the original 1624 text or close reworkings

1624
[Skinner, John, Sir]
A True Relation of the unjust, cruell, and barbarous proceedings against the English at Amboyna In the East-Indies, by the Neatherlandish governour and councel there. Also the copie of a Pamphlet, set forth first in Dutch and then in English, by some Neatherlander; falsly entituled, A true declaration of the newes that came out of the East-Indies, with the pinace called the Hare, which arrived at Texel in June, 1624. Together with an answer to the same pamphlet. By the English East-India Companie. Published by authoritie.
London: Printed by H. Lownes for Nathanael Newberry, 1624.
[The first impression]
With a woodcut (see Figure 3.7).
Quarto
STC 7451

1624
A True Relation of the Late Cruell and Barbarous Tortures and Execution, done upon the English at Amboyna in the East Indies, by the Hollanders there residing. As it hath byn lately delivered to the Kings most Excellent Majesty.
[Saint-Omer]: Printed [at the English College Press], 1624.
No illustration; only the *TR*, not the other two texts.
Quarto
STC 7454

1624
[Skinner, John, Sir]
A True Relation of the unjust, cruell, and barbarous proceedings against the English at Amboyna In the East-Indies, by the Neatherlandish governour and councel there. Also the copie of a Pamphlet, set forth first in Dutch and then in English, by some Neatherlander; falsly entituled, A true declaration of the newes that came out of the East-Indies, with the pinace called the Hare, which arrived at Texel in June, 1624. Together with an answer to the same pamphlet. By the English East-India Companie. The Second Impression. Published by authoritie.
London: Printed by H. Lownes for Nathanael Newberry, 1624.
With a woodcut (see Figure 3.7)
Quarto
STC 7452

1624
[Skinner, John, Sir]
Een waer verhael vande onlancksche ongerechte, wreede, ende onmenschelycke procedure teghen de Enghelsche tot Amboyna in Oost-Indien, door de Nederlanlanders [sic] aldaer ghemaeckt op een versierde pretentie van een Conspiratie vande selve Enghelschen.
[London]: [J. Beale], 1624.
With two different woodcuts (see Figures 3.7 and 3.8)
Quarto
Knuttel 3549
STC 7455

1632
[Skinner, John, Sir]
A True Relation of the unjust, cruell, and barbarous proceedings against the English at Amboyna In the East-Indies, by the Netherlandish governour and councell there. Also the copy of a pamphlet, set forth first in Dutch and then in English, by some Netherlander; falsely intituled, A true declaration of the newes that came out of the East-Indies with the Pinace called the Hare, which arrived at Texel in June, 1624. Together with an answer to the same pamphlet. By the English East-India Company. The third impression. Published by authority.
London: printed by G. Purslowe [and Thomas Cotes] for Nathaniel Newberry, 1632.
With a woodcut (see Figure 4.2), printed twice; some of the frontispieces have red ink, including two copies at the Bodleian (shelfmarks Wood 387 [12] and 4° F 36 Jur. [6]); British Library (shelfmark 8022.a.13); Wolfson Centre, Library of Birmingham; Hertford College, Oxford; Massachusetts Historical Society; University of Illinois; University of Manchester; Trinity College Dublin; New York Historical Society; St. John's College and Trinity College, Cambridge; James Ford Bell Library, University of Minnesota; The National Library of the Netherlands, The Hague.
Quarto
STC 7453

1651
A True Relation of the unjust, cruel, and barbarous proceedings against the English at Amboyna in the East-Indies, by the Netherlandish Governour & Council there. Also the Copie of a Pamphlet of the Dutch in Defence of the Action. With Remarks upon the whole matter. Published by Authoritie.
London: printed by Will. Bentley, for Will. Hope, 1651.
Print run shows two slightly different versions
With engraved frontispiece (see Figure 4.3), and execution scenes around letters in some printings (see Figure 4.4)
Probably produced by John Hall at the order of the English government.
Duodecimo
Wing T3065 and T3065A

1652
A Memento for Holland: or A True and Exact History of the most Villainous and Barbarous Cruelties used on the English Merchants residing at Amboyna in the East-Indies, by the Netherland Governor and Conucel [sic] there. Wherein is shewed What Tortures were used

to make them confess a Conspiracy they were never guilty of; by putting them on the Rack, and by a Water torture, to suffocate them; and by burning them under their Arm-pits, and Soals of their Feet, till their fat by dropping extinguished the Candles.
London: printed by James Moxon, 1652.
With woodcut frontispiece (see Figure 4.3).
Memento contains only the TR, not the other two works
Octavo
Wing M1659

1665
A True Relation of the Unjust, Cruell, and Barbarous Proceedings against the English at Amboyna, In the East-Indies, by the Neatherlandish Govenour and Council there. The Third Edition.
London: printed by Tho. Mabb, for William Hope, 1665.
With frontispiece (identical engraving to the 1651 *TR*; see Figure 4.3).
Contains only the *TR*
Quarto
Wing T3066

1672
[Beamont, John, of Amboyna]
The Emblem of Ingratitude. A True Relation of the Unjust, Cruel, and Barbarous Proceedings against the English at Amboyna in the East-Indies; by the Netherlandish Governour & Council there. Also, a farther Account of the Deceit, Cruelty, and Tyranny of the Dutch against the English, and several others; from their first to their present Estate: with Remarks upon the whole matter. Faithfully collected from Antient and Modern Records. Published by authority.
London: printed for William Hope, 1672.
With frontispiece (see Figure 5.2)
Only the *TR* text, with addition of material about the cruelty of the Dutch at Banda
Beamont is a Wing attribution.
Octavo
Wing B1624A

1672
[Beamont, John, of Amboyna]
The Emblem of Ingratitude: or The Hollanders insolencies & cruelties detected. Being a true relation of their unjust, cruel & barbarous proceedings against the English at Amboyna, &c. to the utter ruin and destruction of the English interest. With a brief account of their perfidiousness to all Christian kings; and to the kings of Ternate and Macassar, in the East-Indies. Also the present condition of Batavia, the principal place of their Indian government and trade. Faithfully collected from antient and modern records. Published by authority.
London: printed for William Hope and Nath. Brooke, 1672.
With frontispiece
Octavo
Wing B1624B

1688

Settle, Elkanah

Insignia Bataviæ: or, The Dutch Trophies Display'd; Being Exact Relations of the Unjust, Horrid, and most Barbarous Proceedings of the Dutch Against the English in the East-Indies. Whereby is plainly Demonstrable what the English must expect from the Hollanders, when at any Time or Place they become their Masters. By Elkanah Settle. Published with allowance. London: printed for Thomas Pyke, 1688.

With frontispiece (see Figure 5.5)

Contains only the *TR.*

Quarto

1712

Beaumont, John

Dutch Alliances: or, a Plain Proof of their Observance of Treaties: Exemplify'd in the Particulars of their Inhuman Treatment of their Friends and Confederates, the English, at Amboyna, in order to dispossess them of that and the other Spice Islands in the East Indies. Made publick from a Manuscript never before printed, and written by Mr. Beaumont, one of the Persons who escap'd that cruel Massacre; and, with several others, made Affidavit of these Barbarities in the High Court of Admiralty. London, 1712.

With illustrations on two pages (see Figure 5.6)

Contains only the *TR.*

Octavo

1712

Hall, R. (Richard)

The History of the Barbarous Cruelties and Massacres, Committed by the Dutch in the East-Indies. I. The Massacre of the English at Amboyna, Batavia, Macassar; and the Taking, Burning, and Destroying several English Ships in the Streights of Mallaca . . . To which is added, The Proceedings of the Council of Amboyna, which the Dutch sent to the English East-India Company, in Defence of the Proceedings against the English there. By R. Hall, B. D. formerly of Queen's Colledge Oxon. [London], 1712.

With image (copied from Crouch, with a different caption; see the original version in Figure 5.4)

Contains only the *TR.*

Octavo

1781

The cries of British Blood; or, An authentic narrative of the horrid massacre of the English by the Dutch at Amboyna: with suitable remarks on that bloody tragedy. Together with a description of the Cape of Good Hope, and of the Islands of Java, Ceylon, Celebes, Banda, and the Molluccas or Spice islands, belonging to the Dutch in the East Indies; with Reflections, proving that they are vulnerable, and may easily be annexed to the Crown of Great Britain. The whole work being well worth the Attention of the Public at this Crisis. Embellished with a striking Representation of the Cruelties inflicted on the English at Amboyna, designed by Mr. Dodd. London: printed for Thomas Lovewell, 1781.

With frontispiece (see Figure 5.8)
Contains only the *TR*.
Octavo
NB: not in any digitized collection; three extant copies according to WorldCat.

Manuscript "True Relations"

Extant:

"A true Relation of the cruell and Barbarous Torture and Execution done upon the English at Amboyna in the East Indies by the Netherlanders there"
[1651–52] (British Library says 1632)
With color illustration (see Figure 4.6). Only the *TR*.
Sloane 3645, British Library

Unlocated:

"A true Relation of the cruel Tortures and Execution done upon the English at Amboyna by the Dutch MS. HH 76"
Listed in Evelyn Pierrepont Kingston, *Catalogus bibliothecæ Kingstonianæ* ([London?, s.n., 1727?]), p. 7.

"The Englishman's Knell, an Account of the Murther of their Countrymen at Amboyna" described as being in fair condition in 1773, valued at 2s.
Listed in Martin Booth, *Bibliotheca Martiniana. A catalogue of the entire library of the late eminent antiquary Mr. Thomas Martin* ([Norwich?], [1773]), np.

A Note on Sources and Methodology

I could not have written this book without access to digitized collections of early printed books and a distinctive word to search. Two databases in particular, *Early English Books Online (EEBO)* and *Eighteenth-Century Collections Online (ECCO)*, were indispensable in my efforts to trace the appearance, use, and meaning of the Amboyna incident over the seventeenth and eighteenth centuries. There are obvious and troubling limitations to these sources, in that many scholars don't have access to these databases at all. The collections themselves are imperfect, a subject analyzed by many scholars.[1] Not all books or periodicals of the period have been digitized (notably in my case the final version of the *True Relation* in 1781, the work titled *The Cries of British Blood*); and many works cannot be text-searched. Nonetheless, for all their limitations these digitized collections not only enabled me to find works that talked about Amboyna and gave me access to them; they also ended up shaping my argument in some unexpected ways because of their distinctive search features. These attributes were especially important as I sought to navigate and make sense of the overwhelming number and varied genres of eighteenth-century printed works that mentioned Amboyna. *ECCO*, for example, shows a short glimpse of the word being searched in context. In the course of a preliminary survey of all of the eighteenth-century appearances of Amboyna, I noticed that "Amboyna, Ireland, Glencoe" appeared frequently together in works I might otherwise have dismissed—almanacs, chronologies, and tablets of memory. I finally started to pay attention to what that collection of names might mean, always together and always in that order, in that period, and the result was my argument about the emergence of Amboyna as the first English massacre by the eighteenth century. *EEBO* and *ECCO* together enabled me to search seventeenth- and eighteenth-century library and book catalogues to trace what I argue was the emerging association of Amboyna with a story of cruelty by the mid-eighteenth century. It is impossible to imagine such an undertaking without these remarkable digital tools.

At the same time, digitized versions of books are no substitute for the real thing, and I visited as many of the seventeenth- and eighteenth-century Amboyna pamphlets as I could. This physical examination also turned out to be crucial, not just in understanding how book buyers made sense of the Amboyna incident through their choices about binding Amboyna pamphlets with other works but also in recovering important aspects of the *True Relation*'s print history. The expertise of librarians was essential in this research. I came to understand how the woodcut featured in the *True Relation*'s first impression thanks to my visit to the Codrington Library at All Souls College, Oxford, and the assistance of the scalpel-wielding librarian there, Gaye Morgan, who gave me a crash course in early book printing and binding. I saw the red ink on the woodcut in one of the Bodleian Library's copies of the 1632 *True Relation*, and Paul Nash, a librarian who happened to be working that morning in the Weston Reading Room, pulled out his magnifying glass, joined me to study the woodcut closely, and shared his expertise as a printer. My subsequent discovery of another ink-covered copy on my next visit led me to hunt for all extant 1632 printings. The *EEBO* version of the 1632 printing, copied from an old microfilm, shows black smudges where red ink appears, so without a physical examination of the works, a reader of the digitized version would not understand this extra dimension of the pamphlet.

Some of the manuscripts I studied have been digitized over the years since I first started reading them, including the *State Papers Online* (Gale Cengage) and the *East India Company* database (Adam Matthew Digital). I didn't rely on these databases for most of my research, although I have appreciated their existence especially as I double-checked references. I am also grateful to the Georgetown librarians who at times arranged temporary access for me to these and other databases. Sometimes the States Papers Online led me to materials I might otherwise never have found. For the most part, though, I worked my way through the relevant manuscript collections systematically and chronologically, looking for Amboyna when it appeared and trying always to situate it in its context, a context too often lost when chasing leads from database results. I used some manuscript collections that have been mined by other scholars, including the original correspondence (E series) and minute books (B series) of the English East India Company, located at the British Library, and the diplomatic correspondence (SP 84) from Holland housed at the National Archives of the United Kingdom. Less frequently used collections included the records for the first decades of the Java factory, which contained material from the trading posts and also the large collection of English and Dutch depositions connected to Amboyna for 1628 and beyond. Finally, a major manuscript collection I relied on is known informally as the Hague Transcripts and is part of the India Office Records at the British Library. This collection was created under the direction of Frederick Charles Danvers, who was the registrar and superintendent of the India Office Records from 1884 to 1898. Danvers made three trips to The Hague, searching the VOC records and looking for relevant material for the history of the English East India Company. He examined 564 volumes and supervised the transcription and translation of materials he identified as especially vital to understanding English activity in the East Indies. The result is 106 volumes (IOR I/3/1-106) covering the period up to 1700, with the odd numbers transcriptions of the original Dutch and the even numbers the translations. While the searcher was especially interested in India, the EIC's main focus in its first decades was the Indonesian archipelago, so the Amboyna incident, and the context that created it, emerge clearly in this remarkable collection.[2] Among the items translated and transcribed, for example, were all the 1625 and 1626 VOC depositions connected to the Amboyna episode. I have double-checked these items against original materials in the National Archives in The Hague when it seemed important to do so, and I also looked through the Amboyna-related materials there in the VOC and States General records, which revealed some important sources that do not exist in the English archives.

Notes

Abbreviations

AHR	*American Historical Review*
BL	British Library
CO	Colonial Office, all at the National Archives, United Kingdom
DNB	*Oxford Dictionary of National Biography*. Oxford University Press. Online Edition.
ECCO	*Eighteenth Century Collections Online*. Gale Cengage Learning.
EEBO	*Early English Books Online*. ProQuest LLC.
EIC	English East India Company
GG	VOC Governor-General
GG and C	VOC Governor-General and Council
IOR	India Office Records, all at the British Library
NAUK	National Archives, United Kingdom
OED	*Oxford English Dictionary*. Oxford University Press. Online Edition.
PC	Privy Council, all at the National Archives, United Kingdom
SP	State Papers, all at the National Archives, United Kingdom
Stationers' Registers	Edward Arber, ed., *A Transcript of the Registers of the Worshipful Company of Stationers of London, 1554–1640 AD,* 5 volumes (London: privately printed, 1875–1894)
TR	*True Relation*
VOC	Vereenigde Oostindische Compagnie (Dutch East India Company)
WMQ	*William and Mary Quarterly*, Third Series

Introduction

1. "Clew" comes from *A Remonstrance of the Directors of the Netherlands East India Company* (London, 1632), 9. For an English defense of the soldier, see *The Reply of the English East India Company, to the said Remonstrance and Defense* (London, 1632), 3.
2. See the confessions in the trial record, *An Authentick Copy of the Confessions and Sentences, Against M. Towerson, and complices, concerning the bloody conspiracy enterprised against the Castle of Amboyna . . . Translated out of their own copy* (London, 1632).

3. The interview with Walter Hicks is at the Australians at War Film Archive, no. 807, September 24, 2003 (http://australiansatwarfilmarchive.unsw.edu.au/archive/807-walter-hicks); his discussion of his memories of learning about Amboyna in school comes in Part 4, between minutes 13:30 and 16:00. For an account of the ordeal of the mostly Australian soldiers in the 2/21st Battalion, see Roger Maynard, *Ambon: The Truth about One of the Most Brutal POW Camps in World War II and the Triumph of the Aussie Spirit* (Sydney: Hachette, 2014).

4. A. P. Newton, "Forgotten Deeds of Empire Building: The Massacre of Amboyna, 1623," *Saturday Review*, May 18, 1935, 633.

5. Entry for "Amboyna massacre," *A Dictionary of British History*, 3rd ed., ed. John Cannon and Robert Crowcroft (Oxford University Press, online, 2015). For a print version of this text, see *A Dictionary of British History*, rev. ed., ed. John Cannon (New York: Oxford University Press, 2009), 18.

6. Hugh Dunthorne, *Britain and the Dutch Revolt, 1560–1700* (New York: Cambridge University Press, 2013), 67.

7. John Pory to Sir Dudley Carleton, Virginia, September 30, 1619, reproduced in William S. Powell, *John Pory, 1572–1636: The Life and Letters of a Man of Many Parts* (Chapel Hill: University of North Carolina Press, 1977), 106.

8. On the cultural dimensions of this entanglement, see Marjorie Rubright, *Doppelganger Dilemmas: Anglo-Dutch Relations in Early Modern English Literature and Culture* (Philadelphia: University of Pennsylvania Press, 2014).

9. Daniel Statt, *Foreigners and Englishmen: The Controversy over Immigration and Population, 1660–1760* (Newark: University of Delaware Press, 1995), 29.

10. Jacob Selwood, *Diversity and Difference in Early Modern London* (Burlington, VT: Ashgate, 2010), 27.

11. Most historical work on the Amboyna incident has been carried out by historians examining it in this domestic political context in England in the 1620s. See especially Karen Chancey, "The Amboyna Massacre in English Politics, 1624–1632," *Albion* 30, no. 4 (Winter 1998): 583–598; Anthony Milton, "Marketing a Massacre: Amboyna, the East India Company and the Public Sphere in Early Stuart England," in Peter Lake and Steven Pincus, eds., *The Politics of the Public Sphere in Early Modern England* (Manchester: Manchester University Press, 2007), 168–190; Miles Ogborn, *Indian Ink: Script and Print in the Making of the English East India Company* (Chicago: University of Chicago Press, 2007), chap. 4; Rupali Mishra, *A Business of State: Commerce, Politics, and the Birth of the East India Company* (Cambridge, MA: Harvard University Press, 2018), chap. 8.

12. This erasure of the Japanese soldiers from British histories of the incident speaks to Nicholas B. Dirks's critique of histories of Europe that omit the history of empire. See *The Scandal of Empire: India and the Creation of Imperial Britain* (Cambridge, MA: Harvard University Press, 2006), 29.

13. "Premeditated" from Beaumont 1624, no. 11 (see Appendix 1 for abbrevations for key depositions used in this book); on the logic of the charge of treason, see *Authentick Copy*, 31–32; "horrible massacre" from 32.

14. Timothy Johnson's confession introduced the word "massacring," *Authentick Copy*, 17; *Reply to the Remonstrance*, 43, outlines the VOC vision of this rampage.

15. Dudley Carleton (Junior) to Conway, The Hague, November 8, 1628, SP 84/138/48.

16. There is a rich body of scholarship on slave conspiracies. For a quick introduction, see "Forum: The Making of a Slave Conspiracy, Parts 1 and 2," *WMQ* 58, no. 4 (October 2001): 913–976; and *WMQ* 59, no. 1 (January 2002): 135–202; and Jason T. Sharples, "Discovering Slave Conspiracies: New Fears of Rebellion and Old Paradigms of Plotting in Seventeenth-Century Barbados," *AHR* 120, no. 3 (June 2015): 811–843.

17. For the certainty of a plot, see F. W. Stapel, "De Ambonsche 'Moord' (9 Maart 1623)," *Tijdschrift van het Bataviaasch Genootschap* 62 (1923): 209–226, translated in M. A. P. Meilink-Roelofsz, M. E. van Opstall, and G. J. Schutte, eds., *Dutch Authors on Asian History: A Selection of Dutch Historiography on the Verenigde Oostindische Compagnie* (Dordrecht: Foris, 1988), 184–195; for belief in the plot but doubt that Coulson took part, see W. Ph. Coolhaas, "Aanteekeningen en Opmerkingen over den Zoogenaamden Ambonschen Moord," *Bijdragen tot de Taal-, Land- en Volkenkunde van Nederlandsche-Indie* 101 (1942): 49–94, translated in the same volume, 196–240. George Masselman describes the episode as a conspiracy, and argues that the English might not have pursued their plot if they had had better information and that the Dutch took too seriously something concocted at a New Year's meeting (*The Cradle of Colonialism* [New Haven, CT: Yale University Press, 1963], 429, 431).

18. See, for example, Chancey, "Amboyna Massacre," 585–586.

19. The only scholar to focus on the Japanese invites us to think about how the plot might be possible if we look at the soldiers' perspectives and motivations. See Adam Clulow, "Unjust, Cruel and Barbarous Proceedings: Japanese Mercenaries and the Amboyna Incident of 1623," *Itinerario* 31, no. 1 (2007): 15–34, espec. 30.

20. For "atrocity" and "Massacre of Amboyna," see George Southgate, *The British Empire* (London: J. M. Dent, 1936), 175 (atrocity), 363 (Massacre of Amboyna); and a later edition of Southgate with identical wording, *The British Empire and Commonwealth* (London: J. M. Dent and Sons, 1963), 188 (atrocity), 418 (Massacre of Amboyna). The 1972 edition of Southgate is identical to the 1963 one. For the same terminology, see also Robert M. Rayner, *A Concise History of Britain to 1939* (London: Longmans, Green, 1938, reprint 1942), 323 ("atrocity" and "Massacre of Amboyna"); and the 1965 edition, Robert M. Rayner, with additional chapters by A. D. Ellis, *A Concise History of Britain* (London: Longmans, Green, 1965), 323.

21. Maynard, *Ambon*, chap. 5.

22. Geoffrey B. Robinson, *The Killing Season: A History of the Indonesian Massacres, 1965–1966* (Princeton, NJ: Princeton University Press, 2018).

23. Descendants of people terrorized and killed in the VOC invasion of Banda in 1621 commemorate the episode annually on Lontor. See John Kampfner, *The Rich: From Slaves to Super Yachts: A 2000 Year History* (London: Little, Brown, 2014), 169, 410n29. He cites a BBC show, *The Spice Trail: Nutmeg and Cloves*, BBC2, February 24, 2011.

24. (New York: Columbia University Press, 2019).

Chapter 1

1. *An Answere to the Hollanders Declaration* ([London], 1622), 10.
2. On the financial booms and resulting competition, see Hugh Dunthorne, *Britain and the Dutch Revolt, 1560–1700* (New York: Cambridge University Press, 2013), 110–112.
3. Claude Guillot, "Banten in 1678," *Indonesia* 57 (April 1993): 89–113; population and comparison to Rouen and Amsterdam from 113; see also Kenneth R. Hall, "European Southeast Asia Encounters with Islamic Expansionism, circa 1500–1700: Comparative Case Studies of Banten, Ayutthaya, and Banjarmasin in the Wider Indian Ocean Context," *Journal of World History* 25, no. 2/3 (June/September 2014): 229–262, especially 232–241.
4. *The Last East-Indian Voyage* (London, 1606), D2r, E2v.
5. Such problems were hardly unique to Java. In 1622, English traders reported a similar problem at Surat, where the people believed the Dutch and English to be "one companie." See Thomas Rastell, Giles James, and Joseph Hopkinson, Surat, to EIC president and council at Batavia, January 24, 1622, William Foster, *The English Factories in India: A Calendar of Documents in the India Office, British Museum, and Public Record Office*, 13 volumes (Oxford: Clarendon Press, 1906-1927), vol. 2, 27.
6. Edmund Scott, *An Exact Discourse of the subtilties, fashishions [sic], pollicies, religion, and ceremonies of the East Indians* (London, 1606), C2v-C3v.
7. On the development of national celebrations surrounding November 17, see Roy Strong, *The Cult of Elizabeth: Elizabethan Portraiture and Pageantry* (London: Thames and Hudson, 1977), espec. chaps. 4 and 5; and David Cressy, *Bonfires and Bells: National Memory and the Protestant Calendar in Elizabethan and Stuart England* (Berkeley: University of California Press, 1989), chap. 4.
8. Scott, *Exact Discourse*, C2v-C3v, J3r. These problems of distinguishing the two companies continued around the Indies. See a discussion of similar difficulties at Ahmadabad, in James Bickford, William Hill, and John Clarke to the EIC president and council at Surat, December 29, 1621, Foster, *English Factories*, vol. 1, 354–355.
9. "Forum: Entangled Empires in the Atlantic World," *AHR* 112, no. 3 (June 2007): 710–799.
10. A remembrance from Sir Henry Middleton to Gabriel Towerson and others, October 1, 1605, Banten, in George Birdwood, ed., *The Register of Letters &c of the Governour and Company of Merchants of London trading into the East Indies, 1600–1619* (London: Bernard Quaritch, 1893, 1965 [reprint]), 93–94, quotation on 93.
11. This cooperative behavior shows what political scientists refer to as "strategic trust." See E. M. Uslaner, *The Moral Foundations of Trust* (New York: Cambridge University Press, 2002). For a helpful overview, see Brian Christopher Rathbun, "Trust in International Relations," *The Oxford Handbook of Social and Political Trust*, ed. Eric M. Uslaner (New York: Oxford University Press, 2018): 687–705.
12. The interaction between these two traits is a central theme of Andrew Van Horn Ruoss, "Competitive Collaboration: The Dutch and English East India Companies and the Forging of Global Corporate Political Economy (1650–1700)" (PhD dissertation, Duke University, 2017).

13. Commission for the fourth voyage, last day of February, 1607/8, Birdwood, ed., *Register*, 241–242.
14. See, for example, "Avizo from Hugh Frayne to Nicholas Downton in the Red Sea," [1610], and "[Fragment of a paper, apparently translated from the Dutch . . .]," n.d., in William Foster, ed., *Letters Received by the East India Company From its Servants in the East*, 6 volumes (London: Sampson Low, Marston & Company, 1896–1902), vol. 1, 68–81; for currencies, see John Hearne to the EIC, Banten, December 4, 1608, *Letters Received*, vol. 1, 19; for cloth, see Tempest Peacock to the EIC, Hirado, December 2, 1613, *Letters Received*, vol. 2, 3.
15. Arthus Gotthard and Augustine Spalding, *Dialogues in the English and Malaiane Languages: or, Certaine Common formes of Speech, first written in Latin, Malaian, and Madagascar Tongues . . . and now faithfully translated into the English tongue by Augustine Spalding Merchant . . .* (London, 1614), 11–12. The original work was Frederick de Houtman, *Spraecke ende Woord-Boeck, in de Maleysche ende Madagaskarsche Talen, met vele Arabische ende Turcsche woorden* (Amsterdam, 1603).
16. The head of the English factory in Japan remarked on the English employees aboard VOC ships. See his entry for June 30, 1617, *Diary of Richard Cocks: Cape-Merchant in the English Factory in Japan, 1615–1622*, ed. Edward Maunde Thompson, 2 volumes (London: Hakluyt Society, 1883), vol. 1, 268–269.
17. Articles between the EIC and Peter Floris and Lucas Antheumis, December 13, 1610; separate commission from the EIC to the principal factors and mariners of the Seventh Voyage, Birdwood, ed., *Register*, 363–368, 369–379, quotation on 375.
18. On this conflict, see Vincent C. Loth, "Armed Incidents and Unpaid Bills: Anglo-Dutch Rivalry in the Banda Islands in the Seventeenth Century," *Modern Asian Studies* 29, no. 4 (October 1995): 705–740.
19. Anthony Reid, *Southeast Asia in the Age of Commerce 1450–1680*, vol. 2, *Expansion and Crisis* (New Haven, CT: Yale University Press, 1993), 4.
20. Michael Krondl, *The Taste of Conquest: The Rise and Fall of the Three Great Cities of Spice* (New York: Ballantine, 2007), 236–241.
21. Leonard Y. Andaya, *The World of Maluku: Eastern Indonesia in the Early Modern Period* (Honolulu: University of Hawaii Press, 1993), 1.
22. Giles Milton, *Nathaniel's Nutmeg, or, The True and Incredible Adventures of the Spice Trader Who Changed the Course of History* (New York: Farrar, Straus and Giroux, 1999), 3.
23. Krondl, *Taste of Conquest*, 217.
24. See Andaya, *World of Maluku*, Part Two, on the conflict between Tidore and Ternate and the role of Europeans.
25. "King of Tidore" to the king of England, n.d., delivered May 1606, in Birdwood, ed., *Register*, 67. England and Spain had been at war until 1604.
26. From the "kinge of Mollocco" (the ruler of Ternate) to the king of England, n.d., delivered May 1606, Birdwood, ed., *Register*, 68–69.
27. One English trader reported from Bacan in 1621 that people there were afraid to gather any cloves because the king of Tidore had threatened to put to death any who did so. Thos. Johnson to Wm. Nichols, June 15/25, 1621, [Bacan], IOR E/3/8, no. 960.

28. Jean Gelman Taylor, *Indonesia: Peoples and Histories* (New Haven, CT: Yale University Press, 2003), 131–135.

29. Willard A. Hanna, *Indonesian Banda: Colonialism and Its Aftermath in the Nutmeg Islands* (Philadelphia: Institute for the Study of Human Issues, 1978), 22–24.

30. John Villiers, "Trade and Society in the Banda Islands in the Sixteenth Century," *Modern Asian Studies* 15, no. 4 (October 1981): 723–750, espec. 730, 745.

31. On the ships, see Villiers, "Banda Islands," 733; and Taylor, *Indonesia*, 132. On trade, see Hanna, *Indonesian Banda*, 19, 24; and M.A.P. Meilink-Roelofsz, *Asian Trade and European Influence in the Indonesian Archipelago Between 1500 and about 1630* (The Hague: Martinus Nijhoff, 1962), 195.

32. Meilink-Roelofsz, *Asian Trade*, 201.

33. John Skinner to Adam Denton, Macassar, July 12, 1615, *Letters Received*, vol. 3, 35.

34. This letter from the *orang kaya* was described in the EIC records as a letter from the "Governour and all the principall states of the Ilande Banda," sent to General Keeling and the main English factors at Banten, probably received at Banten in September 1615, in Birdwood, ed., *Register*, 492–493, quotations on 492. On the Islamicization of the Banda Islands, see Peter V. Lape, "Political Dynamics and Religious Change in the Late Pre-Colonial Banda Islands, Eastern Indonesia," *World Archaeology* 32, no. 1 (June 2000): 138–155.

35. George Cokayne to Sir Thomas Smith, Macassar, July 16, 1615, *Letters Received*, vol. 3, 140–141, 143, quotation on 141 (about a secret meeting with "Captain Hittoe" in the straits of Amboyna).

36. John Skinner to Adam Denton, Macassar, July 12, 1615, *Letters Received*, vol. 3, 133.

37. John Jourdain and others to the EIC, Banten, January 2, 1614/15; Remembrance for George Ball by John Jourdain, Banten, January 24, 1614/15, *Letters Received*, vol. 2, 272–273, 307 (quotation).

38. *The Hollanders Declaration of the affaires of the East Indies. Or A True Relation of that Which Passed in the Ilands of Banda, in the East Indies: In the yeare of our Lord God, 1621. and before. Faithfully Translated according to the Dutch Copie* (Amsterdam [London], 1622), 2.

39. Court Minutes, September 25, 1617, IOR B/6, f. 11.

40. Ordinance from Governor-General Laurens Real at Jakarta, November 19, 1617, IOR I/3/6, XC.

41. Protest from Real at Jakarta to George Ball at Banten, November 20, 1617, IOR I/3/6, XCI.

42. John Jourdain and others to the EIC, Banten, January 2, 1614/15, *Letters Received*, vol. 2, 268–280.

43. George Ball at Banten to Cocks at Hirado, [June 9, 1617], *Letters Received*, vol. 6, 14.

44. Arthur Weststeijn, "The VOC as a Company-State: Debating Seventeenth-Century Dutch Colonial Expansion," *Itinerario* 38, no. 1 (April 2014): 16.

45. Reid, *Southeast Asia*, vol. 2, 274.

46. Adam Clulow, "Unjust, Cruel and Barbarous Proceedings: Japanese Mercenaries and the Amboyna Incident of 1623," *Itinerario* 31, no. 1 (2007): 15–34, especially 16–19.

47. "Mortall enemis" from John Johnson and Richard Pitt at Ayutthaya to John Browne at Patani, May 28, 1617, Anthony Farrington, ed., *The English Factory in Japan, 1613–1623*, 2 volumes (London: British Library, 1991), vol. 1, 606; "professed enemies" and "bewitched" from Nicholas Ufflet at Jakarta to George Ball, Banten, July 24, 1617, *Letters Received*, vol. 6, 17–18.
48. June 30, 1617, *Diary of Richard Cocks*, vol. 1, 269.
49. John Davis, Amboyna, to George Ball, Banten, May 1618, IOR I/3/6, XCIV.
50. John Skinner to Adam Denton, Macassar, July 12, 1615, *Letters Received*, vol. 3, 132.
51. George Cokayne to Sir Thomas Smith, Macassar, July 16, 1615, *Letters Received*, vol. 3, 144.
52. Michael Cooper, "The Second Englishman in Japan: The Trials and Travails of Richard Cocks, 1613–1624," *Transactions of the Asiatic Society of Japan* 17 (1982): 155. Omitted from the Hakluyt Society edition of Cocks's diary, this detail about how the Dutch used the English flag can be found in *Diary Kept by the Head of the English Factory in Japan: Diary of Richard Cocks, 1615–1622*, 3 volumes (Tokyo: Historiographical Institute, 1979), vol. 2, 115.
53. Consultation held at Banten, November 28, 1618, IOR I/3/6, CIV. This assault on flags seems to have been a common ritual. After the Dutch burned the town at Japara, on Java, in May 1620, including the English trading house, they took the English flag, dragged it after them in the dirt through the town, and then towed it off their ship's stern. *An Answere to the Hollanders Declaration*, C4v–D1r.
54. Humphrey Fitzherbert to the EIC, March 27, 1621, IOR E/3/8, no. 948, f. 7r.
55. Court of Committees, September 4, 1618, IOR B/6, f. 195.
56. *An Answere to the Hollanders Declaration*, 11, C4r (quotation), D1v.
57. *An Answere to the Hollanders Declaration*, D4r. On the insult, "tail man," see Elizabeth Staffell, "The Horrible Tail-Man and the Anglo-Dutch Wars," *Journal of the Warburg and Courtauld Institutes* 63 (2000): 169–186. This epithet was used commonly in published pamphlets surrounding the first Anglo-Dutch War, in the same way that the English deployed their own insult, "butterbox," for the Dutch, a slur based on the English belief that the Dutch ate a lot of butter, but butterbox had a much older history. See "buterboxes" in Matthew Duke to the EIC, Petapoli, December 9, 1618, Foster, *English Factories*, vol. 1, 48.
58. Henry Pepwell to Laurens Real, November 20, 1617, *Letters Received*, vol. 6, Appendix V, 311.
59. John Gourney at Banten to Wm. Nicholls at Achin [Aceh], July 23 and 28, 1616, Banten, *Letters Received*, vol. 4, 149.
60. Martine Julia van Ittersum and Adam Clulow have studied European claims to territory in the East Indies, focusing on this period and, in Ittersum's case, on the English and the Dutch in Banda. See Martine Julia van Ittersum, "Debating Natural Law in the Banda Islands: A Case Study in Anglo-Dutch Imperial Competition in the East Indies, 1609–1621," *History of European Ideas* 42, no. 4 (2016): 459–501; and Adam Clulow, "The Art of Claiming: Possession and Resistance in Early Modern Asia," *AHR* 121, no. 1 (February 2016): 17–38.

61. The English made a second historical claim in their assertion to trading rights: the voyage of Francis Drake in the sixteenth century. Traders argued that on the basis of Drake's voyage and the relationships he had forged in the Spice Islands, especially in Ternate, the English had a prior claim to trade there. See Petition from the EIC to Salisbury, [November 1611], Birdwood, ed., *Register*, 429; letter from the "kinge of Mollocco" (the ruler of Ternate) to the king of England, n.d., delivered May 1606, Birdwood, ed., *Register*, 68–69.

62. Cocks to the EIC, February 25, 1616, Farrington, ed., *English Factory*, vol. 1, 383–384.

63. George Ball to the VOC council, responding to Real's protest, November 19, 1617, Banten, IOR I/3/6, XCII.

64. Henry Pepwell to Laurens Real, November 20, 1617, *Letters Received*, vol. 6, appendix item VI, 311.

65. Minutes of a council held by Nathaniel Courthope and others, January 3–April 11/21, 1617, answer of Laurens Real, April 11/21, 1617, *Calendar of State Papers Colonial, East Indies, China and Japan,* ed. W. Noel Sainsbury (London: Her Majesty's Stationery Office, 1870), vol. 3, no. 5.

66. Extract of the resolution passed by Coen and the council at Jakarta, December 16, 1618, IOR I/3/6, CVII. The seizure of the *Black Lion* was something of a debacle. The English had planned to hold the ship hostage, but it was destroyed by accident, and in retaliation the Dutch attacked and destroyed the English trading house at Jakarta, which produced outright war, with the English rallying the Javanese to help them destroy the Dutch fort. See Coen to Thomas Dale and the English council, Jakarta, December 6/16, 1618, IOR E/3/6, no. 714.

67. "A Relation of the Frenchmen . . ." [1618], *Letters Received*, vol. 6, 206–207; also in SP 84/85, f. 212.

68. "Account of the general war the English began against us in December 1618 . . . " IOR I/3/6, XCIX.

69. On these earlier efforts, see Rupali Mishra, *A Business of State: Commerce, Politics, and the Birth of the East India Company* (Cambridge, MA: Harvard University Press, 2018), 210–213.

70. On James I's marriage ambitions in the European context, see Thomas Cogswell, *The Blessed Revolution: English Politics and the Coming of War, 1621–1624* (New York: Cambridge University Press, 1989), 12–20.

71. Loth, "Armed Incidents," 718.

72. Carleton to Lake, December 8, 1617, The Hague, SP 84/81/17.

73. Two letters of Francis Cottington, October 8, 1618, SP 94/23/74 (to Dudley Carleton), SP 94/23/76 (to Lake). When Cottington learned of the treaty, he reported that it would not be well received in Madrid. Cottington to Naunton, July 17, 1619, SP 94/23/215.

74. John Christopher Grayson, "From Protectorate to Partnership: Anglo-Dutch Relations 1598–1625" (PhD dissertation, University College, London, 1978), 250–269. See also Ruoss, "Competitive Collaboration," 73–82; Mishra, *Business of State*, 213–216.

75. VOC directors to GG and C of India, September 10, 1619, IOR I/3/88, pp. 105–108.

76. *CSPC East Indies,* vol. 3, introduction, viii.
77. Fursland used the term "double voice" to describe the ability of the VOC's admiral to determine an outcome the English opposed in President Fursland and the council at Batavia to the EIC, January 11, 1622, Foster, *English Factories,* vol. 2, 17. The treaty is in "Tractaten gemaect tusschen d'Engelsche en de Nederlantse Oost-Indische Compagnien," in Lieuwe van Aitzema, *Saken van Staet en Oorlogh* (The Hague, 1669), vol. 1, 206–8.
78. Reid, *Southeast Asia,* vol. 2, 274.
79. Muschamp told Fursland that the English would have to live in subjection to the Dutch; Fursland to the EIC, Achen [Aceh], July 15, October 15, 1620, IOR E/3/7, no. 881; Edmund Lenmyes to the EIC, Jakarta, February 8, 1623, IOR E/3/9, no. 1098, described the English as subjects to the Dutch.
80. Hanna, *Indonesian Banda,* 49.
81. On this episode, see *A Courante of Newes from the East India* (London, 1622), 2–3; Humphrey Fitzherbert to the EIC, March 27, 1621, IOR E/3/8, no. 948, f. 6r-v; Examination of Robert Randall, merchant, and Abraham Woofe, silk-throwster, of London, before Sir Henry Marten, judge of the Admiralty court, about 13 articles, August 11–14, 1622, SP 84/108/44. A silk-throwster turns raw silk into thread. See also the account of John Cartwright, IOR E/3/7, no. 923. Cartwright wrote his account after the Amboyna episode, and his relation of the events in Banda was part of his catalogue of all of the wrongs done to the English by the Dutch. He made sense of the Banda violence in terms of the later tortures at Amboyna.
82. Loth, "Armed Incidents," 726.
83. On the Dutch occupation of Banda, see Vincent C. Loth, "Pioneers and Perkeniers: The Banda Islands in the 17th Century," *Cakalele* 6 (1995): 13–35. This terrible devastation of 1621 may have been a Dutch act of revenge for the 1609 murder of over forty Dutch on Banda. By the 1610s, a Dutch official had proposed just such a brutal conquest and displacement of the islands' people. Rik Van Welie, "Slave Trading and Slavery in the Dutch Colonial Empire: A Global Comparison," *New West Indian Guide/Nieuwe West-Indische Gids* 82, no. 1 and 2 (2008): 81n65.
84. Humphrey Fitzherbert to the EIC, Neira, March 27, 1621, IOR E/3/8, no. 948, quotation on f. 8r.
85. GG to Houtman in the Moluccas, November 23, 1621, IOR I/3/96, ff. 53v-54r.
86. There were 275 soldiers in March, and 306 in April. Abstract of the general charges at Amboina, March and April, 1621, IOR G/40/25(4), pp. 29–34. The first school in Ambon opened in 1607. See Kees Groeneboer, "The Dutch Language in Maluku under the VOC," *Cakalele* 5 (1994): 1–10.
87. Fursland, Brockedon, Spalding, and Methold, items about payments, debts, Batavia, January 9, 1623, IOR I/3/10, CLXXXVIII. For an earlier reference to the Dutch cheating in the accounts, see Wm. Nicolls to Cocks, July 14/24, 1621, Malayo, IOR E/3/8, no. 971; for other complaints about expenses, see Thomas Brockedon to the EIC, August 26, 1622, Batavia, E/3/9, no. 1073; Fursland, Brockedon, and Spalding to EIC, August 27, 1622, Batavia, IOR E/3/9, no. 1076.

88. Thomas Johnson to William Nicolls, Bacan, October 10/20, 1621, IOR E/3/8, no. 1003; on weighing spices, see Richard Welden at Banda Neira and Pulau Wai, August 20–21, 1622, IOR G/21/3A, pt. 2, f. 249v.

89. John Wetherall, Cambello, to Banten, August 18, 1622, IOR G/21/3A, pt. 2, f. 253r-v.

90. On supporting the Moluccas factories, see GG to Governor Law, May 22, 1621, IOR I/3/96, f. 24v. The VOC was chronically short of cash in its first decades and this policy may have given the VOC agents in the East Indies some flexibility in their operations. See Oscar Gelderblom, Abe de Jong, and Joost Jonker, "The Formative Years of the Modern Corporation: The Dutch East India Company VOC, 1602–1623," *Journal of Economic History* 73, no. 4 (December 2013): 1050–1076.

91. GG to Houtman in the Moluccas, November 23, 1621, IOR I/3/96, ff. 53v-54r.

92. Fursland, Brockedon and Towerson to the EIC, January 11, 1622, IOR E/3/8, no. 1028, quotation on f. 182v.

93. Extract from sentence from Dutch court, September 18, 1620, IOR E/3/7, no. 892.

94. Welden at Banda Neira and Pulau Wai, August 20–21, 1622, IOR G/21/3A, pt. 2, f. 250r-v, quotation on f. 250v.

95. Devenijns and Jocket 1623. See Appendix 1 for abbreviations of depositions.

96. Giles Cole to W. Nicolls, November 16/26, 1621, Bacan, IOR E/3/8, no. 1013. The Billingsgate reference comes from Giles Cole to John Goninge, November 19/29, 1621, IOR E/3/8, no. 1015.

97. Thomas Johnson to William Nicolls, October 10/20, 1621, Bacan, IOR E/3/8, no. 1003, quotation on f. 125v; Giles Cole also described the "christening." See Cole to W. Nicolls, November 16/26, 1621, Bacan, IOR E/3/8, no. 1013, f. 150v.

98. Benjamin Moore at Banda Neira, September 10, 1622, IOR G/21/3A, pt. 2, f. 252r.

99. George Cockayne to Sir Thomas Smith, Macassar, July 16, 1615, *Letters Received*, vol. 3, 141.

100. Cockayne to George Ball at Banten, Sukadana, March 8, 1616/17, *Letters Received*, vol. 5, 167.

101. Court Minutes, October 10, 1621, IOR B/7, ff. 118v-19r; on affairs at Bacan, see Giles Cole to W. Nicolls, November 16/26, 1621, Bacan, IOR E/3/8, no. 1013.

102. Thomas Brockedon, Augustine Spalding, and George Muschamp at Batavia to the EIC, July 20, 1620, Foster, *English Factories*, vol. 1, 196.

103. Note made at Amboyna of VOC resolution sent on March 23 by the GG to various factories, dated Amboyna, April 4, 1619, IOR I/3/96, f. 7v.

104. George Muschampe to the [president and council at Jakarta], June 12, 1621, Amboyna, IOR E/3/8, no. 959, quotation on f. 26r.

105. George Muschampe to the [president and council at Jakarta], June 12, 1621, Amboyna, IOR E/3/8, no. 959, f. 25r.

106. Instructions agreed by the Anglo-Dutch Council of Defense for the "better directions" of the factors in the various factories, Amboina, February 21/March 3, 1621, IOR G/40/25(4), pp. 13–15. Signed by Humfrey Fitzherbert, George Muschamp, and Edward Mead (for the EIC); van Speult, Lawrence Marschalk, and Jan van Bruell (for the VOC).

107. John Wetherall, Cambello, to Banten, August 18, 1622, IOR G/21/3A, pt. 2, f. 253v.

108. Towerson to the EIC council, September 19, 1622, IOR G/21/3A, pt. 2, f. 256r.

109. Fitzherbert to Fursland at Jakarta, April 28, 1621, IOR G/40/25(4), p. 47.

110. John Wetherall, Cambello, to Banten, August 18, 1622, IOR G/21/3A, pt. 2, f. 253r-v.

111. Towerson to the EIC council, September 19, 1622, IOR G/21/3A, pt. 2, f. 256r.

112. Samuel Coulson to the English president at Banten, August 31, 1622, new style, Hitu, IOR G/21/3A, pt. 2, f. 254r-v.

113. Towerson to the EIC council, September 19, 1622, IOR G/21/3A, pt. 2, f. 256r.

114. Thomas Johnson specifically requested a "black" to be sent to him at Bacan, likely for domestic tasks. Thos. Johnson to W. Nicolls at Malayo, November 23/December 3, 1621, Bacan, IOR E/3/8, no. 1016. On domestic services performed by slaves, see EIC president and council at Batavia to Gabriel Towerson at Amboyna, January 21, 1623, IOR G/21/3A, pt. 2, f. 330v. Fitzherbert named the English employees at each post and mentioned the "blacks" there to serve them in his letter to the EIC, March 10, 1621, on the *Royal Exchange* at Amboyna, IOR E/3/7, no. 938. On Welden's plans to send more slaves to Amboyna, see EIC president and council at Batavia to Gabriel Towerson at Amboyna, October 18, 1622, IOR G/21/3A, pt. 2, f. 319v.

115. John Goninge and Joseph Cockram, in the name of the EIC president and council, to Carpentier and VOC council, January 28, 1624, Batavia, E/3/10, no. 1146, f. 94r.

116. *An Answer unto the Dutch Pamphlet* (London, 1624), 14, claimed the English had only six slaves, and they were all boys.

117. John Beaumont to Henry Sill, on the *Royal Exchange*, December 17, 1623, IOR E/3/ 10, no. 1136, f. 68r-v.

118. Joosten 1626, nos. 136–137.

119. Abstract of the general charges at Amboina, March and April, 1621, IOR G/40/ 25(4), pp. 29–34.

120. On the sexual unions created by EIC traders and the policy banning wives, see Alison Games, *The Web of Empire: English Cosmopolitans in an Age of Expansion, 1560–1660* (New York: Oxford University Press, 2008), 104–109.

121. Barry Coward and Julian Swann, "Introduction," in Coward and Swann, eds., *Conspiracies and Conspiracy Theory in Early Modern Europe: From the Waldensians to the French Revolution* (Burlington, VT: Ashgate, 2004), 2.

122. On confessional conspiracies in the sixteenth century, see Penny Roberts, "Huguenot Conspiracies, Real and Imagined, in Sixteenth-Century France," in Coward and Swann, eds., *Conspiracies and Conspiracy Theory*, 55–69; on the crystallization of three strands of conspiratorial thinking in late Elizabethan England, see Peter Lake, " 'The Monarchical Republic of Elizabeth I' Revisited (by its Victims) as a Conspiracy," in Coward and Swann, eds., *Conspiracies and Conspiracy Theory*, 108.

123. Quoted in Mark Knights, "Faults on Both Sides: The Conspiracies of Party Politics under the Later Stuarts," in Coward and Swann, eds., *Conspiracies and Conspiracy Theory*, 153. Important works on seventeenth-century English conspiracies include Rachel Weil, *A Plague of Informers: Conspiracy and Political Trust in William III's England* (New Haven, CT: Yale University Press, 2013); Alastair Bellany and Thomas Cogswell, *The Murder of King James I* (New Haven, CT: Yale University Press, 2015); and Peter Lake, *Bad Queen Bess? Libels, Secret Histories, and the Politics of Publicity in the Reign of Queen Elizabeth* (New York: Oxford University Press, 2016), espec. chap. 2.

124. [John Fletcher and Philip Massinger], *The tragedy of Sir John van Olden Barnavelt* (1619); for the 1623 plot as both a treason and a conspiracy, see *A relation of the late horrible treason, intended against the Prince of Orange, and the whole state of the united prouinces, according to the Dutch coppy printed at the Hage* (London, 1623). This pamphlet includes the Dutch-language account, in addition to an English preface and translation.

125. This strategy, and the fear of proximate, subordinate, and resentful people that animated it, echo the almost chronic fears slaveholders harbored about slave conspiracies, which have been studied extensively by Atlantic and US historians. See, for example, "Forum: The Making of a Slave Conspiracy, parts 1 and 2," *WMQ* 58, no. 4 (October 2001): 913–976 and *WMQ* 59, no. 1 (January, 2002): 135–202; and Jason T. Sharples, "Discovering Slave Conspiracies: New Fears of Rebellion and Old Paradigms of Plotting in Seventeenth-Century Barbados," *AHR* 120, no. 3 (June 2015): 811–843. Fear played a similar role in imperial rule, with implications for both conspiratorial thinking and large-scale violence. For explorations of these correlations in two different contexts, see Adam Clulow, *Amboina 1623: Fear and Conspiracy at the Edge of Empire* (New York: Columbia University Press, 2019); and Kim A. Wagner, *Amritsar 1919: An Empire of Fear and the Making of a Massacre* (New Haven, CT: Yale University Press, 2019).

126. Welden at Banda Neira and Pulau Wai, August 20–21, 1622, IOR G/21/3A, pt. 2, f. 251r-v. See also the report in John Cartwright to EIC council at Batavia, August, 1622, IOR G/21/3A, pt. 2, f. 249r. Flight from Banda had already become a Bandanese strategy after the 1621 invasion. See Wm. Nicolls to Cocks, July 14/24, 1621, Malayo, IOR E/3/8, no. 971.

127. On the executions, see Benjamin Moore at Banda Neira, September 10, 1622, G/21/3A, pt. 2, f. 252r; Richard Welden at Banda Neira, September 11, 1622, IOR G/21/3A, pt. 2, ff. 252v-253r. For "many other plotts," see Richard Welden at Banda Neira and Pulau Wai, August 20–21, 1622, IOR G/21/3A, pt. 2, f. 251v.

128. EIC president and council at Batavia to Richard Welden etc. at Banda Neira, October 1 and 18, 1622, IOR G/21/3A, pt. 2, f. 318r.

129. Towerson to EIC council, September 19, 1622, IOR G/21/3A, pt. 2, f. 255v.

130. President Fursland and the council at Batavia to the EIC, March 6, 1622, IOR E/3/8, no. 1039. Fursland said twelve ringleaders were sentenced to be quartered, the rest condemned to slavery. The EIC later linked this incident to the Amboyna episode as evidence of the Dutch plot against their traders, and in that later document said twenty people were tortured. See "Draft Remonstrance of the English East India Company addressed to His Majesty's Government and to the Upper House of Parliament touching the Exactions and Aggressions of the Dutch East India Company in the East Indies," IOR G/21/2, pt. 2, p. 8. Hanna, *Indonesian Banda*, 55, puts the number of ringleaders at thirteen.

131. For the trial and the quotation, see Extract from the Register of the Town of Batavia, August 24–26, 1622, IOR I/3/8, CXLVII. For an English interpretation of this incident, see Thomas Brockedon to the EIC, August 26, 1622, Batavia, IOR E/3/9, no. 1073.

132. English translation of the fiscal's protest, November 12 and December 30, 1622, Batavia, *CPSC East Indies*, vol. 4, no. 173.
133. Giles Cole to William Nicolls, Bacan, January 8/18, 1622, IOR E/3/8, no. 1025, quotation on f. 176v.
134. Scott, *Exact Discourse*, D1v-D4v; Michael Neill, "Putting History to the Question: An Episode of Torture at Banten in Java, 1604," *English Literary Renaissance* 25, no. 1 (Winter 1995): 70.
135. William Eaton at Hirado to Richard Fursland at Batavia, February 2 and 8, 1622, Farrington, ed., *English Factory*, vol. 2, 877–878.
136. See Muschamp's account, in Muschamp to the EIC [president and council at Batavia], June 8?, 1622, Amboyna, IOR E/3/9, no. 1057, ff. 32–35, quotations on 34v.
137. Powel 1624, no. 11. Powel was deposed after the 1623 trial, and his views were likely colored by that earlier ordeal. It is obvious from van Speult's own correspondence with Coen, however, that he was livid.
138. Extract letter from Jan van Hazel [Harel?] at Surat to GG at Batavia, November 19, 1628, IOR I/3/16, CCLXXIX; Entries for October 21–November 1, 1628, Notes of the main events at Surat, 1628–1630, IOR I/3/18, CCXCVIII.
139. GG to van Speult, October 28, 1622, IOR I/3/98, f. 7r.
140. GG to governors of Moluccas, Banda, and Amboina, January 24, 1622, told the governors that the English were running out of money and expected none from England. IOR I/3/96, ff. 32v-33r.
141. Richard Fursland, Thos. Brockedon, and Augustin Spalding to the EIC, Batavia, February 9, 1623, IOR E/3/9, no. 1099, f. 186v ("chief plotter"), f. 188v ("much exacted uppon"). Muschamp described himself as "disable[d] in bodie," and unable to tolerate the Dutch any longer. [Muschamp] to the EIC, [April 1621], IOR G/40/25(4), pp. 20–27, quotation on p. 26. Another place where Anglo-Dutch relations were especially strained at the same time was Pulicat. See several letters on the subject in Foster, *English Factories*, vol. 2.
142. On closing the factories, see the letters, IOR G/21/3A pt. 2, ff. 327–333; EIC president and council at Batavia to Gabriel Towerson etc. at Amboyna, December 17, 1622, IOR G/21/3A, pt. 2, f. 325r.
143. Letter from GG and Council at Batavia to VOC directors at Amsterdam, February 1, 1623, IOR I/3/10, CLXXXVI; GG to van Speult and Houtman, January 31, 1623, IOR I/3/98, f. 11r, ff. 12–13.
144. This letter fell into English hands. Coen to Martinus Sonck, the Governor of Banda, December 18/28, 1622, IOR E/3/9, nos. 1090 and 1091.
145. George Masselman, *The Cradle of Colonialism* (New Haven, CT: Yale University Press, 1963), 430.
146. VOC directors, Amsterdam, September 8, 1622, to the GG and C of India, IOR I/3/90, ff. 20v (boat)-21r (marriage). For a second reference to the boat, see VOC directors to GG and C, December 10, 1622, IOR I/3/90, f. 22v.
147. VOC directors to GG and C, April 14, 1622, IOR I/3/90, f. 18v.
148. GG to Houtman, October 5, 1622, IOR I/3/98, ff. 4–5.
149. GG to Martinus Sonck, October 28, 1622, IOR I/3/98, f. 8r.

Chapter 2

1. Gerrit Knaap, "Headhunting, Carnage and Armed Peace in Amboina, 1500–1700," *Journal of the Economic and Social History of the Orient* 46, no. 2 (2003): 176.
2. Gerrit J. Knaap, "A City of Migrants: Kota Ambon at the End of the Seventeenth Century," *Indonesia* 51 (April 1991): 109.
3. On the location of the English house, see Forbes, "True Relation"; on the population, see Knaap, "A City of Migrants," 105–106, 111–112, 119. See Appendix 1 for abbreviations for the depositions connected to the trial.
4. On the monsoons, see *A Remonstrance of the Directors of the Netherlands East India Company* (London, 1632), 22; on the four ships at anchor, see Collins 1624, no. 2.
5. Thos. Brockedon, Aug. Spalding, and George Muschamp to the EIC, July 20, 1620, Jakarta, IOR E/3/7, no. 884, f. 231v.
6. M. A. P. Meilink-Roelofsz, *Asian Trade and European Influence in the Indonesian Archipelago between 1500 and about 1630* (The Hague: Martinus Nijhoff, 1962), 220; Anthony Reid, *Southeast Asia in the Age of Commerce 1450–1680*, vol. 2, *Expansion and Crisis* (New Haven, CT: Yale University Press, 1993), 278.
7. The Seventeen to van Speult, December 22, 1620, IOR I/3/88, pp. 137–138.
8. Gerrit Knaap, "The Demography of Ambon in the Seventeenth Century: Evidence from Colonial Proto-Censuses," *Journal of Southeast Asian Studies* 26, no. 2 (September 1995): 227–241, 238 (1634 population). Knaap's evidence is strongest for later in the century, when the population in both 1673 and 1692 was about 90 percent indigenous (233)
9. On VOC fears of English alliances with clove producers, see M. A. P. Meilink-Roelofsz, "The Private Papers of Artus Gijsels as Source for the History of East Asia," *Journal of Southeast Asian History* 10, no. 3 (December 1969): 544. For the death of the VOC servant, see Marschalck 1628, no. 104.
10. *An Answer unto the Dutch Pamphlet* (London, 1624), 7–8; van Santen 1628, no. 104; Joosten 1626, no. 15. On the presents given Vogel on his sickbed, see Vogel 1626, no. 15.
11. Samuel Coulson to EIC president at Banten, August 31 (new style), 1622, Hitu, IOR G/21/3A, pt. 2, f. 254r.
12. Towerson to the EIC council, September 19, 1622, IOR G/21/3A, pt. 2, ff. 254v-58r; EIC president and council at Batavia to Gabriel Towerson etc. at Amboyna, December 17, 1622, IOR G/21/3A, pt. 2, ff. 324v-26r, quotation on f. 325r; *An Answer unto the Dutch Pamphlet*, 17, notes that Towerson was warned "from time to time" by the EIC council, but it is not clear how many of these letters he received.
13. There is considerable inconsistency about his name and identity in the surviving sources. While he is Augustine Peres Marinho (meaning overseer) in the official trial record (*An Authentick Copy of the Confessions and Sentences, Against M. Towerson, and complices, concerning the bloody conspiracy enterprised against the Castle of Amboyna . . . Translated out of their own copy* [London, 1632], 29), he is also described as "a *Neatherlandish Merinho*, or *Captaine* of the *Slaves*," in the VOC's account, *A True Declaration of the Newes that came out of the East Indies* (London,

1624), 8; in the EIC's *An Answer unto the Dutch Pamphlet*, 22, the English complained that in the trial records he was called "the Neatherlandish Marnicho." It seems likely he was Indo-Portuguese.

14. On this motivation for giving Peres a wife, see *Authentick Copy*, 35.

15. Wyncoop 1626, no. 7.

16. Joosten 1626, no. 135.

17. The EIC made this point in *A Reply to the Remonstrance* (London, 1632), 4; and in its published account of the incident, *A True Relation of the Unjust, Cruell, and Barbarous Proceedings against the English at Amboyna In the East-Indies, by the Neatherlandish Governour and council there* (London, 1624), 19. All references in this chapter to the *True Relation* are to this 1624 London printing.

18. Forbes, "True Relation."

19. The EIC's *An Answer unto the Dutch Pamphlet*, 12, a response to the *True Declaration*, addressed this trial record explicitly, and the EIC published the legal record in 1632.

20. The key text here is Samuel Coulson's account in his psalm book, as quoted in the *True Relation*, 21-23, and preserved in States General, 1.01.02, inv. no. 12581.15, National Archives, The Hague; see also William Griggs's notebook, quoted in the *True Relation*, 20-21.

21. The most important depositions, in terms of framing all later debate in Europe about what happened at Amboyna, came from six English survivors, all of whom were deposed in London in July 1624, less than a month after they reached home, willing and eager to provide accounts of their ordeal. Their six depositions were the basis for the EIC's *True Relation of the Unjust, Cruell, and Barbarous Proceedings against the English at Amboyna*, published in 1624, which laid out the EIC's version of events, and the *True Relation*, in turn, led the States General to require VOC officials who had presided over the trial to answer questions specifically concerned with clarifying or disproving allegations in the pamphlet. The VOC directors themselves responded to the States General's complaints and queries in a November 1624 Remonstrance. Thus these six English depositions spawned an extensive debate in Europe, captured also in diplomatic correspondence. The July depositions, moreover, inspired three further series of depositions, in which the interrogatories derived directly from English claims made in the *True Relation*. In the first depositions, seven VOC officials collectively answered ten questions in Batavia in September 1625; in December 1626, five VOC officials testified individually in response to 139 questions in Batavia; finally, ten VOC employees, all of whom had returned to Europe by order of the States General, answered 186 questions in The Hague in 1628. Several other depositions were given in Amsterdam and The Hague between 1628 and 1631 by men with connections to Amboyna, but who were not officials involved in the trials. Some of these depositions were instigated by EIC agents seeking supporting evidence for their own case; others consisted of partial retractions of those earlier depositions.

22. *An Answer unto the Dutch Pamphlet*, 10.

23. From *Authentick Copy*, 2, "divers times, and in divers places asked those questions"; his age is also from *Authentick Copy*, 2; Tieller 1628, no. 25; "younge and rawe" recurs: see Marschalck 1628, no. 24; Tieller 1628, no. 24.

24. Van Speult to Carpentier, June 5, 1623, IOR I/3/12, CXCI.
25. *Authentick Copy*, 2–3, quotations on 2. On how torture fit into European jurispru-
    dence from roughly 1250 to 1800, see Edward Peters, *Torture* (New York: Blackwell,
    1985), 54–62. Roman-Dutch law was based, as the name suggests, on customary
    laws and practices in the provinces that comprised the United Provinces and the
    Roman law pervasive on the European continent. For a helpful introduction to the
    origins of this legal tradition, see Randall Lesaffer, "A Short Legal History of the
    Netherlands," in H. S. Taekema, ed., *Understanding Dutch Law* (The Hague: Boom
    Juridische Uitgevers, 2004), 31–58, especially 43–49.
26. Van Speult to Carpentier, June 5, 1623, IOR I/3/12, CXCI.
27. Van Leeuwen 1628, nos. 29–30; see also Cravanger 1628, nos. 29–30. Hytieso's con-
    fession in the official trial record revealed only English and Japanese co-conspirators;
    the later VOC depositions added these other men. *Authentick Copy*, 2–3.
28. John Skinner to Adam Denton, Macassar, July 12, 1615, William Foster, ed.,
    Letters Received by the East India Company From its Servants in the East, 6 volumes
    (London: Sampson Low, Marston & Company, 1896–1902), vol. 3, 133.
29. Fitzherbert to Fursland at Jakarta, April 28, 1621, IOR G/40/25(4), p. 47.
30. George Muschampe to the EIC [president and council at Jakarta], June 12, 1621,
    Amboyna, IOR E/3/8, no. 959, f. 26r.
31. On Scott's and Towerson's fear of fire, see Edmund Scott, *An Exact Discourse of the
    Subtilties, fashishions [sic], Pollicies, religion, and Ceremonies of the East Indians*
    (London, 1606), C1v–C2r.
32. Jason T. Sharples discusses the centrality of arson as a trope in conspiracies in
    "Discovering Slave Conspiracies: New Fears of Rebellion and Old Paradigms of
    Plotting in Seventeenth-Century Barbados," *AHR* 120, no. 3 (June 2015): 832.
    Jill Lepore explores the intersection between arson and conspiracy in *New York
    Burning: Liberty, Slavery, and Conspiracy in Eighteenth-Century Manhattan* (New York:
    Knopf, 2005).
33. Tieller 1628, no. 5, said it was Towerson's request; on the arson, see Joosten 1628,
    no. 35; for quotation, see *True Declaration*, 12.
34. Joosten 1628, nos. 72–73; *Authentick Copy*, 13–15; for Price's examination and
    torture, see also *True Relation*, 5. Joosten said that Price implicated only those
    merchants in Amboyna.
35. Or so van Speult recalled in June, three months after the executions and six months
    after the warnings, as he created a narrative of events. Van Speult reported that
    he had warned Towerson about two months before the plot was revealed. See
    van Speult to Carpentier, June 5, 1623, IOR I/3/12, CXCI; for van Speult's claims
    that he had frequently warned Towerson about such interactions, see *Authentick
    Copy*, 15–16.
36. Carsten 1623; Duncan 1623; see also *True Relation*, 30.
37. While van Speult said that the English observed this New Year on the English cal-
    endar, that is, January 10 for the Dutch (see van Speult letter of June 5, 1623, IOR I/
    3/12, CXCI), other evidence suggests that the date may have been the Dutch New
    Year's Day—for it was on New Year's Day that van Speult invited Towerson to dine,

and also on that day that the English and Dutch celebrated in the satellite factories. The English started the New Year on March 25.

38. Beaumont 1624, no. 7.
39. Beaumont 1624, no. 7.
40. *True Relation*, 34; van Leeuwen 1628, no. 42; Tieller 1628, no. 42, and van Santen 1628, no. 42, also saw Thompson turned back by the sentry. In van Santen's case, he observed Thompson rebuffed while he was at the examination of the Japanese; the conversation comes from van Santen.
41. See Wyncoop 1626, Vogel 1626, and van Leeuwen 1626, all no. 13.
42. Jauss and Sanderson 1625; Deposition of Ephraim Ramsey, October 14, 1624, Consistory Court of London, deposition book, Sept. 1624–June 1625, DL/C/229, Greater London Record Office.
43. Joosten 1626, no. 139.
44. Marschalck 1628, no. 48.
45. Van Leeuwen 1626, no. 87.
46. Beaumont 1624, no. 9.
47. Corcerius 1625; see also van Santen 1625.
48. Van Nieuwpoort 1625.
49. Sherrock 1624, no. 9.
50. Powel 1624, no. 9
51. Joosten 1628, no. 35.
52. Powel 1624, no. 11.
53. Van Speult to Carpentier, June 5, 1623, IOR I/3/12, CXCI; *True Declaration*, 8.
54. See Beaumont 1624, no. 4, "poore souldiers," "poore fellowes and drudges"; for "meane condition," see Webber 1624, no. 4; see also Collins 1624, no. 4. On failed Dutch efforts to make the Dutch language the lingua franca of Banda and Amboyna, see Kees Groeneboer, "The Dutch Language in Maluku under the VOC," *Cakalele* 5 (1994): 1–10.
55. So the EIC alleged, partly to discredit Price. *An Answer unto the Dutch Pamphlet*, 11.
56. Tieller 1626, no. 16.
57. On their English employment, see Marschalck 1628, no. 18, who described these two men as English slaves.
58. Sidney Miguel may have been the Japanese interpreter named Miguel whom Richard Cocks described on August 15, 1615, as someone too likely to go off carousing and unreliable. See *Diary of Richard Cocks: Cape Merchant in the English Factory in Japan, 1615–1622*, ed. Edward Maunde Thompson, 2 volumes (London: Hakluyt Society, 1883), vol. 1, 40.
59. Van Santen 1628, no. 22; van Leeuwen 1628, no. 22.
60. *Remonstrance*, 6.
61. Adam Clulow, "Unjust, Cruel and Barbarous Proceedings: Japanese Mercenaries and the Amboyna Incident of 1623," *Itinerario* 31, no. 1 (2007): 30.
62. *Authentick Copy*, 10.
63. In 1621, the bakufu limited the ability of the Dutch to recruit such mercenaries, banning their movement in July 1621, primarily, the Dutch concluded, because the

bakufu did not want Japanese soldiers entangled in foreign conflicts, thus risking their own participation. See Clulow, "Unjust, Cruel," 28; For VOC claims of surprise at the alleged betrayal of the Japanese soldiers, see *Remonstrance*, 10.

64. See the confessions of Towerson and Wetherall, *Authentick Copy*, 25, 28.

65. Coen's instructions left in the Indies with Carpentier, January 21/31, 1623, Batavia, IOR E/3/9, no. 1093 +2, f. 164v.

66. Markus Vink, " 'The World's Oldest Trade': Dutch Slavery and Slave Trade in the Indian Ocean in the Seventeenth Century," *Journal of World History* 14, no. 2 (June 2003): 131–177; Rik van Welie, "Slave Trading and Slavery in the Dutch Colonial Empire: A Global Comparison," *New West Indian Guide/Nieuwe West-Indische Gids* 82, nos. 1 and 2 (2008): 78–82.

67. Forbes, "True Relation." On carrying Thompson, see Thomas 1629B; Ideson 1629; Pieters 1629; Jochums 1629; *An Answer unto the Dutch Pamphlet*, 27.

68. Knaap, "City of Migrants," 112, 123.

69. Vink, "World's Oldest Trade," 174.

70. *An Answer unto the Dutch Pamphlet*, 22.

71. *Reply to the Remonstrance*, 21. The EIC believed that Dutch anger about the Spanish match prompted intemperate talk against James I. The EIC also believed that the Dutch council at Amboyna hoped that the Spanish match meant the Dutch would never be held accountable for their actions in Europe, because of what would have been a rupture between England and the United Provinces had the marriage been accomplished (*Reply to the Remonstrance*, 28). For earlier suspicions of an Anglo-Spanish alliance, see Ordinance from GG Laurens Real, Jakarta, November 19, 1617, IOR I/3/6, XC.

72. *True Relation*, 9, 19–21.

73. *Authentick Copy*, 29.

74. Unfortunately, de Bruyn seems to have been in over his head, and there were accusations that he was not a skilled advocate-fiscal. See "A Discourse of the Busines of Amboyna in A.d. 1624," Harley 532, ff. 11–44, BL, for contemporary English derision of the fiscal; and W. Ph. Coolhaas, "Notes and Comments on the so-called Amboina Massacre," in M. A. P. Meilink-Roelofsz, M. E. van Opstall, and G. J. Schutte, eds., *Dutch Authors on Asian History: A Selection of Dutch Historiography on the Verenigde Oostindische Compagnie* (Dordrecht: Foris, 1988), 206, for a historian's later assessment.

75. *True Relation*, 18–19; Powel 1624, no. 9; on hosting the English, see Joosten 1626, nos. 136–37.

76. *True Relation*, 16, called this man Renier; it was likely Renier Corcerius; van Santen 1628, no. 93.

77. John H. Langbein, *Torture and the Law of Proof: Europe and England in the Ancien Regime* (Chicago: University of Chicago Press, 2006, 1976), chaps. 5 and 6. See also Elizabeth Hanson, "Torture and Truth in Renaissance England," *Representations* 34 (Spring 1991): 53–84, especially 55–59. Langbein, 78, notes that the amount of

evidence required to permit the torture of suspects in Roman law was more stringent than that required by juries to convict people in common law.

78. Scott, *Exact Discourse*, F2v–F3r.

79. Welden at Banda Neira and Pulau Wai, August 20–21, 1622, IOR G/21/3A, pt. 2, f. 251r-v.

80. George Willoughby's complaint against Henry Sill and Christopher Read, January 15, 1632/3, IOR E/3/14, no. 1486, quotation on f. 117r; For Read's explanation of why the man was tortured, see his reply to Thomas Grove's accusations, Consultation held January 10, 1632/3, in IOR E/3/14, no. 1484, f. 112r.

81. For "moderate and gentle," see *Remonstrance*, 13; for "touch," see *True Declaration*, 18. For a robust defense of the water torture, see Bailiff et al. 1625. The men argued it was more humane than tortures commonly used in Europe.

82. On Coulson being tortured "gently" with water and fire, see Tieller 1628, no. 87.

83. Collins 1624, no. 9.

84. *Reply to the Remonstrance*, 30.

85. Joosten 1628, no. 161; Marschalck 1628, no 99; Tieller 1628, no. 99 ("some words"). The *True Relation*, 13, described van Nieuwpoort as born in England of a Dutch father.

86. *True Relation*, 7.

87. Beaumont 1624, no. 9.

88. *True Relation*, 13; in the 1626 depositions, the VOC employees in Batavia were asked if Beaumont was tortured with water in such a way "that his inwards did nearly crack." See the 30th interrogatory, and the answers of Joosten, Wyncoop, and the others, 1626.

89. Joosten 1626, no. 42.

90. *True Relation*, 11.

91. Joosten 1626, no. 50.

92. Forbes, "True Relation," f. 140v.

93. On hair: van Leeuwen, Marschalck, Corthals, Cravanger, and Tieller had the same account in their 1628 depositions, answering questions 70–71; on "the Devill playes in this" see Joosten 1628, no. 113.

94. Alison Games, *Witchcraft in Early North America* (Lanham, MD: Rowman and Littlefield, 2010), 15.

95. *The Psalmes of David in Meeter, with the Prose. Whereunto is added Prayers*... (Edinburgh: Andro Hart, 1611), States General, 1.01.02, inv. no. 12581.15, National Archives, The Hague.

96. *True Relation*, 8.

97. Powel 1624, no. 9, related his conversation with Wetherall.

98. Langbein, *Torture and the Law of Proof*, 5.

99. *True Relation*, 17–18.

100. Powel 1624, no. 9.

101. "Write as I will ..." from Joosten 1626, no. 35; "You ly" from *True Relation*, 9.

102. *True Relation*, 13–14, quotation on 13.

103. Sherrock 1624, no. 9. Joosten 1626 and Tieller 1626, nos. 65–66 in each, said Sherrock wasn't tortured; van Leeuwen 1626, no. 65, said he had heard that Sherrock was tortured only with water, but conceded that he was not present himself for the alleged torture.

104. Webber 1624, no. 9; *True Relation*, 16 (quotations).

105. The context of Clarke's employment emerged in the EIC's response to his father's petition to the EIC, Court of Committees, August 25, 1624, IOR B/9, p. 91.

106. *True Relation*, 14.

107. Towerson to Coulson, February 22, 1623 (English style date) States General, 1.01.02, inv. no. 12551.62.1, National Archives, The Hague; For Coulson's rage, see Corcerius 1625. This letter from Towerson to Coulson had a mysterious history, not least since there is no surviving English copy of it. Marschalck claimed to have seen this letter written, and he then saw it in the governor's hands, and in 1628, he deposed that it was in the hands of authorities in the United Provinces (Marschalck 1628, no. 96).

108. *Authentick Copy*, 29.

109. Wyncoop 1628, no. 22; van Santen 1628, no. 99; Forbes 1628; Corthals 1628, "Other Interrogatories," no. 9.

110. Wyncoop 1626, no. 74 (refusing to sign); Forbes 1628 (adding words).

111. Wyncoop 1626, no. 71.

112. Forbes, "True Relation."

113. Beaumont 1624, no. 9.

114. Ramsey 1624, no. 9. The *True Relation* argued that the Dutch deployed this strategy repeatedly, bringing in Japanese men to confront the English, and making the English accuse each other, all through or with the threat of torture. See, for example, *True Relation*, 12. Coulson reported in the text he allegedly wrote before his execution that all of the English had to confess against Towerson, and then Towerson himself confessed. See his *Psalmes of David*, States General, 1.01.02, inv. no. 12581.15, National Archives, The Hague.

115. *Remonstrance*, 23.

116. Joosten 1626, no. 20 (said that Price's confession was written "instantly"), no. 74 (Coulson signed "voluntarily"); In the *Authentick Copy*, each confession (except that of the slave overseer) concludes with a reference to the accused signing his name or his mark.

117. Vogel 1626, no. 80.

118. Vogel 1626, no. 67.

119. *True Relation*, 12.

120. Forbes, "True Relation," f. 140v.

121. Joosten 1626, nos. 55–56.

122. *True Relation*, 27.

123. On Powel's visit, see *True Relation*, 19. For the oral will, see the depositions of Sherrock, Ramsey, and Webber, October 14, 1624, Consistory Court of London, deposition book, Sept. 1624-June 1625, DL/C/229, Greater London Record Office.

124. Court of Committees, October 29, 1624, IOR B/9, p. 175.

125. Forbes 1628; Forbes 1627; Forbes, "True Relation."

126. *True Relation*, 20–21. Towerson's bill of sale, Coulson's prayerbook, and Griggs's notebook found their way to England. See the depositions of Beaumont, Ellam, Forbes, Powel, and Ramsey in 1628. At the king's order, authorized copies of the notebook and Coulson's psalm book were ordered to be sent to the States General's judges with copies kept in the Privy Council's chest; extracts from Mr. Misselden's letter to Secretary Coke, March 3, 1627/8, SP 84/136/53; Privy Council to Carleton (Junior), September 23, 1628, SP 84/138/16.

127. See the petition of John Powel, Court of Committees, August 11, 1624, IOR B/9, pp. 63–64.

128. From the fly-leaf of the book.

129. Towerson to Coulson, February 22, 1623 (English style), States General, 1.01.02, inv. no. 12551.62.1, National Archives, The Hague.

130. *Psalmes of David*, States General 1.01.02, inv. no. 12581.15, National Archives, The Hague.

131. Webber attested to Collins's condition, Court Minutes, November 17, 1624, IOR B/9, p. 203.

132. *True Relation*, 26. See Sherrock's elaborate account, complete with dialogue, in Sherrock 1624, no. 9.

133. Ramsey 1628.

134. Wyncoop 1628, no. 38.

135. Thomas 1629A. Thomas was the smithy.

136. Joosten 1626, nos. 113, 114.

137. This detail about Towerson's assertion of innocence comes from Forbes's "True Relation," not his 1627 examination, and like most of Forbes's statements, is best treated with some skepticism. Forbes later claimed, as he strived to gain favor from the EIC, that it made him cry, and that the fiscal rebuked him and accused him of being part of the English faction. Forbes, "True Relation."

138. *Authentick Copy*, 34–35.

139. *True Relation*, 26.

140. "Old and weak" from Joosten 1626, no. 107; "silly brains" and van Santen's plea in Wyncoop 1626, no. 107. The *True Relation*, 24, garbled this a bit, recalling that Peter Johnson (not van Santen), the Luhu merchant, interceded for Beaumont, as did the Governor's secretary (who was Vincent Corthals, according to his 1628 deposition).

141. John Beaumont to Henry Sill, on the *Royal Exchange*, December 17, 1623, IOR E/3/10, no. 1136, f. 68r-v, quotation on 68v.

142. *Authentick Copy*, 34. The record did not date this action aside from saying it was done "the day aforesaid," which likely referred to the previous item dated March 8.

143. On "mercy" for Thompson, see van Speult et al. 1625, answer 7; *Remonstrance*, 25–26.

144. On Thompson's offer to be a slave, see van Leeuwen 1628, no. 62; Tieller 1628, no. 62 (quotation). The English survivors rejected this story; see marginalia, Wyncoop 1628, no. 37.

145. Joosten 1626, no. 71; Wyncoop 1628, no. 23. Wyncoop reported Towerson's and Collins's conversation verbatim, but the survivors responded that Collins did not

know Dutch and Wyncoop did not know English, so he could not have understood the conversation. See marginalia, Wyncoop 1628, no. 23.

146. Wyncoop 1626, no. 71, gave a detailed account of what Collins told Towerson he had confessed to.

147. *True Declaration*, 19.

148. Joosten 1628, no. 162; van Leeuwen 1628, no. 109 (on Towerson's separate chamber).

149. Vogel 1626, no. 55.

150. Bigwell 1631B, no. 7.

151. Brad S. Gregory, *Salvation at Stake: Christian Martyrdom in Early Modern Europe* (Cambridge, MA: Harvard University Press, 1999), 16–18.

152. Joosten 1626, no. 111; see also Tieller 1626, no. 111.

153. Collins 1624, no. 9.

154. The 1629 depositions and recantations were given by Cornelius Thomas, Ide Ideson, Erasmus Pieters, Frans Jeclunens, Harman Barens, and Lambert Wiggerson.

155. Beaumont 1624, no. 9.

156. Coper 1628, no. 30.

157. Thomas didn't know Thompson's name, but knew him as the "hamburger." See Thomas 1629B, no. 6, no. 14; "shrunck with the fire" is from the same deposition, no. 14; Ideson 1629 deposed that he saw the man he knew as "domini" carried to the execution; Pieters 1629, no. 9, said he was carried by two "blacks," as did Jochums 1629, nos. 5, 6, 7, who also said he was carried by two slaves. The English believed (*An Answer unto the Dutch Pamphlet*, 27) that both Clarke and Thompson were carried to their executions because of the fire torture, but the depositions only provide evidence for Thompson.

158. *Reply to the Remonstrance*, 39.

159. The entry for "scellum" in the *Oxford English Dictionary* (*OED*) notes the word has Belgian origins. "skelm, n. and adj.," *OED*. See also the Lexicons of Early Modern English (https://leme.library.utoronto.ca/).

160. Vander Knijck et al. 1628, no. 10.

161. Thomas 1629B, no. 6; Ideson 1629, no. 8; Pieters 1629, no. 8; Jochums 1629, nos. 6, 7 (gate).

162. Joosten 1628, no. 181; van Santen 1628, no. 116.

163. *True Relation*, 27; quotation from marginal responses to Wyncoop's 1628 deposition, no. 32.

164. Ideson 1629 retracted his first deposition, where he said he followed the English to church in tears, so moved was he by their plight; in his final version, he denied his tears, but confirmed his compassion and the trip to the church. The English believed that the Dutch judges deliberately tried to trip up the pro-EIC witnesses such as Ideson in their second 1629 depositions, but found that core versions of the accounts remained. See Barlow to Carleton (Junior), April 24, 1629, SP 84/139/59. Barlow, the EIC's agent, hoped that these witnesses would come depose in England, which at least one did.

165. Joosten 1626, no. 112. For recurring use of variants on a "stone's cast" see Corthols, Van Santen, Tieller, van Leeuwen, and van Nieuwpoort, 1628, all answering

interrogatory no. 112; Wyncoop 1628, no. 33. It's "steenworp" in the Dutch originals: see the 1628 depositions in States General, 1.01.02, inv. no. 12551.62, National Archives, The Hague.

166. Daniel V. Botsman, *Punishment and Power in the Making of Modern Japan* (Princeton, NJ: Princeton University Press, 2005), 18, 25.

167. On the VOC's many enemies, see *Authentick Copy*, 30; D. K. Bassett, "The 'Amboyna Massacre' of 1623," *Journal of Southeast Asian History* 1, no. 2 (September 1960): 3n8, notes that J. K. J. de Jonge argues that the Dutch carried out the executions in Amboyna in order to terrorize the Ternatans. On the EIC's complaint about the process, see *An Answer unto the Dutch Pamphlet*, 26.

168. Wyncoop 1626, no. 119.

169. *True Relation*, 28.

170. Joosten 1628, no. 180; van Nieuwpoort 1628, no. 115.

171. Corthals 1628, no. 100.

172. This account of Towerson's rebuke of the English appears in "A provisional answer to the attestation of Lawrence Mareschalk and to the rest of the 15 new arguments alledged in justification of the process against the English at Amboyna," enclosed in [EIC] to Carleton, November 20, 1624, SP 84/121/33.

173. Prayer after Towerson's execution comes from Tieller 1626, no. 115; psalm after prayer from Bigwell 1631A; for manner of prayer, see Wyncoop 1626, no. 115.

174. Corthals 1628, no. 114; and Bigwell 1631A, mentioned that Coulson prayed in English.

175. See, for example, Vogel 1626, no. 117; van Leeuwen 1626, no. 117. Powel 1628, no. 9, said Coulson showed him the prayer the day before the execution, and read it to Wetherall and Powel.

176. The VOC councilors denied that the English prayed for a sign. See Joosten 1628, no. 182; van Leeuwen 1628, no. 117; Corthals 1628, no. 117.

177. *Authentick Copy*, 32.

178. Thomas Churchyard, *A generall rehearsall of warres* (London, 1579), Q3v.

179. August 12, 1616, *Diary of Richard Cocks*, vol. 1, 161. This discussion of punishment in Tukugawa Japan draws heavily on Botsman, *Punishment and Power*, 18–25.

180. Anthropologists and others have written abundantly about headhunting in nineteenth- and twentieth-century Indonesia. See, for example, Janet Hoskins, ed., *Headhunting and the Social Imagination in Southeast Asia* (Stanford: Stanford University Press, 1996); and Ricardo Roque, *Headhunting and Colonialism: Anthropology and the Circulation of Human Skulls in the Portuguese Empire, 1870–1930* (Basinstoke: Palgrave Macmillan, 2010). Scholarship on seventeenth-century headhunting in the region is far scanter, with Knaap, "Headhunting," a valuable exception.

181. Knaap, "Headhunting," 169.

182. *An Answer unto the Dutch Pamphlet*, 3.

183. Vander Knijck et al. 1628, no. 2. Wiggerson retracted much of this statement in a third undated deposition in IOR G/21/2, pt. 3.

184. Henrie Hawley, President, and Joseph Cockram, Ric. Bix, and Geo. Muschamp, factors, to the EIC, February 6, 1626, Batavia, IOR E/3/11, no. 1217, f. 93v. Europeans liked to display heads for long periods of time. The head of the New England Indian leader Metacom stood on a staff at Plymouth for some twenty-five years after his execution.
185. Devenijns and Jocket 1623.
186. *Authentick Copy*, 37–38.
187. Letters from Batavia to van Speult, September 26, 1623, IOR I/3/98, ff. 42–44.
188. Powel wrote his employers in Batavia that the English had been condemned for plotting with the Japanese and with natives of the region. EIC Consultations at Java, IOR G/21/3-2, pt. 1, p. 91.
189. *Remonstrance*, 16–17.
190. On meals on Amboyna and on the journey to Batavia, see Marschalck et al. 1623; and *Reply to the Remonstrance*, 41; on Collins's escape see GG to VOC directors at Amsterdam, January 3, 1624, IOR I/3/12, CCXII.
191. John Beaumont to Henry Sill, December 17, 1623, IOR, E/3/10, no. 1136, f. 68r.

Chapter 3

1. Thomas Brockedon, Henrie Hawley, and John Goninge to the EIC, December 14, 1623, Batavia, IOR E/3/10, no. 1130, f. 53v (butcherlie execution), f. 55r (Canniballs); John Goninge to the EIC, December 15, 1623, Batavia, IOR E/3/10, no. 1131, f. 58r (massacre).
2. John Goninge to the EIC, December 15, 1623, Batavia, IOR E/3/10, no. 1131, f. 58r.
3. On waiting for news and the "culture of anticipation," see Michiel van Groesen, *Amsterdam's Atlantic: Print Culture and the Making of Dutch Brazil* (Philadelphia: University of Pennsylvania Press, 2017), chap. 1.
4. When Carleton inspected the trial records and confessions shown him by the Dutch, he saw no evidence of treason, despite what he had been told. Carleton to Conway, May 28, 1624, SP 84/117/83.
5. Carleton to Conway, July 22, 1624, SP 84/118, f. 235.
6. See the endorsement on the December 12, 1623, protest, received in London, May 29, 1624, CO 77/2/71; Court Minutes, May 31, 1624, IOR B/8, p. 542.
7. Chamberlain to Carleton, June 5, 1624, SP 14/167, f. 27.
8. Richard Welden to Sir Wm. Hallidaie, June 16, 1624, IOR E/3/10, no. 1161, f. 136r.
9. Beaumont 1624, no. 11. Thomas Ladbrooke returned to England, but did not give a deposition, and there is no evidence that an eighth survivor, John Sadler, was in England at all in 1624. See Appendix 1 for abbreviations for the depositions connected to the trial.
10. Mark Greengrass, "Hidden Transcripts: Secret Histories and Personal Testimonies of Religious Violence in the French Wars of Religion," in Mark Levene and Penny Roberts, eds., *The Massacre in History* (New York: Berghahn Books, 1999), 69–70.

The pamphlet was *Histoire mémorable de la persécution et saccagement du peuple de Merindol et Cabrières et autres circonvoisins appellez Vaudois* (1556).

11. The 1510 reference is to the massacre of the innocents, in Andrew Chertsey, *Ihesus. The floure of the commaundementes of god* (London, 1510), f. 57r; For the 1567 reference, see Matteo Bandello, *Certaine tragicall discourses written out of Frenche and Latin* (London, 1567), f. 59v. I call the 1510 reference inexplicable because there is a long gap between this work's use of massacre and any subsequent appearance of the word. The *Oxford English Dictionary* (*OED*), moreover, finds the first use of massacre as a noun in 1578 (not in 1567, and certainly not in 1510). "massacre, n." *OED*. I have relied on *Early English Books Online* (*EEBO*) to do word searches in early books. *EEBO* is a remarkable source, although not without its limitations. See Ian Gadd, "The Use and Misuse of *Early English Books Online*," *Literature Compass* 6, no. 3 (2009): 680–692.

12. See the definitions for "*estrágo*" and " *massácre*" as "cruel murther" in John Minsheu, *A Dictionary in Spanish and English* (London, 1599), 122, 166; for horrible murders, see the definition for "massacres" in "A brief explanation of most of the most-difficulties. . .," a section of unfamiliar words and proper nouns, in Guillaume de Salluste du Bartas, *Bartas: His Divine Weekes and Workes* (London, 1605), np.

13. *Prayers and thanksgiving to be used by all the Kings Majesties loving subjects, for the happy deliverance of his Majestie, the Queene, Prince, and states of Parliament, from the most traiterous and bloody intended massacre by gunpowder, the 5 of November 1605* (London, 1606), reprinted in 1610, 1620, and 1623; Christopher Marlowe, *The Massacre at Paris* (London, [1594?]); Edward Waterhouse, *A Declaration of the State of the Colony and Affaires in Virginia. With a Relation of the Barbarous Massacre* (London, 1622); William Russell, *The reporte of a bloudie and terrible massacre in the citty of Mosco* (London, 1607); Ambrosius de Bruyn, *A narration, briefely contayning the history of the French massacre* (London, 1618); *The 27. of September. A relation of letters, and other advertisements of newes. . . . With the lamentable massacre lately committed in the Valtoline . . .* (London, 1622); T. A., *The Massacre of Money* (London, 1602); B. G., *A fig for the Spaniard Wherein are livelie portraihed the damnable deeds, miserable murders, and monstrous massacres of the cursed Spaniard* (London, 1591), reprinted 1592; Jean de Serres, *An historical collection, of the most memorable accidents, and tragicall massacres of France . . .* (London, 1598); William Fulbecke, *An historicall collection of the continuall factions, tumults, and massacres of the Romans and Italians* (London, 1601). For the work with massacre in the subtitle, see *The horrible murther of a young boy of three yeres of age, whose sister had her tongue cut out* (London, 1606).

14. Large-scale massacres took place with greater frequency in Ireland than in the other two kingdoms and with such ferocity that two of them (the 1641 massacre of Protestants and the 1649 massacres at Drogheda and Wexford) are remembered in Ireland to this day. Robin Clifton, "'An Indiscriminate Blackness'? Massacre, Counter-Massacre, and Ethnic Cleansing in Ireland, 1640–1660," in Levene and Roberts, eds., *Massacre in History*, 107, 108.

15. Compare the two words in the Lexicons of Early Modern English (https://leme.library.utoronto.ca/).

16. William Whittingham, *The Bible and Holy Scriptures conteyned in the Olde and Newe Testament* (Geneva, 1561). I searched the 1561 Geneva Bible (STC 2095) using *EEBO*.

17. The reference in 2 Kings 11 is in a headnote to the chapter, not in the text itself. *The Holy Bible conteyning the Old Testament, and the New: newly translated out of the originall tongues* (London, 1611) [STC 2216]. I searched using ProQuest.

18. *Henry VI, Part 1*, V, 4, lines 2835–2836. I searched Shakespeare's works using https://www.opensourceshakespeare.org/.

19. *Richard III*, IV, 3, lines 2728, 2731.

20. EIC Consultations at Java, IOR G/21/3-2, pt. 1, p. 91. The word "butcher" recurred in *The Stripping of Joseph, Or The Crueltie of Brethren to a Brother . . . With a consolatory Epistle, to the English-East-India Company, for their unsufferable wrongs sustained in Amboyna, by the Dutch there . . .* (London, 1625), 11 ("inhumane and wolvish butchering up"), 38 ("butcherly"); and in many EIC communications and later printed works in the context of Amboyna; See also "butcherlie execution," in n.1, above.

21. Nicholas P. Canny, "The Ideology of English Colonization: From Ireland to America," *WMQ* 30, no. 4 (October 1973): 587; Surekha Davies, *Renaissance Ethnography and the Invention of the Human: New Worlds, Maps and Monsters* (New York: Cambridge University Press, 2016).

22. For two references to the Dutch as cannibals, see Thomas Brockedon, Henrie Hawley, and John Goninge to the EIC, December 14, 1623, Batavia, IOR E/3/10, no. 1130, f. 55r; and "A Discourse of the busines of Amboyna in A.d. 1624," Harley 532, f. 42r, BL; for the Dutch as people with "savage hearts," see *Stripping of Joseph*, 12.

23. John Foxe, *The Actes and Monuments* (London, 1563), 1689.

24. Thomas Brockedon, Henrie Hawley, and John Goninge to the EIC, December 14, 1623, Batavia, IOR E/3/10, no. 1130, f. 48r.

25. Depositions of Robert Randall and Abraham Woofe, August 11-14, 1622, SP 84/108/44.

26. *A Second Courante of Newes from the East India* (London, 1622), 2; for "Pagan-like," see *An Answere to the Hollanders Declaration* ([London], 1622), D2v.

27. *A True Relation of the Unjust, Cruell, and Barbarous Proceedings against the English at Amboyna In the East-Indies, by the Neatherlandish Governour and Councel there* (London, 1624). All references in this chapter to the *True Relation* are to this London edition unless otherwise noted. For a different interpretation of how the EIC characterized the two eras of conflict, see Anthony Milton, "Marketing a Massacre: Amboyna, the East India Company and the Public Sphere in Early Stuart England," in Peter Lake and Steven Pincus, eds., *The Politics of the Public Sphere in Early Modern England* (Manchester: Manchester University Press, 2007), 175.

28. Waterhouse, *Declaration*, 14.

29. The English certainly had experience with mass slaughters as perpetrators. There were several such incidents in Ireland, most associated with the Tudor conquest of the kingdom. See David Edwards, "The Escalation of Violence in Sixteenth-Century Ireland," in David Edwards, Pádraig Lenihan and Clodagh Tait, eds., *Age of Atrocity: Violence and Political Conflict in Early Modern Ireland* (Dublin: Four Courts Press, 2007), 34–78.

30. Sir Francis Nethersole to Sir Dudley Carleton, June 25, 1624, SP 14/168, f. 54.

31. Carleton to Conway, July 22, 1624, The Hague, SP 84/118, f. 235.

32. Zuane Pesaro, Venetian Ambassador in England, to the Doge and Senate, October 11, 1624, in *Calendar of State Papers Relating to English Affairs in the Archives of Venice*, vol. 18, 1623–1625, ed. Allen B. Hinds (London: His Majesty's Stationery Office, 1912), no. 608.

33. A second accord, the Treaty of Southampton, was signed in September 1625. It established a maritime alliance.

34. *An Answer Unto the Dutch Pamphlet* (London, 1624), 29.

35. *An Authentick Copy of the Confessions and Sentences, Against M. Towerson, and complices, concerning the bloody conspiracy enterprised against the Castle of Amboyna . . . Translated out of their own copy* (London, 1632), 17.

36. *Authentick Copy,* 32.

37. On the tension between company and state interests, see Rupali Mishra, *A Business of State: Commerce, Politics, and the Birth of the East India Company* (Cambridge, MA: Harvard University Press, 2018), 217–241; and Karen Chancey, "The Amboyna Massacre in English Politics, 1624–1632," *Albion* 30, no. 4 (Winter 1998): 583–598.

38. There are two printings of the *Waerachtich Verhael* from 1624: Knuttel 3547 (in Roman type) was the EIC's printing that accompanied its Dutch-language *True Relation, Een waer verhael vande onlanckse ongerechte, wreede, ende onmenschelycke procedure teghen de Enghelsche tot Amboyna in Oost-Indien, door de Nederlanlanders* [*sic*] *aldaer ghemaeckt op een versierde pretentie van een Conspiratie vande selve Enghelschen* ([London], 1624); Knuttel 3546 (in Gothic, or black letter font, which was more typical in Dutch pamphlets of the era) was the original Dutch printing.

39. Edward Misselden to Carleton, July 27, 1624, Delft, SP 84/118, f. 270. Carleton delivered this manuscript version to the States in August, 1624. Carleton to Conway, August 8, 1624, The Hague, SP 84/119, f. 56.

40. Court Minutes, August 20, 1624, IOR B/9, p. 79. "Libel" (*libellen*, or libels) was one of the words for Dutch pamphlets, along with *maren* (tidings), *paskwillen* (pasquils), *blauwboexkens* (blue books), *briefjes* (little letters), and *boekjes* (little books); a libel was not necessarily libelous, although the States General decided that this one was. Michel Reinders, *Printed Pandemonium: Popular Print and Politics in the Netherlands, 1650–72* (Boston: Brill, 2013), 20.

41. Barlow to Carleton, August 15, 1624, Amsterdam, SP 84/119, f. 113.

42. *Placcaet:* August 18, 1624. There is a copy of this decree in SP 84/119, f. 71; Barlow to Carleton, August 28, 1624, Amsterdam, SP 84/119, f. 164.

43. Court Minutes, October 8, 1624, IOR B/9, p. 151.

44. General Court, December 10, 1624, IOR B/9, p. 251.

45. All of these works were later published in England in 1632.

46. Torture, indeed, was rare, but it was not until 1642 that the distinguished English jurist Edward Coke declared the practice to be in opposition to Magna Carta; two years later, Coke argued that there was no English law that supported it. I have not seen evidence in Coke's work that the Amboyna incident affected his opinions on torture, although it

was certainly a familiar example. Danny Friedman, "Torture and the Common Law," *European Human Rights Law Review* 2 (2006): 180–199, especially 186–187.

47. *A True Declaration of the Newes that came out of the East Indies* (London, 1624), 1–3.

48. *True Relation*, 17; *A Remonstrance of the Directors of the Netherlands East India Company* (London, 1632), Epistle to the reader, A3v.

49. *True Relation*, 1.

50. Miles Ogborn, *Indian Ink: Script and Print in the Making of the English East India Company* (Chicago: University of Chicago Press, 2007), chap. 4, provides a good overview of the EIC's publication and promotional enterprises.

51. *Stationers' Registers*, vol. 4, 87.

52. Harold Love, *Scribal Publication in Seventeenth-Century England* (New York: Oxford University Press, 1993), 187.

53. According to an *EEBO* search there were 488 books printed in 1624 in London, several of which were second printings.

54. Elias Pettit to Henry Pettit, November 1, 1624, *The Oxinden Letters 1607–1642*, ed. Dorothy Gardiner (London: Constable and Company, 1933), 18.

55. On pamphlet formats, see Joad Raymond, *Pamphlets and Pamphleteering in Early Modern Britain* (New York: Cambridge University Press, 2003), 5.

56. It was an era when title pages often had elaborate engravings. See Margery Corbett and Ronald Lightbown, *The Comely Frontispiece: The Emblematic Title-page in England, 1550–1660* (Boston: Routledge and Kegan Paul, 1979).

57. *Een waer verhael vande onlancksche ongerechte, wreede, ende onmenschelycke procedure teghen de Enghelsche tot Amboyna in Oost-Indien, door de Nederlanlanders [sic] aldaer ghemaeckt op een versierde pretentie van een Conspiratie vande selve Enghelschen* ([London], 1624), np.

58. On the St. Omer pamphlet, the press, and a possible creator, see A. F. Allison, "The Later Life and Writings of Joseph Creswell, SJ (1556–1623)," *Recusant History* 15, no. 2 (October 1979): 84; Michael J. Walsh, "The Publishing Policy of the English Jesuits at St. Omer, 1608–1759," *Studies in Church History* 17 (1981): 239–250; A. F. Allison, "John Heigham of St. Omer (c. 1568–1632)," *Recusant History* 4, no. 6 (October 1658): 234–235; C. A. Newdigate, "Notes on the Seventeenth-Century Printing Press of the English College at St. Omers," *The Library: A Quarterly Review of Bibliography and Library Lore*, Third Series, 10, no. 3 (October 1919): 227; A. F. Allison, "A Group of Political Tracts, 1621–1623, by Richard Verstegen," *Recusant History* 18, no. 2 (October 1986): 128–142. A. F. Allison and D. M. Rogers categorize the *True Relation* among "Catholic works in English for which no connection with any particular English Catholic person, institution or group has been found and of which, if a translation, the foreign author has not been identified," in *The Contemporary Printed Literature of the English Counter-Reformation between 1558 and 1640*, 2 volumes (Aldershot: Scholar Press, 1994), vol. 2, Table of Contents; see the book's listing on 189, entry 932.

59. Trumbull to Conway, Brussels, October 3/13, 1624, SP 77/17/353; see also Alastair Bellany and Thomas Cogswell, *The Murder of King James I* (New Haven, CT: Yale University Press, 2015), 148–149. Trumbull reported that this campaign was to be in "sundry languages."

60. On manuscript circulation, see H. S. Bennett, *English Books and Readers, 1603–1640* (New York: Cambridge University Press, 1970), 61. On receiving the manuscript from van Male, see Trumbull to Conway, Brussels, October 3/13, 1624, SP 77/17/353. The EIC made the order for the press to be broken on October 6, 1624, but didn't get its license until a week later. On the press, see Mishra, *Business of State*, 227, 374n86; for the license, see Court of Committees, October 13, 1624, IOR B/9, pp. 159–160.

61. Compare different wording in *True Relation* ([St. Omer], 1624), 18, 26, 27 (quotation), 29; and *True Relation* (London, 1624), 11, 12, 13 (quotation).

62. Compare *True Relation* ([St. Omer], 1624), 55, with *True Relation* (London, 1624), 29.

63. *True Relation* ([St. Omer]), 3 (quotation), 6.

64. (Presborow [Pressburg], 1624). An extant copy is in States General, 1.01.02, inv. no. 12551.62-3, National Archives, The Hague.

65. On news prints, see Henk van Nierop, "Romeyn de Hooghe and the Imagination of Dutch Foreign Policy," in David Onnekink and Gijs Rommelse, eds., *Ideology and Foreign Policy in Early Modern Europe (1650–1750)* (Burlington, VT: Ashgate, 2011), 199, 201.

66. Morris Abbot and various EIC committees to Carleton, February 19, 1625, London, SP 84/122, f. 167; Court of Committees, February 16, 1625, IOR B/9, p. 345.

67. On soldiers as the audience for the St. Omer *True Relation*, see Pamela Neville-Sington, "The Primary Purchas Bibliography," in L. E. Pennington, ed., *The Purchas Handbook: Studies of the Life, Times and Writings of Samuel Purchas, 1577–1626*, 2 volumes (London: Hakluyt Society, 1997), vol. 2, 525n3. Allison and Rogers, *Contemporary Printed Literature*, vol. 2, 189, suggest that the St. Omer pamphlet was intended for English Catholics.

68. The Dutch thought it was bloody, too, but used that adjective to describe the conspiracy. The phrase "bloody conspiracy" appeared in the title of the *Authentick Copy*.

69. President Thomas Brockedon, Henry Hawley, and John Goninge to van Speult, Governor of Amboyna, December 20, 1623, Batavia, IOR E/3/10, no. 1137, f. 70v.

70. Carleton to Conway, June 19, 1624, The Hague, SP 84/118, f. 87.

71. Abbot and other EIC members to Carleton, July 10, 1624, SP 84/118, f. 157.

72. Winge to Carleton, September 28, 1624, Flushing, SP 84/120, f. 138.

73. Morris Abbot and various EIC committees to Carleton, February 19, 1625, London, SP 84/122, f. 167.

74. Morris Abbot and various EIC committees to Carleton, February 19, 1625, London, SP 84/122, f. 167.

75. Court of Committees, April 21, 1626, IOR B/10, p. 372; EIC to Carleton, February 26, 1624, SP 84/122, f. 176.

76. Petition of Edward Clarke to the Lords Commissioners who are authorized to negotiate with the States, [April 1627], CO 77/4/31.

77. The king's secret instructions to Dudley Lord Carleton, May [1627?], SP 84/133, f. 162.

78. Court Minutes, July 6, 1627, IOR B/12, p. 13.

79. Court Minutes, December 12, 1627, IOR B/12, p. 180.

80. *Newes out of East India* (London, [1624]).

81. James Heath, *A Chronicle of the Late Intestine War in the Three Kingdoms of England, Scotland and Ireland* (London, 1676), 308.

82. For the teary reader, see *Stripping of Joseph*, "A Friend of the Publisher . . .," H2r.

83. The EIC's woodcuts probably preceded the Pressburg broadside, because the EIC didn't learn of this continental publication until February 1625 and the company's woodcuts existed by November.

84. The Codrington Library's *True Relation* (London, 1624) (shelfmark h.10.21) is a first impression with the woodcut stitched in. My thanks to the librarian Gaye Morgan at the Codrington Library for taking the time to explain to me the distinction between books being sewn and stitched, and for analyzing this pamphlet's construction. The owner of this pamphlet also carefully went through the work making the corrections in the errata, something that book owners rarely did. See Bennett, *English Books and Readers*, 207-208.

85. The Anabaptist Edward Wrightman was executed in 1612.

86. *Een waer verhael*, frontispiece (of the *Een waer verhael*, not the whole pamphlet), and after p. 34 of the *Antwoorde vande Duytsche Relatie*. Very few copies of this work survive, but the ones that do have this extra woodcut, suggesting that it was part of the binding conventions in 1624 and not something added in later decades or even centuries by book buyers, as was the case with other editions of the *True Relation*. Two copies in the British Library, for example, each contain one copy of the English language woodcut and two copies of this second woodcut. See 9055.b.11 and 106.a.57, 58, BL.

87. *The Book of Common Prayer* (London, [1623]).

88. Jesse Lander, "'Foxe's *Books of Martyrs*: printing and popularizing the *Acts and Monuments*," in Claire McEachern and Debora Shuger, eds., *Religion and Culture in Renaissance England* (New York: Cambridge University Press, 1997), 69-72. Foxe's work was part of an important genre of compilations in prose and image of the suffering of Protestant martyrs, joined a century later by another such work, the *Martyr's Mirror* (1660), which chronicled Anabaptist suffering and executions in the Low Countries.

89. For a serene, tortured man, see Simon Cutbert, depicted in John Foxe, *Actes and Monuments* (London, 1583), 2032; for an exception, see the depiction of Bishop Bonner scourging John Willes, Foxe, *Actes and Monuments*, 2043.

90. For works with illustrations showing Spanish violence in the Netherlands, see *De Spaensche Tiranye Gheschiet in Neder-lant . . .* (Amsterdam, 1621); and *Le Miroir de la Cruelle, & horrible Tyrannie Espagnole perpetree au Pays Bas, par le Tyran Duc de Albe . . .* (Amsterdam, 1620). For the Dutch discovery of Las Casas, see Benjamin Schmidt, *Innocence Abroad: The Dutch Imagination and the New World, 1570-1670* (New York: Cambridge University Press, 2001), 96-99.

91. Laura Caroline Stevenson, *Praise and Paradox: Merchants and Craftsmen in Elizabethan Popular Literature* (New York: Cambridge University Press, 1984), 77.

92. On "martyred" as a synonym for tortured, see *True Relation*, 12, 13, 38; for the martyred Japanese, see *An Answer unto the Dutch Pamphlet*, 41.

93. *A Reply to the Remonstrance* (London, 1632), 33.

94. The ballad instructs the reader to find more information in the printed *True Relation*.

95. On the stock woodcuts, see Alexandra Franklin, "Making Sense of Broadside Ballad Illustrations in the Seventeenth and Eighteenth Centuries," in Kevin D. Murphy and Sally O'Driscoll, eds. *Studies in Ephemera: Text and Image in Eighteenth-Century Print* (Lewisburg, PA: Bucknell University Press, 2013), 169–194. On the relationship between ballads and pamphlets, see Bennet, *English Books and Readers*, 185. This information about the tune comes from http://www.fresnostate.edu/folklore/Olson/BMADD.HTM#BRAGAND, part of http://www.fresnostate.edu/folklore/Olson/index.html, a website created by the now deceased Bruce Olson. John Barry Talley reprints this later song and tune ("Robin and Jeck") from a manuscript history of the Tuesday Club in *Secular Music in Colonial Annapolis: The Tuesday Club, 1745-56* (Urbana: University of Illinois Press, 1988), 94–96. Talley, 96, suggests that the tune was a round, requiring many singers to bring out the full texture, though, he adds, "a clumsy one." For a reference to the tune as lost, see Claude M. Simpson, *The British Broadside Ballad and Its Music* (New Brunswick, NJ: Rutgers University Press, 1966), 743.

96. Helen C. White, *Tudor Books of Saints and Martyrs* (Madison: University of Wisconsin Press, 1963), 165.

97. *True Relation*, 29–30.

98. *Newes out of East India*. Milton, "Marketing a Massacre," 176, remarks on the rhetorical utility for the EIC of these providential rebukes.

99. Deposition of George Furbushe [Forbes] of Aberdeen, February 6, 1628, SP 16/92, f. 76.

100. List of the men who tried the English at Amboyna, [1624], CO 77/3/45; some biographical information about these men, CO 77/3/44. As late as 1628, the English agent in the United Provinces reported that he had gathered attestations by four VOC employees from Amboyna who testified that van Speult was "never well but went as a man troubled w[i]th an evill conscience till the tyme of his death." Burley [Barlow] to Lord Carleton (Junior), March 27/April 6, 1628, SP 84/136/91.

101. On these misfortunes, see *True Relation*, 29–30. Thomas 1629A attested that van Speult prayed for a sign.

102. Joosten 1626, Wyncoop 1626, van Leeuwen 1626, Tieller 1626, and Vogel 1626, nos. 125–29. See also their 1628 depositions (except Vogel), nos. 118–120, 182.

103. Wyncoop 1626 and Joosten 1626, no. 130.

104. *True Relation*, 29; One of the VOC's judges at Amboyna explained emphatically that the English were not charged for the cloth, "as it is distinctly shown in the Company's books." The velvet, he elaborated, had been owned by the Dutch for quite a while. On Sundays, they draped it over the president's chair, and they used it for the funerals of distinguished people. See Tieller 1626, no. 122.

105. *True Relation*, 20–23

106. *True Relation*, 23.

107. Court of Committees, August 1, 1628, IOR B/13, p. 48; Court of Committees, 1 October 1628, IOR B/13, pp. 75–76.

108. Both companies accused each other of forging various documents, and sometimes accusers identified specific culprits. The EIC, for example, accused the VOC council

member Laurens de Marschalck of forging Emanuel Thompson's confession. See the EIC's letter to Carleton, November 20, 1624, SP 84/121/33; for the legitimacy of Coulson's book, see the depositions of John Powel, George Forbes, John Cappur, John Beaumont, and Andrew Ellam, [October 10?] 1628.

109. Privy Council to Carleton (Junior), September 23, 1628, SP 84/138/16. The Privy Council described the items incorrectly as Towerson's Bible and Thompson's Tablebook. The items were Coulson's *Psalmes of David* and Griggs's Tablebook.

110. Elias Pettit to Henry Pettit, November 1, 1624, *The Oxinden Letters*, 18.

111. Court Minutes, September 18, 1624, IOR B/9, p. 116.

112. http://almanac.oremus.org/easter/

113. Maurice Lee Jr., ed., *Dudley Carleton to John Chamberlain, 1603–1624: Jacobean Letters* (New Brunswick, NJ: Rutgers University Press, 1972), 319n3.

114. Marvin Arthur Breslow, *A Mirror of England: English Puritan Views of Foreign Nations, 1618–1640* (Cambridge, MA: Harvard University Press, 1970), 89. This work is Scott, *Symmachia* (Utrecht, 1624).

115. Thomas Cogswell, *The Blessed Revolution: English Politics and the Coming of War, 1621–1624* (New York: Cambridge University Press, 1989), espec. chap. 8; Bellany and Cogswell, *The Murder of King James I*, 1–22.

116. Jacob Selwood, *Diversity and Difference in Early Modern London* (Burlington, VT: Ashgate, 2010), 1.

117. John Chamberlain to Sir Dudley Carleton, London, February 26, 1624/5, in *The Court and Times of James the First . . .*, Thomas Birch, compiler, 2 volumes (London: H. Colburn, 1849), vol. 2, 499–500, quotations on 500.

118. "A Discourse of the Busines of Amboyna in A.d. 1624," Harley 532, BL.

119. "A Discourse of the Busines of Amboyna in A.d. 1624," Harley 532, ff. 29v, 30v, BL.

120. "A Discourse of the Busines of Amboyna in A.d. 1624," Harley 532, ff. 41r-44r, BL.

121. Morris Abbot and various EIC committees to Carleton, February 19, 1625, London, SP 84/122, f. 167.

122. L. H. Cust, "Greenbury, Richard (b. before 1600? D. 1670)?," rev. Sarah Herring, in *DNB*; quotation from Thos. Locke to Carleton, February 21, 1625, SP 14/184, f. 44.

123. Court of Committees, February 18, 1625, IOR B/9, p. 346.

124. Morris Abbot and various EIC committees to Carleton, February 19, 1625, London, SP 84/122, f. 167. For the report of the EIC members who attended the Privy Council, see Court Minutes, February 21, 1625, IOR B/9, pp. 350–351; Abbott and some committees to Carleton, February 26, 1625, London SP 84/122, f. 176; On the Duke of Buckingham's interest in the painting, see Court Minutes, February 28, 1625, IOR B/9, p. 359; On the fainting woman, see William Sanderson, *Graphice. The Use of the Pen and Pensil* (London, 1658), 14; On the painting's disappearance, see *True Relation* (London, 1651), Advertisement to the Reader. Sanderson, *Graphice*, 14, described the painting as "defac'd" by men in power; in his *Compleat History of the Lives and Reigns . . .* (London, 1656), 578, he said the painting was burned on order of the king and council.

125. Neville-Sington, "The Primary Purchas Bibliography," 533.

126. Court of Committees, February 18, 1625, IOR B/9, p. 346.

127. Bartolomé de las Casas, *The Spanish Colonie, or Brief Chronicle of the Actes and Gestes of the Spaniards in the West Indies* (London, 1583); William S. Maltby, *The Black Legend in England: The Development of Anti-Spanish Sentiment, 1558–1660* (Durham, NC: Duke University Press, 1971).

128. *Stripping of Joseph*, 5–11, 12–15, 17, quotations on 10–11. The quotations are italicized in the original.

129. By the First Anglo-Dutch War, English accusations of Dutch cruelty completed the transformation of the Dutch into Spaniards. See Carla Gardina Pestana, "Cruelty and Religious Justifications for Conquest in the Mid-Seventeenth-Century English Atlantic," in Linda Gregerson and Susan Juster, eds., *Empires of God: Religious Encounters in the Early Modern Atlantic* (Philadelphia: University of Pennsylvania Press, 2011), 37–57, espec. 47–57.

130. Richard Dutton, *Licensing, Censorship, and Authorship in Early Modern England: Buggeswords* (Basinstoke: Palgrave, 2000).

131. *Stripping of Joseph*, H2r, [51]. Italicized in the original.

132. Samuel Purchas, *Hakluytus Posthumus or Purchas his Pilgrimes*, 4 volumes (London, 1625).

133. Purchas, *Purchas his Pilgrimes*, vol. 2, 1853–1857.

134. Neville-Sington, "The Primary Purchas Bibliography," 520–533.

135. Proposal to the king by the States General ambassadors, May 10/20, 1628, States General, 1.01.02, inv. no. 12589.45, National Archives, The Hague; Joachimi to Dorchester, January 8, 1630, SP 84/141/8.

136. Margot Heinemann, *Puritanism and the Theatre* (New York: Cambridge University Press, 1982), 209–210. There were riots on over two-thirds of the Shrove Tuesdays between 1606 and 1641. Mishra, *Business of State*, 376n111.

137. *Amboyna*. Lost Plays Database, accessed August 9, 2019, https://lostplays.folger. edu/Amboyna; quotation from Thos. Locke to Carleton, February 21, 1625, SP 14/ 184, f. 44.

138. John Chamberlain to Sir Dudley Carleton, London, February 26, 1624/5, in *The Court and Times of James the First*, vol. 2, 500.

139. On the company's struggles in the late 1620s, see Mishra, *Business of State*, 244–255.

Chapter 4

1. EIC Consultations at Java, IOR G/21/3-2, pt. 1, pp. 91–92, quotations on 91. This letter from Macassar may be the letter of June 19 (the English date), which circulated in Europe but has not survived. There are references to a manuscript letter by the English factors of June 19 ("a briefe Collection of the effect of certaine Letters written by the English Factors at Jaccatra, dated the 19. June 1623") circulating in the period. See *A Reply to the Remonstrance* (London, 1632), 9; VOC council at Batavia to Adrian Jacob van der Dusse, Jambi, June 30, 1623, IOR I/3/98, f. 36, reported the visit and noted the council's desire for the "exact truth."

2. See the 1636 town covenant for Contentment (later Dedham), Massachusetts, *Dedham Historical Register* (Dedham, MA, 1891), vol. 2, 153–154.

3. Even a modern truth and reconciliation commission would not have satisfied them. While these modern commissions normally work to resolve conflicts within a nation, the intimate connection of the English and Dutch in this era makes their conflict over Amboyna akin to these other painful internal struggles. My thinking on the different functions of justice and on truth and reconciliation commissions has been informed by a range of works, including Klaus Neumann and Janna Thompson, eds., *Historical Justice and Memory* (Madison: University of Wisconsin Press, 2015); Birgit Schwelling, ed., *Reconciliation, Civil Society, and the Politics of Memory: Transnational Initiatives in the 20th and 21st Century* (Bielefeld: Transcript Verlag, 2012); and "Forum on Truth and Reconciliation in History," *AHR* 114, no. 4 (October 2009): 899–977.

4. EIC council at Batavia to Henry Sill at Amboyna, January 3, 1623/4, IOR G/21/3-2, pt. 2, pp. 212–214; diary kept by one of the EIC council at Banten, May 30, 1624, IOR G/21/3-2, pt. 1, p. 18.

5. On access to the trial records, see Summary of 26 attestations, act of 4 August, 1623, IOR I/3/10, CXC; and VOC council to Jhebert Visnicht in Persia, August 8, 1623, IOR I/3/98, f. 37.

6. Letter from GG in Council to VOC directors, January 3, 1624, IOR I/3/12, CCXII.

7. By early August 1623, the VOC council was still uncertain about the cast of characters involved in the episode—the English, the Japanese, the captain of the slaves, and unspecified others. Van Speult himself contributed to this uncertainty, explaining in several letters to the council how Towerson had joined with a host of accomplices, including the people of Ternate, Luhu, and Seram, in addition to some of the Bandanese who had escaped the slaughter on their islands in 1621. On this cast of characters, see VOC council at Batavia to van Speult, replying to his letters of June 5, July 8, July 16, and September 15, September 26, 1623, IOR I/3/98, f. 42.

8. Summary of 26 attestations, 1623, IOR I/3/10, CXC. "*Massacre*" appears in the Dutch original, IOR I/3/9, CXC.

9. The timing of this plot is unclear. The VOC council reported that Captain Hitto (as they called an indigenous tributary) had informed them that the people of Luhu had written a letter to Welden, which may have happened before the Amboyna incident. See Letter from GG in Council to VOC directors, January 3, 1624, IOR I/3/12, CCXII.

10. Letter from the EIC council in Batavia, January 17, 1623/24, IOR G/21/3-2, pt. 2, p. 229.

11. Diary kept by one of the EIC council at Banten, IOR G/21/3-2, pt. 1, September 17, 1624, p. 36.

12. See a fight over access to housing, in letter from the EIC council in Batavia [to EIC], January 17, 1623/4, IOR G/21/3-2, pt. 2, pp. 219–220.

13. Protest by John Goninge, Richard Welden, and George Bruen, by order of President Thomas Brockedon, against the Dutch General, Pieter de Carpentier, and Council, December 12, 1623, IOR E/3/10, no. 1128, is missing the first four pages; there is a complete version in CO 77/2/71.

14. VOC council to Coen in the Netherlands, January 29, 1624, IOR I/3/98, f. 72.

15. The English spice trade ended up flourishing in the 1630s and 1640s. On the expansion of trade opportunities after Amboyna, see D. K. Bassett, "The 'Amboyna Massacre' of 1623," *Journal of Southeast Asian History* 1, no. 2 (September 1960): 8–12. For VOC

complaints about English noncompliance, see VOC council to Governor Jacques le Pebure (no location), December 2, 1623, IOR I/3/98, ff. 45–46; VOC council to van den Dusen at Jambi, December 13, 1623, IOR I/3/98, ff. 48–49.

16. Letter from GG in Council to VOC directors, January 3, 1624, IOR I/3/12, CCXII.

17. GG to VOC directors, January 24, 1624, IOR I/3/12, CCXIII. On strategies to deal with the EIC, see VOC council to Jhebert Visnicht in Persia, August 8, 1623, IOR I/3/98, f. 37.

18. VOC council to Peiter van den Broeck at Surat, August 9, 1624, IOR I/3/98, f. 86.

19. VOC council to Bartholomew Kunst at Jambi, March 18, 1625, IOR I/3/98, f. 88.

20. Extract from letter from GG Carpentier in Council to VOC directors, January 17, 1625, IOR I/3/14, CCXXII. It's "anti-batavia" in the Dutch original. IOR I/3/13, CCXXII.

21. The EIC in London signaled these aspirations for permanence when it tried to hire a minister for Lagundy before it learned that the factory had failed. See Court Minutes, March 6 and 8, 1626, IOR B/10, pp. 301, 304.

22. Diary kept by one of the EIC council at Banten, November 26–29, 1624, IOR G/21/3-2, pt. 1, pp. 54–56.

23. Extract from letter from GG Carpentier in Council to VOC directors, January 17, 1625, IOR I/3/14, CCXXII.

24. For this remarkable description of the disease and speculation about its causes, see Henry Hawley, Joseph Cockram, Richard Bix, and George Muschamp to the EIC, Batavia, February 6, 1626, IOR E/3/11, no. 1217, ff. 78v-79r; and Henry Hawley, Joseph Cockram, Richard Bix, and George Muschamp to the EIC, Batavia, August 3, 1625, IOR E/3/11, no. 1203, which also describes how the English took possession of the islands; quotation on f. 42r.

25. VOC directors to GG and C of India, November 19, 1624, IOR I/3/90, ff. 29v-30v; VOC directors at Middelburg to GG and C of India, December 6, 1625, IOR I/3/90, f. 34r.

26. Letter from unnamed author at Batavia to the States General, with copies of evidence about the Amboyna conspiracy, n.d., IOR I/3/14, CCXXIII.

27. Henry Hawley, Joseph Cockram, Richard Bix, and George Muschamp to the EIC, Batavia, October 13, 1625, IOR E/3/11, no. 1210, especially f. 59v.

28. Henry Hawley, Joseph Cockram, Richard Bix, and George Muschamp to the EIC, Batavia, February 6, 1626, IOR E/3/11, no. 1217, f. 93v.

29. For the quotation and the animal metaphor, see extract from a letter from GG to VOC directors, December 13, 1626, IOR I/3/14, CCXXXIII; on despair about having a friendship, see VOC directors at Amsterdam to GG and C of India, April 1626, IOR I/3/90, f. 36r.

30. Henry Hawley, Joseph Cockram, Richard Bix, and George Muschamp to the EIC, Batavia, February 6, 1626, IOR E/3/11, no. 1217, quotation on f. 100r; for a VOC view, see VOC council to Martin Ystrandsen on the Coromandel coast, October 28, 1626, IOR I/3/98, f. 60.

31. Henry Hawley, Joseph Cockram, Richard Bix, and George Muschamp to the EIC, Batavia, February 6, 1626, IOR E/3/11, no. 1217, quotation on f. 100r.

32. Unsigned letter from Batavia to the States General, October 25, 1625, IOR I/3/14, CCXXIII.

33. VOC directors to the GG and C of India, November 1, 1624, IOR I/3/90, f. 28v.

34. The transcripts record this man as "Nieucoop," but it must have been Jan van Nieuwpoort. IOR I/3/14, CCXXIII.

35. *A True Relation of the Unjust, cruell, and barbarous proceedings against the English at Amboyna . . . Also the copy of a pamphlet . . . falsely intituled, A True Declaration . . . Together with an Answer to the same Pamphlet* (London, 1624). All references in this chapter to the *True Relation* are to this London edition unless otherwise noted.

36. Attestation by members of the VOC council, September 10, 1625, IOR I/3/14, CCXXIII.

37. VOC council to van Speult, August 5, 1625, IOR I/3/98, f. 58.

38. Extract from letter from van den Broecke at Surat to GG at Batavia, April 4, 1626, IOR I/3/16, CCXLI.

39. Van Speult at Surat to GG at Batavia, April 4 and 15, 1626, IOR I/3/16, CCXLII.

40. VOC protest against the English leaving Banten, November 28, 1627, Batavia, IOR I/3/16, CCXLVII.

41. Alison Games, "Violence on the Fringes: The Virginia (1622) and Amboyna (1623) Massacres," *History* 99 (July 2014): 523.

42. Beaumont 1624, no. 9. See Appendix 1 for abbreviations for the depositions connected to the trial.

43. William M. Reddy, *The Navigation of Feeling: A Framework for the History of Emotions* (New York: Cambridge University Press, 2001), 123–124.

44. Jane Webber described herself as the executrix for her husband and Sherrock in her petition, April 7, 1652, CO 77/7, no. 23. For William Webber's expenses for Sherrock's sickness and funeral, see Court of Committees, July 24, 1626, IOR B/11, p. 53.

45. *True Relation*, 21.

46. *A Remonstrance of the Directors of the Netherlands East India Company* (London, 1632), 16–17.

47. See the copy of "An order for committing of John Beamont and Edward Collins, merchants," July 30, 1623, IOR G/21/3-2, pt. 1, pp. 96–97.

48. For Collins's and Beaumont's depositions, September 22, 1624, see SP 84/120, f. 114; for Fardo's oral will, see the depositions of Sherrock, Ramsey, and Webber on October 14, 1624, Consistory Court of London, deposition book, September 1624–June 1625, DL/C/229, Greater London Record Office; for the reference to depositions about Johnson's estate, see Petition of Thomas Johnson to commissioners, [April] 1627, SP 16/61, f. 133.

49. See, for example, Powel 1624, no. 9, who tried to recreate Fardo's final words to him verbatim.

50. For Ladbrooke, see Court of Committees, October 29, 1624, IOR B/9, p. 175; for Powel, see Court Minutes, September 18, 1624, IOR B/9, pp. 117–118. The ryal refers to the ryal (or real) of eight, or pieces of eight as they were also known, a primary currency in the Indian Ocean trade. I used D. K. Bassett's work to determine the equivalent value: he wrote that 132,000 reals of eight was equivalent to £33,000 in 1623. See Bassett, "Amboyna," 10.

51. Court of Committees, July 12, 1624, IOR B/9, p. 19.

52. Court Minutes, June 30, 1624, IOR B/8, p. 560.
53. Beaumont and Collins were deposed on July 7, Powel on July 9, Webber on July 10, Sherrock on July 12, and Ramsey on July 13.
54. Court Minutes, November 17, 1624, IOR B/9, pp. 202–203; [EIC] to Carleton, November 20, 1624, SP 84/121, f. 104. There is a French translation of Marschalck's deposition in SP 84/121, f. 27.
55. Court of Committees, September 22, 1624, IOR B/9, p. 135. It seems unlikely Ramsey was tortured.
56. Petition of Sarah Collins and her children, John and Elizabeth Collins, to the Council of State, January 8, 1651/2, SP 84/159/49.
57. Court of Committees, November 17 and 22, 1624, IOR B/9, pp. 202, 209.
58. Court Minutes, September 18, 1624, IOR B/9, pp. 117–118, quotation on 117.
59. Court of Committees, October 18, 1625, IOR B/10, p. 123.
60. A reference to the "Amboyna men" appears in Court of Committees, December 8, 1624, IOR B/9, p. 241; for Ladbrooke's shillings, see Court of Committees, February 21, 1625, IOR B/9, p. 350.
61. Court of Committees, December 8, 1624, IOR B/9, p. 241.
62. Thomas Brockedon, Henrie Hawley, and John Goninge to the EIC, December 14, 1623, Batavia, IOR E/3/10, no. 1131, f. 53v.
63. Meeting to answer petitions, September 25, 1624, IOR B/9, p. 141.
64. "Dilligent" comes from Court Minutes, September 18, 1624, IOR B/9, p. 117; EIC president and council at Batavia to Gabriel Towerson at Amboyna, December 17, 1622, IOR G/21/3A, pt. 2, f. 325r-v.
65. Court of Committees, August 1, 1627, September 12, 1627, IOR B/12, pp. 37, 75–76, quotation on 76.
66. On this practice, see VOC directors to the GG and Council of India, March 4, 1621, IOR I/3/90, f. 11v; VOC directors to the GG and Council, April 14, 1622, IOR I/3/90, f. 17r; VOC directors to GG and C, The Hague, March 15, 1623, IOR I/3/90, f. 24v; for the VOC's instructions after the king's order, see VOC directors to GG and C, Amsterdam, November 1, 1624, IOR I/3/90, f. 28v.
67. Court of Committees, October 22, 1628, IOR B/13, pp. 102–103.
68. In 1625, they were looking especially for Coen (whom the EIC held responsible for plotting the whole affair) and Marschalck. Court Minutes, April 11, 1625, IOR B/9, pp. 419–420; Court of Committees, September 26, 1627, October 26, 1627, IOR B/12, pp. 89, 127.
69. Court Minutes, July 16, 1624, IOR B/9, pp. 23–24. In his deposition on July 10, Webber 1624, no. 9, said that gunpowder was placed in slits of Clarke's toes. Sherrock did not mention this particular torture in his own deposition on July 12: the torture he described here of gunpowder placed in a man's chest and then ignited may have happened on Banda in 1622, or may have been an English atrocity story told after the fact. See Robert Codrington, *His Majesties Propriety, and Dominion on the British Seas Asserted: Together with a true Account of the Neatherlanders Insupportable Insolencies, and Injuries. . .* (London, 1665), 146. This torture, moreover, was not included in the *True Relation*, but rather in *An Answer unto the Dutch Pamphlet* (London, 1624), 27.

70. Court of Committees, July 7, 1626, IOR B/11, p. 10.

71. According to John Beaumont, the two men traveled on the *Elizabeth*. John Beaumont to Henry Sill, on the *Royal Exchange*, December 17, 1623, IOR E/3/10, no. 1136, f. 68r-v.

72. Court of Committees, August 11, 1624, IOR B/9, pp. 62–65, "only for" and "much moved" on 63; "detestacon" on 64.

73. On the many burdens of this post for the two Carletons, see unnamed correspondent to Carleton, Newmarket, February 20, 1624/5, Add. 35,832, f. 176, BL; and notes of Dudley Carleton's [junior] negotiations, 1626–1631, SP 84/144/55.

74. Carleton Junior to Lord Killultagh, April 16, 1627, SP 84/133/50.

75. Edward Misselden to the Privy Council, September 22, 1626, Delft, SP 84/132, f. 59.

76. VOC directors at Amsterdam to GG and C of India, August 10, 1627, IOR I/3/90, f. 44r.

77. Court of Committees, May 11, 21, June 22, 1627, IOR B/11, pp. 523 ("bloody massacre"), 530–531, 571.

78. R. Burley [Barlow] to Lord Carleton (Junior), April 9/19, 1628, SP 84/137/13.

79. Court of Committees, November 2, 1627, IOR B/12, pp. 135–136. The company, always loath to spend money unnecessarily, also thought it might be too expensive to maintain Powel and Ramsey in the United Provinces. May 21, 1627, IOR B/11, pp. 530–531.

80. Extracts from Misselden's letters, presented to Coke on March 3, 1628, SP 84/136/53; quotation from Carleton (Junior) to Conway, November 8, 1628, SP 84/138/48.

81. "In great Jollity" from Extracts from Burley's [Barlow's] letter of February 15, 1628, SP 84/136/52; "English traitors" and "gon laughing" from Extracts from Misselden's letters of January 26 and February 2, 1628, SP 84/136/53. The Amboyna council members who deposed that spring were Coper, Corthals, Tieller, van Santen, Joosten, Marschalk, van Leeuwen, Cravanger, Wyncoop, and van Nieuwpoort.

82. R. Burley (Robert Barlow) to Lord Carleton (Junior), April 6, 1628, SP 84/137/11.

83. VOC directors at Amsterdam to CC and G of India, April 3, 1628, IOR I/3/90, f. 46r.

84. Carleton (Junior) to Dorchester, November 8, 1628, SP 84/138/48; Carleton (Junior) to [Dorchester], November 18, 1628, SP 84/138/51.

85. Carleton (Junior) to Conway, February 22, 1628, SP 84/136/37; Minutes of Privy Council proceedings, November 19, 1628, SP 84/138/52; Court of Committees, November 26, 1628, IOR B/13, pp. 147–148.

86. Barlow to D. Carleton (Junior), April 30, 1629, SP 84/139/57.

87. Anton Poot, *Crucial Years in Anglo-Dutch Relations (1625–1642): The Political and Diplomatic Contacts* (Hilversum: Verloren, 2013), 82. The EIC records are missing for July 1629–June 1630, so unfortunately it isn't possible to track the company's deliberations over this decision.

88. Examination before Lord President (of the Privy Council) and Secretary Coke, Whitehall, October 30, 1627, CO 77/4/40.

89. Powel was sent to Portsmouth on September 22, 1627, IOR B/12, p. 86. For Ramsey's presence, see October 26, 1627, IOR B/12, p. 127.

90. Speeches used by Forbes since his coming to London, October 15, 1627, SP 16/81, f. 144. Barlow named these men as Vincent Corthals, who was a secretary at Amboyna, and Reneir Soreheurs, who said he wasn't a judge at Amboyna. Barlow believed that he must nonetheless have been sympathetic to the judges, "and knew his owne giltines" and thus escaped. It's possible that Reneir Soreheurs was a bungled version of Renier Corcerius. R. Burley [Barlow] to Carleton (Junior), October 11, 1627, SP 84/135, f. 64.

91. For his examination on October 30, 1627, see CO 77/4/40; for his "True Relation," see CO 77/4/75. This text was presented to Coke and Dorchester on November 13, 1629, shortly before Forbes went to The Hague as a witness; "utterly impossible" is from his examination, CO 77/4/40.

92. For "English wittnesses," see Vane to Dorchester, August 18/28, 1630, SP 84/142/14.

93. "Complices der conspiratie," in VOC directors at Amsterdam to CC and G of India, April 3, 1628, IOR I/3/89, no. 82.

94. Vane to [Dorchester], November 20/30, 1629, SP 84/140/43; Vane to [Dorchester], January 27/February 6, 1629/30, SP 84/141/15; Vane to [Dorchester], December 24, 1630, SP 84/140/71.

95. Vane's Memorial to the States about Amboyna, November 28, 1629, SP 84/140/50. See also the negotiations described in Vane's report on leaving Holland, April 25/March 5, 1630, SP 84/141/78.

96. For complaints about expenses, see Robert Burley [Barlow] to the Procurator, February 14/24, 1630, SP 84/141/29.

97. Vane to Dorchester, February 24/March 4, 1630, SP 84/141/37; for Vane's report of orders to return them, see Vane to Dorchester, March 23/April 2, 1630, SP 84/141/55.

98. Court of Committees, August 20, 1630, IOR B/14, pp. 28–29.

99. Vane to Dorchester, August 18/28, with addition on September 2, 1630, SP 84/142/14.

100. Vane to [Dorchester], August 28/September 7, 1630, SP 84/142/18.

101. On Beaumont's language skills, see Captain John Saris to Edmond Camden, November 23, 1612, William Foster, ed., *Letters Received by the East India Company From its Servants in the East*, 6 volumes (London: Sampson Low, Marston & Company, 1896–1902), vol. 1, 200.

102. Deposition of Hendrik Alban, Stadsarchief Amsterdam, 5075 (Archief van de Notarissen ter Standplaats Amsterdam), inv. 847 (Notaris J. Steijns), Testimony, July 8, 1630. My thanks to Susanah Shaw Romney for discovering this document and to Danny Noorlander for his careful translation. For earlier evidence of Barlow soliciting depositions, see Barens 1629, no. 18. For "gnawing of conscience," see the fifth interrogatory posed in the deposition of Vander Knijck et al. 1628.

103. VOC directors at Amsterdam, to the GG and C of India at Batavia, April 27, 1631, IOR I/3/90, f. 59v.

104. The *Amboina* was funded by the Amsterdam chamber. See the database, "Dutch-Asiatic Shipping in the 17th and 18th centuries," http://resources.huygens.knaw.nl/das/detailVoyage/91425.

105. VOC directors at Amsterdam to the GG and C of India at Batavia, November 22, 1631, IOR I/3/90, f. 61v.

106. Court of Committees, October 27, 1630, IOR B/14, p. 74.
107. Court of Committees, October 27, 1630; November 12, 1630, IOR B/14, pp. 74, 85–86.
108. Court of Committees, 13 May 1631, IOR B/14, p. 243.
109. On Ramsey's visit to the king, see Court Minutes, September 18, 1624, IOR B/9, p. 118; Ramsey, a Scot born in Berwick, went to court with Lord Holdernesse, John Ramsay, who may have been a distant kinsman and was a favorite of James VI and I. See A. MacDonald, "Ramsay, John, earl of Holdernesse (c. 1580–1626), courtier," in *DNB*.
110. Court of Committees, July 13, 1632, IOR B/15, p. 15. Powel seems to have ended up in India, according to extant material in the EIC records, and an Ephraim Ramsey was at Japara in December 1634. Ramsey's will, written in 1631, was proven April 14, 1638, PROB 11/176/457, NAUK.
111. Petition of Beaumont, Forbes, Collins, Powel, and Ramsey to the Privy Council [1631], SP 16/205, f. 48; Court Minutes, September 15, 1630, IOR B/14, p. 66; Petition of John Powle of London, merchant, to the king [1633], SP 16/257, f. 228.
112. Poot, *Crucial Years*, 106–108, quotation on 108.
113. *A Remonstrance of the Directors of the Netherlands East India Company, presented to the Lords States Generall of the united Provinces, in defence of the said Companie, touching the bloudy proceedings against the English Merchants, executed at Amboyna. Together, With the Acts of the Processe, against the sayd English. And The Reply of the English East India Company, to the said Remonstrance and Defence* (London, 1632). On the earlier efforts to publish the works, see *Stationers' Registers*, March 1, 1626/27, vol. 4, 135; and discussions at meetings in January 1627, IOR B/11, pp. 303, 348, 362, 376; April 6, 1627, p. 484; "Massacre of Amboyna" from p. 484; Court of Committees, June 22, 1627, IOR B/11, pp. 571–572. See also [November 28], 1628, PC 2/38, p. 602, in which the Privy Council condemned the reprint of the Amboyna pamphlet with pictures, which risked alienating the two nations; Rupali Mishra, *A Business of State: Commerce, Politics, and the Birth of the East India Company* (Cambridge, MA: Harvard University Press, 2018), 245–246. The summer of 1627 also witnessed the preparation of Purchas's work in Latin, part of an interest in making the work available to other European scholars; the translator, a scholar named Edward Elrington, inserted "the bloody passages" describing the conduct of the Dutch at Amboyna, and received a gratuity from the Company for his service. Court Minutes, July 6, 1627, IOR B/12, p. 13. The translation was never printed. On this Latin translation, see Pamela Neville-Sington, "The Primary Purchas Bibliography," in L. E. Pennington, ed., *The Purchas Handbook: Studies of the life, times and writings of Samuel Purchas, 1577–1626*, 2 volumes (London: Hakluyt Society, 1997), vol. 2, 536.
114. Petition of Daniel Buckoke, [1631], SP 16/205, f. 40.
115. Albert Joachimi and Govert Brasser to the States General, London, April 10, 1632, in *Documents Relative to the Colonial History of the State of New York*, ed. John Romeyn Brodhead and E. B. O'Callaghan, 15 volumes (Albany, 1853-1887), vol. 1, 47–50, quotation on 48. The EIC's records are missing for this period so it is difficult to track the publication history.

116. See the evidence of old binding holes in one Bodleian copy (Wood 387 [12]); and the holes and the wear patterns in another copy (History C/124), Wolfson Centre, Library of Birmingham.
117. On the deterioration of woodblocks, see David J. Davis, *Seeing Faith, Printing Pictures: Religious Identity during the English Reformation* (Leiden: Brill, 2013), 32. My thanks to Paul Nash in the Weston Library for helping me understand this context.
118. The colorings are identical in all of the woodcuts, with differences only in the abundance of ink. The exception is a copy in the University of Manchester library (shelfmark 6909.5), which according to a librarian who examined the frontispiece for me is missing the red ink on the hands. See list of copies with red ink in Appendix 2. My thanks to the many librarians and scholars who have helped me make sense of these red markings, and especially to Elizabeth (Upper) Savage. See her article, Elizabeth Upper, "Red Frisket Sheets, ca. 1490–1700: The Earliest Artifacts of Color Printing in the West," *Papers of the Bibliographical Society of America* 108, no. 4 (December 2014): 477–522. For extra costs associated with friskets, as the stencils were known, see Upper, "Red Frisket Sheets," 485–488.
119. See the copies of the *Remonstrance* at Queen's College Library, Oxford (Sel.b.128[1]), and the Folger Shakespeare Library (STC 7450a).
120. On this difficult era, see Andrew van Horn Ruoss, "Competitive Collaboration: The Dutch and English East India Companies and the Forging of Global Corporate Political Economy (1650– 1700)" (PhD dissertation, Duke University, 2017), 93–97; and Mishra, *Business of State*, chap. 10.
121. VOC directors at Amsterdam to GG and C, October 3, 1637, IOR I/3/92, f. 19; J. Sears McGee, *An Industrious Mind: The Worlds of Sir Simonds D'Ewes* (Stanford, CA: Stanford University Press, 2015), 471n40, cites a letter from January 1637 that mentioned anger about the lack of compensation and punishment.
122. For an expression of optimism, see VOC directors at Middelburg to GG and C, September 5, 1641, IOR I/3/92, f. 47a. On the transmission of the news to the Indies in summer 1642, see VOC council to the English President Aron Baker at Banten, July 31, 1642, IOR I/3/100, f. 64.
123. For Boswell's efforts, see the abstract of his negotiations, 1639–1641, SP 84/157/60; for his frustration with his efforts to bring some kind of resolution to a variety of issues between the two nations, see his remonstrance to the States General, October 26/November 5, 1643, SP 84/157/93.
124. For "massacred," see Richard Boothby, *A Breife Discovery or Description of the most Famous Island of Madagascar* (London, 1646), 66; for "Massacre at *Amboyna*," see *Bloudy Newes from the East-Indies* (London, 1651), 4.
125. Court Minutes for the third joint stock, July 5, 1650, IOR B/23, p. 3; EIC petition to Parliament, November 1650, CO 77/7/13, refers to the company's men being "Murthered and Massacred."
126. Memorial from the English Ambassadors to the States General, The Hague, April 15/25, 1651, *A Collection of the State Papers of John Thurloe*, 7 volumes (London, 1742), vol. 1, 179, hereafter *Thurloe Papers*. I found the date December 15, 1651,

in Samuel Rawson Gardiner, *History of the Commonwealth and Protectorate, 1649–1656*, 4 volumes (London: Longmans, Green, and Co.,1903), vol. 2, 169. On this period, see Steven C. A. Pincus, *Protestantism and Patriotism: Ideologies and the Making of English Foreign Policy, 1650–1668* (New York: Cambridge University Press, 1995), chaps. 3–4.

127. Court of Committees, July 16, 1651, IOR B/23, p. 121. Forbes had performed similar work for the VOC as a reader of prayers and comforter of the sick. See his "True Relation," and Forbes 1627.

128. They may even have crossed paths with the survivors in October 1624, when John Clarke's family was at court the same day as John Powel. For references to their petitions and some copies, see Conway to Carleton, June 25, 1624, SP 84/118, f. 113 (petition of Gabriel Towerson's brother); Conway to Carleton, July 19, 1624, SP 84/ 118, ff. 215, 218 (a slightly different copy), with a list on f. 220 (petitions of Henry Billingsley, on behalf of Emanuel Thompson, and of Thomas Johnson, father of Timothy); Court of Committees, October 7, 1626, IOR B/11, p. 138 (petition of Abel Price's mother to the EIC). See also the petition of Thomas Johnson and the inventory of Timothy's estate, [April] 1627, SP 16/61, ff. 133–134; John Fardo's father made his claims to the company at a Court of Committees on May 20, 1625, after John's estate was left to his cousin and the father was left destitute. See IOR B/10, pp. 45–46.

129. Petition of Thomas Billingsley, presented January 6, 1651/2, SP 84/159/48; petition of Sarah Collins, January 8, 1651/2, SP 84/159/49. See the earlier petition of Thompson's family: Petition of Henry Billingsley et al., read at Newmarket February 29, 1627 [1628?], SP 16/94, no. 77. There may have been some connection between Collins, Billingsley, and Thompson, as Collins had a brother-in-law named Billingsley.

130. CO 77/7, nos. 23 (Jane Webber's petition to the Council of State for the estates of Webber and Sherrock, April 7, 1652), 25 (William Powel, on behalf of his brother John Powel), 35 (William Coulson, on behalf of his brother Samuel Coulson) [April 7, 1652?].

131. All in CO 77/7.

132. VOC directors at Amsterdam to the GG and C, April 13, 1652, IOR I/3/92, ff. 62–63.

133. See Carla Gardina Pestana, "Cruelty and Religious Justifications for Conquest in the Mid-Seventeenth-Century English Atlantic," in Linda Gregerson and Susan Juster, eds., *Empires of God: Religious Encounters in the Early Modern Atlantic* (Philadelphia: University of Pennsylvania Press, 2011), 37–57.

134. *A Declaration of the Parliament of the Commonwealth of England, Relating to the Affairs and Proceedings between this Commonwealth and the States General of the United Provinces of the Low-Countreys, and the present Differences occasioned on the States part* (London, 1652), 4.

135. *A True Relation of the unjust, cruel, and barbarous proceedings against the English at Amboyna in the East-Indies, by the Netherlandish Governour & Council there. Also the Copie of a Pamphlet of the Dutch in Defence of the Action. With Remarks upon the whole matter. Published by Authoritie* (London, 1651). Pincus, *Protestantism and Patriotism*, 59–60, says the 1651 *True Relation* was a project of the Council of State.

136. *French Intelligencer*, no. 5, December 16–23, 1651, 39; see 1624 *True Relation*, 21; 1651 *True Relation*, 33–34.

137. There were 278 Dutch pamphlets written about the first war, for example, and 396 about the second. Guido de Bruin, "Political Pamphleteering and Public Opinion in the Age of De Witt (1653–1672)," in Femke Deen, David Onnekink, and Michel Reinders, eds., *Pamphlets and Politics in the Dutch Republic* (Leiden: Brill, 2011), 69.

138. See, for example, *A Declaration of the Parliament*, 3–4; *The Case Stated Between England and the United Provinces...* (London, 1652), 6, 16.

139. Meeting of the Committees for the Dutch Business, July 13, 1653, IOR G/21/2, pt. 4, p. 420. The EIC seems to have envisioned more publications of its own than came to print. On July 20, 1653, the EIC's committees who met specifically concerning affairs with the Dutch ordered the secretary to arrange for 500 copies "of the old Amboyna bookes" to be reprinted, but there is no sign of a 1653 *True Relation*. It's possible that the two versions of the 1651 *True Relation* that exist are actually a 1651 and 1653 reprint, but it would be unusual for the publication date to be incorrect by two years on a book's title page. It's also possible that this reference was to *A Memento for Holland* (London: James Moxon, 1652). Meeting of the Committees for the Dutch Business, July 20, 1653, IOR G/21/2, pt. 4, p. 420.

140. "memento, n." *OED*

141. *Memento for Holland*, A3r–v, quotations on A3v.

142. Henry Robinson, *Certain Proposalls in order to the Peoples Freedome and Accommodation in some Particulars* (London, 1652), 10.

143. (London, 1653).

144. *Second Part of the Tragedy of Amboyna*, 3–5. On this episode, see Simon Middleton, "Order and Authority in New Netherland: The 1653 Remonstrance and Early Settlement Politics," *WMQ* 67, no. 1 (January 2010): 31–68, espec. 55–56.

145. English translation, Letter from the Directors to Stuyvesant and Council, November 4, 1653, New York State Archives. New York (Colony). Council. Dutch colonial administrative correspondence, 1646–1664. Series A1810-78. Volume 11, document 90. Identifier: NYSA_A1810-78_V11_90

146. Both Benjamin Schmidt and Simon Schama use "byword." See Benjamin Schmidt, *Innocence Abroad: The Dutch Imagination and the New World, 1570–1670* (New York: Cambridge University Press, 2001), 295; and Simon Schama, *The Embarrassment of Riches: An Interpretation of Dutch Culture in the Golden Age* (New York: Knopf, 1987), 237.

147. See a character's speech in James Howell, *A German Diet* (London, 1653), 67. [nb pagination starts over again for each speech).

148. *True Relation* (1651), part four, "Remarks upon the fore-going historie," 10–14, quotation on 11. Pincus, *Protestantism and Patriotism*, 59, identifies this compiler as John Hall.

149. On these two images memorializing Isaac Dorislaw, see Malcolm Jones, *The Print in Early Modern England: An Historical Oversight* (New Haven, CT: Yale University Press, 2010), 114–117; and Helen Pierce, *Unseemly Pictures: Graphic Satire and Politics in Early Modern England* (New Haven, CT: Yale University Press, 2009), 199–207.

150. "A true Relation of the cruell and Barbarous Torture and Execution done upon the English at Amboyna in the East Indies by the Netherlanders there," Sloane 3645, ff. 176v (for 1632 date), 177r (illustration), BL.

151. *Anatomia, ofte Ont-ledinge. roerende de saechekn der Engelsche en Hollanders, in Amboyna* (Amsterdam, 1652); *Waerachtigh Verhael* (Rotterdam: Jan van Dalen, 1652); and see the title page, *Waerachtigh Verhael* ([Amsterdam?],1652), which says "Gedruckt tot onderrechtinge tegens de Engelsche Anatomia" (shelfmark 9055. aaa.3, BL). The Rotterdam edition is shelfmark 9056.aa.41, BL. Both have the same Knuttel number (7203).

152. *Engelsche-Duymdrayery, ofte 't geen de Oost-Indische Compagnie in Nederland, van de Engelsche word nageseyd* ... (Amsterdam: Hendrik Stam, 1652).

153. *Journaal ofte Waarachtige Beschrijvinge van de gruwelijke Conspiratien der Engelsche* (Amsterdam: Hendrik Stam, 1652).

154. "Tractait by den advocaat Mr Dirck Graswinckel ingestelt, tot justificatie van de proeduren in Amboina gehouden, ter vergadering van hunne Hoog Mogende geexhibeerd den 9 December 1653," States General, 1.01.02, inv. no. 12581.23, National Archives, The Hague; on not getting permission to publish, see a letter of intelligence from The Hague, June 13, [1653], *Thurloe Papers*, vol. 1, 267; on Graswinckel's labors and his background, see Ruoss, "Competitive Collaboration," 116–118.

155. The importance of this Lagundy history is suggested in a relation in the States General records, "Kort verhael vant gepasseerde tusschen die vande engelsche compe ende de Nederlantsche, nopende der Engelschen vertreck van Batavia na Lagondij ende der selver weder comste.van daer in Batavia," States General, 1.01.02, inv. no. 12576.37C, National Archives, The Hague. This relation contains letters exchanged when the English requested the VOC rescue them from their plight. The letters are in the original English, although copied meticulously into a single coherent volume made (the handwriting suggests) by a Dutch scribe. The letters date to 1625, but the creation of this document itself is not dated. For a 1626 complaint about English ingratitude, see Extract letter from GG to VOC directors, 13 December 1626, IOR I/3/14, CCXXXIII.

156. Demands of the VOC [1652], IOR G/21/2, pt. 4, pp. 399–402; the Answer of the English to the "unjust demands of the Netherlanders," October 14, 1652, IOR G/21/2, pt. 4, pp. 386–389.

157. Extract out of the resolutions of the states of Overyssel, Swoll [Zwolle], January 31 (old style), 1654, read February 17, 1654 (new style), *Thurloe Papers*, vol. 2, 71–72. Italics in original.

158. Extracts out of the secret register of the resolutions of the high and mighty lords the states general of the United Netherlands, February 19, 1654 (new style), *Thurloe Papers*, vol. 2, 77. Italics in original.

159. Jean Dumont, *Corps Universel Diplomatique du Droit des Gens*, 8 volumes (Amsterdam, 1726-31), vol. 6, part 2, 76.

160. "Certified copy of the award of the English and Dutch commissioners appointed under the Treaty of Westminster (1654)," IOR A/1/19A; see printed version in Dumont, *Corps Universel*, vol. 6, part 2, 88–92.

161. A letter of intelligence from The Hague, September 18, 1654, *Thurloe Papers*, vol. 2, 592.

162. Only five families of the ten executed men—those of Wetherall, Griggs, Towerson, Coulson, and Thompson—received settlements. The largest payment went to Towerson's brother, who received £700. The other payments were for the executors of Coulson, £450; John Powel, £350; William Griggs, £200; John Wetherall, £200; George Sherrock, £150; Edward Collins, £465; John Beaumont, £300; William Webber, £200; Ephraim Ramsey, £350; Thomas Ladbrooke, £50; and Emanuel Thompson, £200. Ladbrooke appears in Dumont as Radbroose, but in a manuscript version of this settlement at the British Library, the name is Ladbrooke. IOR A/1/19A. Most families received less than they had claimed. Jane Webber had claimed losses of £658 for William and £415 for George Sherrock in her petition of 1652 (Petition of Jane Weber, CO 77/7, no. 23). In the final settlement, however, she was awarded only £150 for Sherrock, and £200 for her husband. William Coulson received £450, but claimed his brother had had an estate in the Indies worth about £10,000 (Petition of William Coulson, CO 77/7, no. 35); Dumont, *Corps Universel*, vol. 6, part 2, 92.

163. On the emotional and social weight of financial obligations in this era, see Craig Muldrew, *The Economy of Obligation: The Culture of Credit and Social Relations in Early Modern England* (New York: St. Martin's Press, 1998), espec. chap. 7.

Chapter 5

1. Lord Van Gogh, *A Memoriall Delivered to His Majesty (July 21/31 1664) from the Lord Van-Gogh . . . With the Answer which his Sacred Majesty returned thereunto* (London, 1664), 11.

2. John Pory to Sir Thomas Puckering, April 21, 1631, in *The Court and Times of Charles the First* . . . compiler Thomas Birch, 2 volumes (London: H. Colburn, 1849), vol. 2, 109–110, quotation on 109. See wartime versions of this story in Hamon L'Estrange, *The Reign of King Charles* (London, 1655), 113; and *The English and Dutch Affairs Displayed to the Life* (London, 1664), 22–23.

3. Stephen Bradwell, *Helps for Suddain Accidents Endangering Life* (London, 1633), 69–71, quotation on 71. On Bradwell and his medical manual, see also Kristina Bross, *Future History: Global Fantasies in Seventeenth-Century American and British Writings* (New York: Oxford University Press, 2017), 148–158.

4. He approved of those authorities who had the work destroyed because he found it so inflammatory. William Sanderson, *Graphice. The Use of the Pen and Pensil* (London, 1658), 14.

5. Josiah Dare, *Counsellor Manners, his last legacy to his son* (London, 1673), 55–56.

6. Thomas Shadwell, *Sullen Lovers, or, The Impertinents* (London, 1668), 11.

7. A.B., *Covent Garden Drolery* (London, 1672), 33. This same prologue was included two years later in a comedy, although the prologue was "intended, but not spoken." [Thomas Duffett], *The Amorous Old-woman* (London, 1674), A3v.

8. Richard Head, *The Canting Academy* (London, 1673), 75.

9. See Allardyce Nicoll, *A History of English Drama, 1660–1900*, 4th ed., 6 volumes (New York: Cambridge University Press, 1952), vol. 1, 446, which lists this work as a droll. I checked a 1673 collection of drolls by Francis Kirkman, *The Wits* (London, 1673), and didn't find either of these items. There is a copy of the playbill in SP 29/317, f. 219.

10. R. A., *The Valiant Welshman* (London, 1615).

11. John Dryden, *Amboyna: a tragedy. As it is acted At the Theatre-Royal* (London, 1673). His play was entered on June 26, 1673, in the *Stationers' Registers*. (G. E. Briscoe Eyre, ed., *A Transcript of the Registers of the Worshipful Company of Stationers, 1640–1708*, 3 volumes [London, 1913], vol. 2, 462). Scholars disagree about when the play was performed, but perhaps in May or June of 1673. J. A. van der Welle, *Dryden and Holland* (Groningen: J. B. Wolters, 1962), 66.

12. For "pepper'd," see Beaumont and Fletcher, *The Fair Maid of the Inn* (1626) in Francis Beaumont and John Fletcher, *Fifty Comedies and Tragedies* (London, 1679), 397; for "justice," see Ben Jonson, *The Staple of Newes* (London, 1631), 41.

13. I am drawing on Anthony Parr's interpretation of "justice." Ben Jonson, *The Staple of News*, ed. Anthony Parr (Manchester: Manchester University Press, 1988), 168, notes for line 150.

14. The play survived in manuscript and was first published 300 years later. William Mountfort, *The Launching of the Mary*, ed. John Henry Walter (London: Malone Society, 1933).

15. Mountfort was especially concerned with defending the company from its critics, and much of this aspect of the play derived from a 1621 pamphlet, Thomas Mun, *A Discourse of Trade* (London, 1621). On Mun's defense of the company, see Rupali Mishra, *A Business of State: Commerce, Politics, and the Birth of the East India Company* (Cambridge, MA: Harvard University Press, 2018), 134–139. For a helpful introduction to Mountfort and his play, see Matteo Pangallo, "*Seldome Seene*: Observations from Editing *The Launching of the Mary, or the Seaman's Honest Wife*," in Pete Orford, with Michael P. Jones, Lizz Ketterer, and Joshua McEvilia, eds., *Divining Thoughts: Future Directions in Shakespeare Studies* (Newcastle: Cambridge Scholars Publishing, 2007), chap. 1.

16. On the plotline involving women, see Ann Christensen, "'Absent, weak, or unserviceable': The East India Company and the Domestic Economy in *The Launching of the Mary, or The Seaman's Honest Wife*," in Barbara Sebek and Stephen Deng, eds., *Global Traffic: Discourses and Practices of Trade in English Literature and Culture from 1550 to 1700* (New York: Palgrave Macmillan, 2008), 117–136. On Hollandophobia on stage, see A. J. Hoenselaars, *Images of Englishmen and Foreigners in the Drama of Shakespeare and His Contemporaries: A Study of Stage Characters and National Identity in English Renaissance Drama, 1558–1642* (London: Associated University Presses, 1992), 200.

17. Mountfort, *Launching of the Mary*, 8, lines 118–119.

18. I am indebted to Matteo A. Pangallo, *Playwriting Playgoers in Shakespeare's Theater* (Philadelphia: University of Pennsylvania Press, 2017), 3, for this interpretation. It is possible that the EIC had commissioned Mountfort to write the play, but Pangallo is skeptical, 79.

19. Pangallo, *Playwriting Playgoers*, 82, 84; Pangallo, "*Seldome Seene*," 3, 10; Richard Dutton, *Licensing, Censorship, and Authorship in Early Modern England: Buggeswords* (Basingstoke: Palgrave, 2000), 56. The manuscript is in Egerton 1994, BL, and ff. 329v-30r has the excised story about Amboyna; f. 349v contains the censor's note that the play can be performed provided all changes were made.

20. Compare James Shirley, *A Contention for Honour and Riches* (London, 1633), with *Honoria and Mammon* (London, 1659), 15–16.

21. The evidence for Davenant's argument comes from an unsigned letter attributed to him. See James R. Jacob and Timothy Raylor, "Opera and Obedience: Thomas Hobbes and *A Proposition for Advancement of Moralitie* by Sir William Davenant," *The Seventeenth Century* 6, no. 2 (Fall 1991): 205–250; the letter is transcribed and reproduced on 249–250.

22. On Dryden's antipathy to the Dutch, see van der Welle, *Dryden and Holland*, 10–11. On the play, see Shankar Raman, *Framing "India": The Colonial Imaginary in Early Modern Culture* (Stanford, CA: Stanford University Press, 2002), chap. 5; and Robert Markley, *The Far East and the English Imagination, 1600–1730* (New York: Cambridge University Press, 2006), chap. 4.

23. Anne Barbeau Gardiner, "Swift on the Dutch East India Merchants: The Context of 1672–73 War Literature," *Huntington Library Quarterly* 54, no. 3 (Summer 1991): 236; see also Blair Hoxby, *Mammon's Music: Literature and Economics in the Age of Milton* (New Haven, CT: Yale University Press, 2002), chap. 6, espec. 178–190.

24. There was indeed a woman whom Peres called his wife in Amboyna, and a second wife he had left behind, but the names of the women were not mentioned in any of the Amboyna texts. On the characters of Julia and Ysabinda, see Marjorie Rubright, *Doppelganger Dilemmas: Anglo-Dutch Relations in Early Modern English Literature and Culture* (Philadelphia: University of Pennsylvania Press, 2014), 191–192; and Carmen Nocentelli, *Empires of Love: Europe, Asia, and the Making of Early Modern Identity* (Philadelphia: University of Pennsylvania Press, 2013), 142–150. It is tempting to conjecture that Dryden's introduction of Ysabinda is part of what Karl Jacoby identifies in his discussion of a Mrs. Wooster as the trope of the damsel wronged in connection to massacres. See Jacoby, *Shadows at Dawn: A Borderlands Massacre and the Violence of History* (New York: Penguin, 2008), 137–139.

25. On this point, see Candy B. K. Schille, "'With Honour Quit the Fort': Ambivalent Colonialism in Dryden's Amboyna," *Early Modern Literary Studies* 12, no. 1 (May 2006): paragraph 11, https://extra.shu.ac.uk/emls/12-1/schiambo.htm.

26. Mountfort, *Launching of the Mary*, 48, line 1082.

27. See Ayanna Thompson, *Performing Race and Torture on the Early Modern Stage* (New York: Routledge, 2008), chap. 5, for a discussion of Dutch excess and an argument about Dryden's depiction of the Dutch as a racialized other.

28. Derek Hughes, "Rape on the Restoration Stage," *Eighteenth Century* 46, no. 3 (Fall 2005): 227.

29. Dryden, *Amboyna*, 62.

30. Thomas Brockedon, Henrie Hawley, and John Goninge to the EIC, December 14, 1623, Batavia, IOR E/3/10, no. 1130, f. 55r.

31. The specific details about the weapons come from *An Answer unto the Dutch Pamphlet* (London, 1624), 14.

32. Markley, *Far East*, 149.

33. Dryden wrote for the King's Company, whose theater burned in 1672. The company then moved into the theater that had just been abandoned by the Duke's Company, which left behind sets and scenery that wouldn't fit in their new venue. Colin Visser compares the scene settings in Amboyna with some of the works performed by the Duke's Company to argue that Dryden made use of the existing sets and may even have been deliberate in writing Amboyna in order to do so. See Visser, "John Dryden's *Amboyna* at Lincoln's Inn Fields, 1673," *Restoration and Eighteenth Century Theatre Research* 15, no. 1 (May 1976): 1–11; and Elizabeth Maddock Dillon, *New World Drama: The Performative Commons in the Atlantic World, 1649–1849* (Durham, NC: Duke University Press, 2014), 95. The two plays even shared an actor.

34. *Reply to the Remonstrance* (London, 1632), 39. Excluding the *Reply to the Remonstrance*, an *EEBO* search for "schellam" "skelm" "skellum" and "schelm" produces about fifty-three works (out of 132,000 total in *EEBO* as of November 2017) in which the word appears over the course of the seventeenth century. Between 1600 and 1634, six books (one of which was the *Reply to the Remonstrance*) used one of the variants of schelm; between 1635 and 1674, eight books (including two dictionaries) used the word.

35. Mountfort, *Launching of the Mary*, 8, lines 99–100.

36. Hoenselaars, *Images*, 60, 137–138; Rubright, *Doppelganger Dilemmas*, chap. 3.

37. Dryden, *Amboyna*, 2.

38. Dryden, *Amboyna*, 61–62, quotation on 61.

39. On torture on stage during the Restoration, see Rubright, *Doppelganger Dilemmas*, 297n46. These displays became more common after 1678.

40. *A True Relation of the Unjust, Cruell, and Barbarous Proceedings against the English at Amboyna . . .* (London: Thomas Mabb for William Hope, 1665). The 1665 *True Relation* called itself the third edition, which was how the title page of the 1632 edition had also described itself ("the third impression"). Frances Dolan, *True Relations: Reading, Literature, and Evidence in Seventeenth-Century England* (Philadelphia: University of Pennsylvania Press, 2013), 4, notes that most works with "true relations" in the title come from the seventeenth century, although there are sixteenth- and eighteenth-century examples, too.

41. *A collection of voyages and travels, consisting of authentic writers in our own tongue, which have not before been collected in English, or have only been abridged in other Collections. . . Compiled from the curious and valuable library of the late Earl of Oxford*, 2 volumes (London, 1745), vol. 2, 278–352.

42. Each printing had a longer title (see Appendix 2).

43. For the reference to the authorship credited by Wing, see http://estc.bl.uk/ R17875. Wing compiled the invaluable *A Short-Title Catalogue of Books Printed in England, Scotland, Ireland, Wales, and British America and of the English Books Printed in Other Countries, 1641–1700*, 3 volumes (New York: Index Society, 1945–1951). The Yale copy is the version in *EEBO*, where one can see this manuscript attribution.

44. George Coningsby, a Herefordshire clergyman, catalogued the differences between this work and the 1651 *True Relation*. He died in 1766 and left his copy of the book along with the rest of his library to Balliol College. [John Beamont], *The Emblem of Ingratitude* (London, 1672), A3r, Balliol call number 910 a 13(4).

45. Charles Molloy, *Hollands ingratitude, or, A serious expostulation with the Dutch. Shewing their ingratitude to this nation, and their inevitable ruine* (London, 1666).

46. Hugo Grotius, *De Rebus Belgicis* (London, 1665), trans. T. Manley, [A4v].

47. Robert Codrington, *His Majesties Propriety, and Dominion on the British Seas Asserted* (London, 1665), Dedicatory epistle, A3v.

48. The asymmetry in power relations signaled by the invocation of "ingratitude" is evident in its use in imperial contexts. See, for example, Ananya Chakravarti's discussion of the character of Ingratitude in a sixteenth-century play by the Jesuit author José de Anchieta, in *The Empire of Apostles: Religion, Accommodatio, and the Imagination of Empire in Early Modern Brazil and India* (New Delhi: Oxford University Press, 2018), 165–168.

49. For English complaints of Dutch atrocities, see Molloy, *Hollands Ingratitude*, 1; *Emblem of Ingratitude*, 70. The Dutch retorted with their own accusations of English atrocities at Guinea in 1664, when English forces sacked Dutch holdings. For Dutch allegations of English atrocities, see van der Welle, *Dryden and Holland*, 22; Benjamin Schmidt, *Innocence Abroad: The Dutch Imagination and the New World, 1570–1670* (New York: Cambridge University Press, 2001), 300. For Dutch perspectives on the West African atrocities, see [Johan van Valckenborgh], *Waerachtigh Verhael vande Grouwelicke en Barbarische Moorderye, begaen door de Engelschen in Guinea aen Onse Nederlandtsche Natie. . . .* (Middelburg, 1665).

50. Codrington, *His Majesties Propriety*, 150–169.

51. J. D., *A True and Compendious Narration; or (Second Part of Amboyney) of Sundry Notorious or Remarkable Injuries, Insolencies, and Acts of Hostility . . .* (London, 1665).

52. [Henry Stubbe], *A Justification of the Present War against the United Netherlands* (London, 1672) and Henry Stubbe, *A Further Justification of the Present War against the United Netherlands* (London, 1673). On Stubbe, see Mordechai Feingold, "Stubbe [Stubbes, Stubbs], Henry (1632–1676), author and physician," in *DNB*.

53. Head, *Canting Academy*, 115.

54. Carla Gardina Pestana, "Cruelty and Religious Justifications for Conquest in the Mid-Seventeenth-Century English Atlantic," in Linda Gregerson and Susan Juster, eds., *Empires of God: Religious Encounters in the Early Modern Atlantic* (Philadelphia: University of Pennsylvania Press, 2011), 37–57.

55. John Ogilby, *The Swearers. or, Innocence opprest and sacrific'd, in consequence of indulgence to Perjurious Prostitutes* (London, 1681), 6.

56. R. B., *Unparalleld Varieties: or, the Matchless Actions and Passions of Mankind* (London, 1683), 207–208. Crouch cited William Sanderson, *A compleat history of the lives and reigns of Mary Queen of Scotland, and of her son and successor, James the Sixth, King of Scotland . . .* (London, 1656), 577. On Crouch, see Robert Mayer, "Nathaniel Crouch, Bookseller and Historian: Popular Historiography and Cultural Power in Late Seventeenth-Century England," *Eighteenth-Century Studies* 27, no. 3 (Spring 1994): 391–419, quotation on 395; and Jason McElligott,

"Crouch, Nathaniel [pseud. Robert Burton] (c. 1640–1725?), bookseller and writer," in *DNB*.

57. Crouch's illustrations marked something of a departure from comparable tomes, which tended not to be illustrated as his were—with woodcuts, often crude, possibly intended to assist readers making a transition from cheap and popular chapbooks to more substantial works of writing. His Amboyna image seems consistent with this practice, building on the old woodcut with new features. On his illustrations, see Mayer, "Nathaniel Crouch," 399–400.

58. A word on my methodology: I searched both *EEBO* and *ECCO* for title keywords "library," "catalogue," "catalog," and "*catalogus*," and text word "Amboyna." Many library catalogues, especially for the seventeenth century, are not text searchable, and so I selected a few of the larger catalogues to search manually. The technology limited the results in important ways, but the number of catalogues was large enough (138), and included a variety of catalogues—of lending libraries, personal libraries, booksellers' inventories, and auction lists—to capture many different kinds of collections. I also consulted records for two manuscript catalogues, those of Samuel Pepys and Increase Mather.

59. Variants included "Dutch cruel proceedings at Amboyna," "Relation of the Dutch cruelties against the English at Amboyna," "Relation of the cruelties of the Dutch on the English at Amboyna," "The Cruelties of the Dutch at Amboyna," "Cruelties at Amboyna," "Relation of the Cruelties exercised upon the English at Amboyna"; and "Barbarous Proceedings against the English at Amboyna," "Barbarityes of the Dutch towards the English at Amboyna," and "Relation of the Barbarous Proceedings against the English at Amboyna."

60. It is possible that cataloguers were referring to Stubbe's work, but unlikely, because Stubbe's 1672 and 1673 books were quartos, while Beaumont's 1672 work was an octavo, a distinction normally made in the catalogues.

61. The transcriber recorded this title from the manuscript catalogue ("A Catalogue of Books Belonging unto Mr. Increase Mather, 8.18.1664") as "Religion of Proceedings of duty at Amboyna" but there can be no doubt that he meant Relation of the Proceedings of the Dutch at Amboyna and was flummoxed by the seventeenth-century hand. See Julius Herbert Tuttle, "The Libraries of the Mathers," *Proceedings of the American Antiquarian Society* 20 (1910): 269–356, 286 for book title.

62. See Humfrey Babington, *Catalogus variorum librorum Reverendi Dris Babington* (Cambridge, 1692), 23, which listed a 1672 octavo or duo, *The Cruelties of the Dutch at Amboyna* (1672); Edward Millington, *Bibliotheca Ashmoliana a catalogue of the library of the learned and famous Elias Ashmole, Esq.* (1694), 9, which recorded a *Relation of the cruelties at Amboyna* with no year listed, but the work was a quarto and thus likely to be a 1624, 1632, or 1665 *True Relation*; and Edward Millington, *A choice catalogue of the library of John Parsons, Esquire, late of the Middle-Temple, barrister* (1682), 19, which listed a 1672 octavo, *Relation of the Dutch Cruelties against the English at Amboyna*.

63. This title appears in the facsimile of Pepys's catalogue; see his catalogue of works acquired since the last catalogue in 1700, in David McKitterick, ed., *Catalogue of the Pepys Library* (Suffolk: D. S. Brewer, 1991), vol. 7, part i, np. *Catalogue of the Pepys Library*, compiled by N. A. Smith (Suffolk: D. S. Brewer, 1978), vol. 1, 179, lists the 1651 *True Relation*.

64. Cataloguers described 14/17 copies (82 percent) of Stubbe's work as a book about cruelty in the sample I examined.

65. See, for example, the listing for an octavo 1712 publication, *Dutch Cruelty at Amboyna*, in Samuel Baker, *A catalogue of several libraries, and Parcels of Books, lately purchased, Among which are included the libraries of Mansfield Price* ([London], [1766]), 73.

66. David Lloyd, *Memoires of the Lives, Actions, Sufferings & Deaths of those noble, reverend, and excellent personages, that suffered by death, sequestration, decimation, or otherwise, for the Protestant Religion* (London, 1668), 689.

67. Nathaniel Wanley, *The Wonders of the little world: Or, a General History of Man* (London, 1673), 376. This work likely inspired Crouch's book.

68. Reprinted from an English paper, in *Connecticut Journal*, July 3, 1772.

69. From the *South Carolina Gazette*, October 2, 1782, reprinted in the *Pennsylvania Packet*, December 21, 1782.

70. An excerpt from Jedidiah Morse, *The History of America*, Book I, chap. 7, in *Burlington Advertiser, or Agricultural and Political Intelligencer*, July 5, 1791.

71. These sentences distill a vast and contested set of historical circumstances and debates. See Steve Pincus, *1688: The First Modern Revolution* (New Haven, CT: Yale University Press, 2009), for a provocative interpretation and extensive engagement with historiography; see also Tim Harris, *Revolution: The Great Crisis of the British Monarchy, 1685–1720* (New York: Allen Lane, 2006).

72. On Settle's life and politics, see Abigail Williams, "Settle, Elkanah (1648–1724), playwright," in *DNB*. Settle changed his political allegiances again after William and Mary's arrival, and supported them.

73. The title continues: *Whereby is plainly Demonstrable what the English must expect from the Hollanders, when at any Time or Place they become their Masters* (London, 1688).

74. Settle, *Insignia*, B1v. For another author who drew on Amboyna to oppose William and Mary's accession, see Denis Grenville, *The Resigned & resolved Christian, and faithful & undaunted royalist* (Rouen, 1689), 10.

75. Douglas Coombs, *The Conduct of the Dutch: British Opinion and the Dutch Alliance During the War of the Spanish Succession* (The Hague: Martinus Nijhoff for the University College of Ghana Publications Board, 1958), 17–18, 188.

76. [Jonathan Swift], *The Conduct of the Allies, and of the Late Ministry, in Beginning and Carrying on the Present War* (London, 1711). This pamphlet sold 11,000 copies in one month, making it "probably the most influential single publication" of Anne's reign. Coombs, *Conduct of the Dutch*, 277–282, quotation on 281.

77. See, for example, *A vindication of Oliver Cromwell, and the Whiggs of Forty One, to our modern Low Churchmen. With some reflections upon the Bar-r Treaty* (London, 1712), 10. I looked at approximately twenty Whig and Tory pamphlets for this period, primarily those that mentioned Amboyna as identified through an *ECCO* search but also other pamphlets (such as Swift's *Conduct of the Allies*) in order to understand the larger context of the pamphlet exchange.

78. *A Second whigg-letter, from William Prynn to Nestor Ironside, Esq* (London, 1713), 11; *Tit for Tat, or the Lord knows what* (London, [1713]), 2.

79. [Robert Ferguson], *An Account of the Obligations the States of Holland Have to Great Britain . . .* (1711), 34.

80. Coombs, *Conduct of the Dutch*, 347.

81. *The Dutch won't let us have Dunkirk* ([London?], 1712), see 4, 6, 8.

82. John Beaumont, *Dutch Alliances: or, a Plain Proof of their Observance of Treaties: Exemplify'd in the Particulars of their Inhuman Treatment of their Friends and Confederates, the English, at Amboyna, in order to dispossess them of that and the other Spice Islands in the East Indies* (London, 1712), 29. A few changes in wording suggest the vocabulary of a new era—the "four blacks" who carried John Clarke to his cell after his torture became "four Negroes" in this work (11).

83. R. Hall, *The History of the Barbarous Cruelties* ([London], 1712), 32. The new caption read "The manner of Tortering & Executing the English and Japonese At Amboyna, and the Oran-keys and Nobles of Poloroone." Hall drew on William De Britaine, *The Dutch Usurpation; or, A Brief View of the Behaviour of the States-General of the United Provinces* (London, 1672).

84. (London, 1712).

85. Abraham von Golt, *Belga-Britannus: or, the Hollander always in the English interest* (London, [1712]).

86. *The Dutch better friends than the French, to the Monarchy, Church, and trade of England* (London, 1713), 34–35. For a similar complaint about English reliance on old history to criticize the Dutch, see also [John Oldmixon], *Remarks on a False, Scandalous, and Seditious Libel, Intituled, The Conduct of the Allies, and of the Late Ministry, etc.* (London, 1711), 9, 32–33. For seventeenth-century wartime precedents of English pamphleteers defending the Dutch, see [Slingsby Bethel], *Observations on the Letter written to Sir Thomas Osborn . . .* (London, 1673), 4, in which Bethel acknowledged that all deplored what happened at Amboyna, but it was the deed of a few bad actors; and a similar argument in [Peter Walsh], *The Advocate of Conscience Liberty . . .* ([London], 1673), 252.

87. For Amboyna/join-a, see "To the Editor of Lloyd's Evening Post," *Lloyd's Evening Post*, March 31–April 3, 1769.

88. *The World*, February 12, 1756, 981.

89. For a discussion of *Farther Adventures* and *Gulliver*, see Markley, *Far East*, chaps. 5-7.

90. Daniel Defoe, *The Life, Adventures, and Pyracies, Of the Famous Captain Singleton . . .* (London, 1720), 232–233, quotation on 233.

91. Daniel Defoe, *The Farther Adventures of Robinson Crusoe* (London, 1719), 263–265, "blind useless passion" on 263, "appearance of Justice" on 265.

92. Jonathan Swift, *Travels into Several Remote Nations of the World. In four parts. By Lemuel Gulliver . . .*, 2 volumes (London, 1726), vol. 2, 149–154. The scene comes in the final chapter of Part 3.

93. *Chrysal; or, The Adventures of a Guinea by Charles Johnstone*, introduction and notes by Kevin Bourque, 2 volumes (Kansas City, MS: Valancourt Books, 2011), vol. 1, viii, x.

94. For a listing of these novels, see Liz Bellamy, "It-Narrators and Circulation: Defining a Subgenre," in Mark Blackwell, ed., *The Secret Life of Things: Animals, Objects, and*

It-Narratives in Eighteenth-Century England (Lewisburg, PA: Bucknell University Press, 2007), 117–146; bibliography for pre-1800 works is on 135–137.

95. *Chrysal: or, the Adventures of a Guinea*, 2 volumes (Dublin, 1760), vol. 2, 80–89, quotation on 81. On Johnstone's antisemitism and the character of Aminadab, see Ann Louise Kibbie, "Circulating Anti-Semitism: Charles Johnstone's *Chrysal*," in Blackwell, ed., *Secret Life of Things*, 242–264.

96. 2 volumes, (London: Thomas Osborne, 1745), vol. 1, 278–352. In that same period, William De Britaine's *Dutch Usurpation* was reprinted in another collection of the Earl of Oxford's pamphlets. See *The Harleian Miscellany*, 8 volumes (London, [1744]-1746), vol. 3, 1–16.

97. *A voyage to the South-Seas, and to many other parts of the world* (London, 1745), Appendix; John Harris, *Navigantium atque bibliotheca; or, A complete collection of voyages and travels*, 2 volumes (London, 1744–1748), vol. 1, 877–895.

98. https://www.librarything.com/catalog/ThomasJefferson.

99. David Hume, *The History of England, from the Invasion of Julius Caesar, to The Revolution in 1688*, 8 volumes (London, 1767), vol. 6, 125; Catharine Macaulay, *The History of England from the Accession of James I to the Elevation of the House of Hanover*, 8 volumes (London, 1771), vol. 5, 86, 133–135, 202–204.

100. "From Thomas Jefferson to Robert Skipwith, with a List of Books for a Private Library, 3 August 1771," *The Papers of Thomas Jefferson*, vol. 1, 1760–1776, ed. Julian P. Boyd (Princeton, NJ: Princeton University Press, 1950), 76–81.

101. My thanks to April Shelford and Erica Munkwitz for sharing their transcription of Thistlewood's 1777 list of his books. In addition to the engraving in Harris's *Voyages*, Thistlewood owned a copy of *The Dutch Displayed; or, a Succinct Account of the Barbarities, Rapines and Injustices, committed by the subjects of Holland upon those of England* (London, 1766), which also had an engraving.

102. My thanks to Mitch Fraas of the University of Pennsylvania for sharing his database of books owned in India. I focused on books owned in Calcutta and recorded in library and estate inventories in the 1770s and 1780s. There were likely multiple other copies beyond these few recorded in inventories.

103. For a good discussion of this episode, see G. J. Bryant, *The Emergence of British Power in India 1600–1784: A Grand Strategic Interpretation* (Rochester, NY: Boydell, 2013), 162–164; for Clive's account, see "Narrative of the Disputes with the Dutch in Bengal," in John Malcolm, *The Life of Robert, Lord Clive: collected from the family papers . . .*, 3 volumes (London: John Murray, 1836), vol. 2, 74–89, quotation on 89. Clive's narrative probably dates to November 1759 (Malcolm, 74).

104. For "sequel," see *Universal Magazine of Pleasure and Knowledge*, June 1760, 365; for "another Amboyna act," see *Harrop's Manchester Mercury*, July 15, 1760.

105. *Universal Magazine of Pleasure and Knowledge*, June 1760, 364–372; July 1760, 33–37. The incident thwarted by Clive was routinely linked to Amboyna at the time. See *An Impartial History of the Late Glorious War* (London, 1764), 127.

106. The first letter appeared in the *Public Advertiser* on February 6, 1767, and the last one on August 10.

107. "Reply to Coffee-House Orators, [9 April 1767]," *The Papers of Benjamin Franklin,* vol. 14, *January 1 through December 31, 1767,* ed. Leonard W. Labaree (New Haven, CT: Yale University Press, 1970), 102–107. The Portuguese issue pertained to the difficulties British merchants had trading British cloth in Portugal; the American issues derived from the Quartering Act.

108. *The Dutch Displayed; or, a Succinct Account of the Barbarities, Rapines and Injustices, committed by the subjects of Holland upon those of England* (London, 1766), 68.

109. The full title continues, *Since the Commencement of the Dutch Republic to the present Times. With a Plate, exhibiting a view of the Torments inflicted on the English at Amboyna.* See 2–8 for a discussion of the Amboyna incident.

110. *A new collection of voyages, discoveries, and travels,* 7 volumes (London: J. Knox, [1767]), vol. 2, between 426–427. This work also contains a version of the *True Relation,* 421–448. The illustration in the *Dutch Displayed* contained only the top portion of Harris's two-part image.

111. *A Short and Modest Reply* (London, 1766); *Dutch modesty exposed to English view: or, a serious answer to a pamphlet, entitled, A short and modest reply to a book, entitled, The Dutch displayed* (London, [1767]). Jacob Selwood is writing a book about Jeronimy Clifford, tentatively titled *Kingdom's Edge: Suriname, Shifting Sovereignties, and Colonial English Subjecthood, 1650–1780* (Ithaca, NY: Cornell University Press, forthcoming).

112. H. M. Scott challenges this widely shared interpretation that Dutch neutrality prompted Britain to declare war and argues instead that Britain sought to influence Dutch internal politics in "Sir Joseph Yorke, Dutch Politics, and the Origins of the Fourth Anglo-Dutch War," *Historical Journal* 31, no. 3 (1988): 571–589.

113. The full title continues *with suitable remarks on that bloody tragedy. Together with a Description of the Cape of Good Hope and of the Islands of Java, Ceylon, Celebes, Banda, and the Molluccas or Spice islands, belonging to the Dutch in the East Indies; with Reflections, proving that they are vulnerable, and may easily be annexed to the Crown of Great Britain. The whole work being well worth the Attention of the Public at this Crisis* (London: Thomas Lovewell, 1781). The frontispiece was designed, according to the title page, by a Mr. Dodd.

114. *Dutch Displayed,* 67.

115. I am indebted to Jo Ann Moran Cruz, who has been teaching and thinking about legends for many years, for her assistance in understanding the nature of legends as a genre and for reflecting on Amboyna in that context.

116. *True Relation* (London, 1665), frontispiece; George Downing, *A Discourse written by Sir George Downing* (London, 1672), second part of pamphlet ("Of the cruel ingratitude"), with new pagination, 13. The earlier work is *A discourse: vindicating His Royal Master from the insolencies of a scandalous libel. . .* (London, 1664).

117. *Boston Gazette,* November 2–November 9, 1730; *Dutch Displayed,* 15.

118. *Cries of British Blood,* 2.

119. On the role of this relationship with France in defining British identity and nationalism in the eighteenth century, see Linda Colley, *Britons: Forging the Nation* (London: Pimlico, 2003).

Chapter 6

1. The interview with Walter Hicks is at the Australians at War Film Archive, no. 807, September 24, 2003 (http://australiansatwarfilmarchive.unsw.edu.au/archive/807-walter-hicks), Part 4, between minutes 13:30 and 16:00. For an account of the ordeal of the mostly Australian soldiers in the 2/21st Battalion, see Roger Maynard, *Ambon: The Truth about One of the Most Brutal POW Camps in World War II and the Triumph of the Aussie Spirit* (Sydney: Hachette, 2014).

2. Peter Heylyn placed the incident in 1618, not 1623. See Peter Heylyn, *Cosmographie in Four Bookes* (London, 1652), book 3, 251. Charles Leslie, *Delenda Carthago, or, The true interest of England in relation to France and Holland* (London, 1695), 3, put the event in November 1624; *Englands Remembrancer,* in *The Historians Guide in Two Parts* (London, 1676), 42, locates "*Amboyna's* bloody cruelty" in 1624; *A Memento for Holland* (London, 1652), turned Emanuel Thompson into Samuel Tomson, 9. The *Public Advertiser,* March 5, 1767, has Beaumont put to death; William Sanderson, *A Compleat History of the Lives and Reigns of Mary Queen of Scotland, and of her Son and Successor, James the Sixth* . . . (London, 1656), 578, put van Speult on the English coast; for the overseer's confession, see *Britannic Magazine; or, Entertaining Repository of Heroic Adventures and Memorable Exploits,* vol. 4, no. 53 (1796), 335–336.

3. George Downing, *A Discourse Written by Sir George Downing* . . . (London, 1672), second part of pamphlet, 12.

4. William De Britaine, *The Dutch Usurpation* (London, 1672), 15.

5. John Temple, *The Irish Rebellion: or, an history of the beginnings and first progresse of the general rebellion raised within the Kingdom of Ireland . . . together with the Barbarous Cruelties and Bloody Massacres which ensued thereupon* (London, 1646); Kathleen M. Noonan, "'Martyrs in Flames': Sir John Temple and the Conception of the Irish in English Martyrologies," *Albion* 36, no. 2 (Summer 2004): 223–255; for the afterlife of the episode, see John Gibney, *The Shadow of a Year: The 1641 Rebellion in Irish History and Memory* (Madison: University of Wisconsin Press, 2013).

6. Act XVIII, Laws passed in Virginia, March 1661, William Waller Hening, *The Statutes at Large,* 13 volumes (New York: Bartow, 1823), vol. 2, 24.

7. [*Book of Common Prayer*], (London, 1662), np.

8. *Letters of State, written by Mr. John Milton* (London, 1694), 116; Henry Foulis, *The History of the Wicked Plots and Conspiracies of our Pretended Saints* (London, 1662), 4; Roger Manley, *The History of the Rebellions in England, Scotland and Ireland* . . . (London, 1691), 263, invoked the "slaughtering . . . at *Amboyna*"; George Villiers, *A Letter to Sir Thomas Osborn, One of His Majesties Privy Council, upon the reading of a Book, called, The present interest of England Stated* (London, 1672), 7.

9. See the verb form in *The Dutch won't let us have Dunkirk* . . . ([London]), 1712), 6, 8.

10. David Hume, *The History of England, from the Invasion of Julius Caesar, to The Revolution in 1688,* 8 volumes (London: A. Miller, 1767), vol. 8, index, "massacre"; Catharine Macaulay, *The History of England from the Accession of James I to the Elevation of the House of Hanover,* 8 volumes (London: Edward and Charles Dilly, 1771), vol. 5, 134.

11. News from London, December 2, in *Daily Advertiser*, March 13, 1797.

12. *Encyclopedia Britannica*, 1st ed. (Edinburgh: A. Bell and C. Mafarquhar, 1771), vol. 1, 133; *Encyclopedia Britannica*, 3rd ed. (Dublin: James Moore, 1790–98),vol. 1, 531; *Encyclopedia Britannica*, 7th ed. (Edinburgh: Adam and Charles Black, 1842), vol. 2, 598; *Encyclopedia Britannica*, 9th ed. (Edinburgh: Adam and Charles Black, 1875), vol. 1, 661; *Encyclopedia Britannica* (1945), vol. 1, 797; *Encyclopedia Britannica* (1953), vol. 1, 741; https://www.britannica.com/event/Amboina-Massacre; https://www.britannica.com/place/Ambon-island-Indonesia). "Amboyna massacre," in *A Dictionary of British History*, 3rd ed., ed. John Cannon and Robert Crowcroft (Oxford University Press, online, 2015), has an English settlement on Ambon "wiped out." For a print version of this text, see *A Dictionary of British History*, rev. ed., ed. John Cannon (New York: Oxford University Press, 2009), 18.

13. Source for the British ship is the *Bombay Courier*, November 22, 1800; on this era, see James David Wilson, "The Dutch and the Second British Empire in the Early Nineteenth-Century Indian Ocean World," *Journal of British Studies* 58, no. 2 (April 2019): 366–393.

14. Thomas Seccombe, "Kerr, Robert (1757–1813), scientific writer and translator," in *DNB*. Kerr compiled the first ten volumes of this eighteen-volume work; the Amboyna account is in vol. 9.

15. Robert Kerr, *A General History and Collection of Voyages and Travels*, 18 volumes (Edinburgh: Ballantyne and Company, 1813), vol. 9, 537. The Amboyna account is on 537–549.

16. Kerr, *General History*, vol. 9, 537.

17. Kerr, *General History*, vol. 9, 543n3.

18. "Amboyna," *Asiatic Journal*, issue 69, September 1, 1821, 299. For the reprint of portions of the 1651 *True Relation*, see "Barbarous Proceedings against the English at Amboyna in 1622," *Asiatic Journal*, issue 64, April 1, 1821, 330–338.

19. Philip Lawson, *The East India Company: A History* (New York: Longman, 1993), 137–138, quotation on 142.

20. Debate, East Indies Possessions Bill, speech of George Canning, HC Deb June 17, 1824, vol. 11, col 1444. The record says "[a laugh]."

21. T 70/5, f. 17, NAUK. My thanks to Matthew Mitchell for pointing me to this reference.

22. The first colonial volume dealt with the West Indies: *Calendar of State Papers Colonial, America and West Indies: Volume 1, 1574–1660*, ed. W. Noel Sainsbury (London: Her Majesty's Stationery Office, 1860); the first East Indies volume was published in 1864. The entire Calendar is available online at https://www.british-history.ac.uk/.

23. [Alex Charles Ewald], "Records of Early English Adventure," *Edinburgh Review* 152, no. 312 (October 1880), 379–407, quotation on 401. Ewald, who worked at the Record Office, wrote several articles inspired by materials in the *Calendar of State Papers* and gathered them into a single work, *Stories from the State Papers*, 2 volumes (London: Chatto & Windus, 1882). The "massacre of Amboyna" is one of fifteen historical episodes Ewald chose to relate, and it appears in vol. 2, 73–103.

24. On the Victoria County History project and its intermittent history, see https://www.victoriacountyhistory.ac.uk. The project continues under the auspices of the Institute of Historical Research.

25. James Clephan, "The Massacre of Amboyna, 1623," *Monthly Chronicle of North-Country Lore and Legend* 5, no. 51 (May 1891): 195–198. The article explains that the illustration was based on an engraving that originally appeared in the "Cabinet of Curiosities," possibly a reference to the nineteenth-century periodical of that name, suggesting that another version of the depiction of the tortured trader had been created earlier in the century.

26. John Malcolm, *The Life of Robert, Lord Clive: collected from the family papers* . . ., 3 volumes (London: John Murray, 1836), vol. 2, 74–90.

27. See, for example, Clive's biography in the *Encyclopedia Britannica*, 11th ed. (Cambridge, 1910), vol. 6, 532–536. For a modern interpretation, see Mark Grossman's claim that Clive's "victory over the Dutch at Biderra" enabled him to "[avenge] the Dutch massacre of British forces at Amboyna," in Grossman, *World Military Leaders: A Biographical Dictionary* (New York; Facts on File, Inc., 2007), 72–73.

28. P. J. Marshall, "Introduction," *The Oxford History of the British Empire*, vol. 2, *The Eighteenth Century*, ed. P. J. Marshall (New York: Oxford University Press, 1998), 4.

29. G. R. Gleig, *The History of the British Empire in India*, 4 volumes (London: J. Murray, 1835), vol. 1, 348–351; John MacGregor, *The History of the British Empire* . . . 2 volumes (London: Chapman and Hall, 1852), vol. 2, 384–386. Gleig was a minister, which was a typical occupation in his era for authors of schoolbooks; Peter Yeandle, *Citizenship, Nation, Empire: The Politics of History Teaching in England, 1870–1930* (Manchester: Manchester University Press, 2015), 27.

30. E. H. Nolan, *The Illustrated History of the British Empire in India and the East*, 2 volumes (London: James S. Virtue, 1859), vol. 1, 794.

31. Bourchier Wrey Savile, *How India was won by England under Clive and Hastings* (London: Hodder and Stoughton, 1881), 13–14, quotations on 14.

32. On Macaulay's revival of the Black Hole, see Partha Chatterjee, *The Black Hole of Empire: History of a Global Practice of Power* (Princeton, NJ: Princeton University Press, 2012), chap. 6; quotation from Kate Teltscher, "'Fearful Name of the Black Hole': Fashioning an Imperial Myth," in *Writing India, 1757–1990: The Literature of British India*, ed. Bart Moore-Gilbert (Manchester: Manchester University Press, 1996), 30–51, at 30.

33. George Peel, *The Enemies of England* (London: Edward Arnold, 1903), 130.

34. Beckles Willson, *Ledger and Sword*, 2 volumes (London: Longmans, Green, 1903), vol. 1, x; 148–178 (discussion of Amboyna), quotation on 161 ("monument"), 163–164 (verbs and adjectives); for a gratuitous insult, see vol. 1, 161n1; for a more charitable view of the Dutch, see vol. 2, 117.

35. Review of P. J. Blok, *Geschiedenis van het Nederlandsche Volk*, vols. 1–4 (Groningen: J. B. Wolters, 1892–1899), in *The Athenaeum*, May 26, 1900, 650–651.

36. The Boers themselves (as opposed to the Dutch) came to be seen in pejorative ways during the war, especially with their protracted guerrilla resistance. See Aidan Forth, *Barbed Wire Imperialism: Britain's Empire of Camps, 1876–1903* (Berkeley: University of California Press, 2017), espec. chap. 5.

37. See especially the foundational work of John M. MacKenzie, *Propaganda and Empire: The Manipulation of British Public Opinion, 1880–1960* (Manchester: Manchester University Press, 1984); Kathryn Castle, *Britannia's Children: Reading*

Colonialism through Children's Books and Magazines (Manchester: Manchester University Press, 1996); and Yeandle, *Citizenship, Nation, Empire*, 42, from whom I draw "emotional attachment." On the League's activities, see Yeandle, *Citizenship*, 32–33; and MacKenzie, *Propaganda and Empire*, 155–156.

38. Hugh Edward Egerton, *The Origin and Growth of the English Colonies and of their System of Government* (Oxford: Clarendon, 1903), 207n1.

39. A domestic historian was the exception to this pattern. In his minute, detailed ten-volume history of England between 1603 and 1642, Samuel Gardiner followed the narrative in the *True Relation* in his brief summary of Amboyna, and so the Japanese were the starting point of his story. Samuel Rawson Gardiner, *History of England from the accession of James 1 to the outbreak of civil war*, 10 volumes (London: Longmans, Green, 1896–1901), vol. 5, 242.

40. *Cambridge History of the British Empire*, ed. J. Holland Rose, A. P. Newton, and E. A. Benians, 7 volumes (Cambridge: Cambridge University Press, 1929–1961), vol. 1, 134–135 (annoyance, outrage); 142 (massacre, evil usage), 208 (shameful).

41. *Cambridge History of the British Empire*, vol. 4, *British India, 1497–1858*, 654.

42. A. P. Newton, "Forgotten Deeds of Empire Building: The Massacre of Amboyna, 1623," *Saturday Review*, May 18, 1935, 633.

43. A.P. Newton, *A Junior History of the British Empire Oversea* (London: Blackie & Son, 1933), quotations on vii (boys and girls), 279 (diversity); 38 (most atrocious, what they knew was false, shame and cruelty); 37 (turning point); see 97 for his discussion of the Black Hole. Compare Newton's "what they knew was false" with Coulson's assertion in the *True Relation* (London, 1624), 17, that he was forced to confess "that which is as false, as GOD is true."

44. Information on textbook popularity comes from Yeandle, *Citizenship, Nation, Empire*, 152–153.

45. G. T. Warner and C. H. K. Marten, *The Groundwork of British History* (London: Blackie and Son, 1900), part 2, 403–404. Warner and Marten mentioned the Japanese as alleged co-conspirators.

46. Charles Lucas, *The British Empire: Six Lectures* (London: Macmillan, 1915), 64; J. F. Bright, *A History of England for Public Schools* (London: Rivingtons, 1887), 1114.

47. Arthur T. Flux, "Our Pupil Teachers' and Scholarship Course," *The Practical Teacher*, 23, no. 1 (July 1902): 39. For "barbarous act," see Flux, *The Building of the British Empire* (London: Meiklejohn and Holden, 1906), 22.

48. William Harrison Woodward, *A Short History of the Expansion of the British empire, 1500–1911* (Cambridge: Cambridge University Press, 1915), 77, 123. This edition is a reprint of the third edition. MacKenzie, *Propaganda and Empire*, 191; Castle, *Britannia's Children*, 22.

49. George Southgate, *The British Empire* (London: J. M. Dent, 1936), index entry for "massacre," 421; see 51, 175, 185, 202, 224.

50. On the shift to India, see A.F. Pollard, ed., *The British Empire. Its past, its Present, and its Future* (London: League of the Empire, 1909), 643–644; Gerald T. Hankin, *The Story of the Empire* (London: John Murray, 1911), 274; and Flux, *Building of the British Empire*, 22.

51. H. E. Marshall, *Our Empire Story* (London: T. C. & E. C. Jack, [1909]), 371–372, quotation on 371.

52. For a notable exception, see Flux, *Building of the British Empire*, 22, which clarified that ten English, nine Japanese, and one Portuguese were executed.

53. For beginners, see Hankin, *The Story of the Empire*, 274; for students in higher forms, see Edward G. Hawke, *The British Empire and Its History* (London: J. Murray, 1911), 300; for the advanced students, see Pollard, ed., *The British Empire*, 643. On the League, see MacKenzie, *Propaganda and Empire*, 155–156.

54. Robert M. Rayner, *A Concise History of Britain to 1939* (London: Longmans, Green, 1938; reprint 1942), preface, 323.

55. George W. Southgate, *The British Empire and Commonwealth* (London: J. M. Dent and Sons, 1972), 188; Robert M. Rayner, with additional chapters by A. D. Ellis, *A Concise History of Britain* (London: Longmans, Green, 1965), 323.

56. MacKenzie, *Propaganda and Empire*, 180–181.

57. Southgate, *British Empire* (1936), 175.

58. Australians at War Film Archive, no. 807, September 24, 2003 (http://australiansat-warfilmarchive.unsw.edu.au/archive/807-walter-hicks); his discussion of his memories of learning about Amboyna in school and seeing the memorial is in Part 4, between minutes 13:30 and 16:00. He mentions he was fifteen when he started high school in 1936 in Part 1, minute 5:30. There was no one named Hicks killed at Amboyna in 1623. It's hard to know what the stone might have commemorated, or when it was put there.

59. Southgate was going strong into 1972 with the exact wording of his earlier editions; on Southgate and his book's long life, see Castle, *Britannia's Children*, 164; on the endurance of old books until after World War II, see Yeandle, *Citizenship, Nation, Empire*, 151; MacKenzie, *Propaganda and Empire*, 190–194.

60. J. R. Seeley, *The Expansion of England* (Boston: Roberts Brothers, 1883), 126; On the context and impact of the work, see Wm. Roger Louis, "Introduction," *The Oxford History of the British Empire*, vol. 5, *Historiography*, ed. Robin Winks (New York: Oxford University Press, 1999), 8; and Amanda Behm, *Imperial History and the Global Politics of Exclusion: Britain, 1880–1940* (London: Palgrave Macmillan, 2018), chap. 2.

61. F. W. Stapel, "De Ambonsche 'Moord' (9 Maart 1623)," *Tijdschrift van het Bataviaasch Genootschap* 62 (1923): 209–226, translated in M. A. P. Meilink-Roelofsz, M. E. van Opstall, and G. J. Schutte, eds., *Dutch Authors on Asian History: A Selection of Dutch Historiography on the Verenigde Oostindische Compagnie* (Dordrecht: Foris, 1988), 184–195; for belief in the plot but doubt that Coulson took part, see W. Ph. Coolhaas, "Aanteekeningen en Opmerkingen over den Zoogenaamden Ambonschen Moord," *Bijdragen tot de Taal-, Land—en Volkenkunde van Nederlandsche-Indie* 101 (1942): 49–94, translated in the same volume, 196–240.

62. D. K. Bassett, "The 'Amboyna Massacre' of 1623," *Journal of Southeast Asian History* 1, no. 2 (September 1960): 1–19.

63. Charles Corn, *The Scents of Eden: A Narrative of the Spice Trade* (New York: Kodansha International, 1998), 174, gets the year wrong; Harold J. Cook, *Matters of Exchange: Commerce, Medicine, and Science in the Dutch Golden Age* (New Haven,

CT: Yale University Press, 2007), 185, 187, dates the 1619 treaty to 1617 and believes that the Japanese soldiers worked for the English, an error he likely picked up from Coolhaas. Anthony Reid, *Southeast Asia in the Age of Commerce 1450–1680*, vol. 2, *Expansion and Crisis* (New Haven, CT: Yale University Press, 1993), 278, thinks that all of the executed men were from the English factory.

64. See an explanatory note in the Riverside edition of *Gulliver's Travels*, which declares that Amboyna's Dutch governor had "ordered the massacre of a band of English and Japanese traders." Jonathan Swift, *Gulliver's Travels and Other Writings*, ed. Clement Hawes (Boston: Houghton Mifflin, 2004), 214n.

65. http://explore.bl.uk/BLVU1:LSCOP-ALL:BLL01011844770.

66. https://catalogue.leidenuniv.nl/permalink/f/1e3kn0k/TN_chdweebo99849154e. The error is virtually universal. See a similar subject heading for the Folger Shakespeare Library's copy of the 1624 *True Relation*: Ambon Island (Indonesia)—History—Massacre, 1624—Early works to 1800. http://hamnet.folger.edu/cgi-bin/Pwebrecon. cgi?BBID=158242.

Epilogue

1. I use "English" deliberately, despite the obvious fact that the massacres associated with Amboyna by the eighteenth century—Ireland and Glencoe—were part of a larger British experience. I want to invoke not just an English history of massacres but also and especially an English-language history of the word: a linguistic heritage widely shared by English-speakers around the world.

2. *The horrible murther of a young boy of three yeres of age, whose sister had her tongue cut out* (London, 1606), title page.

3. *Prayers and Thankesgiving to be used by all the Kings Majesties loving subiects, For the happy deliverance of his Majestie, the Queene, Prince, and States of Parliament, from the most traiterous and bloody intended Massacre by Gunpowder, the 5 of November 1605* (London, 1606).

4. Robert Dixon, *Canidia, or, The Witches* (London, 1683), the second part, Canto VIII, 26. For the Duke of Ormond's comparison, see Thomas Carte, *An history of the life of James Duke of Ormonde, from his birth in 1610, to his death in 1688*, 3 volumes (London, 1735-6), vol. 2, 84.

5. Although the almanac market dropped by approximately one-third from the seventeenth to the eighteenth centuries, almanac printing nonetheless remained a huge business for the Stationers' Company. By the end of the eighteenth century, the company produced about 238,000 almanacs annually. See Timothy Feist, *The Stationers' Voice: The English Almanac Trade in the Early Eighteenth Century, Transactions of the American Philosophical Society* 95, no. 4 (Philadelphia: American Philosophical Society, 2005), 19.

6. George Wharton, *Calendarium Ecclesiasticum* . . . (London, 1657), np; George Wharton, *Calendarium Ecclesiasticum* . . . (London, 1666), 5 of the Gesta; George Wharton, *Calendarium Ecclesiasticum* (London, 1663), 10 of the Gesta.

7. *Englands Remembrancer*, in *The Historians Guide in Two Parts* (London, 1676), 42.

8. John Josselyn, *An Account of two voyages to New-England* (London, 1674), 249. See Benjamin Schmidt, *Inventing Exoticism: Geography, Globalism, and Europe's Early Modern World* (Philadelphia: University of Pennsylvania Press, 2015).

9. John Pointer, *A Chronological history of England*, 3 volumes (Oxford, 1714), vol. 1, 154; *The complete pocket companion: or, universal almanack* (Dublin, 1738), listing for February events (locates Amboyna in 1622).

10. *An historical and chronological remembrancer of all remarkable occurrences, from the creation to this present year of our Lord, 1775* (Dublin, 1775), 177.

11. *The Examiner*, Friday, July 10–Monday, July 13, 1713.

12. "To the Editor of Lloyd's Evening Post," *Lloyd's Evening Post*, March 31–April 3, 1769.

13. *An historical and chronological remembrancer* (Dublin, 1775), 359.

14. *The Tablet of memory, shewing every memorable event in history, from the earliest period to the year 1783*, 5th ed. (London, [1783]), 80, listed eleven massacres, including Amboyna, Ireland (1641), and Glencoe (1692). This list included one massacre perpetrated by the English against the Danes in 1002. John Trusler, *Chronology: or, the historian's vade-mecum*, listed several massacres in his entry for "Massacre," This work went through multiple editions. The twelfth edition, two volumes [London, 1786] included a range of violent incidents, including the English massacre of Jews in 1189; the other three British massacres continued to be Amboyna, Ireland, and Glencoe, vol. 1, 210.

15. David Hume, *The History of England, from the Invasion of Julius Caesar, to The Revolution in 1688*, 8 volumes (London, 1767), vol. 8, index.

16. James Hardie, *The American Remembrancer, and Universal Tablet of Memory* (Philadelphia, 1795), 93–94.

17. John Gibney, *The Shadow of a Year: The 1641 Rebellion in Irish History and Memory* (Madison: University of Wisconsin Press, 2013), 44–45.

18. Erik Hinderaker, *Boston's Massacre* (Cambridge, MA: Harvard University Press, 2017), 242–255.

19. Hinderaker, *Boston's Massacre,* chap. 10, "mobbish" on 272. On the legacy of Crispus Attucks, see Mitch Kachun, *First Martyr of Liberty: Crispus Attucks in American Memory* (New York: Oxford University Press, 2017).

20. Quoted in Nicholas Canny, "1641 in a Colonial Context," in Micheál Ó Siochrú and Jane Ohlmeyer, eds., *Ireland, 1641: Contexts and Reactions* (Manchester: Manchester University Press, 2013), 65.

21. Ian J. Barrow, *Making History, Drawing Territory: British Mapping in India, c. 1756–1905* (New Delhi: Oxford University Press, 2003), chap. 5.

22. Ari Kelman, *A Misplaced Massacre: Struggling over the Memory of Sand Creek* (Cambridge, MA: Harvard University Press, 2013).

23. Sarah Farmer, *Martyred Village: Commemorating the 1944 Massacre at Oradour-sur-Glane* (Berkeley: University of California Press, 1999).

24. Mustafah Dhada, *The Portuguese Massacre of Wiriyamu in Colonial Mozambique, 1964–2013* (New York: Bloomsbury, 2016), 23, 127–128.

25. Partha Chatterjee, *The Black Hole of Empire: History of a Global Practice of Power* (Princeton, NJ: Princeton University Press, 2012), chap. 10.

26. Edmund Scott, *An Exact Discourse of the Subtilties, fashishions* [sic], *Pollicies, religion, and Ceremonies of the East Indians, as well Chyneses as Javans, there abyding and dweling*... (London, 1606), F2v–F3r.

27. http://biblio.middlebury.edu/record=b3594884~S2. *Middlebury Magazine* 88, no. 3 (Summer 2014) featured a photograph of the book's illustration.

28. A. P. Newton, "Forgotten Deeds of Empire Building: The Massacre of Amboyna, 1623," *Saturday Review*, May 18, 1935, 633. There is no information in the periodical about the source of the pamphlet.

29. *True Relation* (London, 1632). The Sutro Library call number is PE235:2.

30. Thomas Brockedon, Henrie Hawley, and John Goninge to the EIC, December 14, 1623, Batavia, IOR E/3/10, no. 1130, f. 53v (butcherlie execution); EIC Consultations at Java, IOR G/21/3-2, pt. 1, p. 91; *The Stripping of Joseph* (London, 1625), 11; and in many EIC communications and later printed works in context with Amboyna; George Downing, *A discourse written by Sir George Downing* (London, 1672), second part of pamphlet, 3.

31. Carte, *An history of the life of James Duke of Ormonde*, vol. 2, 84.

32. To appreciate the different ways in which people can define massacre, see Karl Jacoby, *Shadows at Dawn: A Borderlands Massacre and the Violence of History* (New York: Penguin, 2008), 224, where he argues that nineteenth-century white Americans thought of massacres as events distinguished not by the numbers of people killed, but rather by the cruelty of the deaths. On violence between intimates, see Wayne Lee, *Barbarians and Brothers: Anglo-American Warfare, 1500–1865* (New York: Oxford University Press, 2011).

Appendix 3

1. See Ian Gadd, "The Use and Misuse of *Early English Books Online*," *Literature Compass* 6, no. 3 (2009): 680–692.

2. On this project, see Nihar-Ranjan Ray, ed., *Dutch Activities in the East, Seventeenth Century: Being a "Report on the Records Relating to the East in the State Archives in The Hague,"* with two appendices by Frederick Charles Danvers (Calcutta: Book Emporium, 1945).

Index

For the benefit of digital users, indexed terms that span two pages (e.g., 52–53) may, on occasion, appear on only one of those pages.

Printed in the USA
CPSIA information can be obtained
at www.ICGtesting.com
JSHW051146180923
48576JS00001B/1

9 780197 507735